Identifying and Serving Diverse Gifted Learners

D1571613

Grounded in a combination of evidence, personal narratives, interviews, data, and research, *Identifying and Serving Diverse Gifted Learners: Meeting the Needs of Special Populations in Gifted Education* is a guiding resource for all stakeholder groups in gifted education to shift the equity needle of gifted programs in America.

Though it is the right of Black, Hispanic/Latinx, twice-exceptional (2e), low-income, and other special populations of students to have access to advanced academic programs in the American educational system, complex and deep-rooted systemic issues often block the way. This seminal text thoughtfully brings the conversation around historically underrepresented students in gifted education to the forefront, drawing on real-world examples to provide an accessible discussion of foundational, interdependent topics, including current research and promising educational practices. Readers will develop a basic theoretical understanding of the issues and be able to advance more responsive programs and experiences for low-income, racially, culturally, and linguistically diverse gifted students, and other diverse gifted populations.

This text serves as a beacon to motivate K-12 educators, researchers, and scholars to carry the torch of advocacy on behalf of those students historically underrepresented in programs for the gifted and talented.

Jaime A. Castellano is a nationally recognized and award-winning educator, principal, author, scholar, and researcher. In 2017 he was recognized as SENG's (Supporting Emotional Needs of the Gifted) National Educator of the Year. He is a preeminent scholar and researcher in gifted education and in identifying and serving diverse/special populations of gifted students.

Kimberley L. Chandler is Senior Director of Federal and Specialized Programs for the Essex County Schools in Tappahannock, Virginia, where she supervises services for gifted students. Her professional background includes teaching gifted students in a variety of settings, serving as an administrator of school district gifted programs, and providing professional development training for teachers and administrators nationally and internationally.

Identifying and Serving Diverse Gifted Learners

Meeting the Needs of Special Populations in Gifted Education

Edited by
Jaime A. Castellano and
Kimberley L. Chandler

Co-published with the National Association for Gifted Children (NAGC)

NEW YORK AND LONDON

Cover image: @Getty Images

First published 2022
by Routledge
605 Third Avenue, New York, NY 10158

and by Routledge
4 Park Square, Milton Park, Abingdon, Oxon, OX14 4RN

Routledge is an imprint of the Taylor & Francis Group, an informa business

© 2022 Taylor & Francis

The right of Jaime A. Castellano and Kimberley L. Chandler to be identified as the authors
of the editorial material, and of the authors for their individual chapters, has been asserted
in accordance with sections 77 and 78 of the Copyright, Designs and Patents Act 1988.

All rights reserved. No part of this book may be reprinted or reproduced or utilized
in any form or by any electronic, mechanical, or other means, now known or
hereafter invented, including photocopying and recording, or in any information
storage or retrieval system, without permission in writing from the publishers.

Trademark notice: Product or corporate names may be trademarks or registered trademarks,
and are used only for identification and explanation without intent to infringe.

Library of Congress Cataloging-in-Publication Data
A catalog record for this title has been requested

ISBN: 978-1-032-20825-1 (hbk)
ISBN: 978-1-032-20823-7 (pbk)
ISBN: 978-1-003-26541-2 (ebk)

DOI: 10.4324/9781003265412

Typeset in Sabon
by Newgen Publishing UK

Dr. Jaime A. Castellano

This book is dedicated to the practitioners, scholars, and researchers whose work with special populations of gifted students has left an indelible mark in the field. You do make a difference! This book is also dedicated to my mother, Lilia Castellano; to my wife, Lillian; to my eldest son, Jaime Jr., his wife Natacha, and their daughter, Leila, my granddaughter; to my son Alejandro and his wife, Kelly, and their children, Freya and Callum; and to my youngest children, twins, Gabriel and Gisell. I also dedicate this book to my sisters, Yolanda, Cynthia, and Olympia; and to my brother, Michael.

Dr. Kimberley L. Chandler

I would like to dedicate this book to my wonderful mother, Cecille Frances Chandler, who always supported me and served as my personal cheerleader throughout my life. In any project I embarked upon, she motivated me with her compassion for all people. Because of her care and encouragement, I have been able to succeed despite some of the barriers I experienced as a gifted child from a rural background.

Contents

About the Editors

Jaime A. Castellano is a nationally recognized and award-winning educator, principal, author, scholar, and researcher. In 2017 he was recognized as SENG's (Supporting Emotional Needs of the Gifted) National Educator of the Year. As a highly sought-after speaker, Dr. Castellano is recognized as one of the leading authorities in the United States on the education of Hispanic/Latino students. He is a preeminent scholar and researcher in identifying and serving diverse gifted students, with particular expertise in identifying gifted Hispanic/Latino students, gifted English Language Learners (ELLs) gifted preschoolers, gifted students from poverty, and gifted students who have trauma, toxic stress, and adverse childhood experiences. With more than 25 years in the field, he has served as a teacher of the gifted, school-based assistant principal and principal supervising gifted education programs; district-level administrator, coordinator, specialist, and director; state department of education specialist in gifted education; and adjunct and/or visiting graduate school professor in gifted education, educational leadership, English to speakers of other languages (ESOL), and special education. Castellano has edited four books on understanding our most able students from diverse backgrounds; written and/or edited multiple chapters, articles, and monographs in the field; and is a peer reviewer for the *Journal for the Education of the Gifted, Gifted Child Today,* and *Roeper Review.* He has also served as a principal investigator or consultant on a number of Javits grants (Jacob J. Javits Gifted and Talented Students Education Program). Castellano continues to consult with school districts across the United States on the inclusion of low-income, racially, culturally, and linguistically diverse students in gifted education. He is a professor at Florida Atlantic University in the Department of Exceptional Student Education. He also works with gifted students with trauma, toxic stress, and adverse childhood experiences as a mental health case manager with Multilingual Psychotherapy Centers, Inc. in West Palm Beach, FL.

Kimberley L. Chandler is the Senior Director of Federal and Specialized Programs for the Essex County Public Schools in Tappahannock, Virginia. She is also an adjunct instructor for the University of Iowa and Johns Hopkins University. Kimberley completed her PhD in Educational Policy, Planning, and Leadership with an emphasis in gifted education administration at William & Mary (a public university in Williamsburg, VA). Her professional background includes teaching gifted students in a variety of settings, serving as a central office administrator of school district enrichment programs, and providing professional development training for teachers and administrators nationally and internationally. She was the 2014 recipient of the NAGC Early Leader Award. Kimberley was formerly the Curriculum Director at the Center for Gifted Education at William & Mary, where she served as the editor and contributing author of numerous curriculum materials. She has served as Guest Editor of the *Journal for the Education of the Gifted* (*JEG*) for special issues focusing on international issues in gifted education and learning resources. She co-authored (with Tamra Stambaugh) the book *Effective Curriculum for Underserved Gifted Students* and is the co-editor (with Cheryll M. Adams) of the book *Effective Program Models for Gifted Students from Underserved Populations*. Kimberley's research interests include curriculum policy and implementation issues in gifted programs, the design and evaluation of professional development programs for teachers and administrators, and the role of principals and superintendents in gifted education.

About the Contributors

Dina Brulles, PhD, Arizona State University and Paradise Valley Unified School District, USA. As Director of Gifted Education at Paradise Valley Unified School District in Arizona, Dina has developed a continuum of gifted education programs, preschool through high school. She is also the Gifted Program Coordinator at Arizona State University. Dina serves on the National Association for Gifted Children (NAGC) Board of Directors as the Governance Secretary. Dina was a co-recipient of the 2019 NAGC Book of the Year Award, the 2014 NAGC Gifted Coordinator Award and also the NAGC Professional Development Network Award in 2013. Dina co-authored the books: *A Teacher's Guide to Flexible Grouping and Collaborative Learning*; *Designing Gifted Education Programs: From Purpose to Implementation*; *Differentiated Lessons for Every Learner*; *The Cluster Grouping Handbook*; *Teaching Gifted Kids in Today's Classroom*; and *Helping All Gifted Children Learn*.

Kristina Henry Collins, PhD, Texas State University, USA, is an Associate Professor of Talent Development at Texas State University, San Marcos. She is also a Lyndon B. Johnson (LBJ) Institute Faculty Research Fellow, serving as the NASA STEM Educator Professional Development Collaboration Research and Strategic Projects Specialist. She earned her PhD in Educational Psychology at the University of Georgia, in addition to an EdS degree; both specializing in Gifted and Creative Education. Dr. Collins also holds an MSEd degree in Mathematics from Jacksonville State University, and a BS degree in Engineering from the University of Alabama, specializing in Cryptology and Electronic Surveillance with the United States Navy. Dr. Collins has 25 years of teaching, leadership, and formal mentoring experience in PK-20 education. Dr. Collins' research foci include social, emotional, and cultural (SEC) contexts of gifted and talent development, STEM identity development in underrepresented students, and mentoring across the lifespan. Dr. Collins is a member of the NAGC Board of Directors and a former Jenkins Scholar Awards Chair sponsored by the NAGC Special Populations Network/GRACE SIG. She is the 2020–2021 President for Supporting the Emotional Needs of the Gifted, Inc. (SENG).

Megan Foley-Nicpon, PhD, University of Iowa, USA, is a professor in Counseling Psychology and Department Executive Officer for Psychological and Quantitative Foundations at the University of Iowa. She also serves as the Associate Director for Research and Clinic at the Belin-Blank Center for Gifted Education and Talent Development. Dr. Foley-Nicpon is a licensed psychologist whose research and clinical interests include assessment and intervention with high-ability students with disabilities, and the social and emotional development of talented and diverse students. She is an Associate Editor for the *APA Handbook of Giftedness and Talent*, and has written more than 60 peer-reviewed articles and book chapters and given more than 100 presentations at international, national, and state professional meetings in the areas of talent development, counseling psychology, and twice-exceptionality.

Erik M. Francis, MEd, MS, Maverik Education LLC, USA, is an international author and presenter with more than 20 years of experience working as a classroom teacher, a site administrator, an education program specialist with a state education agency, and a professional development trainer. He is the author of *Now THAT'S a Good Question! How to Promote Cognitive Rigor through Classroom Questioning*, published by ASCD. His book *Deconstructing Depth of Knowledge: A Method and Model for Deeper Teaching and Learning* was published by Solution Tree International in 2021. Erik was also ranked as one of the World's Top 30 Education Professionals for 2019 (#13) and 2020 (#3) by the research organization Global Gurus. Erik is the owner of Maverik Education LLC, providing academic professional development and consultation to K-12 schools, colleges, and universities on developing learning environments and delivering educational experiences that challenge students to demonstrate higher- order thinking and communicate depth of knowledge (DOK). His areas of expertise include teaching and learning for depth of knowledge (Webb's DOK), higher-level questioning and inquiry, authentic learning, differentiated instruction, personalized learning, and talent development.

Anne Gray, PhD, New Mexico Institute of Mining and Technology, USA, is the Educational Assessment Specialist on a Title V grant at New Mexico Institute of Mining and Technology. She has been an active member of NAGC since 2010, was a member of the Diversity and Equity Committee, is an organizing member and secretary of the Native American, Alaska Native, and Indigenous Peoples Special Interest Group (SIG), and an organizing member for the Gifted and Native: Research, Practices, and Partnerships (NAGC 2020, Albuquerque, NM), and Identifying and Serving Gifted and Talented Native American Students conferences (NAGC 2015, Phoenix, AZ). Her research focuses on American Indian/Alaska Native, Indigenous, and minority youth with gifts and talents, equity in gifted education, and critical theory.

Nancy B. Hertzog, PhD, University of Washington, USA, is Professor and Director of Learning Sciences and Human Development and the former Director of the Robinson Center for Young Scholars at the University of Washington. She received her Master's degree in Gifted Education from the University of Connecticut, and her PhD in Special Education from the University of Illinois. In addition to studying the outcomes of Robinson Center alumni, her research focuses on teaching strategies designed to dif-ferentiate instruction and challenge children with diverse abilities. Specifically, she has studied teachers' implementation of the Project Approach in classrooms with both high-achieving and low-achieving children. From 1995 to 2010, she was on the faculty in the Department of Special Education and directed the University Primary School, an early childhood gifted program, at the University of Illinois at Urbana-Champaign. She has published three books and several chapters on early childhood gifted education, and numerous articles in gifted education.

Tiombe Bisa Kendrick-Dunn, PhD, Miami-Dade County Public Schools, USA, is a prac-ticing school psychologist who resides in Miami, Florida. She is employed by Miami-Dade County Public Schools, where she has practiced since 2005. She also operates a private practice that includes a sub-specialization in gifted and talented children and culturally competent services. Ms. Kendrick-Dunn currently serves on the Board of

Directors for the Florida Association for the Gifted (FLAG) and the Children's Trust of Miami-Dade County. She also holds leadership positions with the National Association of School Psychologists (NASP) and the National Association for Gifted Children (NAGC). She has dedicated her entire professional career to helping children reach their potential.

Kimberly Lansdowne, PhD, is the founding Executive Director of the Herberger Young Scholars Academy, a secondary school for highly gifted students at Arizona State University, USA. She has a lengthy career in teaching and administration at universities, colleges, public and private schools. At ASU she develops and teaches undergraduate- and graduate-level education classes for Mary Lou Fulton Teachers College. She typically teaches education courses on curriculum, instruction, testing, measurement, and special needs. Along with being featured in multiple media events focusing on her work at the Herberger Academy, Kimberly has authored articles, books, and book chapters. She co-authored *Helping All Gifted Children Learn* and the *Naglieri Tests of General Ability–Quantitative* with co-authors Jack Naglieri and Dina Brulles.

Ching-Lan Rosaline Lin, MEd, PhD, University of Pennsylvania, USA, is a Psychology Postdoctoral Fellow at the University of Pennsylvania's Student Counseling Center. Rosaline has gained specialty experience in mental health and wellness of twice-exceptional students, international student populations, and students of color. As a beginning scholar and clinician who advocates for psychological health and social justice, Rosaline is passionate about supporting individuals in building their strengths and coping with adversities in life.

Melanie S. Meyer, PhD, Johns Hopkins University, USA, is a Postdoctoral Research Fellow at Johns Hopkins University. Her doctoral program was in Educational Psychology at the University of North Texas. She has been a teacher in gifted and advanced academic English classrooms at the middle and high school level for over 20 years. Her research focuses on adolescent identity development, school-based talent development, and the college, career, and military choice process for talented students.

Rachel U. Mun, PhD, University of North Texas, USA, is an Assistant Professor in Educational Psychology. She received her PhD in Education, Learning Sciences, and Human Development from the University of Washington. Her research interests are two-tiered and best described as an intersection between culture, gifted education, and socioemotional well-being. At the micro-level, she explores socioemotional development and decision-making for high-ability students (emphasis on immigrants) within family, peer, and academic contexts with the goal to promote well-being. At the macro-level, she examines ways to improve equitable identification and services for K-12 high-ability learners from diverse populations. She has published a variety of articles in gifted education and most recently received the NAGC 2017 doctoral dissertation award (first place).

Paul James (PJ) Sedillo, PhD, has published an article titled "The 'T' is Missing from Gifted/Gifted Transgender Individuals: A Case Study of a Female to Male (FTM) Gifted Transgender Person" in *The Journal of Education and Social Policy*. He has also published an article in *Parenting for High Potential* titled "Why Is There a Gay Rainbow Sticker on My 9 Year-Old Child's Backpack?" His book *40 years of Solidarity*, published with ABQ Press, was awarded the 2018 Best Book for New Mexico and Arizona Award; it is a historical account of the GLBTQ Albuquerque Pride movement from 1976 to 2016. He is currently Past President for the New Mexico Association for the Gifted (NMAG), representative for the National Association for Gifted Children (NAGC) Legislative and Advocacy Committee, and Co-Chair for the NAGC GLBTQ Network.

Glorry Yeung, University of North Texas, USA, is a research and teaching assistant in the Department of Educational Psychology. He is pursuing a PhD in Educational Psychology – Gifted and Talented. His return to academia after an extended hiatus was driven by an avidity for the advocacy for gifted education and advanced academics intervention. Identifying talents and serving the needs of the gifted learner population are his current research interests. Glorry aims to leverage his experiences in international business, advocacy work, interest as a stakeholder, and newly acquired knowledge for meaningful contributions to the field of educational psychology.

Foreword

It is with pleasure that I write to introduce this important new book. In it, Castellano and Chandler have assembled an impressive array of chapters united around the theme of meeting the needs of diverse gifted learners. Importantly, they broaden the conception of diversity beyond that of income, race, language, multi-exceptionalities, and culture by including chapters about students who identify as LBGTQ, have experienced trauma, are members of military families, are highly gifted, or are very young. These additions to the traditionally underserved population groups provide for a comprehensive look at diversity in the field of gifted education. Equally impressive to the content in the book are the experts who have contributed their best thinking, research, and advice to their chapters. Kudos to the editors for including such a strong cadre of authors, each bringing their important perspectives, knowledge, and experiences in a manner completely relevant and accessible to the reader. Having such a broad and comprehensive view of diversity written by experts in each of these respective areas is clearly a strength of this book.

Another thing I like about this collection of chapters is their relevance to educators, researchers, and in some cases, students themselves. In each chapter, authors tell a story providing a very human narrative for their population of underserved learners. For example, Sedillo's proposed Stages of Gifted–GLBT Identity (Chapter 4) provides educators, parents, and adolescents themselves with insights into identity, struggles, and others who have come before them. This is important, and perhaps, lifesaving work. Similarly, in her chapter (7) on gifted American Indian/Alaska Natives, Gray encourages adopting strength-based, non-colonial views of giftedness. She demands that the cloak of invisibility be removed from these children and their educators seek to understand and recognize their gifts and talents. Castellano included a chapter (3) on gifted children and youth who experience trauma, toxic stress, and adverse childhood experiences, reminding us that despite these events, these youth are resilient. In his chapter he shares the powerful voices of trauma survivors, reminding us that some youth must overcome horrific life experiences. The stories throughout the chapters in this book, with their author and student voices, are powerful reminders that parents and educators must be concerned about the whole child – their social and emotional well-being, their academic interests, their passions and their person.

Through understanding of and caring for students from diverse circumstances, we can all develop better and more responsive programs and experiences suited for their individual needs. This book provides a basis for this important work. Kudos to Castellano and Chandler and their fantastic collection of authors for contributing this important work. I believe it will help educators, families, and youth.

Marcia Gentry
Director of the Gifted Education Resource Institute and
Professor of Educational Studies at Purdue University

Acknowledgements

Dr. Jaime A. Castellano

I would like to first acknowledge the contributing writers to this project for helping make this book a reality. Without their passion, commitment, and professionalism, this book would not have been possible. A special thanks goes to Dr. Kimberley L. Chandler, a friend and colleague, who agreed to serve as both a contributing author and co-editor. We share a commitment to the field of gifted and talented education that is reflected in this book. I would also like to thank Dr. Scott Peters, Chair of the NAGC Publication Committee, Joel McIntosh, then Prufrock Press publisher, and Routledge for their patience and support. Thanks for helping us see this project through.

My wife, Lillian, has been steadfast in her support of this project. Therefore, I must acknowledge and thank her for her patience and understanding. For the past year I have spent the majority of my weekends in the local public library, often at the expense of missing family functions. Thank you from the bottom of my heart. Additional thanks go to the National Association for Gifted Children (NAGC) which has allowed me to grow and flourish through various leadership roles and which has informed my work in the field for more than 20 years.

Dr. Kimberley L. Chandler

I would like to extend my appreciation to Dr. Jaime Castellano, who honored me by asking me to be a co-editor of this book. Jaime and I share a wealth of experiences at the K-12 and university levels that have informed our work with populations of diverse gifted learners. Jaime is an enthusiastic supporter of gifted children and has devoted his life's work to advocating for students from populations that are often underserved. I am inspired by his passionate advocacy in this arena and am delighted to share the work of this special project with him!

Introduction

Why does the inclusion of low-income, racially, culturally, and linguistically diverse students, along with other special populations, continue to be a conundrum in the field of gifted education? Research, policy, and hundreds of millions of dollars spent over the past 20-plus years, primarily in the form of federally funded Javits grants to school districts and universities across the United States, has put only a small dent in this effort. Why does this goal continue to be elusive?

Elusiveness, in the context presented here, implies a "break in the link" or "a chink in the armor" as to where the disconnection presents itself. Where on the continuum of advocacy, research, practice, policy, and politics does elusiveness exist in gifted education? And does it present itself at the local, state, or federal level? Perhaps it's a combination of "some or all of the above." Here is where this edited volume comes into play. Its laser-like focus on a dozen special populations found in gifted education aims to help educate others who participate in advocacy, research, practice, policy, and politics. This contribution to the field is meant to inform and empower them with the kind of knowledge that they can use to make a difference and help advocate for more diversity, inclusion, and equity in gifted education for low-income, racially, culturally, and linguistically diverse students; and other special populations.

Furthermore, national reports created by the U.S. Department of Education and other national policy centers highlight the growing need for students to achieve their full potential, and specifically for the reduction of race- and ethnicity-based achievement gaps, in order to maintain global competitiveness and a growing economy (Paik, 2004; Paik & Walberg, 2007). These achievement gaps also exist in gifted education and are often referred to as an "excellence gap" (Plucker & Peters, 2016). Developing the gifts and talents of our most able students from all walks of life must be a national imperative. The benefits to our nation and to the world require us to put forth our best effort as educators. An increase to our nation's intellectual capital, social capital, and economic capital, among others, further validates what has always been a basic tenet in gifted education – the use of gifts and talents to better humanity.

When one achieves a certain level of success in a particular field of study there is a sense of responsibility to give back to the field. This book represents that responsibility. It comes from the heart with nothing expected in return. It comes from a place where wanting to make a difference in the lives of children/students is authentic and is the force that drives us. In part, it is our way of saying thank you. As current practitioners, scholars, and researchers in gifted and talented education it is also our intention to promote dialogue among all stakeholder groups in gifted education, who like us, are concerned about equity,

DOI: 10.4324/9781003265412-1

access, and opportunity. In the end, we hope this book will make a difference for those who historically have been disenfranchised, neglected, and often prevented from enacting their individual and collective talent and potential.

One innovative aspect of this publication resides in providing real-life stories about special populations of gifted students that offer a synopsis and accessible discussion of foundational, interdependent topics, including current research and educational practices. It is intended to be seminal to the field, bringing the discussion of these issues to the forefront in one single volume. However, simple solutions to increasing the numbers of historically underrepresented students in gifted education do not exist. This book may offer some small steps in the right direction by informing all stakeholder groups about some of the salient issues related to equity and access for each special population identified.

Contents of the Book

Throughout this book we have attempted to develop a guiding resource for all stakeholder groups in gifted education, based on thorough reviews of the literature, theory-driven works, and applications to practice. In addition, we hope that educational researchers and policy makers will view this book as a basic reference to pertinent issues. In the end, we hope this book will enable readers to develop a basic theoretical understanding of the issues and to advance more responsive programs and experiences for low-income, racially, culturally, and linguistically diverse gifted students, and other diverse gifted populations.

For purposes of organization, chapters have been arranged in the way they seem to fit best or that helps ideas to flow. All invited authors were provided with a template designed to guide their writing; but were also invited to champion their own style in presenting explicit information about each of the special populations identified. The book is divided into four parts.

- Part I: Supporting Gifted Students from Historically Underrepresented Populations
- Part II: Expanding the View of Special Populations: Connecting and Understanding
- Part III: Special Populations of Gifted Students
- Part IV: Reflections for Practice, Policy, and Research

Part I: Supporting Gifted Students from Historically Underrepresented Populations

In *Chapter 1, Jaime A. Castellano* writes that supporting the identification and education of gifted students from historically underrepresented populations should be a national priority; an imperative that reflects a standing commitment to educate our nation's gifted students regardless of their income level, zip code, sexual orientation, or their racial, ethnic, or linguistic background; even their mental health status.

Part II: Expanding the View of Special Populations: Connecting and Understanding

The three chapters (2–4) in Part II focus on expanding the view of special populations beyond identification and assessment. The scant research and resources for each of the three groups requires us to take a deeper dive to increase our own level of commitment and advocacy. Each chapter leads the reader on a journey that highlights the circumstances associated with a unique special population. In *Chapter 2, Melanie S. Meyer* writes that children from military families move an average of six to nine times between kindergarten and high school graduation. This geographic mobility may be even more difficult for students receiving gifted and talented services. Meyer examines how school personnel can proactively plan for transitioning military-connected and other highly mobile students who need gifted and advanced academic services by providing continuity of curriculum, high-quality academic services, enrichment activities, social and emotional support, scaffolding to meet current academic needs, and help with record keeping for future transitions.

Jaime A. Castellano (Chapter 3) presents gifted students with trauma, toxic stress, and adverse childhood experiences (ACEs) as a new special population in the field of gifted education. The chapter will be framed more like a toolbox for teachers of the gifted and any other educator who serves this population. Contents will include frequently asked questions; types of trauma; case studies and vignettes; the causes and effects of childhood trauma, and strategies that promote resiliency, relationships, and perseverance.

In *Chapter 4, Paul James (PJ) Sedillo* theoretically proposes Identity Stages for Gifted–GLBT individuals. Currently, there are very few proposed theories illuminating GLB stages of identity and even fewer pertaining to Transgender persons. Furthermore, there are no theoretical applications of stages of identity that exist for Gifted–GLBT individuals. Therefore, this chapter brings forth information to assist all who either are Gifted–GLBT, their family and friends, counselor/therapists, and educators.

Part III: Special Populations of Gifted Students

Dina Brulles and Kimberly Lansdowne (Chapter 5) discuss the need, purpose, and rationale for providing highly gifted and profoundly gifted learners with radically differentiated learning experiences and educational opportunities. The authors launch into the plight of this vastly underserved population by describing who these students are and why their learning needs so dramatically differ from others.

In *Chapter 6, Kimberley L. Chandler* reviews the unique place-based components that must be considered when considering identification protocols and programming for students from rural settings: physical isolation, proximity of extended family, limited transportation options for specialized programs, lack of specialized training for teachers, and the intersection of poverty. An examination of current practices is suggested, including a call for the development of more robust distance-learning options and regional programming, emphases on teacher and administrator professional learning, and the recognition of the ways that some federal Title funds can be used to support programming.

Anne Gray (Chapter 7) writes that American Indian and Alaska Native (AIAN) students with gifts and talents experience barriers to their identification and the services provided as a result of their invisibility, relegation to the historic past, and the lack of cultural competence among non-Native educators. Gray identifies actionable steps that can be taken to help mitigate these barriers such as policies and practices that increase equitable identification and policies/practices that align with the cultural norms of Native communities.

In *Chapter 8, Kristina Henry Collins and Tiombe Bisa Kendrick-Dunn* explore why, despite an increased awareness regarding the underrepresentation of Black students in gifted and talented programs, little has changed. This chapter addresses the myriad critical issues that serve as barriers to increasing the recruitment and retention of Black students in gifted programs and offers culturally responsive solutions to lessen the gaps. Highlighted barriers include deficient identification methods, piecemeal assessments, and culture-blind curriculum.

Rachel U. Mun and Glorry Yeung (Chapter 9) present strategies for identifying and serving Asian American students in gifted programs using student vignettes. While Asian Americans are highly diverse with origins in more than 20 countries from East, South, and Southeast Asia, they are often perceived as a homogeneous group in American schools and stereotyped as "model minorities" who are generally successful in academics, overrepresented in gifted and talented programs, self-sufficient, and mentally healthy, despite contrary evidence particularly for certain sub-groups (e.g. children of refugees).

Megan Foley-Nicpon and Ching-Lan Rosaline Lin (Chapter 10) review current research on best practice identification and assessment of Attention-Deficit Hyperactivity Disorder, Autism Spectrum Disorder, and Specific Learning Disability among high-ability youth, as well as potential co-existing mental health concerns. They review recommended curriculum and instructional strategies for educators as well as the role parents and family play as both student advocates and supports. The authors conclude with overall recommendations for identification, intervention, and advocacy for twice-exceptional children that are applicable for educators and parents alike.

In *Chapter 11, Nancy B. Hertzog* provides an equity lens to serving young children in gifted education. The author questions historic conceptions of school readiness, and discusses the systemic barriers to advanced learning opportunities including policies and practices of early identification which label young children gifted. Using a framework for advancing equity in early childhood education, the author proposes action steps to creating welcoming, enriching, and academically challenging early child environments for all young children.

Jaime A. Castellano and Erik M. Francis (Chapter 12) aim to inform readers on the identification, assessment, nature and needs, programming, and instruction of gifted English Language Learners (ELLs). Gifted ELLs are in every school they attend; in urban, suburban, and rural America. They come from culturally and linguistically diverse backgrounds and their families sometimes have values that differ from those represented in U.S. schools. As such, teachers, principals, and other educators who serve gifted ELLs need to learn about students' cultures, teach in a manner that is responsive to those cultures, and acknowledge and value their classroom and school diversity.

In *Chapter 13, Jaime A. Castellano* emphasizes that to meet the needs of gifted Hispanic/Latino students, identification, assessment, and instruction cannot be one-dimensional. A variety of assessment strategies should be considered based on language proficiency patterns, a variety of instructional approaches should be used to challenge these students and to meet their instructional goals, and teachers should receive the professional development required to identify them in the first place. Building a programmatic infrastructure that includes these practices builds a foundation which increases the possibility that the gifts, talents, and potential that gifted Hispanic/Latino students possess will be recognized, nurtured, and honored.

Part IV: Reflections for Practice, Policy, and Research

In *Chapter 14, Kimberley L. Chandler* offers final thoughts about special populations in gifted education. Chapter authors examined these groups through two lenses: 1) equity; and 2) supporting their identification and education. Equity could be considered to be the backdrop for every discussion in the book, as this must be the driving force for all decision-making; it requires a deliberate, systemic approach to making sure that every child has the opportunity to achieve success. In the case of gifted education specifically, it refers to the equitable representation of diverse student populations in programs.

Concluding Remarks

Based on research and practice, this book highlights important information about 12 special populations of students found in gifted education. It represents a coordinated effort among the editors, authors, Routledge, and the National Association for Gifted Children (NAGC) Publication Committee. The United States is a country in transition because considerable demographic changes are taking place. Its racial, cultural, and linguistic diversity is unparalleled. Although this diversity vitalizes the United States, it also poses serious challenges to deeply rooted habits of mind, to assumptions, and to conduct. An example of this is the educational challenge posed by increasing numbers of culturally and linguistically diverse students in U.S. schools and their subsequent underrepresentation in advanced academic programs like gifted education. Data on their educational status indicate that a primarily disabling approach has been used to face this challenge, and, as a result, these students have been thwarted from tapping into cultural, linguistic, and cognitive resources. Nevertheless, this book offers a better understanding of 12 special student populations by offering a clear understanding of them through an expanded body of knowledge and increased awareness.

References

Paik, S. J. (Ed.). (2004). *Advancing educational productivity: Policy implications from national databases*. Information Age Publishing.

Paik, S. J., & Walberg, H. (Eds.). (2007). *Narrowing the achievement gap: Strategies for educating Latino, Black, and Asian students*. Springer.

Plucker, J. A., & Peters, S. J. (2016). *Excellence gaps in education: Expanding opportunities for talented youth*. Harvard Education Press.

Chapters at a Glance

		A Focus on Equity	Research Connection	Instructional Connection
I	A Standing Commitment to Special Populations in Gifted Education	Five main pillars of equity	Equity through research practices	
2	On the Move: Helping Military-Connected Gifted Students Navigate Non-Promotional School Transitions	Promoting equity and access	Managing non-promotional school transitions for military-connected gifted and talented students	Strengths-based intake protocols and mastery learning approaches
3	Educating Gifted Students with Trauma, Toxic Stress, and Adverse Childhood Experiences	A focus on equity	Frequently Asked Questions	Student vignettes; An exercise for teachers of the gifted
4	The Why, Who, What, Where, and How for this Under-identified Underserved Population: Sedillo's Gifted–GLBT Stages of Identity	Strategies for equity	Based on the Cass Identity Model; however, no theoretical applications of stages of identity that exist	Information to assist counselors/ therapists, educators, or family and friend(s) who support Gifted–GLBT persons, Table 4.1. Strategies
5	Serving Our Highly Gifted Learners: A Practitioner's Guide	Equity issues with highly gifted learners	Literature review on highly gifted	Teaching the highly gifted learners
6	Growing Up Gifted in Rural America: Mitigating Challenges Posed by Geography	Lack of equity exacerbated by challenges of geography	Limited research about this population: Recent studies related to teachers of rural gifted students, place-based instruction, and case studies about rural gifted education programs	Need for the development of more robust distance- learning options and regional programs

DOI: 10.4324/9781003265412-2

WWW Connection	Collaboration	Social-Emotional Learning	Practical Application
Interstate Compact on Educational Opportunity for Military Children (2016)	Record keeping to facilitate communication between families, school personnel, and School Liaison Officers	Suggestions for monitoring transition-related stress and student adjustment	Examples of elementary, middle, and high school transition experiences
Hattie, J. (2009). *Visible Learning: A Synthesis of over 800 Meta-Analyses Relating to Achievement*	The Five-Minute Measurement	Creating social-emotional strength and resiliency	Ten practical, low-cost or no-cost strategies for offering social-emotional learning
Gay–Straight Alliance (GSA) https:// gsanetwork.org	Engaging and informing counselors/therapists, educators, and parents, Table 4.1. Strategies	Stages of identity, pp. 81–82 (Table 4.1)	Sedillo's Gifted–GLBT Stages of Identity, Table 4.1
Programming options for highly gifted	Collaborating with school district departments	Vignettes Belonging and Identity	Gifted Programming: In Search of the Right Fit Questions for discussion
Online courses for gifted students	Leveraging partners to expand academic options: finding viable options for supplemental and out-of-school programming, building partnerships with parents and the community, and making use of federal grant funds	Rural milieu and impact on social-emotional aspect	Need for culturally responsive pedagogy and materials

		A Focus on Equity	*Research Connection*	*Instructional Connection*
7	Meeting the Needs of American Indian and Alaska Native Youth with Gifts and Talents	Promoting equity with AIAN students	Invisibility, relegation to historic past, lack of culturally competent educators	Differences, pp. 136–137 student vignette
8	Fostering Cultural Capital and Creativity for Recruitment and Retention: A Holistic Approach to Serving Gifted Black Students in Gifted Education	Utilize equity goals	Larry P. v. Riles (court case)	Culturally responsive curriculum development
9	Gifted Identification and Services for Asian Americans	Asian American diversity and need to focus on equity	Research-based identification and assessment	Curriculum and instruction, and classroom strategies
10	Identifying and Providing Instructional Services for Twice-Exceptional Students	Equity, belonging, and identity	Twice-exceptionality	Curriculum and instruction
11	Young, Curious, and Resilient: The Population of Early Learners	A focus on equity, pp. 202–203	Issues in identification of young learners, pp. 206–207	Pedagogy to elicit strengths of young children, pp. 209–210
12	Identifying and Serving Gifted English Language Learners (ELLs)	A focus on equity	Exploratory study on the identification of ELLs for Gifted and Talented Programs	Educating gifted ELLs about self-efficacy
13	Gifted Hispanic/Latino Students	Gifted Hispanic/ Latino students and issues of equity	Use different tests; use tests differently	Relational pedagogy
14	Shifting Paradigms for Special Populations of Gifted Learners	Equity as the backdrop for all discussions: Requires a deliberate, systemic approach	Research history in gifted education versus research agenda moving forward with new paradigms emphasizing equity	

WWW Connection	Collaboration	Social-Emotional Learning	Practical Application
Table 7.3: American Indian and Alaska Native Helpful Resources	With families, pp. 142–143	Belonging and identity	Recommendations
America's teacher–student racial gap	Interviews with parents and guardians	Social and emotional growth and development of Black gifted students	Principles advocated by E. Paul Torrance
U.S. Census and Pew Research Center (Lopez et al., 2017)	Understanding and engaging parents and families with emphasis on cultural and structural influences	Understanding belonging and cultivating ethnic identity	Seven recommendations for practice including disaggregation and culturally responsive pedagogy
National Center for Educational Statistics (2016)	Roles of parents and family	Recommend-ations	Curriculum and instruction
Critical pedagogies and equity lens, p. 206	Valuing partnerships and collaboration with families, p. 210	Classroom strategies to design positive learning environments, pp. 211–213	Recommendations, pp. 213–214
United States Department of Education, Office for Civil Rights	Communicating and collaborating with parents and families of gifted ELLs	Teacher Saul Ramirez and students at Henderson Middle School, El Paso, TX	Questioning and inquiry: Applications to gifted ELLs
Education Week Research Center (2019)National Survey in Gifted Education	Engaging Hispanic/Latino parents/families	Belonging and identity	Tenways to incorporate student choice
NAGC's Equity and Social Justice Initiative			

Part I

Supporting Gifted Students from Historically Underrepresented Populations

Chapter 1

A Standing Commitment to Special Populations in Gifted Education

Jaime A. Castellano

Supporting the identification and education of gifted students from historically underrepresented populations should be a national priority; an imperative that reflects a standing commitment to educate our nation's gifted and talented students regardless of their income level, zip code, sexual orientation, or their racial, ethnic, or linguistic background; even their mental health status. Ethically, we have a responsibility to ensure that these students are provided with an education that develops their gifts and talents to the highest possible level and that improves their quality of life. In gifted education, ethics should also reflect equity – equity in the form of taking action as practitioners, researchers, and advocates that results in gifted education programs reflecting the diversity of the local student population. In working with a Virginia school district in January of 2020 struggling with issues of equity and access in the participation rate of Hispanic/Latino students in Advanced Placement (AP) courses, I was asked to define or give an example of equity during a town-hall meeting with the community. My response was in the form of an example; "Equity means that if 40 percent of the high school students are Hispanic/Latino, then 40 percent of the students enrolled in the school's AP program should be Hispanic/Latino." That response received a loud round of applause, leading me to believe that there were many like-minded individuals in the auditorium during the district's town-hall meeting on how to redesign their only high school.

The following Pillars of Equity in Gifted Education for Special Populations (Table 1.1) by no means represents an exhaustive list. Rather, it serves as a starting point that teachers, school and district-based administrators, and school boards can consider as they initiate conversations about the equity issues that surround gifted education. These pillars promote measures that ensure equity, quality, and evaluation of progress being made in the education of special populations of gifted students. Castellano (2018) adds that every stakeholder group – from classroom teachers of the gifted to superintendents and school boards deciding on district policy – should include these pillars in their planning and decision-making.

Pillar 1: Identification – Teachers and administrators are at the heart of quality identification practices that impact the referrals and nominations of special populations of gifted students, particularly those that are racially, culturally, and linguistically diverse; as well as low-income. As such, training and professional development are key elements in promoting equity – ensuring that teachers and administrators have the skill, ability, and desire to identify diverse gifted learners.

DOI: 10.4324/9781003265412-4

Table 1.1 Five Pillars of Equity in Gifted Education for Special Populations

Pillar 1 Identification	Pillar 2 Assessment	Pillar 3 Curriculum and Instruction	Pillar 4 A Healthy Class/ School Environment	Pilar 5 A Healthy Infrastructure
• Teacher training about identification and characteristics of special populations • Communicating access and opportunity to the greater school community • Identifying and working with advocates: local, state, national • Educators working with gifted students should examine personal background and biases • Policy development through an equity lens	• Professional development for psychologists on special populations • Disaggregation of local school gifted education district data by race, ethnicity, language, and income. • Flexibility in intelligence tests used with special populations • Use of alternative assessments other than IQ tests • Policy development through an equity lens	• Honor and respect the abilities of students • Use culturally responsive pedagogy and practices • Teachers engage in self-reflection and self-assessment on how they are impacting student learning • Reinforce qualities that are key to resilience • Collaborate with other stakeholder groups to meet the social, emotional, academic, and cognitive needs of special populations of gifted students	• Engage in open and respectful communication • Promote opportunities for students that instill a sense of pride and passion where they learn discipline toward something important to them • Recognize and value student input • Recognize student diversity and promote/display contributions of all groups through the use of symbolism	• School and district administrators engage in professional development opportunities specific to local diverse gifted student populations • School boards of education identify a vision and strategy that include policies for educating special populations of gifted students • A school and/ or district identifies strengths and areas of improvement and has a direction for how teachers and administrators can continuously improve their practice

Pillar 2: Assessment – The decision to refer a student from a diverse background for gifted education services must include a comprehensive evaluation of what that student knows and is able to do. Considerations include areas to be assessed, sources for obtaining assessment data, and who gathers the information. This collection of evidence at the point of service will help a school's or district's child study team to determine if a placement in gifted education is warranted. Furthermore, the information found in Pillar 2 should become non-negotiables and tied to policies, practices, and procedures.

Pillar 3: Curriculum and Instruction – When instruction is developmental and flexible and infused with multicultural education; and uses culturally responsive pedagogy and practices, students are held accountable for their own learning and progress. This allows diverse gifted students in the same classroom and in the same school to work on a range of concepts and skills according to their own individual abilities, readiness levels, needs, and interests – the foundational ideal of fluid teaching through an equity lens.

Pillar 4: A Healthy Class/School Environment – The dynamics of the classroom and school offering gifted education programming can work either in favor of or against special populations of gifted students. Today, there is a call to action to get classroom teachers of the gifted and school administrators to realize that in order to actualize the talent of its diverse gifted students, the raising of the ceiling must occur. Pillar 4 offers foundational, structural actions, and promotes behaviors that teachers and principals should consider in their efforts to educate their diverse gifted student population.

Pillar 5: A Healthy Infrastructure – In working within the system to build equitable policies and procedures in gifted and talented education for underserved populations, a healthy infrastructure is essential. In designing a flowchart of programmatic infrastructure for serving diverse gifted students, a district's governing board, superintendent, building principals, and classroom teachers of the gifted should not only focus on increasing student achievement, but also on developing the innate talents, abilities, and skills of their gifted students from diverse populations.

According to Castellano (2018), one of the most disturbing trends is our continued lack of commitment at all levels in identifying and serving special populations of students who are gifted. How and why we fail to properly serve these student populations is the subject of serious debate among stakeholder groups. If nothing else, the Five Pillars of Equity in Gifted Education for Special Populations should serve to make the reader aware of how we can combat the uncountable nuances and confounding factors that impact how we view special populations in gifted education.

The Role of School- and District-Based Practitioners in Promoting Equity

Practitioners in gifted education are "boots on the ground." They provide direct services to gifted students. Teachers, for example, connect with parents, families, school and district administrators, and often collaborate with community partners. Principals, coordinators, and directors serve as resource providers and as a "web of support" for the teachers they supervise. They are an important niche in the district's infrastructure for supporting advanced academic programs like gifted education. They are in the unique position to promote equity by making sure that the constituents of their school community get information about such programs. They use, for example, Spanish language radio and other social media outlets and/or partner with the faith institutions of the community to "get the word out." These individuals are also in the position to advocate for and plan professional development opportunities that help identify special populations of students for gifted education. In these efforts, practitioners often rely on the work of researchers.

In her Education Week Editor's Note, Samuels (2020a) writes that educational equity isn't about forcing all students to the same destination. It's about making sure all students have access to the educational foundation they need to reach their individual potential. It's a belief that's easy to embrace. It's more complex to put it into action. Overall, white, Asian, and affluent students had greater access to schools with signs of quality. Black students, Hispanic students, and students from low-income backgrounds had less access to schools with quality educators and a positive school climate.

In a different article in the same publication, Samuels (2020b) included research from the Education Trust, a group that advocates for students of color and students of poverty who looked more closely at students' access to advanced coursework: gifted education, Algebra I in 8th grade, and Advanced Placement courses. It found that nationally, Black and Hispanic students are less likely to attend schools where rigorous coursework is offered, but when they do, they are less likely to be enrolled in those courses. In using 2015–2016 federal data to track student enrollment in rigorous classes by race and ethnicity, the Education Trust (2020) documented the following information:

- Black students in elementary school account for 16% of all students; but only 9% are identified as gifted.
- Black students in middle school account for 15% of all students; but only 10% are enrolled in 8th Grade Algebra I.
- Black students in high school account for 15% of all students; but only 9% are enrolled in AP courses.
- Hispanic students in elementary school account for 28% of all students; but only 18% are identified as gifted.
- Hispanic students in middle school account for 25% of all students; but only 18% are enrolled in 8th Grade Algebra I.
- Hispanic students in high school account for 24% of all students; but only 21% are enrolled in AP courses.

(Education Trust, 2020, cited by Samuels, 2020b, p. 3)

A growing interest in educational equity has coincided with the release of federal data on every school. These data offer a valuable perspective on state efforts to identify and serve historically underrepresented students in advanced academic programs like gifted education. The data presented above tell us what we already know; that more research is needed on how to move the equity needle in gifted education.

The Role of Researchers in Promoting Equity

According to Andrews et al. (2019), researchers working to address issues of equity have a responsibility not to perpetuate disparities, inequalities, and stereotypes about populations of color. While disaggregating data is a necessary component of understanding disparities in outcomes by race and ethnicity, it is not wholly sufficient. Researchers must think critically about how they collect, analyze, and present data to avoid masking disproportionalities or disparities that different racial and ethnic groups experience. While there is no "one-size-fits-all" approach to incorporating a racial and ethnic equity perspective into research, the following five guiding principles, the stages of the research process, and their connections to research in gifted education (see Tables 1.2, 1.3, 1.4, and 1.5) can help researchers better identify where inequities exist, their structural cause, and the environments and conditions that perpetuate those inequities.

1   Examine your own background and biases.
2   Make a commitment to dig deeper into the data.
3   Recognize the impact the research process itself has on communities, and acknowledge your role in ensuring that research benefits communities.
4   Engage communities as partners in research.
5   Guard against the implied or explicit assumption that white is the default position.

Racial and equity perspectives in gifted education can be seen in the research-based Jacob K. Javits grants awarded to school districts and universities across the United States. The

Table 1.2 Stages of the Research Process: Connections to Equity in Gifted Education: Stage 1: Landscape Assessment

Components	Characteristics	Connections to Equity in Gifted Education
Know the context	• Examine the history and values of the community • Acknowledge power difference • Has the community agreed to participate?	• Identify the targeted gifted special populations • Identify allies in that community and respectfully request their assistance
Use context to define research problem	• Issues under examination are defined appropriately for the community • Collect background data • Review publicly available datasets and reports • Gather key stakeholders' perspectives • Hold community forums to receive feedback on the issue	• Disaggregate school district information by race, ethnicity, language, and income • Form an advisory committee, reflective of the community/special population, as a form of checks and balances; accountability
Identify root causes of the issue, along with contributing causal factors	• Identifies the conditions that allow the issue to occur or persist • Researchers dig deeper to uncover the systematic and societal root causes of the issue they are researching	• Acquire information and data from community stakeholders impacted by the research • Results from "drilling down" into the data to identify root causes is publicly shared

Table 1.3 Stages of the Research Process: Connections to Equity in Gifted Education: Stage 2: Study Design and Data Collection

Components	Characteristics	Connections to Equity in Gifted Education
Develop ethical research questions	• Research questions should reflect the community's values and perspectives • Actively encourages community to engage in research process	• Research questions account for race, power structures, language, and privilege • Identifies how the community/special population will benefit from research
Determine the research design by gathering community input	• Researchers must ensure that the community respects and trusts the design and type(s) of data collected	• Avoid randomized control trials that perpetuate disproportionality • Be sensitive to study participants who may have experienced discrimination in the past
Decide who will collect the data	• Avoid homogeneous research teams • Have discussions on how life experiences may impact perspective on research	• Researchers reflect the ethnic and racial diversity of the community where the research is taking place
Identify data collection instruments	• Select methodology that answers the research questions but also eliminates method or measurement biases	• Identifies and makes public the relationship between the measurement tools and scales used and the community/special population

Table 1.4 Stages of the Research Process: Connections to Equity in Gifted Education: Stage 3: Data Analysis

Components	Characteristics	Connections to Equity in Gifted Education
Confront implicit bias in data analysis	• Researchers engage in self-reflection • Identify their assumptions and implicit bias and how that may influence how they conduct research	• Researchers share their discussions with community stakeholders, advisory group • Both parties come to a common agreement on moving forward
Quantitative data analysis	• Disaggregate data by race, ethnicity, language, etc. • This allows researchers to examine important variables by different racial and ethnic sub-groups	• Researchers also look at structural and societal determinants that might explain data findings
Qualitative data analysis	• Asks explicit questions that cannot be captured through quantitative means	• Questions are delivered in the languages of the communities impacted by research study
Community involvement in data interpretation	• Research that involves community participants must be respectful and transparent	• Involve stakeholder groups/advisory committee to assist with data analysis and interpretation

Table 1.5 Stages of the Research Process: Connections to Equity in Gifted Education: Stage 4: Dissemination

Components	Characteristics	Connections to Equity in Gifted Education
Audience	• Identifies the audiences they hope their research will reach • Considers what information will be most useful for the community	• Researchers maintain communication with community representatives after the research has been completed – strengthens trust
Messaging	• Researchers are sensitive to the demographics of a community	• The language researchers use with their audiences must be comprehensible; make sense
Medium	• The medium used to disseminate findings should match the needs of the community and audiences for whom the research is intended	• When sharing information and data with community participants, researchers implement a variety of media (forums, town halls, interviews, etc.)
Sustainability	• Findings are accompanied by recommendations or actionable items • Researchers sustain their engagement with policy makers and community representatives	• To promote equity as a result of data findings, researchers work with community participants to engage policy makers to sustain action

major emphasis of the Jacob K. Javits Gifted and Talented Students Program, from the U.S. Department of Education's Office of Elementary and Secondary Education (2006), is on identifying and serving students traditionally underrepresented in gifted and talented programs. The focus is to promote equity and access where researchers have developed concrete steps to embed a racial and ethnic equity perspective within their work. The result typically is an increase in the number of low-income, racially, culturally, and linguistically diverse students who are identified as gifted. The five guiding principles, the stages of the research process, and their connections to research in gifted education can strengthen and sustain the overall research experience.

The Role of Professional Associations in Promoting Equity

Applying research and practices that are responsive to the unique needs of historically underrepresented students is the mantra of local, state, and national associations and organizations dedicated to gifted education. Through their advocacy work they apply an understanding of cultural, social, and economic diversity and individual learner differences to inform the development and improvement of programs, supports, and services. For example, in 2019, the National Association for Gifted Children (NAGC) restructured its Diversity and Equity Committee to oversee efforts to ensure that the association is an equitable organization on issues related to underserved populations, including honoring and cultivating diversity within student populations. The committee will focus on diversity and underrepresented populations, in part, in the following ways:

- Work to raise awareness of the presence of giftedness in diverse, underserved populations and to highlight programs and models that have nurtured success in those populations.
- Recommend to staff and NAGC Committees appropriate ways to further the goals of specific diversity initiatives and opportunities, with the outcome of affecting underrepresented populations more directly.

(NAGC, 2019, n.p.)

Along with other structural changes, the NAGC continues to move forward with its standing commitment to special populations. The Association for the Gifted (TAG), linked with the Council for Exceptional Children (CEC), is another national association that is committed to diversity within gifted education school-based programs. In their seminal publication titled, *Diversity and Developing Gifts and Talents: A National Call to Action*, TAG (2009) believes that diversity and excellence are each essential to the realization of ideals in a democratic society. These ideals have been the cornerstone of our achievements as a society. Diversity has been a topic of discussion in America for decades. Embedded in discussions of diversity and excellence are race, culture, ethnicity, class, gender, sexual orientation, and linguistic issues. Nowhere are these issues more evident than in education. As our society continues to become more diverse, it is even more important that we develop the great variety of gifts and talents of all children and youth in our nation.

The need for a national call to action about diversity and developing gifts and talents derives from the continuing and significant underrepresentation of specific groups receiving educational services for the gifted and talented. This underrepresentation belies the premise that the capacity for exceptional achievement exists across racial, ethnic, language, and economic groups as well as some categories of disability. With all children and youth, expressions of potential differ as a result of family background and experiences with social institutions. As we continue to implement traditional educational policies and practices, we ignore these differences and contribute to the inequities. Our schools must reflect society's changing values about excellence and the needs of its people (TAG, 2009).

Mordechay et al. (2019) write that American society is in the midst of profound demographic changes, and our younger generations are the most diverse generations that we have ever seen. As our diversity grows, a return toward the vision of *Brown v. Board of Education* (1954) becomes more imperative. We need to create schools that will build a society where the gifts, talents, and assets of all are developed, and where students of all races, ethnicities, and social classes receive an equitable education. This can only be achieved by reconceptualizing our ideas of race and place in America and creating integrated communities where all have access to opportunity-rich schools.

Conclusion

A standing commitment to special populations in gifted education means that they will benefit from the work of researchers and scholars; from local, state, and national associations and practitioners in the field; and from policies and practices that promote equity, access, and opportunity. For gifted students of color, this imperative is even more important. Although policy development is an important consideration in addressing equity, changing enrollment policies doesn't address the lack of gifted education and advanced coursework at some schools. Nationwide, high-poverty schools often have fewer rigorous courses than those in more- affluent and higher population areas. The chapters in this book advocate for particular special populations in gifted education. All, in their own way, present information, strategies, and/or recommendations on how we can identify, serve, and advocate for these students. Equity is at the heart of our collective work.

References

Andrews, K., Parekh, J., & Peckoo, S. (2019). *A guide to incorporating a racial and ethnic equity perspective throughout the research process*. Child Trends.

Brown *v*. Board of Education of Topeka, 347 U.S. 483 (1954).

Castellano, J. A. (2018). *Educating Hispanic and Latino students: Opening the doors to hope, promise, and possibilities*. Learning Sciences International.

Mordechay, K., Gandara, P., & Orfield, G. (2019). Embracing the effect of demographic change. *Educational Leadership, 76*(7), 34–40.

National Association for Gifted Children. (2019). Diversity and equity committee structure. Retrieved from: www.nagc.org/diversity-equity-committee-structure

Samuels, C. A. (2020a). Pursuing equity. *Education Week, 39*(24), 1.

Samuels, C. A. (2020b). A clear-eyed view of the inequities in school. *Education Week, 39*(24), 2–3.

The Association for the Gifted [TAG]. (2009). *Diversity and developing gifts and talents: A national call to action*. Council for Exceptional Children.

United States Department of Education. (2006). Jacob K. Javits Gifted and Talented Students Education Program. Retrieved from: www.ed.gov/programs/javits/awards.html

Part II

Expanding the View of Special Populations

Connecting and Understanding

Chapter 2

On the Move

Helping Military-Connected Gifted Students Navigate Non-Promotional School Transitions

Melanie S. Meyer

When a parent serves in the armed forces, their children also make sacrifices. Over 200,000 children with a parent or guardian in the United States military experience non-promotional school transitions each year (Center for Public Research and Leadership [CPRL], 2017). In addition to transitioning from elementary to middle and middle to high school, these students move six to nine times, on average, during their K–12 education. These military job-related moves are referred to as a permanent change of station (PCS), but despite the name, these duty station changes are often temporary and military families may have to make subsequent moves. The Department of Defense Education Activity (DoDEA) operates a limited number of schools on the East Coast and outside the contiguous United States (OCONUS), but about 80% of military-connected pupils are served in their local public schools (CPRL, 2017). State definitions of giftedness and service models can vary drastically (Rinn et al., 2020), so the portability of gifted identification from district to district is often limited by local education agency policies. Consequently, students from military families may have to be reevaluated by their new schools, creating the potential for discontinuity of services (Borland, 2005; Military Child Education Coalition [MCEC], 2020; Plucker & Peters, 2016). School districts that are closer to military installations or those with higher percentages of military-connected students may be more aware of the needs of this student population, but there are military-connected students in most public school systems. For example, in Texas, there are military-connected gifted and talented students in every education service center region in the state, even in districts not geographically close to military installations (Rodriguez & Brewer, 2019). Regular promotional transitions can be challenging, even for well-adjusted students, but the addition of non-promotional transitions can present social, emotional, and academic challenges for gifted and talented military-connected students and their families.

School Transitions

In the civilian population, students move from school to school for a variety of reasons, including parental job changes, shifts in the family, such as divorce, or fluctuations in financial resources. Sometimes these moves are across town and other times across the state or country. Family stress theory suggests that transition-related stress, added to the stress of everyday life, creates a cumulative effect that may make it more difficult for students experiencing non-promotional school moves to focus on academic achievement (Bradshaw et al., 2010). In addition, the timing of school changes (e.g., elementary, middle, or high

DOI: 10.4324/9781003265412-6

school) may also impact student reactions to transition-related stress. In one study, middle school movers, compared to elementary movers, showed decreases in academic achievement, an effect that was more pronounced for girls in the sample (Anderson, 2017). As students move into high school, academic performance is more directly linked to critical milestones (e.g., high school graduation, entry into college, career training, or the military), so even temporary performance decreases can be difficult for students to overcome (MCEC, 2020). Children from military families are three times more likely to experience geographic mobility than their civilian peers (CPRL, 2017), so although changing schools is difficult for children of all ages and genders, military-connected children face additional challenges.

School Transitions for Military Children

Military family moves may be made to a new area of the country, to an overseas duty station, or back to the United States after being stationed abroad, so families have to adjust to regional differences while also managing the practical aspects of daily life, including school (Anderson, 2017). For military families, geographic mobility is part of the job, and with every move, school-aged military-connected students must adjust to new homes and new schools simultaneously (CPRL, 2017; Lester & Flake, 2013). Consequently, the climate of the receiving school plays a critical role in facilitating smooth transitions for students from military families (MCEC, 2020). Education professionals must understand that military families are not a homogeneous group. Although there are similarities between the experiences of individual military families, there are also notable differences in their lived experiences based on a combination of factors, including the service member's career field, military branch, and duty station. Due to the complexity of the phenomenon, the information and examples provided in this chapter cannot begin to address the experiences of all military families, but they will provide a broad overview of common issues faced by military-connected gifted students experiencing school transitions.

Elementary and secondary students from military families have lived their entire lives with the possibility of an active duty, National Guard, or Reserve parent deploying to a conflict zone due to U.S. involvement in military campaigns in Iraq, Afghanistan, and other global hotspots in the international war on terror since 2001 (Torreon, 2018). Some military-connected students transitioning to new schools will experience the deployment of a parent. Other military families may be assigned to duty stations farther from on-base support (e.g., college Reserve Officers' Training Corps [ROTC] assignments). Traditional National Guard and Reserve members who are not full-time employees may not live in close proximity to the military installation where they report for monthly drill and annual training. Military families can "experience a sense of aloneness" when moving to a new community or when they live "in a community with no military affiliation" (Harrison & Vannest, 2008, p. 19). Military family experiences may be quite different, so when working with military-connected students in transition it is critical to understand the family's unique situation rather than making assumptions. In a survey of more than 5,000 military-connected students, parents, veterans, and education professionals who work with military families (see MCEC, 2020), students emphasized that "not all military kids come from the same background or education" (p. 8), but encouraged educators to "look for the positive" (p. 9). For students receiving school-based gifted, advanced academic, or talent development services, there may be additional concerns related to placement and continuity of services.

Military-Connected Students in Gifted Education

The unique challenges faced by military-connected gifted students have not been fully explored in gifted education literature, but it is clear that transitions can cause a loss of educational opportunities, such as gifted program participation. Varying identification protocols are frustrating for parents and students, who might qualify for gifted services in one state, but not in another (Borland, 2005; CPRL, 2017; MCEC, 2020; Rinn et al., 2020). One study noted that military-connected students reach college entrance milestones at a rate comparable to their peers, due in large part to academic socialization in the home (e.g., talking about college and career goals) and the military culture of mission-readiness (Cabrera et al., 2018). Another study found that on state assessments for math and reading, military-connected students consistently passed at higher rates than their non-military peers (Muller et al., 2016a). Using three years of achievement data, the same researchers determined that military-connected students were less likely to be labeled at-risk than their non-military peers (Muller et al., 2016b). However, gifted and talented program participation was lower for military-connected students than for other student groups (Muller et al., 2016a, 2016b). Taken together, these studies indicate that military-connected students may exhibit higher academic achievement than their civilian peers, but they may also participate in gifted programs at lower rates. When asked about their top academic concerns, military parents and students both listed "accessing gifted education programs" and "accessing advanced academic programs" (MCEC, 2020, p. 18). These findings emphasize the need for education policies that support the unique needs of this population of geographically mobile high-ability students.

For readers unfamiliar with the challenges faced by children from military families, it may be helpful to have a few concrete examples of real-life situations that military-connected students routinely face as a result of school transitions. Three vignettes will examine the diverse needs of military-connected elementary, middle, and high school students in transition:

Three Vignettes

Alisha's story

Alisha is a third grader whose family received PCS orders to move to a new state. Her father and his new unit are preparing for an overseas deployment. Alisha's sending school served gifted and talented students in her grade through a twice-weekly pull-out enrichment program, but her receiving school uses a self-contained gifted and talented class model. Although her parents are concerned about Alisha's academic transition, they also worry about her social adjustment to the new school and her emotional adjustment to her father's upcoming absence.

Jason's story

Jason is an eighth grader whose mother received PCS orders to move to a new state. Jason's new middle school offers a general enrichment elective for gifted services, but does not offer the accelerated math and science options that were available at his old school. In addition, wrestling, a sport he has participated in for two years, is not offered at the middle school level in his new school either. Jason and his mother are concerned about his academic options for math and science, his extracurricular choices, and his opportunities to build a new social network.

Grace's story

For her senior year, Grace and her family will relocate to a new state so her father can teach courses on a military base. The Advanced Placement French language and literature course Grace has been preparing to take is not offered at the new school. With high school graduation approaching, Grace and her parents are concerned about the new state's graduation requirements, as well as how her recalculated grade point average (GPA) and class rank may impact the college admissions process.

After the discussion of policy and best practices for supporting military-connected students experiencing school transitions, we will revisit the stories of these young people to describe best case scenarios and how those outcomes can be achieved through collaboration between students, their families, and school personnel.

The Interstate Compact

Fortunately, there are educational provisions specifically created for students from military families. The Interstate Compact on Educational Opportunity for Military Children [Interstate Compact] (2016) was introduced in 2008, adopted by all 50 states and the District of Columbia by 2014, and updated in 2016 (Military Interstate Children's Compact Commission [MIC3], n.d.). The compact is intended to "remove barriers to educational success imposed on children of military families because of frequent moves and deployment of their parents" (Interstate Compact, 2016, § 89.4). When a state adopts the compact, the provisions are added to the educational code, but the compact does not supersede state and local education agency policies, nor does it take away local control of education decisions. However, the compact does educate local school districts on the challenges that military-connected students face and offers a guide as to how schools might best support this special population of high-ability students. While there are many other interstate compacts in federal regulations, for the purposes of this chapter, the terms "compact" and "interstate compact" refer to the Interstate Compact on Educational Opportunity for Military Children (2016).

Individuals Covered by the Interstate Compact

The provisions of the compact only apply to the children of active duty service members and National Guard and Reserve members on active duty orders. Single-year provisions are granted to the children of medically discharged or medically retired service members injured on active duty and the children of members who died on active duty (Interstate Compact, 2016, § 89.3). The compact does not apply to the children of National Guard and Reserve members who are not on active duty orders, to the children of military contractors, or to transitions made as a result of voluntary separation or retirement from the armed forces.

Educational Provisions in the Interstate Compact

The provisions of the interstate compact include moves from public or DoDEA schools to other public or DoDEA schools, but do not cover transitions to or from private or home-based educational settings. The compact addresses how school district personnel should approach enrollment documentation (e.g., transcripts, vaccinations), academic placement (e.g., advanced courses, prerequisite courses), program eligibility (e.g., extracurricular participation, gifted services), attendance (e.g., additional excused transition and deployment-related absences), and on-time graduation (e.g., state testing, required course completion) for military-connected students moving into and out of their school systems. However, each of these provisions is followed by a caveat stating that after receiving schools initially "honor placement," they "may perform subsequent evaluations to ensure the child's appropriate course placement" (Interstate Compact, 2016, § 89.8). Although the compact is not solely dedicated to students receiving gifted and talented or advanced academic services, many of the provisions have the potential to positively impact gifted military-connected students in transition.

Support for Students with Gifts and Talents

The following compact provisions highlight the support available to military-connected students who have previously participated in gifted, advanced academic, and talent development services in school.

Early Entry and Acceleration

The compact recommends allowing students who move mid-year to continue their enrollment in the grade level from the sending state. If a student has "satisfactorily completed the prerequisite grade level in the sending state," they should be promoted to the next grade level. The compact further clarifies that these provisions should be honored "regardless of the age of the child" (Interstate Compact, 2016, § 89.8). Some states and districts have restrictions on the age at which a student can enroll in kindergarten, or a minimum age for placement in particular grades. For example, in one state a student may be allowed to enter kindergarten at age four, while in other states, the earliest age for entrance is five. If a four-year-old child successfully completes kindergarten in the sending state, the compact advises that they should be allowed to enroll in first grade for the following school year in the new state. The compact explicitly addresses potential age and grade disparities and encourages districts to allow students to continue the academic trajectory started in the sending state.

Enrollment in Advanced Academics

The compact emphasizes that "as long as the course is offered" by the receiving school, personnel enrolling military-connected students should "honor placement of a transfer student in courses based on the child's placement" from the sending state by enrolling them in a similar course, awarding credit for completed courses, or allowing the student to advance to the next course in a series (Interstate Compact, 2016, § 89.8). For example, if a student was participating in an Advanced Placement course or a series of career and technical education (CTE) courses, they should be allowed to continue in the course or series, provided that the classes are offered. The problem arises when course offerings differ between sending and receiving schools. For example, an advanced world language course that was available in the sending school might not be offered by the receiving school, but the school can help the military-connected student to find a comparable course online or at a local community college or university. The chief consideration for placement decisions under the compact is "continuing the child's academic program from the previous school and promoting placement in academic and career challenging courses" (Interstate Compact, 2016, § 89.8). The purpose of these provisions is to alert school districts to locally created barriers to participation in advanced academic or career development courses that can be removed for military students.

Gifted and Talented Programs

Schools are encouraged to "honor placement of the child in educational programs based on current educational assessments and placement in like programs in the sending state" (Interstate Compact, 2016, § 89.8). This section of the compact specifically addresses gifted and talented program participation and gives local education agencies the option to honor identification test results from the sending state and forgo reassessment. Districts may also temporarily place the student in gifted services, reassess the student according to the receiving school's criteria, and keep or adjust that placement based on the results. Retesting for gifted services is an added strain on a military-connected student making a non-promotional school transition (MCEC, 2020). However, since gifted services can vary drastically between local education agencies, testing that is aligned with the local service model may help ensure appropriate placement in the new learning environment (Peters et al., 2014).

Extracurricular Talent Development

The compact recognizes the importance of the social and talent development opportunities provided by extracurricular participation. The interstate compact instructs school districts to "facilitate the opportunity for transitioning military children's inclusion in extracurricular activities, regardless of application deadlines, to the extent the children are otherwise qualified" (Interstate Compact, 2016, § 89.8). This provision allows students to try out for teams or groups (e.g., band, choir, sports) as soon as they move to the school, even if tryouts have been held or paperwork deadlines have passed. For example, band auditions may have been held in the spring semester of the prior school year, but a student enrolling in the fall semester who has previously participated in band activities should have the opportunity to audition for placement in a band. Schools are not required to hold spots for transferring students, nor are they required to accept students who do not have the requisite skills for participation, but this provision removes some barriers to talent development activities for transitioning military-connected students.

Best Practices for Supporting Military-Connected Student School Transitions

Although military-connected students may have experienced discontinuity of curriculum and may face social and emotional challenges, they also bring strengths, which include resilience, diverse life experiences, and individual gifts and talents. Schools and individual educators must understand that mobility is part of the job description for military service members and that when parents serve in the military, the children, in a sense, serve too (Jagger & Lederer, 2014). The following sections will discuss best practices for addressing identification and assessment, equity and access, curriculum and instruction, and belonging and identity for gifted and talented students from military families.

Identification and Assessment

In order to help families navigate non-promotional transitions most effectively, school personnel need to be aware of a student's military-connected status. The Every Student Succeeds Act (ESSA, 2015) requires schools to collect data on students from military families. If a parent or guardian on active duty or connected to a National Guard or Reserve unit self-reports military-connected status when a student enrolls, a military identifier is linked to the student's educational records. However, this information is often kept for reporting purposes only and is not shared with teachers, administrators, and counselors (De Pedro et al., 2014). If education professionals are aware of a student's military-connected status and the provisions of the interstate compact, they will be better equipped to walk military families through the transition process and to act in the best interest of the military-connected child (CPRL, 2017; MCEC, 2020).

Previously Identified Students

The compact instructs receiving schools to initially place transitioning military students in gifted services similar to those they were receiving in the sending school, if at all possible. When there are differences in identification protocols and service models, communicating with the sending school, reviewing assessment records, and observing the student in the initial placement can allow receiving schools to determine appropriate placement without the added burden of reassessment. When reassessment for services is required, school personnel should communicate with the student and family about the specific differences between identification and services in the two districts and the rationale for retesting. The goal of reassessment should be to "predict success in the program" (Peters et al., 2014, p. 25).

Students Not Previously Identified

For students who were enrolled in gifted and talented services in the sending district, the options for receiving districts are clearly outlined in the compact. However, some military-connected students may come into receiving schools and demonstrate a need for gifted services in the new context. An elementary student from a military family who has never been identified for gifted services may move to a new state and show signs that evaluation is warranted; or a military-connected high school student may be placed in a grade-level math course, but quickly demonstrate a need for single-subject acceleration. Therefore, it is essential that professionals who interact with transfer students (e.g., teachers, gifted specialists, school psychologists) and personnel enrolling military-connected students (e.g., counselors, registrars) are aware of identification processes and gifted service models within the district to ensure that transitioning students have equal access to educationally appropriate placements (MCEC, 2020).

Academic Record-Keeping

Many military families will make subsequent school transitions so gifted program coordinators can assist families by providing copies of educational assessments, such as gifted and talented program testing reports. These reports, combined with a parent handbook or detailed description of the gifted identification process and service model by grade level and subject-area will be valuable tools for future school enrollment conferences (MCEC, 2020). Counselors and registrars can encourage secondary students to select challenging courses that are also more likely to transfer across schools and districts, such as Advanced Placement options, when possible (CPRL, 2017). Teachers can help military-connected students record mastered skills, course readings, and other relevant class content. They can also provide parents and older students with a syllabus or scope and sequence document for the course to keep on file for future enrollments (CPRL, 2017). In addition, for older high school students who are withdrawing, it is helpful to supply contact information or letters of recommendation for use in the college application process (MCEC, 2020). When schools welcome military families to collaborate with them on placement decisions and provide tools to navigate future transitions, parents will have the information they need to participate in enrollment meetings and students can advocate for themselves in conversations about course credit, grade point average, and class rank.

Equity and Access

Students from military families often encounter obstacles related to gifted and talented programming (MCEC, 2020) and students from culturally, linguistically, and economically diverse backgrounds may face additional challenges, particularly if they transition into gifted and talented classes where they do not see themselves reflected in the curriculum or the composition of the group (Ford et al., 2018). Gifted and talented programs need to be evaluated regularly for inclusiveness and other factors related to the retention of students from diverse cultural backgrounds (Ford et al., 2008), including geographically mobile military families.

Underrepresentation and Deficit Thinking

Ford et al. (2018) noted that "gifted students of color" are "extensively underrepresented in gifted education" (p. 125) and identified systemic practices in education, including "deficit thinking," that are "fueling underrepresentation" in gifted and advanced academic programs (Ford, 2010, p. 32). Ford and Grantham (2003) defined "deficit thinking" by describing situations "when educators hold negative, stereotypic, and counterproductive views about culturally diverse students and lower their expectations accordingly" (p. 217). Educators may inadvertently engage in deficit thinking when working with highly mobile students, including those from military families, due to students' perceived gaps in knowledge and skills that stem from differences between the curriculum in sending and receiving schools. When student mobility is viewed as a deficit, rather than a strength, the entire learning community misses out on the rich experiences that military-connected students bring with them (MCEC, 2020). Schools have an obligation to create learning environments that are safe, culturally responsive spaces for students with a variety of lived experiences. Gifted program coordinators and education professionals involved in gifted identification and program planning must carefully evaluate their programs to ensure that they are accessible, equitable, culturally responsive, and not grounded in underlying beliefs that reflect deficit thinking (Ford, 2010; Ford et al., 2018).

Challenging Identification and Placement Decisions

Military organizations are mission-focused and function according to a hierarchy and chain of command (Astor et al., 2012). As a result, some military parents may be reluctant to question the decisions of receiving schools with regards to course placement or program participation. However, high-ability students who are academically talented need opportunities to learn and grow in school environments, so families and students themselves may have to advocate for inclusion in gifted education programs (Plucker & Peters, 2016). The School Liaison Program can assist families of gifted and talented students. School Liaison Officers (SLOs) provide a bridge between military families and local education agencies and can be an important source of information about gifted and talented services in local school districts (Jagger & Lederer, 2014; MCEC, 2020). For families who live farther from on-base supports, resources are available through military education and family organizations (e.g., Military Child Education Coalition, www.militarychild.org/; National Military Family Association, www.militaryfamily.org/). Transition resources may also be available through the state education agency or the local school district, but service members have to know about these resources and be able to access them.

Curriculum and Instruction

Once a military-connected student is placed in a gifted or advanced academic program, there are additional curriculum and instruction considerations to examine. Many students from military families are resilient, but school personnel must be aware of potential transition-related issues at school and at home, and have structures in place that support the continued academic achievement of military-connected students (Astor et al., 2012; De Pedro et al., 2014; Garner et al., 2014; Russo & Fallon, 2015). Due to potential differences between the sending and receiving districts' curriculum, it is important for schools and individual educators who receive military-connected students in gifted and advanced academic programs to focus on student strengths and to provide opportunities for mastery learning.

Create Strength-Based Intake Protocols

Discontinuity of curriculum between schools can create the perception of gaps in student knowledge and skills, but teachers can help military-connected students by implementing flexible, data-informed instructional plans (Garner et al., 2014). When assessing military students in transition, teachers should consider the experiences and strengths of the individual student and use a variety of approaches, methods, and materials in combination to help students achieve academically (Russo & Fallon, 2015). Student learning is a dynamic process, and while it might be tempting to focus exclusively on perceived student skill gaps or deficits (Ford, 2010; Ford & Grantham, 2003), students are better served when instructors adopt strength-based intake protocols. Teachers can use diagnostic assessments to identify areas of strength and possible knowledge and skill gaps. These assessments can be formal or informal, and should account for both the scope of the curriculum and the sequencing of the content and skills. Teaching professionals can use the results of these assessments to confer with students and parents, and to develop an instructional plan specific to the transfer student and the course (Russo & Fallon, 2015). Proyer et al. (2017) described several key elements of successful strength-based interventions, which include identifying student strengths, allowing students to share common experiences with peers, facilitating academic interventions, and collaborating to discuss growth and set new goals. Military-connected gifted students likely have areas of interest that can be channeled into guided and independent investigations to facilitate content mastery. Dynamic, rather than deficit, thinking is the key to designing instruction that allows transitioning military students to work in areas of strength and talent, while also addressing content they may have missed in school-to-school moves (Baum et al., 2014; Ford & Grantham, 2003).

Adopt Mastery Learning Approaches

Mastery learning approaches are instructional systems that prioritize the mastery of content and skills and minimize the negative consequences of creative risk-taking and initial failures as learners gain competence in a domain (Beghetto, 2013; Schlechty, 2012). These approaches can be used with any incoming student to gather data on academic abilities and create personalized instruction plans. Diagnostic assessments allow students to demonstrate mastery of skills and concepts that will be covered throughout the academic year in order to identify strengths. In many cases, a military-connected student may not have mastered content from one unit, but they may have mastered content from a later unit, so the time reserved for that later unit can be used to return to the earlier unit's concepts and skills. These flexible approaches can be adapted for any course content to allow transitioning military students to demonstrate mastery of the curriculum they have already covered in previous schools, but also to move flexibly through content that is new to them. Mastery learning approaches that incorporate differentiated instruction and prioritize students' strengths can help mobile high-ability students continue to show academic achievement during a school transition (Baum et al., 2014).

Belonging and Identity

Academically advanced students may experience the exploration of identity differently, particularly where their academic, social, and emotional lives intersect. At times, gifted students may face a "forced-choice dilemma" in which they feel they must choose between academic achievement or fitting in with their same-age peers (Gross, 1989, p. 189; Neihart, 2006). Military-connected children who "start over and over again, just getting comfortable when it is time to move again" (MCEC, 2020, p. 28) may have difficulty figuring out where they belong in the new school context. For gifted and talented students from military families, the process of trying to develop a new social support network adds yet another layer of complexity to school transitions. Many military-connected children navigate transitions successfully and develop new social networks, but this requires resilience and supportive home and school environments (De Pedro et al., 2014).

Support Social and Emotional Adjustment

When teachers welcome new students into their classrooms, they set the tone for the transition. Teachers should be sensitive when asking students to introduce themselves and say where they are from, since there may be differences between the place where students lived most recently and the place they identify as home (Astor et al., 2012; CPRL, 2017). Depending on classroom culture, it may be more appropriate for the teacher to hold these conversations one-on-one with the new student. It can be difficult for military-connected students experiencing a non-promotional transition to develop academic support networks and make friends (MCEC, 2020). Classroom teachers can pair new students with helpful classmates so that they have someone to eat lunch with and someone to answer questions about the school or their classes (Astor et al., 2012; Hébert, 2011). It is also critical for education professionals to evaluate and explicitly discuss aspects of the hidden curriculum with new students, including rules, procedures, school climate, and practical considerations, such as bathroom locations and lunch options. It may be helpful to enlist the aid of students, particularly those who have experienced school moves themselves, in developing orientation programs for new students (CPRL, 2017; MCEC, 2020). Schools can host peer-led Student 2 Student® programs that partner incoming students with other students from military families for support (www.militarychild.org/programs/student-2-student). When teachers design learning experiences that recognize and celebrate the unique social and cultural capital each student brings to the learning environment, military-connected students may feel more welcomed and supported in their new schools (Cabrera et al., 2018; Lester & Flake, 2013). When an individual's academic, social, and family life are all in a state of change, having a constant becomes increasingly important (Bradshaw et al., 2010; Cabrera et al., 2018). Extracurricular activities can be a lifeline for transitioning military students and participation in these activities has been positively correlated with successful outcomes, including "educational attainment" and "future earnings" (Snellman et al., 2015, p. 195). However, activities may not be consistent across states and districts and students may have to explore new options (Bradshaw et al., 2010; CPRL, 2017). Military-connected children have unique needs, and schools can provide a stable and supportive learning environment as they adjust socially and emotionally.

Provide Social and Emotional Interventions

Non-promotional school transitions can build resilience, but may also increase mobility-related stressors in children and adolescents. For high-ability students engaged in talent development in academic or extracurricular domains, psychosocial skills are critical. These psychological, social, and emotional skills, such as self-regulation, motivation, and adaptation, are necessary for academic achievement and the development of talent (Rinn, 2020; Subotnik et al., 2018). A social-emotional curriculum (e.g., Dai & Speerschneider, 2012) and mentoring programs (Hébert, 2011) may be helpful for students from military families who are adjusting to new schools. However, teachers and counselors need training and strategies for coaching student psychosocial skill development and supporting their social and emotional needs (Rinn, 2020). Some military-connected children transition with little difficulty, whereas others may experience temporary transition-related stress, and still others may benefit from professional intervention (Gewirtz et al., 2018). Families should maintain open lines of communication with children and their classroom teachers. While there will be transition-related stress, particularly for academically advanced students adjusting to new academic programs and services, this stress may subside after an initial adjustment period (Dai & Rinn, 2008). If stress-related issues worsen, families can reach out to school counselors, gifted program coordinators, and classroom teachers.

Access Military Support Networks

There are established resources for military families that may be helpful for school personnel as well. Base SLOs can also provide information about extracurricular and wellness programs in the community for military families and students. Military families have access to organized social support networks. The Army, Navy, and Marine Corps have Family Readiness Groups/Programs and the Air Force has a Key Spouse Program (Cabrera et al., 2018; Lester & Flake, 2013). One of the many benefits of these programs is a network of other families who have experienced school transitions with their children, in many cases to or from the same schools in different regions of the country or overseas. These families can be a resource when navigating gifted program placement with the new school, particularly if they have experienced the process themselves. In addition, online resources, such as SchoolQuest, can help military families plan school transitions by providing a free platform to research schools, gather academic records, and make enrollment decisions (https://schoolquest.militarychild.org/about-schoolquest).

Military-Connected Student Vignettes

Earlier in the chapter, three scenarios were introduced to illustrate common issues that students from military families experience as a result of non-promotional school transitions. In light of the research, policy, and best practice recommendations discussed in the chapter, we revisit each student to identify ways that school personnel can collaborate with students and their families to facilitate positive transition experiences.

Alisha's Story

Alisha, a third grader attending a public elementary school on the West Coast, and her family received PCS orders and moved to a new state where her father prepared for deployment. Alisha was placed in a self-contained gifted and talented class pending retesting. Her teachers and parents monitored her social and academic adjustment closely since her old school had provided gifted services in a pull-out enrichment program two times per week, while her new school served students through ability-grouped and accelerated instruction in all subject areas each school day. Alisha thrived in some aspects of the new gifted and talented class, but she also benefitted from targeted interventions to address perceived gaps in content knowledge and skills resulting from differences in the curriculum between her sending and receiving schools (Astor et al., 2012; De Pedro et al., 2014; Garner et al., 2014; Russo & Fallon, 2015). At the end of the school year, Alisha was performing at a level comparable to her academically advanced peers and the school chose to maintain her placement in the gifted and talented class rather than retesting her (Interstate Compact, 2016, § 89.8). She also received coaching in psychosocial strategies to help her cope with the increased rigor of the academic program and her father's upcoming deployment. Alisha met one-on-one with her classroom teacher for targeted work on academic skills and participated in small-group guidance counseling with other military-connected students on her campus (Astor et al., 2012; De Pedro et al., 2014; Garner et al., 2014; Russo & Fallon, 2015). Her parents and school personnel maintained open lines of communication with Alisha and each other about her academic, social, and emotional adjustment throughout the school year (Astor et al., 2012; De Pedro et al., 2014; Garner et al., 2014; Russo & Fallon, 2015). Alisha's story illustrates the importance of addressing social and emotional adjustment alongside academic achievement, particularly for students from military families who are experiencing non-promotional school transitions.

Jason's Story

Jason, an eighth grader enrolled in accelerated math and science courses, and his mother received PCS orders to move to a new state. Although he had been a wrestler on his school team for two years, in Jason's new middle school, there was no wrestling team, so he decided to give technical theater classes a try. The school paired Jason up with a fellow student for the first week after he transferred and this student showed him around the school and answered questions (MCEC, 2020). In contrast to the accelerated math and science courses at his old school, the new middle school offered a general enrichment elective for gifted services. For Jason, the enrichment elective offered opportunities to explore his interest in mechanical engineering, but he and his mother discussed with his counselor the issue that he was not being adequately challenged in his new math and science courses. After demonstrating mastery and earning credit by exam for his current math and science courses, he was given the option of taking accelerated courses at the high school or online (Interstate Compact, 2016, § 89.8; National Association for Gifted Children [NAGC], 2019). Theater courses provided a way for Jason to start building a new social network and he continued strength and conditioning training on his own in hopes of joining the high school wrestling team the following year (Interstate Compact, 2016, § 89.8; Snellman et al., 2015). Jason's story illustrates the benefits of creating proactive systems to welcome new students into school learning communities (CPRL, 2017; MCEC, 2020) and the importance of gifted education service models that provide flexible options for academic talent development and acceleration (NAGC, 2019).

Grace's Story

Right before her senior year in high school, Grace and her family moved to the Northwest so that her dad, recently home from deployment, could teach training courses on a military base. Grace was on track to graduate with honors and was ranked in the top 5% of her class. Upon enrolling in her new school, the registrar notified Grace and her parents that the school did not offer advanced courses in French, a language she had been studying for three years. She also found out that she would have to take two state-mandated courses and an end-of-course test in order to graduate. Her grade point average was recalculated according to the new district's procedures, which caused her class rank to drop. Grace was able to try out for varsity swim and made the team. Through swim, Grace met other military-connected students who had also moved to the school recently. Between work and a military family organization, her parents met other families who were new to the area. Grace and her parents talked to the SLO at the military base and learned about options under the compact to substitute for similar testing from the sending state, how to petition for credit for coursework she has already done, or to join a state exam study group with other transitioning students (Jagger & Lederer, 2014; MCEC, 2020). Grace was able to continue her French studies at a local community college. She still worried about her chances of getting into her top choice for college, so for her college applications, Grace contacted teachers from her old school to help with recommendation letters (CPRL, 2017; MCEC, 2020). She also enlisted her new composition teacher who helped her to write a compelling application essay on how military-connected geographic mobility impacted her high school experience. Grace's story illustrates the importance of understanding the big picture and acknowledging that local policy decisions at the secondary level have the potential to impact students' postsecondary talent development opportunities for better or worse. It also emphasizes the fact that local education agencies have considerable flexibility in how they approach the handling of transfer student records, and that whenever possible, they should make decisions that support the best interests of all students, including those from military families (Interstate Compact, 2016).

Conclusion

There has been a call for stronger policy research in gifted education, with a specific focus on the possible unintended consequences of policy decisions (Plucker et al., 2017). School district policies related to enrollment, course placement, course credit, and program participation may inadvertently penalize military-connected students who have had to change schools as a result of parental job-related moves. However, local education agencies can examine their policies and use the guidance provided in the Interstate Compact on

Educational Opportunity for Military Children (2016) to act in the best interest of gifted students from military families. School personnel can proactively plan how they will assist students who move into and out of their school districts. Transitioning students can benefit from a flexible curriculum within high-quality academic programs, scaffolding to meet current academic needs, social and emotional support, and help with record-keeping for future transitions. Former president Ronald Reagan (1987, n.p.) said, "Freedom is never more than one generation away from extinction. It has to be fought for and defended by each generation." For educators and school personnel who interact with the gifted and academically talented children of members of the armed forces, caring for this special population of students and showing respect for their lived experiences is one way to demonstrate gratitude to those who serve.

References

Anderson, S. (2017). School mobility among middle school students: When and for whom does it matter? *Psychology in the Schools, 54*(5), 487–503. https://doi.org/10.1002/pits.22010

Astor, R. A., Jacobson, L., Benbenishty, R., Atuel, H., Gilreath, T., Wong, M., ... Estrada, J. N. (2012). *The teacher's guide for supporting students from military families.* Teachers College Press.

Baum, S. M., Schader, R. M., & Hébert, T. P. (2014). Through a different lens: Reflecting on a strengths-based, talent-focused approach for twice-exceptional learners. *Gifted Child Quarterly, 58*(4), 311–327. https://doi.org/10.1177/0016986214547632

Beghetto, R. A. (2013). *Killing ideas softly? The promise and perils of creativity in the classroom.* Information Age Publishing.

Borland, J. H. (2005). Gifted education without gifted children: The case for no conception of giftedness. In R. J. Sternberg & J. E. Davidson (Eds.), *Conceptions of giftedness* (2nd ed., pp. 1–19). Cambridge University Press.

Bradshaw, C. P., Sudhinaraset, M., Mmari, K., & Blum, R. W. (2010). School transitions among military adolescents: A qualitative study of stress and coping. *School Psychology Review, 39*(1), 84–105. https://doi.org/10.1080/02796015.2010.12087792

Cabrera, A. F., Peralta, A. M., & Kurban, E. R. (2018). The invisible 1%: A comparison of attaining stepping stones toward college between military and civilian children. *Journal of Higher Education, 89*(2), 208–235. https://doi.org/10.1080/00221546.2017.1368816

Center for Public Research and Leadership [CPRL]. (2017). *The challenges of supporting highly mobile, military-connected children in school transitions: The current environment.* Columbia University.

Dai, D. Y., & Rinn, A. N. (2008). The big-fish-little-pond effect: What do we know and where do we go from here? *Educational Psychology Review, 20,* 283–317. https://doi.org/10.1007/s10648-008-9071-x

Dai, D. Y., & Speerschneider, K. (2012). Cope and grow: A model of affective curriculum for talent development. *Talent Development & Excellence, 4*(2), 181–199.

De Pedro, K. T., Esqueda, M. C., Cederbaum, J. A., & Astor, R. A. (2014). District, school, and community stakeholder perspectives on the experiences of military-connected students. *Teachers College Record, 116*(5), 1–32.

ESSA (2015). Every Student Succeeds Act of 2015, Pub. L. No. 114–95 § 114 Stat. 1177 (2015–2016).

Ford, D. Y. (2010). Underrepresentation of culturally different students in gifted education: Reflections about current problems and recommendations for the future. *Gifted Child Today, 33*(3), 31–35. https://doi.org/10.1177/107621751003300308

Ford, D. Y., Dickson, K. T., Davis, J. L., Trotman Scott, M., & Grantham, T. C. (2018). A culturally responsive equity-based bill of rights for gifted students of color. *Gifted Child Today, 41*(3), 125–128. https://doi.org/10.1177/1076217518769698

Ford, D. Y., & Grantham, T. C. (2003). Providing access for culturally diverse gifted students: From deficit to dynamic thinking. *Theory Into Practice, 42*(3), 217–225. https://doi.org/10.1207/s15430421tip4203_8

Ford, D. Y., Grantham, T. C., & Whiting, G. W. (2008). Culturally and linguistically diverse students in gifted education: Recruitment and retention issues. *Exceptional Children, 74*(3), 289–306. https://doi.org/10.1177/001440290807400302

Garner, J. K., Arnold, P. L., & Nunnery, J. (2014). Schoolwide impact of military-connected student enrollment: Educators' perceptions. *Children and Schools, 36*(1), 31–39. https://doi.org/10.1093/cs/cdt026

Gewirtz, A. H., DeGarmo, D. S., & Zamir, O. (2018). After deployment, adaptive parenting tools: 1-year outcomes of an evidence-based parenting program for military families following deployment. *Prevention Science, 19*, 589–599. https://doi.org/10.1007/s11121-017-0839-4

Gross, M. U. M. (1989). The pursuit of excellence or the search for intimacy? The forced choice dilemma of gifted youth. *Roeper Review, 11*, 189–194. https://doi.org/10.1080/02783198909553207

Harrison, J., & Vannest, K. J. (2008). Educators supporting families in times of crisis: Military reserve deployments. *Preventing School Failure, 52*(4), 17–24. https://doi.org/10.3200/PSFL.52.4.17-24

Hébert, T. P. (2011). *Understanding the social and emotional lives of gifted students*. Prufrock Press.

Interstate Compact on Educational Opportunity for Military Children, 32 C. F. R. § 89 (2016).

Jagger, J. C., & Lederer, S. (2014). Impact of geographic mobility on military children's access to special education services. *Children and Schools, 36*(1), 15–22. https://doi.org/10.1093/cs/cdt046

Lester, P., & Flake, E. (2013). How wartime military service affects children and families. *The Future of Children, 23*(2), 121–141. https://doi.org/10.1353/foc.2013.0015

Military Child Education Coalition [MCEC]. (2020). *Military kids now 2020 survey: Summary report*. Retrieved from: www.militarychild.org/upload/files/MCEC_2020EdSurvey_digital.pdf

Military Interstate Children's Compact Commission [MIC3]. (n.d.). *Organization timeline*. Retrieved from: www.mic3.net/assets/ldc-graphic-rev-14-nov.pdf

Muller, R., Tong, F., & Irby, B. J. (2016a). *Military student achievement report 2014–2015*. Educational Leadership Research Center. http://elrc.tamu.edu/wp-content/uploads/2017/02/Military-Acheivement-Report-.pdf

Muller, R., Tong, F., & Irby, B. J. (2016b). *The military student identifier: A Texas study*. Educational Leadership Research Center. http://elrcprod.wpengine.com/wp-content/uploads/2017/02/The-Military-Student-Identifier.pdf

National Association for Gifted Children [NAGC]. (2019) *Pre-K to grade 12 gifted programming standards*. Retrieved from: www.nagc.org/sites/default/files/standards/Intro%202019%20Programming%20Standards%281%29.pdf

Neihart, M. (2006). Dimensions of underachievement, difficult contexts, and perceptions of self: Achievement/affiliation conflicts in gifted adolescents. *Roeper Review, 28*, 196–202. https://doi.org/10.1080/02783190609554364

Peters, S. J., Matthews, M. S., McBee, M. T., & McCoach, D. B. (2014). *Beyond gifted education: Designing and implementing advanced academic programs*. Prufrock Press.

Plucker, J. A., Makel, M. C., Matthews, M. S., Peters, S. J., & Rambo-Hernandez, K. E. (2017). Blazing new trails: Strengthening policy research in gifted education. *Gifted Child Quarterly, 61*(3), 210–218. https://doi.org/10.1177/0016986217701838

Plucker, J. A., & Peters, S. J. (2016). *Excellence gaps in education: Expanding opportunities for talented students*. Harvard Education Press.

Proyer, R. T., Gander, F., & Tandler, N. (2017). Strength-based interventions: Their importance in application to the gifted. *Gifted Education International, 33*(2), 118–130. https://doi.org/10.1177/0261429416640334

Reagan, R. (1987, July 6). Remarks at the annual convention of Kiwanis International. Retrieved from: www.reaganfoundation.org/ronald-reagan/reagan-quotes-speeches/remarks-at-the-annual-convention-of-kiwanis-international/

Rinn, A. N. (2020). *Social, emotional, and psychosocial development of gifted and talented individuals*. Prufrock Academic Press.

Rinn, A. N., Mun, R. U., & Hodges, J. (2020). *2018–2019 State of the states in gifted education.* National Association of Gifted Children and the Council of State Directors of Programs for the Gifted.

Rodriguez, A., & Brewer, M. (2019, June 18–20). *Serving the gifted/talented military child* [Conference session]. Texas Association for the Gifted and Talented Gifted Plus Equity Conference, San Antonio, TX, United States.

Russo, T. J., & Fallon, M. A. (2015). Coping with stress: Supporting the needs of military children and their families. *Early Childhood Education Journal, 43,* 407–416. https://doi.org/10.1007/s10643-014-0665-2

Schlechty, P. C. (2012). *Leading for learning: How to transform schools into learning organizations.* Jossey-Bass.

Snellman, K., Silva, J. M., Frederick, C. B., & Putnam, R. D. (2015). The engagement gap: Social mobility and extracurricular participation among American youth. *The Annals of the American Academy of Social and Political Sciences, 657*(1), 194–207. https://doi.org/10.1177/0002716214548398

Subotnik, R. F., Olszewski-Kubilius, P., & Worrell, F. C. (2018). The talent development framework: Overview of components and implications for policy and practice. In P. Olszewski-Kubilius, R. F. Subotnik, & F. C. Worrell (Eds.), *Talent development as a framework for gifted education: Implications for best practices and applications in schools* (pp. 7–23). Prufrock Academic Press.

Torreon, B. S. (2018). *U.S. periods of war and dates of recent conflicts* (RS21405, Version 27, Updated). Congressional Research Service.

Chapter 3

Educating Gifted Students with Trauma, Toxic Stress, and Adverse Childhood Experiences

Jaime A. Castellano

Vignette: Jennyffer's Story

I was eight years old when my mother passed away. She passed three days after my birthday. The day she died I was at school, but I remember every single thing. My uncle picked up me and my brother from school. Instead of taking us home he drove to the home of a family friend. I recall asking him why he didn't take us to our house since we lived right down the street from the school. He didn't respond. We spent a couple of hours at that house before my father arrived. He told me and my brother that something happened to my mother and grandmother, my mother's mom, but wouldn't say what. After prodding him, he said that someone broke into our home to perform a robbery and that my mother and grandmother were there at the time. My father started crying and said, "They are no longer with us." Saying those words broke me. "They are no longer with us." I remember looking at a picture on the wall saying over and over again, "No, it's not true." My brother had stopped crying and asked how they died. My father answered that my mother got shot twice and that her mother got shot in the chest. We cried some more. At the mortuary my father claimed my mother's body and my uncle claimed my grandmother's body. I remember them having an open casket funeral.

After the funeral, we fled Honduras for the United States. My father wanted to keep us safe. Two years later, my father traveled back to Honduras to find us a new place to live. He does and he sends for me and my brother. We were trying to adjust the best we could but it was difficult. One day, my dad went to pick us up from school. In the car was my new stepmother. My brother and I were sitting in the back seat as my father drove to his brother's house. Midway to my uncle's house my father pulls over to let a car pass us by. Instead of continuing down the road the car stops, a guy jumps out and begins shooting at our car. My stepmother got shot once in the knee and my father got shot eight times, dying in front of us. The guy in the other car got back in his car and sped away. I was 12 years-old when this happened. With my uncle, we fled again and returned to the United States. A few months later my father's mother died. I spiraled downward soon after that. I believed my life was filled with sadness and death. I could

---

DOI: 10.4324/9781003265412-7

not handle it. At 12 years of age, I started sneaking out, smoking weed, and hanging out with the wrong crowd. Life didn't seem to matter anymore. What made it worse was that no one understood me. I was a wild child who wanted to be heard. I am 16 years old now and still in pain. Those memories still hurt but I am pushing forward.

When my mother and father died, we lived in Honduras. In both cases the school was informed of what happened. When my mother died, they sent flowers. When my father died representatives from the school came to our house. I vividly remember returning to school and my teachers acting like nothing happened; like it didn't matter and that it was not important enough to offer me support. My advice to teachers, counselors, and principals would be to think about what students go through in their lives. Pull them aside and talk to them. Arrange for them to get some help or support during school hours. Advocate for them and help students with trauma know that you care.

During the 2019–2020 school year, Jennyffer was in my religion education class where she was studying to make her first Holy Communion and Confirmation through the Catholic Church. At times she offers glimpses of her intelligence, gifts, and talents. She spends a lot of time trying to be "cool" and "street." She does not want her classmates to know that she is smarter than she appears. However, she felt safe enough with me to agree to share her story of a gifted student with trauma and PTSD (Post-Traumatic Stress Disorder). She hopes that her story will impact teachers, counselors, and all educators in a positive way by helping those students with trauma, toxic stress, and ACEs.

What Can We Learn from Jennyffer's Story?

My experience as a teacher and administrator in gifted education is that the school is often the last one to know that a student has gone through a traumatic event, or has had an adverse childhood experience. However, once the information is received it is incumbent that they immediately make available school-based support services to address any mental health issues that students like Jennyffer may manifest during the school day. Like she says, *"My advice to teachers, counselors, and principals would be to think about what students go through in their lives."*

This chapter presents gifted students with trauma, toxic stress, and adverse childhood experiences (ACEs) as a new special population in the field of gifted education. Identification and assessment for gifted education eligibility will not be a focus. The assumption is that they have already been identified and are sitting in gifted education classrooms or are enrolled in other Honors, advanced (middle school), and Advanced Placement programs. The chapter will be framed more like a toolbox for teachers of the gifted and any other educator who serves this population. Content will include frequently asked questions; types of trauma; case studies and vignettes; the causes and effects of childhood trauma; and strategies that promote resiliency, relationships, and perseverance. The purpose of the chapter is to inform and educate; to reflect on past and current gifted students; to become advocates; and to become more trauma-sensitive.

In my coursework as a university professor instructing undergraduate pre-service candidates in teacher education, considerable time is spent on how to identify and educate students who experience trauma, toxic stress, or have adverse childhood experiences (ACEs). Students identified as gifted are always part of the conversation. This expanded view of inclusion is important because of the sheer numbers of students who have experienced events in their lives that often leave them emotionally scarred, vulnerable, and susceptible to both short-term and long-term problems with their physical health, mental health, education, and relationships. These students are in our schools and they transcend intelligence and achievement levels, zip-code, and socioeconomic status.

As a behavioral health care case manager for a community-based social service agency that offers mental health services, I work directly with gifted students who have mental health challenges resulting from childhood trauma. My role is to identify and assess client and family needs; evaluate, coordinate, and oversee that necessary services and/or treatment are provided; provide in-home services to clients; complete required assessments; and assist and counsel individuals and families. My clients are in elementary, middle, and high school and are enrolled in gifted education, Honors programs, magnet programs, and Advanced Placement. Face-face visits are held in their homes and in their schools.

I feel fortunate that I am able to work with these gifted students and their families. I know firsthand about suffering from toxic stress and adverse childhood experiences. I was one of these gifted students during my K-12 years. I lived in a dysfunctional home where abuse, neglect, violence, addiction, mental illness, and abject poverty were the norm. It wasn't until I left home at 18 years of age that the nightmares stopped. It was a matter of survival and I chose to leave my family. I went to a state university and never returned home other than to visit my mother for a couple of hours once or twice a year. I suppose my own experiences explain, in part, why I am effective in working with this population of student. When I tell them my story, the connection is almost immediate, allowing me to cultivate a positive, supportive relationship with them. Some of their stories will be shared later in this chapter.

For clarification purposes, the National Institute of Mental Health (2019) defines two basic kinds of trauma. The first comes from a single incident, often a disaster such as a hurricane or a school shooting. These affect many students or a whole community and often involve broad community responses. The second type, which is more common but often much harder for school staff to spot, is complex trauma, such as chronic neglect, housing or food instability, or physical and sexual abuse. Complex trauma can lead to so-called "toxic stress," defined (NIMH, 2019, n.p.) as a response to "severe, prolonged, or repetitive adversity with a lack of the necessary nurturance or support of a caregiver to prevent an abnormal stress response." The term "Adverse Childhood Experiences" (ACEs) was coined by the federal Centers for Disease Control and Prevention and the health provider Kaiser Permanente (CDC, 2019a) in the mid-1990s. ACEs are traumatic events occurring before the age of 18. They include all types of abuse and neglect; as well as parental mental illness, substance use, divorce, incarceration, and domestic violence, among others.

Gifted Students with Adverse Childhood Experiences: Orchids or Dandelions?

Driving home one evening from the university after teaching a class during the spring of 2019, I was listening to NPR (National Public Radio) on the radio. The host was interviewing Dr. W. Thomas Boyce, a pediatrician and researcher, about his new book titled, *The Orchid and the Dandelion: Why Some Children Struggle and How All Can Thrive*. I was enthralled that many of the cases he described involved highly intelligent children whom he identified as either orchids or dandelions. I immediately purchased the book to learn more. As I read the book, I was constantly reflecting on the hundreds of gifted students I have encountered over my career. Which were orchids and which were dandelions? The characteristics he described for each made it easier for me to distinguish and identify individual gifted students, many of them Hispanic.

Boyce (2019) identifies a special group of children – "orchids" – who are outliers among groups of more typically developing children, or "dandelions." Orchid children are uniquely fragile, needing special nurturing to achieve their best. Dandelions are more rugged and likely to overcome any difficulty. Most (gifted) children – in our families, classrooms, or communities – are more or less like dandelions; they prosper and thrive almost anywhere they are planted. Like dandelions, these are the majority of children whose well-being is all but assured by their constitutional hardiness and strength. There are (gifted) others, however, who, more like orchids, can wither and fade when unattended by caring support, but who – also like orchids – can become creatures of rare beauty, complexity, and elegance when met with compassion and kindness.

Most of our gifted children can, like dandelions, thrive in all but the harshest, most bestial circumstances, but a minority of others, like orchids, either blossom beautifully or wane disappointingly, depending upon how we tend and care for them. For orchid children, the world is sometimes a frightening and overwhelming place, but with loving and supportive help, they can, as we have discovered to our great surprise, do as well as or thrive even more than their dandelion peers. In the end it is not vulnerability but sensitivity that defines the orchid, and when given the right support, that sensitivity can blossom into lives of great joy, success, and beauty.

I was reading Boyce's book as I was engaged in writing this particular chapter for a book on special populations of gifted students. How coincidental that it happened to be on gifted students with trauma, toxic stress, and adverse childhood experiences. Throughout the writing process, my mind kept on drifting to the gifted students I was currently working with; all of them suffering from a variety of mental health issues. Who were the orchids and who were the dandelions? In the two stories and multiple student vignettes presented in this chapter, is it possible to determine who the orchids are and who the dandelions? We begin, however, with responses to questions that are designed to educate and empower teachers of the gifted and administrators supervising gifted programs, so that they may increase their advocacy for this vulnerable group of gifted students.

Frequently Asked Questions (FAQs)

Child Trends (2016) reports that the level of toxic stress one is exposed to early in life, particularly when the brain is developing, impacts learning and achievement, both academically and socially. Children suffering from anxiety or depression may have trouble sleeping, feelings of worthlessness, and poor eating habits. These cognitive and behavioral changes serve to distance traumatized children from their peers, leading to feelings of abandonment and isolation. They also make classroom learning difficult; often, learning will be the last priority for these vulnerable youths. Any combination of these mental health issues confounds an already complex educational process. Some of our gifted education colleagues may believe that these are simply more excuses for why they underachieve, do less well in school. Others would argue that you cannot separate these realities from the gifted students we serve and that it is our collective responsibility to accommodate their needs by ensuring that they fully understand these students. The following frequently asked questions (FAQs) may help empower us to effectively serve gifted students who experience trauma, toxic stress, and have ACEs.

Q1: What are adverse childhood experiences (ACEs)?

A1: Adverse Childhood Experiences, or ACEs, are potentially traumatic events that occur in childhood (0–17 years) such as experiencing violence, abuse, or neglect; witnessing violence in the home; and having a family member attempt or die by suicide. Also included are aspects of the child's environment that can undermine their sense of safety, stability, and bonding such as growing up in a household with substance misuse, mental health problems, or instability due to parental separation or incarceration of a parent, sibling, or other member of the household. Adverse Childhood Experiences have been linked to risky health behaviors, chronic health conditions, low life potential, and early death (CDC, 2019b).

Q2: Can ACEs impair learning?

A2: Yes, chronic exposure to traumatic events, especially during a child's early years, can adversely affect attention, memory, and cognition. In addition, it reduces a child's ability to focus, organize, and process information, interfere with effective problem solving and/or planning, and result in overwhelming feelings of frustration and anxiety (National Child Traumatic Stress Network, 2008).

Q3: How common is it to have a student with ACEs?

A3: Research shows that 45 percent of all children in the United States have experienced at least one adverse childhood experience, such as parental divorce, death, or incarceration; mental illness, substance abuse, or domestic violence in their household; being a victim of violence or witnessing violence in their community; or experiencing economic hardship (Sacks et al., 2014).

Q4: What are the limitations as a teacher when it comes to ACEs?

A4: As a teacher you cannot diagnose or serve as a counselor. What you can do is refer the student to the proper professionals within the school who can help the student. In any situation where there is a possibility of abuse, you are legally required to report the information to the Department of Children and Family (DCF), social services, or law enforcement.

Q5: At what grade level may a student experience ACEs?

A5: Students with ACEs range from preschool to high-school grade levels. In my role as a targeted case manager working with a community-based social services agency which provides mental health support to students, I have worked with gifted, advanced, and high-ability children as young as three years old.

Q6: Are effects of ACEs immediately evident?

A6: Not all effects of ACEs are immediately evident. Some children show signs of stress in the first few weeks after a trauma, but return to their usual state of physical and emotional health. Even children who do not exhibit serious symptoms may experience some degree of emotional distress, which may continue or even deepen over a long period of time. Other children who have experienced traumatic events may experience problems that impair their day-to-day functioning. Still others may have behavioral problems, or their suffering may not be apparent at all (National Child Traumatic Stress Network, 2008).

Q7: Do students who experience ACEs have visible effects?

A7: Many students who experience traumatic events show visible effects in the classroom. Some of the behaviors I have observed include inconsistent academic performance, impulsive behavior, overreacting to instructions or directions, disrupting the classroom, verbal or physical aggression, and being overly sensitive, among others.

Q8: How can I make my classroom more inclusive for students who have experienced ACEs?

A8: Provide positive and constructive feedback to guide students' learning and behavior. Effective feedback must be strategically delivered and goal- directed; feedback is most effective when the student has a goal and the feedback informs the student regarding areas needing improvement and ways to improve behavior and/or performance (Council for Exceptional Children, 2017). Maintaining usual routines that promote a sense of normalcy will communicate the message that the child is safe. Give students choices. Often traumatic events involve loss of control and/or chaos, so you can help children feel safe by providing them with some choices or control when appropriate.

Q9: Where are ACEs prevalent?

A9: Just under half (45 percent) of children in the United States have experienced at least one ACE. In Arkansas, the state with the highest prevalence, 56 percent of children have experienced at least one ACE. One in ten children nationally has experienced three or more ACEs, placing them in a category of especially high risk. In five states – Arizona, Arkansas, Montana, New Mexico, and Ohio – as many as one in seven children had experienced three or more ACEs. Children of different races and ethnicities do not experience ACEs equally. Nationally, 61 percent of Black non-Hispanic children and 51 percent of Hispanic children have experienced at least one ACE, compared with 40 percent of white non-Hispanic children and only 23 percent of Asian non-Hispanic children. In every region, the prevalence of ACEs is lowest among Asian non-Hispanic children and, in most regions, is highest among Black non-Hispanic children (Sacks & Murphey 2019).

Types of Childhood Stress

Poag (2018) is a social worker and therapist who distinguishes between acute and chronic trauma:

1. **Acute trauma.** Is often a single incident that occurs in life, such as an accident, being a victim of a crime or even a natural disaster. You may have experienced one of these in the past, and find yourself still trying to make sense of it. These incidents can have a lasting negative impact on your psyche if left unprocessed, and impact the way you live your life. Some patients have been told that they should just get over it, especially if the acute trauma happened a while ago. Unfortunately, resolving trauma is not so simple, and many times trying to just "get over it" can do more harm than good. I caution my patients against trying to put the trauma out of their mind by ignoring the incident. When a trauma goes ignored, and is not processed in a therapeutic manner, our brain responds by holding on to the memory, in hopes of addressing it at a later time. The more you ignore it, the more your body will show physical manifestations of it.

2. **Chronic trauma.** Is trauma that is repetitive, and occurs over an extended period of time. Examples of chronic trauma can include such things as domestic violence, childhood

abuse, and war. Chronic trauma can even be made up from several instances of acute traumas, happening one after the other. Often times my clients will feel as though there was no end in sight, and the only thing they could do was to continue to endure the trauma. Just like the acute trauma, leaving chronic trauma unresolved can have a long-term negative impact on the quality of your life. When you are ready to begin treatment, it's important that you work with a qualified trauma therapist. A seasoned clinician will assist you in developing a plan to address the many traumas you have survived.

3. **Complex trauma.** Describes both children's exposure to multiple traumatic events—often of an invasive, interpersonal nature—and the wide-ranging, long-term effects of this exposure. These events are severe and pervasive, such as abuse or profound neglect (Wamser-Nanney & Vandenberg, 2013).

4. **System induced trauma.** The traumatic removal from home; admission to a justice or treatment facility; or multiple placements within a short time. Occurs when the systems that were designed to assist trauma victims end up causing trauma. In order to best serve the individuals and families who end up in the system, it is important to understand how procedures and practices within the system can potentially re-traumatize them.

(Poag, 2018, p. 2)

Causes, Effects, and Building Resiliency

Table 3.1 identifies the causes of trauma, toxic stress, and ACEs that negatively impact children. The root cause is often confirmed by the parents and is consistent with the psychologist or psychiatrist's summary or conclusion based on all the data obtained.

Table 3.2 helps teachers identify the effects of trauma, toxic stress, and ACEs and the behaviors that may manifest themselves in the classroom, in the home, and in the community. Communication and collaboration with outside agencies through case management practices assist the student by identifying natural and institutional support systems.

Flannery (2020) documents an incredible one in six high school students reported as "seriously considering suicide" in 2017, including nearly one in four girls and almost half of gay, lesbian, and bisexual students, according to the U.S. Centers for Disease Control and Prevention (CDC) data. Today's teens, including those identified as gifted and talented,

Table 3.1 Causes of Trauma, Toxic Stress, and ACEs

Challenges in the Home	Abuse	Neglect	Relationships	Violence/ Bullying	Natural Disasters
• Domestic violence • Substance abuse • Mental illness • Parent separation • Parent divorce • Parent incarceration • Poverty • Homelessness • Undocumented	• Emotional • Physical • Sexual	• Emotional • Physical • Nutritional	• Loss of friendships; including death • Separation from parents/families • Deportation • Unaccompanied minors • Reunion with parents/families	• Victim • Witness • In the home • In the community • In the school • Online	• Death • Loss • Separation • Resettlement

Table 3.2 Effects of Trauma, Toxic Stress, and ACEs

• Identified as Emotionally Disturbed (IDEA)	• Succumbs to peer pressure	*Cultural Consideration*
• Identified with Behavioral Disability (IDEA)	• Juvenile Justice System	For many Hispanic and Black males, talking about or
• Post-Traumatic Stress Disorder	• Teenage pregnancy	sharing feelings; talking about
• Acting-out behavior	• Truancy	experiencing emotional or
• Self-harm	• Disruptive in school	psychological issues is counter-
• Cutting	• Underachieves	cultural; a violation of pride.
• Promiscuity	• Eating disorders	The mentality may be to "rub
• Drugs/alcohol	• Suicide	some dirt on it and be quiet."
• Violence/drugs	• Depression	Because of cultural factors it
	• Addiction	emasculates them.
	• Nightmares	

are the most anxious and depressed ever, according to health surveys. In 2017, about 10 percent experienced "a major depressive episode with severe impairment" according to the National Institute of Mental Health (NIMH, 2019, n.p.). This means at least two weeks with little sleep, energy, and low self-esteem, and an inability to participate in life's activities, including school. Meanwhile, a CDC report (2019a) shows that the number of young people dying of suicide jumped 56 percent between 2007 and 2017, outpacing any other group. Researchers have struggled to say why, but point to a variety of root causes, including social media and smartphones, bullying, and lack of community. Consider the following statistics from the CDC (2019b, n.p.) on the percentage of students, grades 9–12, who report they thought seriously about suicide in 2017.

- 17.1 Total number of students
- 22.1 Female students
- 11.9 Male students
- 19 American Indian students
- 18.4 Native Hawaiian or Pacific Islander students
- 17.4 Asian students
- 17.3 White students
- 16.4 Hispanic students
- 14.7 Black students
- 47.7 Students who identify as gay, lesbian, or bisexual

This author (Castellano) has not come across any statistics specific to students identified as gifted and talented. However, deduction dictates that they are represented in the data listed above.

Table 3.3 presents important information by providing teachers with classroom strategies, online resources, and selected additional readings. Serving as a toolbox for educators, additional strategies that promote resiliency and perseverance that support gifted students will follow. Gifted student vignettes and case studies will also be presented.

As you read this sentence, know there are gifted, advanced, and high-ability students in your school who have experienced trauma. I know because I support them in the home and in the school. In my role as a targeted case manager, I have worked with the gifted, advanced, and high-ability students identified in Table 3.4 who have experienced trauma, toxic stress, and ACEs.

Table 3.3 Creating Social-Emotional Strength and Resiliency: A Toolbox for Educators

Strategies	Online Resources	Additional Reading
• Create confidential, judgment-free spaces • Identify those whom students trust and respect • Model/show empathy • Feedback and solutions are personalized • Intentional engagement • Storytelling • Bibliotherapy • Cinematherapy • Songs of inspiration	*National Child Traumatic Stress Network* • Natural disasters • Mental health needs assessment (Grades 3–12, includes teachers) www.nctsn.org *Oakland Unified School District* • Overview of ICE Protocol (for undocumented students and families) www.ousd.org/Page/16192	*ASCD: Educational Leadership* *Mental Health in Schools* Dec. 2017/Jan. 2018 Vol. 75, No. 4 (special issue) • Responding with Care to Students Facing Trauma (p. 32) • Who in Your Class Needs Help? (p. 12) • Combatting Race-Related Stress in the Classroom (p. 51) • When Teacher Self-Care Is Not Enough (p. 38) • A "Special" Answer for Traumatized Students (p. 78)

Table 3.4 Examples of Gifted Students with Trauma, Toxic Stress, and Adverse Childhood Experiences

	Label	Grade	Diagnosis	Cause	Effect
Maya	Gifted	Grade 10	Generalized anxiety; depression; Asperger's; ADHD	Home life	• Suicide ideology • Baker-Acted • Self-mutilation • Depression • Anxiety • Poor short-term memory
Gage	Gifted	Grade 2	Adjustment disorder with mixed disturbance of emotions and conduct	Home life	• Anxiety • Nightmares • Difficulty following rules
Anthony	Advanced/ High- Ability	Grade 6	Major depressive disorder; ADHD	Home life; bullied in school	• Poor interpersonal relationships • Suicide ideation • Depression • Anxiety • Poor short-term memory
Patricia	Advanced/ High- Ability	Grade 7	Disruptive mood; Dysregulation disorder	Home life; DCF removal	• Poor short-term memory
Eric	Advanced/ High- Ability	Grade 6	Unspecified mood disorder	Home life	• Nightmares • Anxiety • Sleep disturbance • Poor short-term memory
Christofer	Gifted	Grade 6	Anxiety disorder; Asperger's; ADHD	Home life	• Depression • Anxiety • Panic attacks • Phobias • Impulsive • Poor short-term memory

Vignettes: An Exercise for Educators of the Gifted

Maya

Maya is 15 years old and in the 10th grade. She has an active Individualized Education Plan (IEP) and is twice-exceptional. She becomes easily bored in school despite being enrolled in AP classes. As a freshman she scored at the 99th percentile on the PSAT; scoring a 1260/1440. She is disorganized, identifies as transgender, and has very few friends. Strengths include drawing, creating fantastical stories of science fiction, and she is a detailed storyteller. She believes she can overcome her mental health conditions without any assistance from doctors, therapists, or teachers. If Maya is in your class, what would you do?

Gage

Gage is 8 years old and enrolled in a full-time, self-contained gifted education program. He has an advanced sense of humor, often wants to be the center of attention, and can be characterized as the class clown. He is an organizational mess, has no sense of time management, and easily manipulates language in inappropriate ways. He is divergent in his responses, has an advanced vocabulary, and easily picks up new concepts. Gage is athletic, social, and has many friends. He would rather be social than pay attention in class. If Gage is in your class, what do you do?

Anthony

Anthony is 11 years old and in the sixth grade. He excels in math, is currently in an advanced math class, but is failing because his teacher is "a yeller." As a result, he becomes anxious and shuts down. He refuses to do his work and is falling further and further behind. Anthony is very manipulative and often resorts to tantrums to get what he wants. In school he is being bullied because of his weight. Instead of reporting the bullying to his parents or school personnel, he resorts to name calling in the form of homophobic slurs toward the bullies. How can the school support Anthony?

Patricia

Patricia is 13 years old and in the seventh grade. She is enrolled in advanced civics and language arts. Patricia is shy, has very few friends, and has poor interpersonal relationship skills. She lives in abject poverty and often goes to school in dirty clothes. Her stepfather is bipolar and rules the house with an iron fist. She fears him. Mother says she bullies her younger siblings and must be told repeatedly to help clean the house. She enjoys drawing. Patricia currently stays after school four days a week to participate in the coin club and robotics club. When asked questions about school or her home life, her most common response is, "I don't know." If Patricia is in your class, what do you do?

Eric

Eric is 11 years old and in the sixth grade. He is enrolled in advanced math and world history. His adjustment to middle school was uneventful. He has a laissez faire attitude about his education. In other words, he realizes the importance of an education, but does not worry about it; whatever happens, happens. He is a wonderful storyteller and presents a maturity beyond his years. He enjoys Japanese anime, video games, and playing soccer, which he states he is quite good at it. He only does enough school work to get through it. If Eric is in your class, what do you do?

Christofer

Christofer is 12 years old and in the sixth grade. He is enrolled in advanced reading, math, and world history. He is an introvert and has problems talking to others. He does not like loud noises, crowds, and prefers to be left alone. He often states how bored he is at home and at school. He has only two or three friends; none in his neighborhood. In school, he will not volunteer any responses during lessons and prefers to eat lunch alone in the school cafeteria. Rarely does he smile or laugh. And once he sets his sight on a task he will not deviate until it is completed. His math teacher is "a yeller" which causes him anxiety and he shuts down. If Christofer is in your class, what do you do?

The Gifted Education Classroom: Creating Social-Emotional Strength and Resiliency: A Toolbox for Educators (see Table 3.3) as part of the teaching and learning process for gifted students with trauma, toxic stress, and ACEs promotes a positive mental health environment. The following classroom practices provide a platform for educating the whole child that complements their academic skill and cognitive ability.

- **Create confidential judgment-free zones.** This practice allows for communication style options that include one-on-one, small-group, or whole-group interactions. The importance of a judgment-free zone is that often students are taking a risk in sharing their personal story. They need to know they will not be judged for telling their "truth." Feedback is in the form of asking questions to inform clarity and understanding.
- **Identify the persons whom students trust and respect.** Gifted students, with their heightened sense of justice and fairness, need to know that their confidentiality will be honored. To this end, who can they be honest with? To whom are they willing to open up? In my experience as a teacher of the gifted, a principal, and a targeted case manager, the individual that these students trust and respect the most may come from outside the classroom. That said, the teacher of the gifted should acknowledge that it's about the students, not about them and what they think they can offer. Secure relationships with caring adults they can trust may restore their passions, interests, and excitement about learning.
- **Model/show empathy.** Through their body language, use of facial expressions, the use of "I" statements, and by the questions asked and the words used, teachers of gifted students demonstrate empathy. Communicating understanding by sharing personal

stories also helps to develop perseverance and resiliency in students. Listening is purposeful and used to reaffirm and support students in their time of need.

- **Feedback and solutions are personalized.** Teachers working with gifted students who have experienced trauma and toxic stress need to notice the little things about their students. They need to be observant because every situation is unique and this may help them identify resources that can assist the student socially and emotionally. One of the practices that I use is children's, teen, or young adult literature intentionally chosen, based on what the presenting challenge is for any given student in real time. This personalized approach lets the students know they are not alone.

Hickman and Higgins (2019) write that as education researchers have found, stress can change the brain architecture, making it more difficult for children to focus and learn. When a child's fight or flight response is triggered by adverse experiences such as abuse or neglect, the child's nervous system can become dysregulated, which can also affect thinking, decision-making, emotional control, and learning. This will make it more likely that students will experience negative academic outcomes such as poor grades, underachieving, an increased risk of suspension, or dropping out of school altogether. To prevent this from happening, they list the following ten practical, low-or no-cost strategies for offering social-emotional learning.

1. **Immerse your school in trauma-informed practices.** Such approaches focus on infusing the values of safety, trust, collaboration, choice, empowerment, and equity into all learning environments. Trauma-informed teaching is less about following a checklist than adopting a new way of doing business as a school.
2. **Create a positive school climate that offers long-term, secure relationships between teachers and students.** These relationships support academic, physical, cognitive, and social-emotional development that can help children overcome trauma and toxic stress.
3. **Incorporate practices that address belonging and safety.** Students need a feeling of safety and connection in order to thrive. Something as simple as greeting students at the door with a high-five or personalized handshake can help develop an atmosphere of trust, safety, and caring.
4. **Implement one-on-one time with the teacher.** Giving students a few moments of private time each day will help students feel cared about.
5. **Create "safe" corners in the classroom.** Students should have space if they need to take a break and regroup. This respite is particularly important if students are suffering from trauma or toxic stress.
6. **Be predictable.** Consistency and routine are important. This predictability may help students navigate their day and balance their emotions.
7. **Make sure your students are eating nutritious food and have time to move and play at school.** Healthy students perform better in the classroom, attend school more often, and behave better. With this in mind, schools should ensure that students have nutritious meals as well as regular opportunities to be physically active.
8. **Boost engagement with phrases like "I wonder" and "I notice."** Encouraging students to use these phrases in conversation can clue in teachers about what and how students are learning. This can make it easier to pinpoint gaps and reach out to students who need help, which may reduce their anxiety about learning.

9. **Hang up reminders to use "talk moves" for classroom discussions.** Taping helpful conversational formulas to the wall for kids to refer to – "What do you think?" or "I heard you say X – could you explain that?" – can help students feel more connected socially.

10. **Teach and model social-emotional learning.** Showing students how to calm themselves, work out conflicts, and name emotions helps everyone in the classroom better focus on learning and promotes academic and social development. It also allows them to learn about resiliency and perseverance.

(Hickman & Higgins, 2019, p. 19)

For gifted students, the application of these practices provides a comfort level that encourages them to share their thoughts and emotions in a safe way. Furthermore, they allow teachers to advocate for their gifted students, which is another important skill for children to acquire. Classrooms structured in this way allow students to grow socially and emotionally. Support and development of a gifted student's social and emotional growth after they have experienced trauma and toxic stress helps them navigate complex feelings, social situations, and cope with their mental health issues.

Building Resiliency

Trauma is a sensory memory, not a cognitive memory, and is manifested in one of two ways: hyperarousal – which is characterized by irritability, depression, nightmares, and even a reversion back to childish behaviors; or the child shuts down emotionally. In either case, the gifted classroom should be a safe and nurturing place. Because behavior is a form of communication, never downplay problems and be a good listener. Students need an opportunity to tell their story on their own terms, so don't force them, as healing takes time. Above all, nurture them and provide them with love while building resiliency. Building resiliency is the capacity for children to adapt successfully and overcome severe stressors and risks. Longitudinal studies document that as many as two-thirds of children growing up with trauma overcome these adversities and turn their life from one characterized by extreme risk to one of resilience or successful adaptation. Cognitive and behavioral factors that promote resiliency include a sense of optimism, social-emotional problem-solving skills, a quality relationship with significant adults, and access to services.

Linking Resiliency to Motivation

According to Frey et al. (2019), an underlying principle of social and emotional learning, and linking resiliency to motivation is developing the identity and agency of students in ways that open them up to learning. Teachers can assist children and adolescents in developing the ability to recognize their strengths and accurately weigh current abilities with knowledge of their internal and external resources. When this is done well, students develop a sense of motivation, self-confidence, and self-efficacy that fuels learning while reducing factors that get in the way. Perseverance and grit factor into young people's developing confidence and sense of efficacy, in turn empowering students and building their resiliency in the face of challenge. For gifted students with trauma, toxic stress, and ACEs, the following strategies (see Table 3.3) link resiliency to motivation.

- **Bibliotherapy.** An effective strategy that teaches an explicit point. The goal is to promote normal development and self-actualization or to maintain positive mental health. Here are some examples of books I have used with my gifted, advanced, and high-ability students.
  - *A Family That Fights* by Sharon Chesler Bernstein. An 8-year-old boy and his two younger siblings who live at home where the father abuses the mother. Ages 4–12
  - *When I Was Little Like You* by Jane Porett. About sexual abuse of a child by a family member; helps children understand what sexual abuse is and what they can do. Ages 3–6
  - *The Hurt* by Teddi Doleski. A boy whose feelings get hurt when his friend calls him a name. A simple story with a moral/behavioral message. Ages 6–8
  - *Dear Bully* by Megan Kelley Hall & Carrie Jones. Today's top authors for teens and young people come together to share stories about bullying – as bystanders, as victims, and as the bully themselves – in a moving and deeply personal collection.
  - *My Family Divided: One Girl's Journey of Home, Loss, and Hope* by Diane Guerrero. Successful actress (*Jane the Virgin* and *Orange Is the New Black*) is traumatized as a teenager when parents and siblings are deported. This caused severe mental health issues, struggles with depression and cutting, and thoughts of suicide. In the end, Diane triumphs with the help of others.
  - *What Do You Do with a Problem?* by Kobi Yamada. This is the story of a persistent problem and the child who isn't sure what to make of it. The longer the problem is avoided, the bigger it seems to get. But when the child finally musters up the courage to face it, the problem turns out to be something quite different than expected.
  - *Dear Girl: A Celebration of Wonderful, Smart, Beautiful You* by Amy Krouse Rosenthal and Paris Rosenthal. This book is a celebration of being a girl; of embracing who you are without making excuses. The book is meant to inspire, enrich, and to accept who you are as a girl.
- **Cinematherapy.** Commonly known as videotherapy, this has been used as a medium for counseling adolescents for quite some time. The roots of this method stem from bibliotherapy. In cinematherapy, students view films or film clips to vicariously experience conflicts and situations they may have experienced, in a secure and safe way. Films that I have used include:
  - *Freedom Writers*
  - *Stand and Deliver*
  - *To Sir with Love*
  - *The Blackboard Jungle*
  - *McFarland U.S.A.*
  - *Matilda*
  - *Akeelah and the Bee*
  - *Disney movies*
  - *Underwater Dreams*
- **Songs of Hope, Inspiration, and Self-Efficacy.** Here, music is the source that gives students hope and inspiration. It helps them to identify their feelings and the lyrics of the songs they chose inspire them and make them feel better. There is an example in Table 3.5 from a gifted student I have worked with.

Table 3.5 Songs of Hope, Inspiration, and Self-Efficacy

Student	Song	Artist	Year	Genre	Hope, Inspiration, Efficacy
Paul El Salvador Grade 10 Age=17	Fight Song	Rachel Platten	2015	Pop	At one of the lowest points in my life I felt as if my world was taken from me. My parents divorced after 25 years of marriage. One day, while crying in the bathtub, after my world seemed to crash, listening to the radio, "Fight Song" by Rachel Platten began to play. The words spoke to me. When the artist sang of taking back her life, saying she was alright, this lifted my spirits up in a different way. After listening to "Fight Song" numerous times, my head became clear and depression, as well as my suicidal thoughts, drifted away. This song honestly saved my life. Any challenge that I face now, I listen to "Fight Song." This song inspires, empowers, and gives me strength that better days are ahead. The song helps me believe I can survive anything.

Other strategies related to gifted students that link their resiliency to motivation include:

- Identifying mentors to work with students
- Supporting friendships with high-achieving peers
- Encouraging students' engagement with family
- Providing instruction in specific skills to foster effective teamwork
- Teaching positive coping strategies
- Differentiated instruction
- Academic acceleration
- Enrichment opportunities
- Allowing students to make choices
- Capitalizing on preferred learning styles
- Capitalizing on student interests
- Collaboration and cooperative learning
- Flexibility in allowing students to demonstrate what they know and are able to do
- Grouping practices

The Five-Minute Measurement

I developed the Five-Minute Measurement (Figure 3.1) as an informal, qualitative tool to assist teachers, administrators, and other school personnel in starting conversations about their gifted, advanced, and high-ability students who are experiencing trauma, toxic stress, and ACEs. Deductions based on the prevalence of ACEs across the United States lead me to believe that these students exist in the gifted education classroom. Based on observations, interactions, and data collection, how would you rate the student in each of the following ten areas using a scale from 1–10, with 1 being the student does not exhibit the characteristic or behavior; and 10 being the student meets/exceeds age and grade level expectations?

Student Name:	Date	School	Grade Level
Teacher Completing Checklist:	Birthday	Age	Score

Instructions

1. Based on your observations, interactions, and data collection, how would you rate the student in each area using a scale from 1–10, with 1 being the student does not exhibit the characteristic or behavior; and 10 being the student meets/exceeds age and grade level expectations.

Physical health

1	2	3	4	5	6	7	8	9	10

Mental health (happiness)

1	2	3	4	5	6	7	8	9	10

Productivity

1	2	3	4	5	6	7	8	9	10

Ability to cope with setbacks (resiliency)

1	2	3	4	5	6	7	8	9	10

Academic aptitude

1	2	3	4	5	6	7	8	9	10

Cognitive growth (benefits from meaningful and challenging learning experiences)

1	2	3	4	5	6	7	8	9	10

Social relationships

1	2	3	4	5	6	7	8	9	10

Emotional understanding (of self and others)

1	2	3	4	5	6	7	8	9	10

Self-understanding (possesses appropriate understanding of how they learn and grow)

1	2	3	4	5	6	7	8	9	10

Demonstrates complex learning and understanding

1	2	3	4	5	6	7	8	9	10

Out of 100 points, how did the student score?

Use of Results

1. The results are simply an informal qualitative reference point; an opportunity to get a holistic and whole child overview of an individual gifted student.
2. Observations, interactions, and data collection are widely accepted in the field as reliable and valid informal assessment practices that may be shared with other professionals.

Scores

80–100	Overall, the student is in the green zone cognitively, academically, socially, *and* emotionally where no major concerns manifest themselves.
60–79	The student is in the yellow zone either cognitively, academically, socially, *or* emotionally; a pattern of where the student is challenged may exist in one area. Identify the area and provide interventions and monitor progress.
<60	The student is in the red zone either cognitively, academically, socially, *or* emotionally; a pattern of where the student is challenged is evident in at least one area, perhaps two. Identify the area(s) and provide interventions and monitor progress. Seek assistance from the school's multidisciplinary team.

Figure 3.1 The Five-Minute Measurement: An Informal Qualitative Whole Child Assessment of Gifted, Advanced, and High-Ability Students

Source: Developed and Copyrighted © by Dr. Jaime A. Castellano, January 2020.

The Five-Minute Measurement

The Five-Minute Measurement was designed as an informal, qualitative tool to assist teachers, administrators, and other school personnel in starting conversations about their gifted, advanced, and high-ability students who are experiencing trauma, toxic stress, and adverse childhood experiences (ACEs). Deductions based on the prevalence of ACEs across the United States leads me to believe that these students exist in the gifted education classroom.

1. **Physical health.** Has the appearance of the student changed in some way? Does the student experience appetite disturbance, is he/she engaged in self-mutilation/cutting? Do they appear tired in class; perhaps falling asleep? What are your observations based on their physical health?
2. **Mental health (happiness).** What is the status of the student's mental health based on what you see, what you hear, your interactions, and any other data you collected?
3. **Productivity.** Is the student able to keep up with classroom assignments; what is their participation like in both small group and whole group instruction? Have their grades slipped? What is their attitude about completing assignments?
4. **Ability to cope with setbacks (resiliency).** How difficult is it for the student to "bounce back" from a setback? Do they feel overwhelmed about school? Do they engage in healthy coping mechanisms when feeling anxious or stressful?
5. **Academic aptitude.** Has their knack for learning decreased; even in their area of interest? Do they pursue any form of study that is meaningful to them?
6. **Cognitive growth (benefits from meaningful and challenging learning experiences).** Does the student engage in critical-thinking and problem-solving exercises that complement their intelligence. Are they benefitting from/or participating in meaningful and challenging learning experiences?
7. **Social relationships.** Is the student able to maintain positive, healthy, and productive interpersonal relationships with classmates and teachers? Are they collaborative or do they isolate themselves?
8. **Emotional understanding (of self and others).** Based on your observations and interactions with the student, do they acknowledge their change in behavior and/or emotions? How do they engage others in the classroom socially and emotionally? Are they extremely sensitive? Do they anger easily?
9. **Self-understanding (possesses appropriate understanding of how they learn and grow).** Are they underachieving in core academic areas? Can they articulate why they are underachieving?
10. **Demonstrates advanced and complex learning.** Does the student accept the challenge of advanced and complex learning? What is the quality of their work? Have they given up easily; or refuse to do the work?

Out of 100 points, how did the student score? The results are simply an informal qualitative reference point; an opportunity to get a holistic and whole child overview of an individual gifted student. Observations, interactions, and data collection are widely accepted in the field as reliable and valid informal assessment practices that may be shared with other professionals. The purpose of the Five-Minute Measurement is to use the results to start a conversation; to make the recommendations that will help the student develop resiliency and perseverance; and to be successful in school.

Figure 3.1 Cont.

1   **Physical health.** Has the appearance of the student changed in some way? Does the student experience appetite disturbance, is he/she engaged in self-mutilation/cutting? Do they appear tired in class; perhaps falling asleep? What are your observations based on their physical health?

2   **Mental health (Happiness).** What is the status of the student's mental health based on what you see, what you hear, your interactions, and any other data you collected?

3   **Productivity.** Is the student able to keep up with classroom assignments; what is their participation like in both small group and whole group instruction? Have their grades slipped? What is their attitude about completing assignments?

4   **Ability to cope with setbacks (Resiliency).** How difficult is it for the student to "bounce back" from a setback? Do they feel overwhelmed about school? Do they engage in healthy coping mechanisms when feeling anxious or stressful?

5   **Academic aptitude.** Has their knack for learning decreased; even in their area of interest? Do they pursue any form of study that is meaningful to them?

6   **Cognitive growth.** Does the student engage in critical-thinking and problem-solving exercises that complement their intelligence. Are they benefitting from/or participating in meaningful and challenging learning experiences?

7   **Social relationships.** Is the student able to maintain positive, healthy, and productive interpersonal relationships with classmates and teachers? Are they collaborative or do they isolate themselves?

8   **Emotional understanding (of self and others).** Based on your observations and interactions with the student, do they acknowledge their change in behavior and/or emotions? How do they engage others in the classroom socially and emotionally? Are they extremely sensitive? Do they anger easily?

9   **Self-understanding (Possesses appropriate understanding of how they learn and grow).** Are they underachieving in core academic areas? Can they articulate why they are underachieving?

10   **Demonstrates advanced and complex learning.** Does the student accept the challenge of advanced and complex learning? What is the quality of their work? Have they given up easily; or refuse to do the work?

Out of 100 points, how did the student score? The results are simply an informal qualitative reference point; an opportunity to get a holistic and whole child overview of an individual gifted student. Observations, interactions, and data collection are widely accepted in the field as reliable and valid informal assessment practices that may be shared with other professionals. The purpose of the Five-Minute Measurement is to use the results to start a conversation; to make the recommendations that will help the student develop resiliency and perseverance; and to be successful in school.

Promoting Equity

To create an equitable school experience for gifted students with trauma, toxic stress, and adverse childhood experiences we must first determine what their social and emotional needs are and then identify and implement ways to meet those needs. Despite the challenge that these students may present in the classroom, it is our ethical responsibility to show that we value them by our actions and behaviors. We must not only talk the talk, but walk the walk.

Bachtel (2019) writes that the impact of trauma on the physical and emotional health of gifted students reinforces the body of research calling for early identification practices. It also reiterates the invaluable nature of parent and educator partnerships – schools and families both need data from each other to inform decision-making. If an individual is exhibiting any combination of the behaviors and signs associated with trauma, meet them with compassion. For a variety of reasons, including mental health stigma, students and their families may feel reluctant to share information about traumatic events. Until adequate healing has occurred, it is unlikely caregivers will have an accurate approximation of a student's abilities. In the interim, educators can reduce unnecessary exposure to individuals or situations that may remind the student of the trauma. Consider finding a substitute for content that may remind a student about traumatic events and potentially re-traumatize them or cause regression in the healing process.

Equity for this population of students cannot be a stand-alone professional development experience. In this author's experience, professional development must be a sustained practice, empowering teachers of the gifted with the tools they need to make a difference in the lives of the students who come to school having witnessed domestic violence, who are victims of physical abuse, or have experienced the death of a parent, among other traumatic events. Equity calls for solutions based on individual circumstances that often require collaboration with other professionals such as mental health therapists, counselors, and other community-based agencies. Equity also calls for measuring the success of the interventions by how it impacts the whole child socially, emotionally, academically, and cognitively. Throughout this chapter, readers will be offered a number of strategies that they can employ when working with gifted students who have experienced trauma, toxic stress, and adverse childhood experiences. Bachtel (2019), also adds the following ideas:

Learning Environment Considerations

- Spaces mindful of sensory sensitivities support youth healing from trauma and also sensitive gifted learners. Attention to environmental elements can make the classroom less taxing on a student's nervous system. Remove fluorescent lights and utilize natural lighting whenever possible. Insure volume levels are kept low. Avoid chemical cleaning supplies. Reduce any potential upsetting or distracting auditory and visual stimulation. Decorate with soothing colors and images.
- Prepare or signal student for changes, transitions or class surprises (It is important to use a calm, soft tone of voice and to rehearse when possible).
- Avoid unnecessary exposure to upsetting stimuli.
- Identify patterns that result in student shutting down.
- Use non-verbal cues to signal the student when he or she might be starting to shut down.
- Identify staff the student feels safe discussing traumatic events and flashbacks with and a procedure for accessing those staff as needed.
- Provide an appropriate fidget item.
- Teach and practice calming techniques and emotional literacy skills.
- Provide opportunities for alternate modes of expression including art and music.
- Support students in creating a Calming Toolbox with resources to aid in self-soothing such as puzzles, art supplies, yoga poses, guided meditations, tea, mindfulness practices, inspirational quotes, etc.
- Encourage students to take breaks and ask for help as needed.
- Celebrate Mistakes.
- Include the student in decision-making and encourage them to track progress independently.
- Practice Unconditional Positive Regard.

(Bachtel, 2019, n.p.)

Professional Development

I concur with the work of Frey et al. (2019) that teachers unquestionably influence students' social and emotional development, and have a responsibility to do so in a way that is positive and deliberate. Some teachers are naturals and have a skillset that empowers them to make a difference. Others need additional training and opportunities to practice what they learn through professional development experiences. Still others are novices and perhaps need someone to model or demonstrate the behavior, strategy, or action that potentially will positively impact students.

In serving gifted students with trauma, toxic stress, and ACEs, the following categories are designed to stimulate thoughts and actions while pursuing individualized professional growth and development. This is important because where a teacher is at in their career informs the kind of professional growth they need. One size does not fit all.

Which one are you?

The Novice

- Define trauma, toxic stress, and ACEs; including key characteristics of culturally responsive schools who serve these students.
- Reflect on one's own viewpoints and biases about serving gifted students with trauma; including the role that personal and family histories and group membership play in the formation of these identities.
- Determine how ready you are to invest in your gifted students who are in distress.
- Identify one professional development opportunity beyond the school day, based on your professional need, that you are willing to commit to.

The Capable and Proficient Practitioner

- Demonstrate an awareness of expectations for serving gifted students with trauma, toxic stress, and ACEs, and the degree to which those expectations are or are not being met.
- Reflect on and explain why cultural responsiveness is a critical responsibility of all teachers and administrators when serving these students.
- Analyze, synthesize, and evaluate program information and data and determine how the information will be used in promoting social and emotional growth and development in students with mental health challenges.

The Highly Skilled Practitioner

- Examine a variety of strategies for building relationships with students, including learning about their cultures, employing culturally responsive pedagogy, and involving parents, families, and communities.
- Access ongoing resources to support gifted students with trauma, toxic stress, and ACEs.

- Share qualitative and metacognitive strategies with teachers and administrators that demonstrate effective cross-cultural communication and understanding.
- Lead a professional development exercise for your colleagues that focuses on gifted students with trauma.

The Expert

- Write an action plan for fostering a classroom culture that addresses the social and emotional needs of gifted students with trauma in a sustained and meaningful way.
- Access and assess resources that purport to support these students. Build and share a library of resources.
- Share instructional strategies and processes with school and district colleagues on how to develop resiliency and perseverance in students via blogs, YouTube, or other social media outlets.
- Add to the national discussion on serving gifted students with trauma, toxic stress, and ACEs by writing a position paper for a professional association/organization. Present at a state or national conference.

Teachers have to teach students how to make decisions about the choices and problems they face. A gifted student who has excellent content knowledge but poor social skills and mental health challenges is a student at risk of being manipulated. Similarly, gifted students who are able to predict the possible consequences of their actions may be better equipped to make good decisions (Frey et al., 2019). Durlak and colleagues (2011) add that teacher implementation of social-emotional learning resulted in statistically significant outcomes. When teachers teach social-emotional skills, students learn them (effect size of 0.62). Effect sizes are a measure of magnitude, or how much gain is realized based on the influence being studied. According to Hattie (2009), the average effect size in educational "influences" is 0.40, and as educators, we generally focus on actions, strategies, or practices that are above average. Professional growth and development play a role in how we influence learning.

A Case Study

The following case study may be painful to read, and is offered as a training exercise for teachers, coordinators, directors, principals, and any other educator associated with serving gifted, high-ability students. It will give them the opportunity to share thoughts and ideas, and create plans for advocacy and classroom supports that will address the unique needs of gifted students with trauma, toxic stress, and adverse childhood experiences. Both the student and mother granted permission to use their story. Following are the questions and responses:

1   Age, grade at the time of the event.
    I was a sophomore at School ABC and was 15 years old at the time.
2   Please describe the traumatic event as briefly as possible. Where were you?
    I was at my private girls' school in my dorm room when a friend from back home called me after having driven past my house and seeing nearly a dozen police cars parked outside. My mother had come home from work to find my father sitting on

the couch waiting for her. Earlier that day he had received divorce papers from her. They spoke briefly and she left for the closet in her bedroom to pack an overnight bag with the intention of staying at her mother's house that night. He followed her into the bathroom, which preceded the closet, holding a gun in his hand that had been tucked in the side of the couch. His actions were premeditated. He then began what would be nearly an hour of physical and verbal abuse that was an intended murder-suicide, which my mother survived through her sheer grit, level-headed and collected demeanor, and determination. He shot my mom in both feet and our family dog, Sam, five times. Sam had been lying with his head on my father's lap when my mom got home minutes before and had followed them both into the bathroom. Sam was not aggressive; rather, was just confused by the situation and died in the most painful and cruel manner. He attempted to run up the back stairs on the other side of the house and fell down to the bottom where he died. I cleaned the spattered arc of his blood off the walls of that back stairway. The cleaning crew must have missed it. My father drug my mom by her hair out into the living room and up the main stairs to the landing just to throw her down those same stairs. He pistol-whipped her eight or nine times, causing deep lacerations in her scalp, screaming at her all the while and informing her that he intended to kill the family cat, her mother (my grandmother), our horses, and basically anything that my mother loved within reachable distance so as to cause her the most pain possible prior to killing her. He tortured her intentionally. My mom did not yell back and held eye contact with him through all of this. For some reason, which we presume was his own lack of fitness, he became tired, his self-proclaimed plans of going on to kill my grandma along with other familial loved living things changed, and my father proclaimed that my mother would think of him every time she took a step from that moment forward right before shooting her in the knee and then, in quick succession, putting the gun in his mouth and shooting himself in the head.

On two shattered feet, my mom walked across the house to her phone, which sat on the kitchen table. She tried to call emergency services but was unable to properly work the phone that had quickly been covered by her own blood. She was able to make a call to my grandma, who then called emergency services and was the first person on the scene, living less than two miles away. My mom walked to the back door and opened the garage door before laying down by the open back door, still within the house, as she bled out on the tile, while speaking with a first responder on the phone who without data assured her that she was not bleeding out, while she was in the process of losing over 40 percent of her blood volume.

3   How were you informed? What was your reaction?
I received a call from an old friend of mine, who had driven past my house and seen 11 cop cars outside. She told me that something horrible had happened and that I needed to look at the news. I think she herself could not bear to tell me what had happened. The news article I read said that there had been a fatal shooting where one person was killed, and another was left in critical condition. It did not specify who had died and who was in critical condition. I immediately felt violently ill and terrified. I believe I was crying. I don't remember if or when I hung up the call with my friend. I remember feeling like I could not breathe and trying repeatedly to call my grandma. She did not answer. I had woken up my roommate, who went to get our dorm mom. I believe one of our security officers eventually showed up as well. At this point, I was

definitely having a panic attack. I did not want anyone to touch me and did not care that any one was watching me.

It was like the world around me had gone blank, like I knew nothing at all, and was incapable of thinking coherently or doing anything other than feeling the immense weight of the fact that I knew nothing, except that everything was horribly wrong and would never be the same again. The anguish I felt in that moment was worse than any physical pain I have ever had before or since. My mind had been presented with something it did not know how to process. My synapses over loaded and failed to process anything around me. Every schema I had ever built for processing the world was broken to bits in that moment and I was quite literally left with nothing; the knowledge that I no longer knew anything.

I do not remember who informed the dorm director in my dorm; presumably my roommate, but I cannot remember this. While I was physically present in Connecticut, my mind was absent. I believe I tried and failed to make contact with my mom and then grandma. I knew I probably would not be able to reach my mom but did so anyway, almost as if to confirm my own fears. I do not remember when I did finally make contact with my grandma.

The female security officer took ahold of me to try to move me over to the health center, which was a building located directly next to my dorm. I remember being pulled back to myself by her touching my arm and feeling defeatedly angry, not at her but at how this was the second time in less than a year when I had had all my autonomy and control taken from me. There was absolutely nothing I could do. I half slammed my arm across the door as I walked out, which is the closest I had ever been to hitting any stationary object. Reflectively I did not really hit it that hard but it made a loud enough noise and was a stark enough contrast to my blank teary stare that it startled the security officer, who once again took ahold of my arm to try to get me out of the dorm.

The school counselor, Victoria, sat with me most of the night. My emotions ranged wildly, and I remember even laughing at certain points. It did not seem real. At some point that night, I spoke with my mom on the phone as well prior to her surgery and transfer to Methodist Hospital in Indianapolis. She sounded tired. Hearing her voice helped slow my mental spiraling, because I knew at the very least, she was alive. I did not sleep at all for the next three days.

I was flown home to Indiana from Connecticut the following morning. My school booked the flight and a member of staff drove me to the airport. I believe someone even packed for me. The duration of the trip felt painfully and terribly long. I alternated between crying and staring blankly at the back of the seat in front of me. I remember a flight attendant showed me particular kindness that day.

In the hospital, I asked my mom two questions: 1) Can we change your relationship Facebook status? 2) Can I change my last name? We also laughed over the emergency operator's commentary that my mother was not bleeding out and her response that he did "not have the data to support such a claim." Seeing her in the hospital, I knew everything was going to be okay. She looked better than I had expected her to after such an ordeal, but I did not yet know the upcoming long and arduous recovery process she was to face. I posted an update on her condition shortly after arriving at the hospital and fielded hundreds of messages from concerned and supportive family, friends, colleagues, and acquaintances.

I washed dried blood out of my mom's hair in the hospital, which to this day is one of the hardest things I have ever done. Her hair, always worn in a long braid that reached her lower back, came out in my hands in clumps having been pulled out as she was suspended by it by a man twice her size.

My later reaction was to take it on as my personal mission to put a face to stories like this one, by which we so often find ourselves fascinated as we watch the news. It does happen and people rarely survive what my mom did. I chose to use what occurred in my family as motivation and became a high honor roll graduate of School ABC, going on to become an Honors student graduating a full semester early from Purdue University with an additional three minors to my degree, amidst other chaos of my mom having stage 3 cancer during my sophomore and junior year.

At School ABC, I helped found an organization dedicated to helping end violence and sexual assault against women through advocacy and education. I also led another organization whose purpose it was to encourage and develop leadership skills in young women. I gave a speech in front of several hundred people during my second to last year at the school telling my story and took back the narrative that too often was said for me.

There are certain moments when you know your life has changed and will never be the same, and you are keenly aware of that change taking place in a given moment. This event was one such moment for me.

4   How did this event change you, i.e., mental health, physical health, socially-emotionally? The word "parents," as a plural, became almost knife-stabbingly painful after January 30, 2014. I developed a deeper sense of empathy for the pain and trauma of others, generally speaking, but more significantly my understanding [of] the power of language grew ten-fold. Mentally, I do not believe I actually processed what had happened until a significant temporal delay from the incident itself. I was in survival mode for the first few months following the incident, during which my energies were focused on supporting my mother as she recovered. I feel like that is the day my childhood/adolescence ended, but I am not resentful for that. The way I viewed the world shifted irrevocably. In a way, it became a less safe place, because one of the people who was never supposed to hurt me did so in the most gruesome and violent ways possible. I grew up being screamed and sworn at nearly daily, but this event took that violence and abuse to a level I could never have imagined.

I despise the sound of fireworks, as they are reminiscent of the sounds of the gun shots that I have played over in my mind a hundred times. I initially blamed myself for what had happened, as many in my situation do as they try to make sense of what happened. I cannot stand to be screamed at or to be on the receiving end of strong, negative emotions, which is more a result of his abusive parenting style that I grew up with than the incident itself, but it does affect how I handle certain tense social interactions. At times, I struggle to feel lovable, though logically I know this is not the case. I hate the idea of ever being pitied and the fact that so many people looked at me with pity, when I first returned to school, one week after the incident; I did not even last two days on campus, before returning home and staying there until after spring break. Emotionally, it was too much.

In terms of physical effects, I have always been an avid athlete. Running and general physical activity were and always have been my escape. I ran to escape my emotions to

the extent that I broke both of my feet from overuse and required two orthopedic sur-
geries during my junior year of high school that effectively ended my athletic career.
This in and of itself was horrifically difficult on me, as I had lost my emotional outlet.

5   Was the school you attended at the time informed of the incident? If so, what services
went into effect?

As the school I attended was a boarding school, the faculty and staff immediately
knew of what happened. The dorm director, security officer, my advisor, health center
staff, counselor, a woman from admissions, and administrators were involved in the
process of getting me home from campus to be with my mom, making it possible
for me to keep up with academic responsibilities, and my reintegration to academic
life when I was ready to return in full as a student. As I mentioned previously, on
the night the incident took place, my dorm mom and [a] security officer facilitated
moving me over to the health center and helped me pack my bags, a counselor and
several members of the health center staff sat up with me all night, and a woman from
admissions drove me to the airport that following morning. When I came back earlier
than I was truly ready to be back and was not able to handle the pressure of being
back, I stayed in the health center with several members of staff who kept me company and cooked me food prior to my return home.

When I came back in full, the school tried to institute mandatory counseling services as a condition of my return. I had been seeing a counselor back home and this
mandate was detrimental to my mental well-being, making it difficult to reintegrate
in campus life, with the expectation that I see a stranger twice a week to "deal" with
my problems interrupting that reintegration process to a schedule that really did not
allow time for such diversions. Additionally, the counselor I had seen during my time
back home had cleared me to return without the need for further psychological services. The counselor I saw in Connecticut shared similar sentiments, saying that counseling was unnecessary and not productive for me at the time, going so far as to cancel
appointments on my behalf, so I did not have to attend them. The Dean of Students
was responsible for this mandate and threatened to send me home if I did not comply.
It took several correspondences with these aforementioned counselors, meetings with
me, and phone calls with my mother before she agreed to remove this mandate that
was in place purely for legal reasons and not to protect and support me as a student
who had been through trauma. School ABC, while a wonderful and valuable insti-
tution that supports girls' education, has a habit of disposing of students who they
perceive to have problems and therefore pose legal risks. If you want to be a student
there, you had better never show any sign of psychological weakness, or your status
as a student there will be seriously threatened.

6   How were you treated by each individual teacher upon returning to school? Does anything stand out?

One of the strongest aspects of an education from School ABC is their teaching staff.
The teachers gave me a list of missed readings and assignments to catch up on and
many of them worked with me one on one in the evenings to facilitate and support
me. They gave me great flexibility in terms of deadlines as well.

My advisor did not really know how to handle what I had been through and
was a bit odd around me. I ended up switching advisors to the woman who was my

substitute dorm mom. I am grateful the school offers this as an option, not just for me given my situation, but to all students. I think it is an incredibly supportive structure in place on behalf of the student population. My English teacher in particular was a great source of kindness and support for me. She took time to warn me and talk to me about potentially upsetting moments in the texts that we read for her course.

Having the opportunity to turn my trauma into a teaching experience for others was incredibly helpful as I healed from it. I appreciate that the school offered me the opportunity where I was able to speak about my experience in front of the student body, staff, and faculty – most of whom already knew about my experience but were able to hear it first hand from my perspective, really, for the first time. These talks were not unique to me. They are known as journey talks and in some ways are comparable to TED Talks, just within the context of our own community.

7   If you could give teachers advice on what to do or what not to do when one of their gifted students has experienced trauma, toxic stress, and psychological distress, what would it be?

Please do not treat us differently and be cogn[izant] of how that stress, trauma, and pain may relate to materials encountered in the course and how we go about participating/integrating in collaborative and/or participative academic environments. Peer relationships change quite a bit following such an event. Please be flexible and give the student autonomy and encouragement over their academics. Be a source of support, compassion, and understanding. Please do not act in a pitying way toward a student who has been through a traumatic event. While validating feelings and recognizing the event is important, treating a student who has experienced trauma as though they are broken or defined by this event puts that idea in their mind. I did not want to be defined by what happened in my family. More than anything, I needed control over my own narrative. Create a safe space where the student can share with you if they need to and understand that the emotions result[ing] from such an event often come in waves. Some days will be better than others. Sometimes it is easier to talk to an adult than to one's peers, so if you are capable of doing so be that person to whom a student can talk and with whom they can process these emotions. Sometimes just providing a space where the student can process on their own is enough as it can be a bit overwhelming and isolating to have experienced something to which none of one's peers can relate.

Questions for Discussion

1   What was your first "gut level" feeling after reading the case study above?
2   How did you cognitively process the case study?
3   Why might some teachers have difficulty in making a commitment to help a gifted student with trauma, toxic stress, and ACEs?
4   Do you believe teachers of gifted students suffering from trauma, toxic stress, and ACEs should only deal with the student's classroom behavior, or should they also try to address the underlying reasons? Support your response.
5   How might the principal help or hinder how gifted students with trauma, toxic stress, and ACEs are handled?

Conclusion

The information presented in this toolbox affirms that collaboration is essential when serving gifted students with trauma, toxic stress, and ACEs. Teachers of gifted students are the experts in the classroom, focusing on academic achievement, cognitive development, and social-emotional learning. Knowing when to involve others is important and informs referrals for outside help. School psychologists, counselors, mental health therapists, targeted case managers, and the like, offer other types of expertise. Joining forces to build a "web of support" for students with trauma is essential and in their best interest. Ultimately, we want these gifted students to be self-aware, have a healthy self-image, and to be able to access the resources they need to promote a positive and strong mental health.

Teachers of gifted students need to be flexible and ready to implement action should the need arise. Often, this means instituting those lessons, experiences, and activities that allow the student to express what they are going through in a meaningful way. The information presented in this chapter provides a plethora of ideas on how they can do that. Of course, working with families is crucial and should be a priority in the collaboration between school personnel and the local community's mental health services. Community agencies work with schools and families to help each gifted child be successful.

Gifted students who experience trauma, toxic stress, and ACEs need support. They need resources devoted to offsetting the effects of damaged mental health. They need informed educators to help them navigate and understand their complicated personal identity. We can help them by acknowledging the influence of their struggles on academic performance, by investing the time to constantly improve, by being responsive and proactive, and by raising our expectations of how much these students can flourish during challenging times. When teachers of gifted students with trauma choose to make a difference, they are increasing that students' chance to be happy, healthy, and mentally strong.

References

Bachtel, K. (2019). Trauma: A call for collaboration. Retrieved from: www.sengifted.org/post/bachtel-trauma-collaboration

Boyce, W. T. (2019). *The orchid and the dandelion: Why some children struggle and how all can thrive*. Borzoi Books.

Centers for Disease Control and Protection [CDC]. (2019a). *About the CDC–Kaiser ACE study*. Retrieved from: www.cdc.gov/violenceprevention/childabuseandneglect/acestudy/about.html

Centers for Disease Control and Protection [CDC]. (2019b). *Adverse childhood experiences (ACEs)*. Retrieved from: www.cdc.gov/violenceprevention/childabuseandneglect/acestudy/

Child Trends. (2016). *Moving beyond trauma: Child migrants and refugees in the United States*. Author.

Council for Exceptional Children. (2017). *High-leverage practices in special education*. Author.

Durlak, J. A., Weissberg, R. P., Dymnicki, A. B., Taylor, R. D., & Schellinger, K. B. (2011). The impact of enhancing students' social and emotional learning: A meta-analysis of school-based universal interventions. *Child Development, 82*(1), 405–432.

Flannery, M. E. (2020). "Are you thinking about suicide?" YES! *NEA Today, 38*(3), 34–39.

Frey, N., Fisher, D., & Smith, D. (2019). *All learning is social and emotional: Helping students develop essential skills for the classroom and beyond*. ASCD.

Hattie, J. (2009). *Visible learning: A synthesis of over 800 meta-analyses relating to achievement*. Routledge.

Hickman, J., & Higgins, K. (2019). 10 simple steps for reducing toxic stress in the classroom. *Education Week, 39*(14), 19.

National Child Traumatic Stress Network. (2008). *Child trauma toolkit for educators.* Author.

National Institute of Mental Health. (2019). *Helping children and adolescents cope with disasters and other traumatic events: What parents, rescue workers, and the community can do.* Retrieved from: www.nimh.nih.gov/health/publications/helping-children-and-adolescents-cope-with-disasters-and-other-traumatic-events/index.shtml

Poag, G. (2018). What is the difference between acute trauma and chronic trauma? Columbia Center for EMDR Therapy. Retrieved from: www.columbiaemdr.com/single-post/2017/07/26/what-is-the-difference-between-acute-trauma-and-chronic-trauma

Sacks, V., & Murphey, D. (2019). *The prevalence of adverse childhood experiences, nationally, by state, and by race or ethnicity.* Available from: www.researchgate.net/publication/330397979_The_prevalence_of_adverse_childhood_experiences_nationally_by_state_and_by_raceethnicity

Sacks, V., Murphey, D., & Moore, K. (2014, July). *Adverse childhood experiences: National and state-level prevalence* (Research Brief). Child Trends. Retrieved from: https:// childtrends-ciw49tixgw5lbab.stackpathdns.com/wp-content/uploads/2014/07/Brief-adverse-childhood-experiences_FINAL.pdf

Wamser-Nanney, R., & Vandenberg, B. R. (2013). Empirical support for the definition of a complex trauma event in children and adolescents. *Journal of Traumatic Stress, 26,* 671–678.

Chapter 4

The Why, Who, What, Where, and How for this Under-identified Underserved Population

Sedillo's Gifted–GLBT Stages of Identity

Paul James (PJ) Sedillo

Introduction

This chapter theoretically proposes Identity Stages for Gifted–GLBT (Gay, Lesbian, Bisexual, Transgender) individuals. Currently, there are very few proposed theories illuminating GLB (Gay, Lesbian, Bisexual) stages of identity and even fewer pertaining to Transgender persons. The most widely accepted theory for GLBT identity development is the Cass Identity Model (CIM) established by Vivienne Cass in 1979 (see also Cass, 1984). The model has never been applied to Gifted-GLBT people, who also represent an invisible minority. The CIM was applied to gifted identity development in a survey of 742 high-IQ society members who were 16 to 79 years of age.

Since there are no theoretical applications of stages of identity that exist for Gifted–GLBT individuals, this chapter brings forth information to assist all who either are Gifted–GLBT, their family and friends, a counselor/therapist, or an educator. All current research on gay and gifted stages of identity were collected, dichotomized, magnified, and validated in order to theoretically introduce Sedillo's Gifted–GLBT Stages of Identity which are as follows:

Stage 1: Discovery and Awareness of One's Self and Self-Denial as a Gifted–Gay, Lesbian, Bisexual, or Transgender Individual

Stage 2: Stress, Social Isolation, and Questioning for Being a Gifted–Gay, Lesbian, Bisexual, or Transgender Individual

Stage 3: Revelation or Being Uncovered by Others, Further Questioning of Self Which Leads to Self-Acceptance as a Gifted–Gay, Lesbian, Bisexual, or Transgender Individual

Stage 4: Seeking and Discovering Others Who Are Similar in Intelligence and Sexual/Gender Identity.

Stage 5: Identity Acceptance/Tolerance as a Gifted–Gay, Lesbian, Bisexual, or Transgender Individual

Stage 6: Socialization with other GLBT, Gifted, or Gifted–GLBT People

Stage 7: Positive Self-Identification, Synthesis, and Pride as a GLBT, Gifted, or Gifted–GLBT Person

Stage 8: A Revelation as a Self-Directed Independent Learner of Life: Living Out and Open, Autonomously and Becoming a Positive Teacher/Servant to Society.

GLBT sexuality identity development is a multifaceted and often problematic process. There are commonalities that exist between gay/lesbian and gifted children which make

DOI: 10.4324/9781003265412-8

members of both groups prone to suicidal ideation. Feelings of being different, isolation, sexuality (which includes sexual-identity formation), numerous school issues and depression may all be present in gay/lesbian and gifted adolescents. Therefore, the major question posed utilizing Sedillo's Gifted–GLBT Stages of Identity Theory and asked by Gifted–GLBT individuals is, "Who Am I?" both in terms of their sexual orientation/gender identity and their giftedness. This is a common element during the stages of reflection and observation. Further questions that follow are the "Why, Who, and How Am I?"

Many GLBT persons are born into families that do not harmonize with their sexual or gender identity. Therefore, questions need to be asked – from whom do they acquire information about their gender/sexual identity and who ultimately supports them, especially in an environment that might show hostility? Also, to whom do they go to learn about their intelligence and find out specifics about their giftedness?

Adolescents who feel that it is not "cool" to be smart may hide their abilities in order to blend in (to become friends) with others their own age, and girls may not work up to their academic potential (Earle, 2003). Parents, teachers, and other educators may need to encourage students who are gifted to keep showing their bright sides and building on their strengths (Earle, 2003). In the same way that gifted youngsters see the possibilities, they also see potential problems in undertaking those activities.

Webb (2004) and Whitmore (1980) emphasize that avoidance of potential problems can mean avoidance of risk-taking and may result in individuals hiding the fact that they are gifted. The development of these individuals' sexual/gender identity and giftedness is in many cases underprepared, unsupported, and defamed. The individual's progression through this stage is inconsistently characterized and incongruent with emotional, intellectual, and behavioral factors and may not always coincide with their intellectual, emotional, and/or sexual/gender identity. It must be noted that individuals can be at the same or different stages in terms of their giftedness and gender/sexual identity. Evidently, no Gifted–GLBT individual is exactly the same as any other and each has his/her own unique patterns and characteristics.

Stages of Identity

There are eight stages of development. These eight stages include discovery/awareness of self versus self-denial, anger/resentment/questioning versus self-actualization, revelation versus questioning of self, seeking others who are similar, socialization, positive self-identification, and finally living autonomously. This chapter will also discuss strategies that can be utilized and applied to assist individuals who identify as Gifted–GLBT, their family members, educators, administrators, and counselors/therapists.

Stage 1: Discovery and Awareness of One's Self and Self-Denial as a Gifted–Gay, Lesbian, Bisexual, or Transgender Individual

Erikson (1968) stated that identity formation is "a process located in the core of the individual and yet also in the core of his [her] communal culture" (p. 22). The major question that is posed during this stage for Gifted–GLBT persons is "Who Am I?" both in terms of their sexual orientation or gender identity and their giftedness. Individuals in this stage usually possess a conflict of internal denial which may lead them to try to "pass" as a heterosexual or deny the fact that they could be gifted in any way. This occurs because of social interactions in their lives –with family, friends, peers, their church and their faith (to name a few) which restrict the individual from experiencing his/her true self. Some Gifted–GLBT individuals may consider their sexual behaviors as "experimenting" and try to hide their giftedness from others and "play dumb."

Hiding one's giftedness is known as the "Chameleon Effect." Students who feel that it is not "cool" to be smart may hide their abilities to blend in (and become friends with) others their own age (Chartrand & Bargh, 1999). Ultimately, this may lead them to avoid risk-taking which may result in underachievement. Middle school girls may not meet their potential by not revealing their true intelligence, as this is the time in their life when girls become interested in boys and look at the chance to date, feeling that boys do not like smart girls. In essence, girls opt out of working on their passion for science and replace it with make-up kits (Kerr, 1997).

These feelings may lead to emotional conflict resulting in confusion, anxiety, and denial of feelings. Gifted–GLBT people are usually "in the closet" at this stage in terms of either their sexual orientation, gender identity, or their giftedness; however, because of their intelligence they usually seek out information online, locate books (bibliotherapy), watch movies, conduct research, and seek out mentors and individuals who have dealt with a similar issue.

Gay–Gifted adolescents have difficulty in coming to terms with being different from the majority of their age mates in both ability and sexual orientation (Peterson & Rischar, 2000).

This stage is one that is the most private and sacred until the Gifted–GLBT individual becomes more independent and feels confident enough to "come out" to others either with their giftedness, or their sexual/gender identity or both. This usually occurs during college and young adulthood; however, in recent times, Gifted–GLBT persons are coming out at an earlier age (Benfer, 2009). Regardless of whether GLBT youth develop their identity based on a model, the typical age at which youth in the United States come out as GLBT has been dropping. High school students and even middle school students are coming out (Benoit, 2009).

For transsexuals/transgender persons there is an abiding anxiety during this stage which can be characterized by unfocussed gender and sex discomfort. Preference for other gender activities and companionship might take place. Identity confusion about one's originally assigned gender and/or sexual orientation brings forth doubts about suitability of one's original assigned gender and sexual orientation.

Once the discovery and acceptance of one's self as a Gifted–Gay, Lesbian, Bisexual, or Transgender person is made, it can lead to the questioning of one's self. Reservations and uncertainties might come up to make such individuals feel that there is no way that they are gifted or gay, lesbian, bisexual, or transgender. If they are ready to come to terms with being Gifted–GLBT, then what does it really matter that they are Gifted–GLBT? Notably, setbacks might occur because gifted individuals are usually easily wounded and need emotional support (Clark, 2008), something which is similarly experienced by GLBT persons.

Individuals who are Gifted–GLBT do not realize the importance of their self-discovery and acceptance. It must be noted that some individuals might choose to stay in this stage by hiding either their sexual orientation/gender identity, or their giftedness, or by choosing to hide both attributes; therefore, they become "imposters" in society (Sedillo, 2013). Another case scenario might be that because gifted individuals often have an extreme sensitivity to the feelings of others and advanced levels of moral judgement, they have the ability of acceptance. This characteristic could lead to and assist with the acceptance of other inherent attributes for Gifted–GLBT or other sexual/gender identity persons.

Counselors/therapists, educators, and parents must be aware and comprehend the effect of life's development for an individual's giftedness and sexual and/or gender identity. The primary focus and strategy should be that of understanding themselves. Furthermore, counselors/therapists, educators, and parents must assess how the complexities of a person's giftedness and/or sexual/gender identity are relevant to healthy or unhealthy individual development. Upon completion of this period, the individual moves to Stage 2 and will experience one of the most difficult stages of growth. This includes coping with anger and resentment about being Gifted–GLBT, and questioning oneself about why this has happened and dealing with the question of whether this is a curse or a blessing.

Stage 2: Stress, Social Isolation, and Questioning for Being a Gifted–Gay, Lesbian, Bisexual, or Transgender Individual

In this stage individuals who were identified as gifted feel stress, social isolation, and question if they are truly gifted (this is similar to GLBT persons). Added pressures for them to succeed and be perfect can cause stress and lead to underachievement. There are even more difficulties for individuals who were never identified as gifted during their childhood and who are now adults. This results in anger pertaining to suffering experienced about their questioning intelligence and consequently being judged by themselves and others. Twice-exceptional adults who are diagnosed with a disability *and* giftedness in their adulthood experience the same type of resentment and anger.

Similarly, GLBT individuals also experience anger and resentment and question their gender/sexual identity. It can become painful to hide personal and intimate aspects of one's life and then make every effort to hide one's true self from others. This constant "hiding" brings forth anger and difficulties in assessing perceptions of other people and of oneself. Lack of self-esteem, invisibility, losing one's voice, encountering walls from society and walls self-created eventually become barriers to one's true acceptance (Dresher, 1998). This experience is similar to that of those who are gifted and talented.

At this stage people who are either gay, gifted or Gifted–GLBT proceed with actions of bargaining, depression, and anxiety. Some individuals might experience panic attacks, question their God/spirituality, question their self, and pose doubtful reservations like "Can I give this 'gift' back, I don't want it, or can I be cured?" either with their intelligence or sexual/gender identity. One must consider the negative results of anger. This emotion can result in the destruction of creativity; therefore, the person becomes destructive toward him/herself which can inhibit him/her from overcoming disgrace, resentment, and self-harm.

Identity comparisons and questioning also occur during this stage for persons who are transsexual/transgender. This questioning pertains to one's originally assigned gender and sex. The difference between sex and gender is that sex is a biological concept based on characteristics such as difference in genitalia in the male and female. Gender, on the other hand, primarily deals with personal, societal, and cultural perceptions of sexuality.

The individual seeks out and weighs alternative gender identities – made easier by their superior intelligence to locate, research, and find information. Individuals might also during this stage experiment with alternative gender identities. Gifted individuals, who are sometimes androgynous, make this stage easier for those who are transgender to cope with because of non-conforming attire.

During this stage, all those involved with the Gifted–GLBT person should be conscientious, aware, and have an understanding of the existential depression and panic disorders which might occur. These fears and intellectual/sexual concepts become an inward experience. This is a time when Gifted–GLBT individuals must come to terms with who they are and accept the gift of having a superior intelligence and own their personal sexual/gender identity. Acceptance of being either gay, gifted, or Gifted–GLBT might occur. Usually, acceptance of one's intelligence will come first, and then the individual can utilize his/her intelligence and proceed to accept his/her new-found sexuality/gender identity (Sedillo, 2013). Notably, an individual might accept his/her giftedness and move into the next stage, but will remain in the anger, resentment, and questioning stage pertaining to their sexual/gender identity.

Social issues are common in gifted, gay, and Gifted–GLBT individuals. Difficulties arise with the meeting of peers who are compatible. The chance of meeting someone who is similar is difficult. The chances of meeting a similar sexual/gender-identified and intellectual peer is even less likely to occur. The higher the IQ, the less chance there is that an individual will meet someone who is similar or like-minded. The following levels apply with a standard deviation of 15 on a standardized IQ test. Each level of Sedillo's Scale of Giftedness (grounded on Galbraith, 2013) represents a difference of one standard deviation from the mean.

1 Bright: 115+ or one in six (84th percentile)
2 Moderately gifted: 130+ or one in 50 (97.9th percentile)
3 Highly gifted: 145+ or one in 1,000 (99.9th percentile)
4 Exceptionally gifted: 160+ or one in 30,000 (99.997th percentile)
5 Profoundly gifted: 175+ or one in 3 million (99.99997th percentile)

Gifted individuals, adults, or adolescents live lives that are comparatively isolated from society. If they are more gifted than one out of 1,000 individuals, many of the people they meet within their lifetime will not be comparable. If they are more gifted than one in 30,000, they may not come across anyone in their lives who is as gifted as they are unless they attend places where gifted people congregate. If they are more gifted than one in 3 million, it is certain that they may never encounter anyone with a similar giftedness in their lifetime. Therefore, gifted individuals will find themselves more isolated in terms of intellectual stimulation.

Consequently, loneliness and disconnection from peers can have drastic results leading to underachievement, suicidal ideation, or the suicidal act of completion. Difficulties meeting compatible peers with similar aspirations for greater intimacy, loyalty, and stability can hinder close friendships/relationships (Gross, 2000). This occurs similarly for GLBT persons.

Whether anger and resentment are the most difficult emotions to control is dependent on the situation at hand and even more so on the person's intellect. Emotions become a stressful situation that creates anxiety. The emotion of anger becomes an added fuel which makes it the most difficult emotion to control. Thus, anger drives anxiety and more anger.

During this stage, it is important to locate mentors. Mentors can provide understanding for these individuals who can then share their emotional stories. Mentors who are themselves tuned in to their sexuality/gender identity, giftedness, or the combination can provide an awareness, supportiveness, and a comprehensive understanding of the mentor's self, helping individuals understand exactly how they can accept their uniqueness and positive self-worth.

Furthermore, Gifted–GLBT individuals can channel their anger into finding a solution to whatever problem they are facing (Sedillo, 2013). They can easily adopt new or improved understandings by researching, learning about, and comprehending the many differences that exist in the universe; therefore, being exposed to many rudiments that will lead to their own personal strength and acceptance.

Strategies to overcome this stage of anger and resentment must include the individual observing that one's giftedness, gender, and/or sexual orientation can be accepted as their own. This must take place within the individual who can then decrease their feelings of anger and resentment. This can lead to acceptance of one's gender and/or sexual orientation and giftedness. Counselors/therapists, family members, teachers – or most importantly a positive role model in their life – can support these individuals through this stage (Sedillo, 2013). Upon completion the individual will be able to have a metamorphosis and an eye-opening experience which leads to self-acceptance in Stage 3.

Stage 3: Revelation or Being Uncovered by Others, Further Questioning of Self which Leads to Self-Acceptance as a Gifted–Gay, Lesbian, Bisexual, or Transgender Individual

At this stage, Gifted–GLBT persons comprehend the feelings that they are experiencing; however, as gifted individuals, they seek justification and reasons for why they are having them. They do not want to let others know how smart they are, and they realize that in the current society they live in, it is not "cool" to be smart (especially with peers in middle and high school).

In terms of being gay or lesbian, they might state at first that they might be bisexual (it must be noted that the individual might actually be bisexual); however, the individual might feel that it is easier for a person to come out as bisexual – which could mean that there is still a chance to be heterosexual. This proclamation of bisexuality might also be used as a defense mechanism – that they might not be gay, lesbian, or transgender. Therefore, the individual might choose the other sex in a relationship so as not to be uncovered by others. Furthermore, someone who is transgender might question whether they are gay or lesbian. Ultimately, this leaves these individuals feeling isolated, alienated, and pondering, "Is this only a phase?"

During this stage for transsexual/transgender persons, after locating research and facts during the previous stage, the individuals continue to have more questions about their identity. These questions pertain to the discovery of transsexualism or transgenderism and its existence. Testing one's transsexual identity might occur because one starts to dis-identify with individuals of the same sex.

Furthermore, when Gifted–GLBT persons realize the importance of their own self-discovery and acceptance, they choose to stop hiding either their sexual orientation/gender identity or their giftedness. They break away from being a charlatan – known as the "Chameleon Effect," as previously described.

This is still a stage in which the individual will choose a select few individuals to "come out" to. It must be mentioned that revealing or sharing one's own giftedness or sexual/gender identity is an ongoing process. Gay, gifted, or Gifted–GLBT individuals will possibly encounter one or more of the following steps when sharing their self-identity with a close friend, mentor, teacher, counselor/therapist, or family member:

1 Rejection/denial may cause a return to Stage 1, either in terms of their sexual orientation, gender identity, or giftedness (or all characteristics).
2 A positive response from others might lead to higher self-esteem and a greater acceptance of self.
3 The person's superior intellectual ability will be able to process and evaluate the situation. The individual may choose to disclose to others. Through the process of evaluating the situation, they will be able to provide disclosure and be validated in terms of their sexual/gender identity.

Gifted students routinely exhibit academic and emotional traits that may be described as intense and, at times, even extreme. They are more curious, demanding, and sensitive than their typical developing peers. When gifted individuals are identified as gifted, it provides an explanation that they can intellectually comprehend; this can then lead to an understanding about their sexuality/gender identity. Thus, they are aware of whom to come out to and can evaluate what to do next, depending on whether the response is positive or negative. Gifted children are unique and require parents and educators to modify both home and school environments to meet their strong need to know. Modification is imperative if gifted students are to reach their full potential (Manning, 2006).

Interestingly enough, when individuals learn that they are gifted, they usually experience that "Aha! moment" when they realize that they have not been crazy after all. This experience can be liberating and moves them forward to understand their new-found world so much that they want to share with others, even though they may be afraid of proclaiming that they are gifted because they might be viewed as a nerd, as arrogant, or as an elitist. If this happens, they might then minimize communication with others who do not understand giftedness. This negative experience might cause the individual to shift back to Stage 1, Stage 2, or a combination.

If a positive experience occurs, with others welcoming their new-found self-discoveries, the individual will be able to look at his/her gifted qualities and share them with family, friends, and others with whom they feel confident and comfortable. This sharing of self will continue in this stage as they choose to come out to others pertaining to their intelligence. However, this can make it difficult for educators to provide appropriate gifted services in the educational setting. Locations, services, or the settings where one's intelligence is revealed vary, ranging from gifted programs (nationally), organizations, workplace, the family home, and gifted peers.

This very social dynamic becomes a life-long problem for the majority of gifted persons to figure out as an adult: Do they come out to their boss, someone on a date who might be a future mate, or during a job interview? This revelation to others is similar to the experience of those who are GLBT. Also, during this stage, individuals who are Gifted–GLBT need to understand how to cope with others who can be less enthusiastic or even hostile to their new self-discovery. Many misunderstandings can take place, and the individual needs to be able to communicate effectively.

On a positive note, if individuals are able to successfully meet the needs of Stage 3, they are in a better position to understand their sexual/gender identity. Based on my own research findings, it has been revealed that Gifted–GLBT individuals first deal with their acceptance of giftedness and then can easily use their intelligence to support, understand, and advocate for their sexual orientation or gender identity.

They also realize they can use their intelligence to work out with whom to share this information. Persons within this stage require positive individuals in their life to help them acquire a covenant of acceptance with their emotions of anger which are usually based on questions of "Why, why, why?" In essence they are trying to validate, tolerate, and make sense of their identities, and anyone in their life who is a supporter or advisor can assist the individual to move to the next segment of identity.

Stage 4: Seeking and Discovering Others Who Are Similar in Intelligence and Sexual/Gender Identity

Gifted children are very particular when locating friends. They specifically seek those who understand their humor, share the same feelings and concerns, stand up for one another, and can share secrets and successes. Evidently, the brighter the children, the more likely they are to seek a smaller number of older friends. On the other hand, they see that "being smart" makes it more difficult to acquire and keep new friends (Janos et al., 1985).

An inability to locate friends can bring forth a withdrawal from society – this person is then seen as one who is superior or "stuck-up." Research suggests that gifted individuals who are introverts reveal more independence and need fewer social relationships than others (Mills et al., 1996; Sak, 2004). Gifted individuals who are introverts are usually not popular and prefer to focus on their passionate interests and learning. Because of this, gifted individuals have the most difficult time leaving this stage because it is more comfortable to be safe than to take risks. This is even more evident with gifted individuals who are perfectionists.

However, gifted individuals need to learn how to work with others in society or "how to play the game" in order to succeed. Ultimately, it is the responsibility of society to ensure that all children are treated with respect and dignity and given opportunities to thrive in order to become resilient beings; this can occur by providing gifted programs and services. Without gifted programs and services adolescents may encounter a world of disrespect and intolerance. Furthermore, without the necessary support provided in programs like gifted education, they would be unable to develop the skills needed to confront opportunities, leading to them becoming defeatist individuals, and in the worst-case scenario, they would have notions of suicidal ideation or even commit suicide (Sedillo, 2013). Gifted programs and services are important because they can help in preventing such negative results, and ensuring that the individual can move out of this stage to the next one.

Gay, lesbian, and bisexual individuals have difficulty locating others who have similar sexual identities. Many segments of U.S. society still do not accept GLBT individuals. In

28 states it is still legal to fire GLBT individuals, kick them out of an apartment, or deny them services. It is even more difficult for transgender individuals who hide their true selves from family members, friends, peers, colleagues, and teachers. In 2013, more than one in five GLBT Americans told Pew researchers (Pew Research Center, 2013) that they'd been mistreated by an employer because of their sexual orientation and gender identity. The Pew Research Center is a nonpartisan organization that provides information on social issues and demographic trends that profile the Unites States and the world by conducting public opinion polling, demographic research, and analyze the content from the media.

One safe haven might be the fact that many gifted adolescents are androgynous; this can make it easier for them to fit in with other Gifted–GLBT adolescents and others on the fringes of society, despite the fact that they are still not accepting who they are. Another safety net is participation in a Gay–Straight Alliance (GSA). GSAs are clubs found in middle and high schools across the United States for gay, lesbian, bisexual, transgender, queer individuals and allies. The club becomes a support network for those who attend. However, only three states have Gay–Straight Alliances in more than half of their high schools (Temkin et al., 2017). Gifted children and adolescents (who might or might not be GLBT) usually support certain groups because of their keen sense of empathy and awareness to support those who are being bullied or marginalized by others and society (Niles & Jolly, 2019). Upon completion of Stage 4, the individual will be able to accept him/herself and move to Stage 5.

Stage 5: Identity Acceptance/Tolerance as a Gifted–Gay, Lesbian, Bisexual, or Transgender Individual

In this stage, the new-found acceptance of identifying as GLBT might have the individual accept some aspects of his/her sexual/gender identity, while some other aspects might not be fully embraced. An individual might be encountering same-sex sexual experiences and feel that it is okay, but he or she might not be able to identify as gay, or lesbian; therefore, living "out of the closet" with one foot still in the door. A transgender person might be gender non-conforming, gradually learning feminine presentation while living as a "feminine man;"; thus, living a double life.

This double life is similar to the acceptance of one's intelligence/giftedness. There might be a few other people of similar intelligence who associate with the gifted person and know that they are gifted; however, the gifted individual might hide his/her intelligence from others who are not gifted. An example might be an athlete who is academically gifted hiding his/her superior intelligence from team mates. They might even dumb themselves down so as to seem to be "just one of the guys."

This stage involves individuals in being open and not defensive about their sexual orientation or gender identity. Manifestation might occur in the following different ways:

1   Proclamation of one's sexuality orientation or gender identity to self and others
2   Proclamation of one's gender change to self and others
3   Announcement of sexual orientation or gender identity which leads to supporting others who are similar (empathy takes place)
4   No need to be invisible and hide their sexual orientation or gender identity from self and others after proclamation

5   Validation and affirmation with relationships with family and friends
6   Integration of one's self within his or her chosen community

Gifted individuals during this stage come to the realization that if they are going to accept this "gift," then they must figure out how they are going to use it to improve and benefit their life. They are able to investigate and use their intelligence to assist with clarification about their personal values and preferences which will assist them to become their authentic self.

Connections for the gifted individual are made on how they think, process information, understand strengths and weaknesses, and accept both the emotional and logical reasons why they are gifted; thus, they shatter any previous misconceptions and doubts. During this stage the acceptance of one's intelligence usually occurs before one's acceptance of gender identity or sexual orientation. However, a person's acceptance of his or her superior ability can lead to his/her acceptance of gender identity or sexual orientation.

During this stage individuals tolerate their transsexual or transgender identity. They might identify as probably transsexual while dis-identifying as their originally assigned gender and sex. Furthermore, the individuals might be waiting and hoping for their circumstances to change, seeking others for confirmation, or looking for signs to offer validity and approval for their actuality as a transsexual/transgender person. Thus, there might be a slight delay before *true* acceptance of the transsexual or transgender identity will occur.

Consequently, individuals who are Gifted–Transsexual/Transgender are able to utilize their giftedness or superior ability to be able to sift through what is logical and not logical. Because of their comprehensive knowledge, they are able to realize and acquire substantial positive support by locating trans mentors, peer-reviewed journal articles, books, and others met via social media (not mentioned before, but for any of these stages one must be aware of the positive and negative use of social media). Next steps might be to reveal their "true identity" to specifically chosen others.

At the Identity Acceptance/Tolerance Stage it is common for individuals to seek out similar others to socialize with, whether they be lesbian, gay, bisexual, transgender, gifted, or Gifted–GLBT. Social groups are important to assist with the exploration of their new-found identity and acceptance by similar and like-minded peers/groups provides support and validation. In this stage the person's acceptance helps them to tolerate their sexual orientation, gender identity, or giftedness. They realize that they can and will be accepted by others. This stage also assists them with realizing that their life can be happy and fulfilling and that it is okay to come out to a few trusted individuals. Socializing with others who are similar leads to Stage 6. Socialization is a process whereby an individual acquires a personal identity and learns the norms, values, behavior, and social skills appropriate in the realm of the GLBT and gifted communities.

Stage 6: Socialization with Other GLBT, Gifted, or Gifted–GLBT People

During this stage the individual consciously seeks and begins to connect with others who have similar identities. This, in turn, diminishes the feelings of isolation and discord. Their new-found positive sense of self is strengthened by their comprehension of the situation, their own validation of self and from others, and locating support and acceptance from other community members with shared experiences of being gay, lesbian, bisexual, transgender, gifted or Gifted–GLBT. It is important to have positive role models and mentors during this stage. For gifted individuals this stage brings forth how he/she sees him/herself in relation to others.

During the stage of socialization with other GLBT, gifted, or Gifted–GLBT people, it is common for individuals to become comfortable and complacent. It becomes the stage for one to take a breath and re-evaluate the previous stages. However, gifted individuals have a tendency to be perfectionists and might be stuck in this stage of constantly re-evaluating the previous stages and are now exhausted and tired of taking risks. Complacency makes it easier to deal with life; however, this complacency hinders individuals from reaching the final stage of positive self-identification, synthesis, and pride.

Seeking socialization with others and sharing one's actual existence as an experienced transsexual or transgender person becomes intensified during this stage, especially for those who are gifted. Some individuals have queries about dealing with transition – especially on how to transition in terms of money, support, or whether ultimately one is making the right decision.

During this stage, the individual finally has anticipation toward his or her final transsexual/transgender identity. This is deepened by the person's final dis-identification of his or her original gender and sex; therefore, he or she is figuring out how to conduct his or her transition (notably, an individual who is transgender does not have to complete gender and sex reassignment to go to the next stage).

Gifted individuals who have excellent, intensified expectations and standards look closely to appreciate what they have accomplished. During this stage, the tendency to criticize one's self becomes a desired emotion. These individuals tend to look at all mistakes through a microscope, leading them to ponder their true accepted self and how this new profound self might assist in serving others or even "humankind." Their own existence leads them to find out how they can help others fulfill their self-acceptance of being GLBT, gifted, or Gifted–GLBT. Individuals can, however, become stagnant by being comfortable and complacent during this stage of socialization with similar others which makes it easier to deal with life; however, this complacency hinders them from reaching the next stage of positive self-identification, synthesis, and pride. A strategy to move forward is to make a strong effort to work on perfectionism issues by taking risks and realizing that the individual has the capacity and ability to move to Stage 7.

Stage 7: Positive Self-Identification, Synthesis, and Pride as a GLBT, Gifted, or Gifted–GLBT person

This stage is one where the individuals feel good about their self-identity. They have consciously located others for relationships that are positive. It becomes an understanding that Gifted–GLBT persons can experience reconciliation, harmony, and normalcy with others whether it be in a same-sex relationship, being openly transsexual/transgender, or providing support and becoming an advocate for gifted or GLBT people.

Individuals during this stage feel a sense of pride with their sexual orientation and comfort from interaction within the GLBT community. This is a time when individuals will start coming out to others in their lives and eventually make their sexual orientation known publicly. Furthermore, this is the stage where individuals are ready to rebuild their lives based on who they are as a Gifted–GLBT person. This might occur through building up their career, education, self-esteem, family, and personal relationships or by sharing their revelation to assist others with positive connections and true inner callings both professionally and personally.

This stage for transsexual/transgender formation of identity brings forth "transition." At this stage individuals have successfully changed their gender and sex. This might be for the completion of gender and sex reassignment, or acceptance of one's gender and sex identity (without surgery). This moves forward by integration and transsexuality becoming visible. The individual successfully lives as a transsexual or transgender person. This leads to becoming openly transsexed and prideful which leads to Transsexual advocacy. Finalization for Gifted–GLBT persons during this stage leads to one becoming autonomous and self-serving in order to help others.

Stage 8: A Revelation as a Self-Directed Independent Learner of Life: Living Out and Open, Autonomously, and Becoming a Positive Teacher/Servant to Society

Individuals who have successfully managed the realization of self-discovery have experienced the exuberance of reaching the mountain top, but questions remain: What are their next steps, if any? Is there more to explore with this new-found knowledge of self? Do they help others up the mountainous struggles using what they know and have just accomplished?

Gifted individuals tend to be overexcitable, leading them to pile question upon question, which does not give them time to let their minds rest. This can become both exhilarating and exhausting. They have reached the mountain top, so what's next?

One can at this stage began to search for spiritual questions which can lead to an unsettling revelation of self. Although this is the final stage, because of one's giftedness, there is a constantfight to accept whether one is *truly* autonomous. Therefore, self-metacognition or the awareness and understanding of one's own thought process can become debilitating and cumbersome during this stage. The problems that arise during this stage can, however, be transformed by using one's creative expression, critical thinking, and deep empathy and understanding of self.

Significantly enough, Gifted–GLBT individuals who reach this stage (interestingly similar to the highest level of Bloom's [new] Taxonomy) (Anderson & Krathwohl, 2001) are capable of incorporating creativity throughout their daily life experiences to create a new unique self. One's creativity thrives during this stage as a self-directed independent learner by tapping into the ability to produce a large number of ideas (fluency) which leads to one's originality in thought. This, in turn, helps the individual to be flexible – acquiring the ability to change and stretch one's creativity which leads to the addition of meaningful details to one's idea. Ideas that are novel and unique are created by individuals who express an unrestrained vision which can produce innovations in society.

This final stage can incur personal challenges – feeling that one is being pushed and pulled by life's experiences from one's autonomy in life. This final stage with one's giftedness might bring forth past experiences of avoidance, denial, or fear of risks which may become "barricades" for any future opportunities to articulate one's autonomy.

Evidently, society makes assumptions that everyone is heterosexual, lives in their birth gender, or is of average intelligence. Using each stage as a precursor, Gifted–GLBT persons do not "come out" only once; they might have to reveal who they are on a daily basis. Furthermore, they must be able to quickly think whether or not to reveal themselves and respond to every new situation or person they encounter. Therefore, coming out becomes a life-long process of discovery, acceptance, and the sharing of one's gender identity, sexual orientation, and giftedness with others. Situations must continuously be questioned as to the circumstances under which and with whom disclosure is made.

Self-acceptance and/or one's autonomy are constantly questioned at this stage (as in previous stages). Questioning one's self-acceptance also has individuals looking deeply at their emotional and physical stability, and their healthy faith and spirituality. The empowerment of coming out assists in ending one's secrecy of pain and isolation. Notably, because of the finality of this stage, it becomes easier for one to constantly come out.

The most challenging confrontations during this stage are the constant questioning of self, thoughts, and actions. Gifted–GLBT persons during this stage might feel anger and resentment because of the lack of legal and social rights for people like them; this can lead to becoming a positive advocate through involvement and becoming a source of inspiration to others (all based on theoretical, realistic, planning standards).

For Gifted–Transsexual/Transgender persons during this stage, acceptance of identity deepens into final dis-identification from one's original gender and sex, and this becomes an anticipatory part of socialization. Because there is a revelation about being a self-directed independent learner of life, these individuals learn how to conduct their transition by saving money, locating or organizing personal support, and being able to live autonomously as a Gifted–Transsexual/Transgender person. During one's transition and acceptance of changed genders and sexes, one might consider or not consider gender and sex reassignment. This final stage will see the person accepting their own post transition of gender and sex identities by establishing the next steps of integrating in society, and proclaiming that they are no longer dealing with being invisible as a transsexual/transgender person. He or she will have pride by being openly transsexed through Transsexual advocacy.

During this stage the Gifted–GLBT person also ponders continuously, "Where am I at on this journey?" – exploring all the possibilities of his or her intelligence, actively rebuilding and creating truth on the journey depending on inner and outer situations and conditions. Because of this continual assessment of his or her unique autonomous cognitive profile, the next step involves becoming a mentor for other Gifted–GLBT persons. Ultimate growth occurs by providing community support, advocating for others, or by providing essential and needed support for those who might be stagnating in prior stages due to their gender identity, sexual orientation, giftedness, or a combination of the lot.

Table 4.1 presents the various stages, situations, and strategies to support Gifted–GLBT persons.

Strategies for Equity

Notably, there are few extant empirical studies that exist pertaining to the identity formation of Gifted–GLBT individuals (Sedillo, 2013) and more research is needed. Furthermore, there are no studies pertaining to Gifted–GLBT issues of equity. As stated throughout

Table 4.1 Sedillo's Gifted–GLBT Stages of Identity

Stages	Situations	Strategies
Stage 1: Discovery and Awareness of One's Self and Self-Denial as a Gifted–Gay, Lesbian, Bisexual, or Transgender Individual	The major question that is posed during this stage for Gifted–GLBT persons is, "Who Am I?" both in terms of their sexual orientation or gender identity and their giftedness.	The primary focus should be on the strategy of understanding themselves. They should seek out assistance from counselors, therapists, educators, and parents who can help assess the complexities of their giftedness, sexual/gender identity, and how this is relevant to their healthy or unhealthy individual development.
Stage 2: Stress, Social Isolation, and Questioning for Being a Gifted–Gay, Lesbian, Bisexual, or Transgender Individual	In this stage individuals who were identified as gifted experience stress, social isolation, and question if they are truly gifted (this is similar to GLBT persons).	During this stage, it is important to locate mentors. Mentors can provide an understanding for these individuals who can then share their emotional stories. Furthermore, Gifted–GLBT individuals can channel their anger into finding a solution to whatever problem they are facing (Sedillo, 2013). They can easily adopt new or improved understandings by researching topics important to them. Networks such as PFLAG, Safe Zones, GSAs are available to provide support.
Stage 3: Revelation or Being Uncovered by Others, Further Questioning of Self Which Leads to Self-Acceptance as a Gifted–Gay, Lesbian, Bisexual, or Transgender Individual	At this stage, Gifted–GLBT persons comprehend the feelings that they are experiencing. This is still a stage in which the individual will choose a select few individuals to "come out" to. It must be mentioned that revealing or sharing one's own giftedness or sexual/gender identity is an ongoing process.	During this stage individuals who are Gifted–GLBT need strategies to understand how to cope with others who can be less enthusiastic or even hostile to their new self-discovery. Also, provide strategies to assist with communicating effectively because of the many misunderstandings that can take place.
Stage 4: Seeking and Discovering Others Who Are Similar in Intelligence and Sexual/Gender Identity	At this stage Gifted–GLBT individuals have difficulty locating others who have similar sexual/gender identities and intelligence.	Strategies for their giftedness assist them in learning how to work with others in society or "how to play the game" in order to succeed. This learning should be acquired by providing gifted programs and services. Another strategy is to identify a "safety net" such a participation in a Gay–Straight Alliance (GSA) club.

(continued)

Table 4.1 Cont.

Stages	Situations	Strategies
Stage 5: Identity Acceptance as a Gifted–Gay, Lesbian, Bisexual, or Transgender Individual	In this stage, individuals who are Gifted–GLBT need to understand how to cope with others who can be less enthusiastic or even hostile to their new self. This new-found acceptance with identifying as gifted and/or GLBT might have the individual accept some aspects of their sexual/gender identity, while some other aspects might not be fully embraced.	Identifying social groups is important to assist with the experience of exploring their new-found identity; acceptance by similar and like-minded peers/groups provides support and validation.
Stage 6: Socialization with other GLBT, Gifted, or Gifted–GLBT people	During this stage individuals consciously seek and begin to connect with others who have similar identities. This in turn diminishes the feelings of isolation and discord. Their new-found positive sense of self is strengthened by their comprehension of the situation, validation of self and by others, and locating support and acceptance from other community members with shared experiences of being GLBT, gifted, or Gifted–GLBT.	Their existence leads them to find out how they can help others fulfill their self-acceptance of being Gifted–GLBT. Strategies such as becoming a mentor, volunteering for a local Pride Organization, attending GLSEN (Gay, Lesbian, Straight Education Network). Assist with Safe Zones and anti-bullying at local schools. Get involved with legislation locally, statewide, and nationally.
Stage 7: Positive Self-Identification, Synthesis, and Pride as a GLBT, Gifted, or Gifted–GLBT person	This stage is one where individuals feel good about themselves. They have consciously located others for relationships that are positive. It becomes an understanding that Gifted–GLBT persons can experience reconciliation, harmony, and normalcy with others, whether it be in a same-sex relationship, being openly transsexual/transgender, or providing support and becoming an advocate for the gifted.	Individuals who will start coming out to others in their lives and eventually make their sexual orientation known publicly need a support network and the ability to take risks. Mentors, family members, and friends can assist individuals who are ready to rebuild their lives again based on who they are as a Gifted–GLBT person.
Stage 8: A Revelation as a Self-Directed Independent Learner of Life: Living Out and Open, Autonomously and Becoming a Positive Teacher/Servant to Society	The importance of self-acceptance or one's autonomy is constantly questioned at this stage. Furthermore, questioning one's self-acceptance also has individuals looking deeply at their emotional and physical stability, and their healthy faith and spirituality. The empowerment of "coming out" assists in ending their secrecy of pain and isolation. The most challenging confrontations during this stage are the constant questioning of self, thoughts, and actions.	Strategies during this stage assist with personal self-growth which can occur by providing community support, advocating for others, or by providing essential and needed support for those who might be stagnated in prior stages due to their gender identity, sexual orientation, giftedness, or a combination of the lot. In essence, this stage is when the individual can become a mentor for others.

this chapter, Gifted–GLBT people continue to face discrimination, marginalization, and violence. A standing commitment to this special population is needed. So how can one support equity for those who are Gifted–GLBT? This can be accomplished by:

1   Learning more with support from organizations led by GLBT and gifted people
2   Getting connected with GLBT- and gifted-led organizations
3   Joining with other allies who support each other
4   Joining with other Gifted–GLBT individuals
5   Reviewing and taking action informed by these GLBT and gifted organizations
6   Advocating for Gifted–GLBT individuals

Since there is limited research about what is available for Gifted–GLBT individuals, the applicable strategies for equity are as follows:

1   Family counseling or organizations such as Parents and Friends of Lesbians and Gays (PFLAG) could support family members with this issue (Sedillo, 2013).
2   Counselors, therapists, and teachers must help these adolescents to cope by instilling in them a healthy, positive attitude about sex and who they are, while teaching them to make appropriate choices (Cross, 1996; Sedillo, 2013).
3   Gay gifted adolescents do not ask for help from adults because of a lack of mentors who match the student (Levy & Plucker, 2003). Locating positive mentors could assist as a deterrent against suicide or suicidal ideation (Sedillo, 2013).
4   These adolescents need specialized counseling and emotional support (Whittenburg & Treat, 2009).
5   Gay gifted adolescents may need rules to safeguard them from bullying, violence, neglect, and persecution.
6   Queer–Straight Alliances (QSAs) and Gay–Straight Alliances (GSAs) could help deter gay gifted adolescents from suicide or suicidal ideation (Sedillo, 2013).
7   Burdens of being gay and gifted seem to add emotional problems. Some individuals will respond to these problems by suicide (Kerr & Cohn, 2001). Parents, teachers, and counselors should be mindful of the general suicide correlations.
8   Information about a gifted adolescent who is suicidal must be made available to the parents immediately (Coleman & Cross, 2001).
9   The limited research conducted about gay–gifted adolescents suggests the need for teachers to become more aware of situations that Gifted–GLBT youth face (Friedrichs & Etheridge, 1995; Sedillo, 2013).
10 Parents must help their adolescents have a healthy, positive attitude about sex and teach them to make responsible appropriate choices for themselves.
11 Children must be shown and taught about relationships, intimacy, gender roles, sexual orientation, and privacy from their parents' sensitive and caring examples.
12 Gay, gifted, and Gifted–GLBT elementary-age children should be provided with more complex information about things like reproduction, birth, death, HIV (human immunodeficiency virus), and other sexually transmitted diseases.
13 As they get closer to middle school age, it is not too early to talk with them about pregnancy, sexually transmitted diseases, condoms, and birth control. Research has shown that giving young people honest information about sex – including information about sexual orientation – does not promote early sexual activity.
14 When parents notice the onset of puberty, they must keep the lines of communication open between themselves and their child. This will likely become more and more

difficult, but it is important that children feel that it is safe to bring questions and concerns to parents. If parents have an expectation of abstinence, "Just say no" is not enough. Teaching children the skills they will need, including decision-making, effective communication, assertiveness, and negotiation is valuable.

15   If parents are unsure about their children's sexual activity or sexual orientation, they should not push the child to tell them. Parents must not probe deeper than children are comfortably willing to share. If answers are demanded and their children are not ready to be straightforward about their feelings, they will be forced to lie and this will set an uncomfortable precedent.

Conclusions

Utilizing Sedillo's Gifted–GLBT Stages of Identity, the major question asked by Gifted–GLBT individuals is, "Who Am I?" – both in terms of their sexual orientation/gender identity and their giftedness. This is a common element during the stages of reflection and observation. Further questions provided in this chapter were "Why, Who, and How Am I?"

This chapter's theoretically proposed Identity Stages for Gifted–GLBT youth revealed that there are very few proposed theories illuminating GLB stages of identity and even fewer pertaining to Transgender persons. Furthermore, there are no theoretical applications of stages of identity that exist for Gifted–GLBT individuals. Therefore, this chapter aims to provide information to assist all who are either Gifted–GLBT, or their counselors/therapists, educators, family members, and friends, providing strategies for equity. All current research collected has been dichotomized, magnified, and validated in order to theoretically introduce Sedillo's Gifted–GLBT Stages of Identity.

Personal Vignette: Gifted and Gay

It is another night, and PJ is exhausted. All day, he has been running around like a chicken with his head cut off. He thrives on doing and doing and doing – anything for his work, community, spouse, and himself. PJ Sedillo thrives on stress. When he is not active, his mind begins to wander, and he realizes that rest is not an option.

PJ Sedillo makes sure to give himself personal time; however, this is usually penciled in on his date book and usually only happens once a month if the time is available. PJ Sedillo has not only one day planner but two. He has two because there is a backup if he loses one. Always on the go, he sometimes loses important items, something that frustrates him no end, but life goes on, and one must continue to serve. To call him ADHD (Attention-Deficit Hyperactivity Disorder) would be an understatement.

PJ Sedillo, who was known as Paul James (which was what his mother called him when he was in trouble, which was often), grew up in a household that was as close to the 1950s sitcom *Leave it to Beaver* as possible. Paul James grew up in a stable household with a mother, father, brother, and himself. Paul James just happened to be gay. No divorce, no drugs, no fighting (at least not severe), just normal living or as normal as it would be viewed by the audience of the world. The only problem that Paul James encountered was that he did not fit in. He somehow felt that he, *The Beav*, was different and did not belong in this normal sitcom family. He was a Technicolor kid living in a black-and-white world.

His earliest recollection of his life of being gay–gifted was when he was about four or five. He was sent to preschool at his local Catholic church. Kindergarten did not exist when he was young, but preschool at the Catholic church did.

Every day, Paul James would wait by the television to watch the relationship between Big Bird and Mr. Snuffleupagus grace the screen during a daily routine of watching *Sesame Street*. For some reason, Paul James was plucked out of his world and sent off to another place, where *Sesame Street* was not shown or considered a priority. He was disappointed by this new environment which was boring because the kids were learning the alphabet and Paul James was reading at a 3rd grade level.

Paul James left the preschool and walked two miles home to watch his television show. Little did he realize that the police and other agencies had been contacted because he was missing from his preschool. When Paul James was located, his parents were angered. He was eventually spanked with the belt that his father reserved for that purpose. When Paul James was sent to preschool the next day, he again left without notice and walked home. Mr. Snuffleupagus and Big Bird were not to be missed. After the third time of leaving the facility, Paul James was eventually excused and not asked to return to Catholic preschool. He had flunked preschool. This stubbornness would plague him for the rest of his life.

When Paul James entered elementary school, he was already labeled as different or, as his parents said, "special." He typically played girl activities and was often criticized by his father for being effeminate. Paul James's mother loved him and tried to dissuade his father from being so critical about his son's feminine behavior. Paul James was forced to participate in sports. Paul James was unlike his brother, who was extremely sports-oriented and a success at baseball, swimming, basketball, and golf (which was *the* sport loved by his father). Paul James tried and tried to be good at sports. He hated the fact that he did not fit in.

During baseball practice in the Pee Wee leagues, Paul James was once singled out and told that he needed to learn how not to throw like a girl. For half an hour (which seemed endless), he had to throw rocks at a field while being reminded constantly to stop throwing like a girl. Tears streamed from his eyes which only made matters worse. Paul James began to hate anything that had to do with sports.

Eventually, because of his mother, Paul James would be able to drop out of baseball and take up the violin. His mother told his father that one day Paul James would make his father proud because of other accomplishments that had nothing to do with sports. This would turn out to be true.

During his elementary school years, he was known as Paul by the other children. However, at school he attracted other names. He was inundated by hateful name calling from the boys in his classroom. *Sissy boy*, *faggot*, *gay boy*, *joto* (slang in Spanish), and *queer* were commonly thrust upon him. He lacked the skills to be successful in sports and hid during recess with the girls. Almost every day when Paul would walk home after school, just when he was about to get home, he would pee in his pants. His father would notice, and Paul would get the belt. This happened regularly for about two years, not every day, but at least twice a month.

It was at this time that, because of his intelligence, he decided to research as much as he could locate about being a homosexual. The local library would become his haven. Although Paul James was never identified as gifted because children were not identified as such in the 1970s in New Mexico, he was often provided enrichment for all of his work since he was years ahead of his peers.

The females in his class would become his saviors because they accepted him and protected him. Paul did have a close friend, a best friend, who was as butch as could be. They lived on the same street, and this boy, named Robert, would defend Paul on many occasions. Paul eventually had enough of the torments and finally decided to defend himself by going against the most powerful boy of his school. Despite the fact that Paul had beaten the hell out of the boy who was the most powerful, the other boys reported that Paul had won the fight because he fought like a girl (scratching, biting, and pulling hair).

Nevertheless, this small but glorious victory ensured that Paul was able to defend himself; however, others continued to single him out. He would always have to be on his guard. The sad thing is that the boys who persecuted Paul would also be present in his middle school and his high school years.

Paul would constantly try to prove that he was worthy of fitting in. Sometimes he was so discouraged that he contemplated suicide. Paul dated many girls so that he would be perceived as heterosexual. He often picked the girls who most needed to be loved (mostly the misfits who were given that title by the more popular members of the class system that existed within the school). Up until high school, Paul had gone back and forth through Stages 1 (Discovery and Awareness of One's Self and Self-Denial as a Gifted–Gay, Lesbian, Bisexual, or Transgender Individual), Stage 2 (Stress, Social Isolation, and Questioning for Being a Gifted–Gay, Lesbian, Bisexual, or Transgender Individual), and Stage 3 (Revelation or Being Uncovered by Others, Further Questioning of Self Which Leads to Self-Acceptance as a Gifted–Gay, Lesbian, Bisexual, or Transgender Individual).

Eventually, Paul decided to come out to his close circle of friends during his senior year. However, he was required to leave his hometown and attend a university in a different city. He would have to go back in the closet. At the university, Paul pretended to be heterosexual to survive. Being beaten up for being gay was common in this city. Such beatings could even result in death, a consequence for being an "out" homosexual in this small town.

Paul knew that he was gay and had a boyfriend who was 90 miles away; Paul would go to him every weekend just to survive by living out the gay life. He did this for three years, calling his mother, who knew that he was gay, almost every night. His mother, brother, and sister-in-law had a meeting where Paul finally revealed who he was. It was decided by the group not to tell his father. Paul eventually graduated from college and was extremely tired of denying the love of his life and his sexual orientation. This part of Paul's life was Stage 4 (Seeking and Discovering Others Who Are Similar in Intelligence and Sexual/Gender Identity).

While attending a Gay Pride parade in his hometown, Paul watched from the sidelines. The six o'clock camera crew had arrived, so Paul hid behind the side of a building so they would not film him. When he went home after the event was over, he started to cry. He then realized that his life needed to change. While walking around with his head hanging low, heartbroken with an aching soul, knees shaking in case people would find out, and ready to quit living, Paul James finally realized he was tired of not being true to himself.

His misery and pain changed to an internal anger which eventually became a positive self-actualization. He had an eye-opening and life-awakening experience revealing that he was a proud gay man. God loved both Paul and Paul James; he was an awesome human being. He did not deserve to hide in the shadows for fear of revealing his true self. This transformation of his total being revealed to him that he needed a new name. He changed his name from Paul James, and just Paul, to PJ. This rebirth moved him into a new light, giving him a new identity and hope that would help him survive. This was Stage 5 (Identity Acceptance/Tolerance as a Gifted–Gay, Lesbian, Bisexual, or Transgender Individual).

PJ graduated with his BA at the top of his class in three years and entered the field of elementary education at the age of 20. PJ would no longer accept anything in his life that restricted him because he was gay. He was out and proud. He hated anyone who did not accept him for who he was. He gave his family an ultimatum: His father must know about his son's homosexuality, or PJ was no longer to be part of the family. The sky did not fall, and his father did not die with the information given to him.

PJ started attending meetings at the local GLBT community center, attending service at the Metropolitan Community Church (a gay-affirming church), volunteered for Pride and started a chapter of GLSEN (Gay, Lesbian & Straight Education Network). Being part of the GLBT community would assist him to move through Stage 6 (Socialization with Other GLBT, Gifted, or Gifted–GLBT People), and Stage 7 (Positive Self-Identification, Synthesis, and Pride as a GLBT, Gifted, or Gifted–GLBT Person).

PJ Sedillo would reach Stage 8 (A Revelation as a Self-Directed Independent Learner of Life: Living Out and Open, Autonomously and Becoming a Positive Teacher/Servant to Society). He decided to challenge the Albuquerque Public Schools (APS) System to include a policy of nondiscrimination against persons based on sexual orientation. With the help of his mentor, Neil Isbin, PJ got the statement of nondiscrimination included in the APS negotiated contract. The process would lead PJ to fight against other inadequacies within the public school system. PJ Sedillo would marry the love of his life in a ceremony in Canada. PJ and his spouse would receive a proclamation from the mayor of Albuquerque for their union. Thirteen years later, PJ Sedillo would win, with the support of his spouse, full spousal health benefits. Together, they would earn the deserved rights for his spouse and get full health benefits and change the process in their state.

PJ Sedillo became an openly gay teacher, a female impersonator (known as Fontana DeVine), and an advocate who was as proud of his life as he could be. He would obtain his PhD and become a professor at the university where he received his BA in elementary education. He now does Safe Zone Training with students, staff, administration, and faculty. He has come full circle from the student at the university who had to lead a double life for fear of being outed.

He still constantly fights the bullies whom he encounters on a daily basis. He must be on the go to assist all those who have been persecuted because they are gay. Whether serving as Gay Pride president for 21 years, working at a booth at the New Mexico State Fair for the GLBT Community, working with the legislature to pass hate crime bills, or traveling to different counties and states that need a positive presence of GLBT adults, PJ lives out and open as a positive teacher and servant to society. He desires to befriend those isolated, friendless, ignored boys who are forced to throw rocks into oblivion. He wants to assist them in believing that they are okay and not sissy boys, gay boys, girly men, degenerates, or queers.

All people deserve to be shown dignity, and Paul James Sedillo will not rest until all homosexual men are respected by society. This story is about his life as a gay–gifted man, his personal journey, and the struggles that will affect his future and the future of others. Coming to terms with his own sexuality has taken years of blood, sweat, and tears. The fact that he is homosexual or gay, the term that he prefers, has been a struggle of acceptance that has made him a stronger and more compassionate individual.

References

Anderson, L. W., & Krathwohl, D. R. (Eds.). (2001). *A taxonomy for learning, teaching, and assessing: A revision of Bloom's Taxonomy of Educational Objectives*. Boston, MA: Allyn & Bacon.

Benfer, A. (2009). We're here! We're queer! We're 13! Retrieved September 27, 2009 from: www.salon.com/2009/09/24/gay_teens/

Benoit, D. L. (2009). Coming out in middle school. *The New York Times*. Retrieved from: www.nytimes.com/2009/09/27/magazine/27out-t.html

Cass, V. (1979). Homosexual identity formation: A theoretical model. *Journal of Homosexuality, 4*(3), 219–235.

Cass, V. C. (1984). Homosexual identity formation: Testing a theoretical model. *Journal of Sex Research, 20*, 143–167. doi:10.1080/00224498409551214

Chartrand, T. L., & Bargh, J. A. (1999). The chameleon effect: The perception-behavior link and social interaction. *Journal of Personality and Social Psychology, 76*, 893–910.

Clark, B. (2008). *Growing up gifted* (7th ed.). Prentice Hall.

Coleman, L. J., & Cross, T. L. (2001). *Being gifted in school*. Prufrock Press.

Cross, T. (1996). Social/emotional needs: Examining claims about gifted children and suicide. *Gifted Child Today, 19*(1), 46–48. doi:10.1177/107621759601900114

Dresher, J. (1998). I'm your handyman: A history of reparative therapies. *Journal of Homosexuality, 36*(1), 19–42.

Earle, S. (2003, November). *Affective issues: A baker's dozen*. Paper presented at the annual conference of the National Association for Gifted Children, Danbury, CT.

Erikson, E. (1968) *Identity, youth and crisis*. New York: W.W. Norton & Company.

Friedrichs, T. P., Etheridge, R. L. (1995, Winter). Gifted and gay: Reasons for educators to help. *Council for Exceptional Children/The Association for Gifted (TAG) Newsletter, 17*(1), 4–5.

Galbraith, J. (2013). *The survival guide for gifted kids: For ages 10 & under*. Minneapolis, MN: Free Spirit Publishing Inc.

Gross, M. U. M. (2000, Winter). Exceptionally and profoundly gifted students: An underserved population. *Understanding Our Gifted, 12*(2).

Janos, P. M., Marwood, K. A., & Robinson, N. M. (1985). Friendship patterns in highly intelligent children. *Roeper Review, 8*(1), 46–49.

Kerr, B. (1997). *Smart girls: A new psychology of girls, women, and giftedness*. Tucson, AZ: Great Potential Press.

Kerr, B., & Cohn, S. (2001). *Smart boys: talent, manhood, and the search for meaning*. Tucson, AZ: Great Potential Press.

Levy, J. J., & Plucker, J. A. (2003). Assessing the psychological presentation of gifted and talented clients: A multicultural perspective. *Counselling Psychology Quarterly, 16*, 229–247.

Manning, S. (2006). Recognizing gifted students: A practical guide for teachers. *Kappa Delta PI Record, 42*(2).

Mills, C. J., Moore, N., & Parker, W. D. (1996). Psychological type and cognitive style in elementary age gifted students: Comparisons across age and gender. *Journal of Psychological Type, 38*, 13–23.

Niles, K., & Jolly, J. (2019). *The success strategies for parenting gifted kids*. Washington, DC: Prufrock Press.

Peterson, J. S., & Rischar, H. (2000). Gifted and gay: A study of the adolescent experience. *Gifted Child Quarterly, 44,* 231–244.

Pew Research Center. (2013). A survey of LGBT Americans. Retrieved from: www.pewsocialtrends.org/2013/06/13/a-survey-of-lgbt-americans/8/#top-issues

Sak, U. (2004). A synthesis of research on psychological types of gifted adolescents. *Journal of Secondary Gifted Education, XV*(2), 70–79.

Sedillo, P. J. (2013). *A retrospective study of gay gifted, young adult males' perceptions of giftedness and suicide.* Retrieved from: www.proquest.com/openview/05cb6ff0f1e7ea27ceffb5fd8ed94869/1?pq-origsite=gscholar&cbl=18750?

Temkin, D., Belford, J., McDaniel, T., Stratford, B., & Parris, D. (2017, June). Improving measurement of sexual orientation and gender identity among middle and high school students: Executive summary. *Child Trends.*

Webb, J. T. (2004). *Misdiagnosis and dual diagnosis of gifted children.* Great Potential Press Inc.

Whitmore, J. F. (1980). *Giftedness, conflict and underachievement.* Boston, MA:Allyn & Bacon.

Whittenburg, B., & Treat, A. R. (2009). Shared characteristics of gifted and sexually diverse youth. In N. L. Hafenstein & J. A. Castellano (Eds.), *Perspectives in gifted education: Diverse gifted learners* (Vol. 4, pp. 130–165). Denver, CO: University of Denver.

Part III

Special Populations of Gifted Students

Chapter 5

Serving Our Highly Gifted Learners

A Practitioner's Guide

Dina Brulles and Kimberly Lansdowne

Equity Issues with HG Learners

What's the problem? When considering equity issues with highly gifted learners, we can separate the problem into two categories. This question speaks loudly to the inequitable services for highly gifted students of diverse and underrepresented populations. The question also makes us consider the vast differences in serving gifted and highly gifted children in general, as the majority of gifted programs do not effectively cater to the disparate learning needs of highly and profoundly gifted learners. In this section we first address the lack of equity among the highly gifted students represented in our schools. We then consider how gifted programming can hinder or advance instructional opportunities for highly and profoundly gifted learners.

Coordinators of gifted programs throughout the United States struggle in their efforts to make gifted education more inclusive. Despite well-intentioned outcomes, most tests used for measuring ability in our schools are designed for fluent English-speaking students and high achievers. Schools systematically underestimate the degree to which language represents a barrier to identification of underrepresented populations when assessing a student's level of ability (Naglieri & Otero, 2017). Hence, high-ability students from diverse backgrounds are often inadvertently overlooked for gifted programming. This naturally results in their ability levels often remaining underestimated by educators.

Human nature sometimes leads to a view of life colored by one's own unique experiences; thus, the importance of using objective measures to identify learning potential in those who differ from us (Padilla & Borsato, 2008). This disconnection becomes glaringly apparent with students from diverse backgrounds and perpetuates the social injustice that prevails in our schools. Researchers such as Ortiz et al. (2012) encourage authors to design test questions that are usable for all regardless of gender, age, language background, socioeconomic status, or disability. Creating inclusive educational environments that enfranchise diversity in gifted education programs is the outcome of affirmative action that champions equity and justice. This outcome requires that schools put into place proactive measures, such as equitable access to identification.

The second big issue when considering equity for highly gifted students pertains to programming and services commonly provided in the schools. Included in this chapter you will find Table 5.1, titled "Levels of Giftedness," which shows that the higher the IQ, the fewer people will be identified at that level. We see a dramatic decrease in population represented in each level of giftedness as the levels increase. These numbers have practical

DOI: 10.4324/9781003265412-10

implications for highly gifted children in gifted programs. Generally speaking, the higher the IQ, the more modifications will be needed for the students in an educational setting (Gross, 2000). With that in mind, consider that the structure of most gifted programs typically relies on a single modality directed toward the vast majority of our gifted students who have an IQ in the range of 130–145. However, educators and parents recognize that students with IQs exceeding 145 usually require dramatically different curriculum and instruction. The level of giftedness greatly impacts the type of instruction, education placement, and supports that the student needs. A gifted program that appropriately addresses the learning needs of a student with an IQ of 130 may need to be radically modified for a student with an IQ of 160. Later in the chapter you will find several examples of gifted program models specifically designed for highly gifted learners. Additionally, some strengths and limitations of commonly practiced program models are provided to understand the types of modifications schools can make for highly gifted learners in the schools' existing programs.

Introduction

The late Dr. James Webb, a recognized expert in the field of gifted education, focused on the social and emotional needs of gifted children. Webb's work on highly and profoundly gifted children emphasized their unique affective needs and sensitivities. In *A Parent's Guide to Gifted Children*, he wrote:

> Gifted children view the world in different ways than other children, and their thoughts, actions, and feelings are more intense. It has been said that an exceptionally gifted child seems to see the world not only as an adult might, but also as if he is looking through an electron microscope, as compared with normal vision. This child sees what others do not see, and what others cannot even imagine.
>
> (Webb, 2007, p. 118)

In this chapter we discuss the views, perceptions, and learning needs of these exceptional students.

Meet Lars, Anya, Yesenia, and Rex:

- While in fourth grade, Lars and three other students participated in Honors Algebra at their local high school. Lars had to stand on a chair to reach the pencil sharpener. He and his fourth-grade peers scored the highest grades in the course.
- Anya graduated from high school at the age of 13 and from college at 16. Though completing her coursework was never a challenge, Anya struggled socially and emotionally throughout her schooling.
- Yesenia moved to the United States in first grade. Although her parents spoke no English, by the spring of her first year she achieved perfect scores on all three batteries of the Cognitive Abilities Test (CogAT) and was placed in her school's gifted program. (She was the only ELL [English language learner] student in the program.)
- Rex is on the Autism Spectrum with a 155 IQ. Rex truly struggles at school (and at home). Though his very high intelligence allows him to do well academically, he has extreme challenges managing his behaviors, feelings, and interactions.

Decades of debate over the necessity of gifted programs continue to plague our schools. Throughout this time there have been strong and compelling voices of parents and educators who advocate passionately for gifted services. One wonders about the reasons for the disconnection between the believers and the nonbelievers. The answer lies in the numbers. Gifted students in general make up a small proportion of our students, approximately 8% nationwide, depending upon the criteria used to designate the identification. And who are the voices advocating for gifted services in the schools? They are commonly parents of gifted children, along with educators who have had personal or professional experience with giftedness. Most often, the voices we hear advocating are those with experience with highly gifted learners, who make up a very small percentage of our gifted learners, but who are those in greatest need of differentiated learning experiences. This chapter helps to answer the questions: "Who are the highly gifted?" and "What do they need differently in their schooling?"

Literature Review

What does it mean to be highly gifted and why is the distinction important? *Highly gifted* is a term used as one of the ways to convey the degree to which one is gifted, writes Beverly Shaklee (2009). Research conducted by David Lubinski and Camilla Benbow (2006) and colleagues shows that highly gifted students generally have extremely high levels of ability in one or more domains, such as mathematics, and moderately high abilities in other areas. These students also commonly manifest "an extreme need for constant mental stimulation, insatiable curiosity, precision in thinking and expression, inability to concentrate on mundane tasks, and a propensity toward underachievement" (Davidson Academy, 2020, n.p.). Highly gifted students are typically aware that they are different from their peers in many ways, which can lead to social isolation (Gross, 1994; Webb et al., 2007). Hollingworth (1942) and Gross (1994) found that feelings of social isolation diminish when highly gifted students are placed in higher grade levels and allowed to accelerate in their learning.

It is not uncommon for highly gifted students – those with very high potential – to perform poorly at school, especially when they are expected to participate in grade-level curriculum and instruction that neither interests them nor challenges them. When schools fail to make appropriate instructional provisions for these students, their academic performance will likely lag (Hollingworth, 1926; Gross, 1994) due to a lack of mental stimulation and interest. Numerous studies show that when highly gifted students are required to remain in grade-level classes their motivation and self-esteem diminish. In contrast, when allowed to accelerate, these students have positive attitudes toward school and establish strong relationships with their intellectual peers and their teachers (Cross, 2017).

Levels of Giftedness: Why It Matters

The question is often asked, "If we know that a child is gifted, does it really matter that we know *how* gifted she is?" Although obtaining an accurate IQ of a highly gifted child may be difficult for a variety of reasons, the answer is, "Yes." Consider the following IQ stratifications and consider how those breakdowns can impact curriculum, instruction, and pacing throughout a child's educational years. Miraca Gross (2015) writes:

Researchers, school administrators and parent organizations involved in the education of intellectually disabled students and students with some form of physical disability, explicitly acknowledge the various levels and degrees of the condition. Hearing impairment, for example, is classified as mild, moderate, severe and profound. It is important to note that this is neither intended nor perceived as labeling but rather as a means of clarifying the degree to which the individual differs from the norm in terms of her condition.

(Gross, 2015, p. 4)

Discussing the degree of a student's disability then, is not labeling. In general, teachers recognize that an accurate assessment of the nature and extent of a student's disability is a vital first step in discussing the types of support – and indeed the levels of support – the child may require if he or she is to achieve to the level of his or her potential. Assessment is a vital first step in designing an individualized and developmentally appropriate curriculum.

Most educators enter the field with little to no experience with gifted learners (Peters & Brulles, 2017; Siegle, 2015). The vast majority of our gifted students learn well in their schools' gifted programs when those programs exist (Peters & Brulles, 2017). However, a small percentage of those gifted learners need additional interventions that may stretch even beyond typical gifted programs. Generally speaking, the vast majority of intellectually gifted individuals fall between two and three standard deviations from the norm on the right side of the bell curve as shown in Figure 5.1. Highly and profoundly gifted individuals are at least three standard deviations from the norm.

The bell curve in Figure 5.1 shows that the mean, or average IQ, is 100. The majority of the population, 95.44%, falls within two standard deviations of the mean (IQ 70–130). This represents the range typically addressed by the standards-based grade-level curriculum in most schools. Consider that 2.14% of the population is between the second and

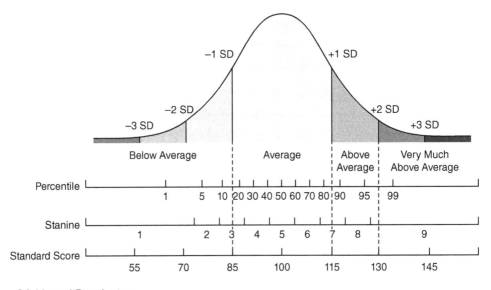

Figure 5.1 Normal Distribution.
Source: Copyright @ 2021. Multi-Health Systems, Inc. All Rights Reserved. Image reproduced with Permission from MHS.

third standard deviation below the mean (IQ 55–70), and 2.14% is between the second and third standard deviation above the mean (IQ 130–145). These exceptional students on both sides of the curve require an individualized curriculum to address their specific needs.

Students between two and three standard deviations above the mean are considered gifted and benefit from gifted programs or services. Just 0.13% of the population is more than three standard deviations below the mean (IQ <55), and 0.13% of the population is more than three standard deviations above the mean (IQ 145–160). Thus, 13 out of 10,000 individuals score above 145 and are considered profoundly gifted. Approximately one out of 30,000 individuals (.003%) is positioned more than four standard deviations above the mean (IQ >160). Students more than three standard deviations from the norm on both sides of the curve are very exceptional and require individualized accommodations to address their needs.

For the purpose of this chapter, we will consider students with an IQ of 145 or higher as highly or profoundly gifted. Students with an IQ of 145 and above require extremely exceptional educational accommodations to meet their needs. Consider that a 160 IQ is as far away from a 130 IQ, as a 130 IQ is to a 100 IQ. Schools need gifted programs because students with a gifted identification, which typically begins with an IQ in the high 120s, require differentiated, extended, and/or accelerated curriculum and instruction because their learning needs fall outside the norm.

Table 5.1, "Levels of Giftedness," shows that the higher the IQ, the fewer people will be identified at that level. We see a dramatic decrease in population represented in each level of giftedness as the levels increase. This has practical implications for children both in schools and in their social lives. Generally speaking, the higher the IQ, the more modifications will be needed for the students in an educational setting, including both academic and socialization needs (Gross, 2000).

Students at the Basic levels can generally be challenged within the regular classroom with only slight modifications to their curriculum. Students at this level are more likely to find intellectual peers with whom they can interact. Students at the Moderate level can also be sufficiently challenged in a regular classroom when the gifted students are cluster grouped together into one gifted cluster class (when the cluster teacher has participated in professional learning opportunities in gifted education and is able to differentiate the curriculum and instruction for the gifted students placed in the class). They are also more likely to feel accepted by other gifted students in their setting, especially when a number of gifted students are grouped together in the classroom. Students in the High, Exceptional, and Profound levels of giftedness require a dramatically different curriculum and instruction than other students. Later in this chapter we discuss a variety of methods for reaching and teaching highly and profoundly gifted students.

Table 5.1 Levels of Giftedness

Level	IQ Score	Ratio to total population
Basic	115–129 IQ	1:6–1:30
Moderate	130–144 IQ	1:40–1:1000
High	145–159 IQ	1:1000–1:10,000
Exceptional	160–179 IQ	1:10,000–1:1 million
Profound	180+ IQ	1:1 million+

Regardless of their educational placement, these students share a few basic traits. They learn at a much faster pace than others; they process information to a much greater depth; and they demonstrate higher levels of intensity, imagination, and intellectual ability. They are also likely to show heightened sensitivity and emotions at levels not typical in the general population. For these reasons, they need curriculum, instruction, and understanding outside the norm in order to learn.

The level of giftedness greatly impacts the type of instruction, education placement, and supports that the student needs. Most gifted programs are designed for students with IQs around 130. A gifted program that appropriately addresses the learning needs of a student with an IQ of 130 may need to be radically modified for a student with an IQ of 160. Later in the chapter you will find several examples of gifted program models specifically designed for highly gifted learners. Additionally, the chapter describes the strengths and limitations of commonly practiced program models to shed light on the types of modifications schools can make for highly gifted learners in the schools' existing programs.

Highly and profoundly gifted students' accelerated intellectual development typically presents some degree of asynchronous development. Asynchrony in gifted children increases with the levels of giftedness. A child may have the intellect of an adult, the social and emotional development of a child, and the intensities of a highly gifted individual. Having teachers who understand the asynchronous development these students experience greatly improves their school experiences and dramatically impacts learning.

Vignettes

Lars

Throughout his elementary and middle school years Lars was enrolled in a self-contained gifted program that was designed for highly and profoundly gifted children. In this program Lars was able to work at his challenge levels in all subjects. Lars, along with three others in his class, took Honors Algebra as a fourth grader. By the time he entered high school, he had successfully taken all Advanced Placement math courses provided in the district. While in high school he enrolled in dual placement at the local community college so that he could continue with math coursework.

Lars's teachers allowed him to build time into his day to study for the State Geography Bee. Year after year Lars climbed in the standings until he won the State Bee, competed at nationals several times, and eventually won the National Geography Bee. During weekends and school breaks Lars studied for the Bee for eight to ten hours every day, even during family vacations. By the time he began high school, Lars dual enrolled in an Ivy League university where he flourished. Lars was a highly motivated student who thrived when allowed to build on his interests and work at his personal challenge level. He never lost his passion for learning.

Anya

Anya's family moved to the United States from India when she was four years old. At this young age, Anya was fascinated by learning about the brain. Her parents nurtured this interest by providing her with brain-related books, coloring books, games, and puzzles; regularly visiting their local library; and spending countless days at the science museum. Anya's parents routinely attended local gifted parent events, the state gifted conference, read books on parenting gifted children, and reached out to local experts in the field of gifted education. They were highly motivated to cultivate their daughter's strengths, abilities, and interests. At 16 years old, Anya graduated from a private gifted high school that was located at the state university where she was dual enrolled in the honors program. At 18, she graduated from a private women's college and immediately applied for medical school where she planned to follow her lifelong dream to become a brain surgeon.

Yesenia

Yesenia kept to herself at school. Her parents immigrated to the United States when Yesenia was in first grade. The family spoke only Spanish. Once at school Yesenia learned English very rapidly, and by second grade, her teacher recognized her high potential and nominated her for gifted testing. Identified as gifted with very high abilities on all areas of the gifted test, Yesenia was placed in the gifted program throughout her elementary school years and then participated in honors and AP classes throughout middle and high school.

Despite her academic successes, Yesenia suffered tremendously at school. None of the other students in the gifted program were Latinx, which meant she looked, behaved, and spoke differently. The other gifted students could not connect with her. Meanwhile, the other Latinx students who had previously been her friends viewed her as different from them because of her status in the gifted program. She was lonely and felt she did not fit in with either of her peer groups. For one full year while in middle school, Yesenia resisted speaking Spanish to anyone, including her parents. (Her siblings translated so that her parents could understand her when she spoke.) While in high school Yesenia seriously considered suicide.

Rex

Rex was identified as gifted during Special Education testing. Rex is on the Autism Spectrum with a 155 IQ. Rex truly struggles at school (and at home). Though his very high intelligence allows him to do well academically, he has extreme challenges managing his behaviors and social interactions. Rex is fortunate that his school district has a program for twice-exceptional gifted students. The teachers are certified in gifted and in special education, there is a very small teacher/student ratio, and there are aids in the classroom to assist when students are distressed. Without this program, Rex would have been placed in a program with other autistic students but without intellectual peers or a teacher who understands how gifted students learn. Still, Rex's behaviors are so extreme that the school has to call Rex's mother nearly daily to pick him up from school early due to severe behavior incidents that render Rex inconsolable. Rex's mother is overwhelmed due to her son's behavioral challenges and caring for Rex's two young siblings.

Lars, Anya, Yesenia, and Rex are all considered highly gifted, though clearly they have radically distinctive learning needs. No one single type of gifted program will effectively provide appropriate instruction for these four students. Later in the chapter we discuss programming options that schools can make and families can seek based on student needs.

Identification and Assessment

We have recently witnessed an increased attention and focus on the assessment and identification of gifted students. Many U.S. states now mandate the assessment and identification of gifted learners. Historically and still today, states' identification criteria have fluctuated between IQ and/or aptitude requirements. In many states, IQ has been or currently is the only score used for gifted identification. Lately, however, giftedness has been seen as a combination of factors including IQ, aptitude, social/emotional well-being, and other traits resulting in high performance in academics, the arts, leadership, social action, and creativity (NAGC, 2019).

The federal Elementary and Secondary Education Act (ESEA) defines gifted and talented students as:

> Students, children, or youth who give evidence of high achievement capability in areas such as intellectual, creative, artistic, or leadership capacity, or in specific academic fields, and who need services and activities not ordinarily provided by the school in order to fully develop those capabilities.
>
> (ESEA, 2002, Title IX, Part A, Definition 22)

Many states and districts follow the federal definition. However, remember that there is as much difference between an average student and a gifted student as there is between a gifted student and a highly gifted student. Highly gifted students do not match the prototypical characteristics of a gifted student. For this reason, schools need to closely consider the tools they use in the identification process. Due to the high costs of assessments, many school districts use group administered aptitude tests, which is a good place to start, but for the highly gifted, individualized testing should take place. An individually administered assessment with a high ceiling, or extended norms, provided by a psychologist familiar with gifted education, is recommended to accurately assess a highly or profoundly gifted individual (Shaughnessy & Fickling, 1991).

Dr. James Webb, a psychologist and leading expert in the social and emotional needs of gifted students, described a full neuropsychological evaluation as being equivalent to a medical test, as it provides prescriptive information regarding a child's learning needs. Ideally, families should find a licensed psychologist who understands highly gifted children and knows how to ascertain the necessary information to make educational decisions based on testing results. A full psycho-educational evaluation requires that a neuropsychologist administer and analyze the evaluation results, which is clearly cost prohibitive for most families. Therefore, many students must rely on the testing procedures provided by the schools, which may contribute to the underrepresentation of some populations in the highly gifted ranges.

In addition to cost being a barrier to adequately assess a student's level of ability, language also presents an issue. Most assessments used in the United States are designed for fluent English-speaking students and high achievers. Hence, students from diverse backgrounds are often overlooked for gifted programming. Human nature sometimes leads to a view of life colored by one's own unique experiences; thus, the importance of using objective measures to identify learning potential in those who differ from us.

Using ability tests that are free of language and culturally specific content allows objective assessment to occur. Someone who has not acquired verbal and quantitative skills due to limited opportunities or a disability will probably do poorly on a traditional ability test. Many students will likely fail to reach their potential when these students of high ability who have had limited educational experiences go unidentified. They may then miss opportunities for higher education and promising futures. Many of these individuals are likely to be from culturally and linguistically diverse populations (e.g., Hispanics and other ethnic and cultural groups that make up a significant portion of the United States population). Using a standardized nonverbal measure of general ability as part of the identification process helps to identify gifted children from a wide variety of cultural and linguistic groups, especially those who may have limited academic and English language skills (Naglieri & Ford, 2005).

Belonging and Identity

Considering the very small number of individuals identified as highly to profoundly gifted, it is reasonable to understand that they may harbor feelings of isolation and disenfranchisement. When was the last time you were at an event with 10,000 people? This may have been at a large concert, parade, or sporting event. How long would it take you to find someone like you? This is how highly gifted children feel on a daily basis when they are not in a specialized program for highly gifted students.

Due to their asynchronous development, highly gifted students tend to feel lonely when they are with age-peers in the general population. Most prefer to associate with bright, older children or adults. The lack of intellectual peers at the same age can be very isolating for children and can lead to depression, poor social behaviors, and underperformance in schoolwork (Hollingsworth, 1942). Even with the best intentions, teachers who have had little or no experience with highly gifted students are unfamiliar with how they learn, thus unintentionally exacerbating the students' uneasiness at school.

Feelings of isolation and loneliness take on different forms depending on the students' personal lives, the school setting, support system, and culture. Yesenia reported that she was so lonely she contemplated suicide while in her elementary years. Being the only Hispanic student in her gifted class, she felt different and not accepted by the other gifted students. At the same time, her Hispanic friends treated her differently once she entered the gifted program. In her efforts to feel accepted in her gifted program she stopped speaking Spanish for an entire year. Clearly, Yesenia was confused about her identity and longed for acceptance and belonging. An activity included at the end of this chapter encourages readers to consider how family, school, and identity groups influence the highly gifted student's attitudes toward school and learning.

Collaborating with School District Departments

Collaboration with school district administrators is important when developing and supporting gifted programs in general. For highly gifted students this collaboration becomes imperative because this population is learning at radically accelerated and/

or advanced levels. For example, the selection and pacing of content and the academic achievement testing procedures must be drastically modified in order to provide information to the teachers and be of value for these students. Radical acceleration and advanced academics typically require collaboration with the directors of several departments, including special education, assessment, curriculum, and sometimes language acquisition, and student services. Through these collaborative efforts our highly gifted students can receive the differentiated curriculum, instructional resources, and alternative assessment methods they need. Working closely with the other departments, schools can continually address these needs and obtain access to resources that support their learning goals (Peters & Brulles, 2017).

Collaborating with School Administrators

Opportunities for gifted education coordinators to interact with other school district administrators who oversee the departments can yield significant outcomes for highly gifted learners. Methods of collaboration with departments such as special education, assessment, language acquisition, and curriculum are described here. The suggestions included here discuss and provide a rationale for ways that school district departments can expand their efforts to plan and provide more effectively for highly gifted students. Radically accelerated and advanced learning needs require significant modifications to existing departmental structures to support teachers when designing instruction for these students.

Collaboration with School Psychologists

Collaboration between the gifted education department and special education can be very important in numerous ways. Ideally, the gifted coordinator would meet yearly with school psychologists to share information on gifted identification procedures, placements, and services. Some highly gifted students become identified through special education referrals; this is especially common with twice-exceptional learners, some of whom are on the Autism Spectrum or diagnosed with Asperger's Syndrome.

When school psychologists, special education teachers, and classroom teachers are familiar with the characteristics and learning needs of highly gifted twice- exceptional students, they can better recommend appropriate interventions and academic placement (Siegle, 2015). Too often when these professionals are not well informed on the gifted, they prioritize areas of weakness at the expense of the areas of strength. The students then often become disillusioned about learning, and they may become frustrated from the lack of intellectual stimulation which can cause behaviors detrimental to their learning.

One suggestion for middle- and large-sized school districts is to implement a program for twice-exceptional students, as many of these twice-exceptional students are highly gifted. Placement into twice-exceptional programs is typically determined through collaboration between the special education director and the gifted coordinator. The programs are staffed by teachers who hold certification or endorsements in both special education and gifted education. Class sizes typically replicate self-contained special education numbers. However, instruction in these programs builds on the students' strengths, interests, and background knowledge and should incorporate interactive and engaging instructional methods such as project-based and problem-based learning, critical and creative thinking, and appropriately accelerated and advanced instruction.

Collaboration with the Administrator Overseeing Assessments

Collaboration with the director of assessment can occur in various ways. Since highly gifted students are typically accelerated in their learning, schools need to develop methods for assessing growth beyond grade-level metrics; this requires out-of-level testing. Gifted coordinators or principals can work with assessment directors to request or jointly develop testing structures that allow for assessing growth in the core content areas for students who are radically accelerated.

Administrators can also seek existing assessments that are designed for this out-of-level testing. Additionally, schools may rely on the assessment department for examining student achievement levels to identify those who might excel in a more radically accelerated class. This system allows schools to monitor program and teacher efficacy and provide intervention and support where needed.

Collaboration with the Administrator Overseeing Language Acquisition

Language acquisition departments typically employ testers who travel to schools to test English language learners for proficiency levels. These testers are in a unique position to recognize when students acquire English at much faster rates than others. This rapidity in language acquisition can signify gifted tendencies, similarly as an individual's primary language development is typically accelerated and advanced in young gifted children. In fact, the majority of highly gifted students enter school with the reading accuracy and comprehension of children several years older (Gross, 1999).

The rate at which these students acquire English should be identified and monitored so that the students can be tested for gifted services when the time is appropriate. In these cases, a nonverbal ability test or a test that is free of language and cultural biases should be used. Placing gifted English language learners in educational settings along with other gifted students can significantly impact and improve their rates and levels of learning.

Collaboration with the Administrator Overseeing Curriculum and Instruction

Collaborate with the curriculum department to seek out appropriately challenging material for highly gifted students. Given the relatively small numbers of highly gifted students in the schools, and given that these students' learning needs may differ widely, collaboration for these unique students typically occurs informally through meetings with the curriculum director to consider what is most appropriate for the student. This type of collaboration requires some flexibility in planning but can make a world of difference to the student.

Another aspect to consider when collaborating with the curriculum department is the pathway the student will take in a radically accelerated trajectory. First, understand the vertical alignment of instructional materials. The curriculum department can advise on the different instructional pathways existing in the district. Later in this chapter we discuss several possible alternatives that students can seek out when they have completed the highest levels of coursework the district offers.

Collaboration with Student Services

School districts typically have a district-level administrator assigned to addressing student issues that routinely arise. A gifted coordinator's interaction with the director of student services on behalf of highly gifted students may be sporadic, but is imperative in certain circumstances. As an administrator, this author (Dina Brulles) oversees 504 Accommodation Plans, early entrance procedures, parent concerns, and disciplinary actions such as those involved with behavioral problems.

With highly gifted students, these topics/issues sometimes involve different considerations that require nuanced approaches. Highly gifted students may have social and emotional concerns, such as high intensities of feeling, that require modifying approaches for managing these issues. The director of student services may have extensive experience addressing these topics, but may not have the background in gifted education to know how to resolve such issues when they arise with highly gifted students.

Collaboration with Instructional Technology

Highly gifted students inherently seek innovative methods for learning because they have typically mastered grade-level (and even beyond grade-level) material prior to entering the classroom. Grade-level textbooks often lack the depth and rigor these students need to learn at their challenge and interest levels. Highly gifted students rely heavily on technology to access primary sources that are up to date, relevant, and free of prior interpretation. They also need meaningful ways to demonstrate their learning and many thrive on the creative possibilities to do so through the use of technology. Teachers of gifted students commonly understand this and many naturally seek out these opportunities for their highly gifted students. This can be the impetus for considerable collaboration between the two departments, as IT directors commonly look for students to pilot new technologies.

Gifted Programming: In Search of the Right Fit

Gifted program options for Basic gifted students are often found in elementary schools in the form of push-in, pull-out, enrichment, cluster grouping, and single subject acceleration. However, these programs might not sufficiently challenge highly gifted students, which forces some families to investigate other options. Some families of highly gifted children make drastic changes in their living arrangements in search of the right educational environment where their children can find intellectual stimulation and thrive academically. Families seeking services for highly gifted children may move across districts, cities, and even states to find the ideal educational setting for their child. They typically seek out programs that are flexible, yet rigorous enough to meet their child's distinctive needs (Schultz, 2018).

Grouping practices for gifted students vary based on learning needs. As noted, while Basic and Moderately gifted students' learning needs can usually be met with differentiated instruction in the regular classroom, in a gifted cluster class or through Honors classes, highly gifted students need more radical programming modifications. Brief descriptions of common gifted education programming models are described next. As you consider these models, think about the range of ability levels, achievement levels, behaviors, and characteristics of highly gifted students. The advantages pertain to Basic and Moderately gifted students; the limitations noted for each model pertain solely and specifically to highly and profoundly gifted students.

Content Replacement

In content replacement services, students usually receive accelerated learning opportunities in a specific subject area in an alternative classroom setting. Gifted students are typically pulled out of the regular classroom for replacement of services in mathematics, and/ or reading and writing based upon their area(s) of strength. On average, the curriculum is one to two grade levels beyond the student's assigned grade.

Advantages for Basic and Moderately gifted learners:

- Provides an appropriate challenge level
- Gifted students spend time learning with others at the same level of achievement
- Does not require additional staffing; low cost to district
- May allow middle school students to earn high school credit

Limitations for highly gifted learners:

- Students may need a higher level of challenge than provided
- This model typically only addresses math and reading

Enrichment

Enrichment programs vary widely and may take the form of pull-out (of the classroom) or push-in (to the classroom). They typically emphasize critical thinking skills, creativity, and project-based learning, and can provide gifted students with opportunities to learn with their peers. Enrichment classes can have a great impact on student learning when critical thinking activities are connected to learning in content areas.

Advantages for Basic and Moderately gifted learners:

- Gifted students spend time learning with others of like ability
- Topics are typically student-centered and engaging
- Students have time for extended learning

Limitations for highly gifted learners:

- Highly gifted students will not be consistently challenged every day and in all content areas

Cluster Grouping

Cluster grouping is an inclusion model in which gifted students are integrated into mixed-ability classrooms with teachers trained to provide appropriate differentiated learning opportunities. Cluster grouping allows teachers with specialized training in gifted education to challenge gifted students in all content areas. The pacing of instruction and the depth of content that gifted students need is made possible through compacting, differentiation, and flexible grouping arrangements (Winebrenner & Brulles, 2018).

Advantages for Basic and Moderately gifted learners:

- Challenges gifted students every day when implemented with fidelity
- Teachers are better able to meet all students' needs when there is a group clustered in their classes
- Gifted students spend time learning with others of like ability

Limitations for highly gifted learners:

- Highly gifted students will not be sufficiently challenged
- There is insufficient opportunity to learn with intellectual peers

Self-Contained Gifted Programs

Self-contained gifted programs typically target highly and profoundly gifted students. Instruction provided in self-contained gifted programs is generally between one to three grade levels advanced. Effective teachers in self-contained gifted classes encourage students to delve deeper into content. Students who succeed in these programs usually demonstrate achievement well beyond grade-level expectations.

Advantages for Basic and Moderately gifted learners:

- Challenges most gifted students every day
- Gifted students spend time learning with others of like ability
- Students make social connections with same-age peers
- Students learn with intellectual peers

Limitations for highly gifted learners:

- Unless the district is large, there are usually too few highly gifted students identified to create a sufficiently rigorous program

Radical Acceleration Practices/Grade Skipping

Radical acceleration can occur within a subject area or by skipping an entire grade level. Students who benefit from radical acceleration are typically defined as being two to three years advanced in curriculum in comparison to their age peers. Radical acceleration can be accomplished in any subject, but is most easily described and implemented in mathematics. Consider a scenario where a sixth grade student is given an end-of-the-year assessment during the first week of school and shows mastery of 90–100% of the curriculum. As a result, she is given an end-of-the-year exam for the next level of mathematics. Again, she shows mastery of 90–100% of the curriculum. As a sixth grader, she has demonstrated mastery of sixth and seventh grade math standards. Based on this information, along with her socially and emotionally advanced development, she is placed in a high school algebra class. Despite her age, she performs as well as, if not better than, the typical ninth grade algebra student.

Other forms of radical acceleration include early admission into kindergarten, graduating from high school early, and early entry into university classes.

Advantages for highly gifted students:

- Provides continual challenge
- May allow students to earn high school and/or college credit

Limitations for highly gifted students:

- Students' social and emotional needs may not be sufficiently developed to learn with older children on a full-time basis
- Despite the research showing its effectiveness, many educators are reluctant to provide radical acceleration

Based on these gifted programming options, it is clear that a combination of some method for grouping, along with subject acceleration, is needed for highly gifted learners (Gross, 2015; Rogers, 2006). Research supports acceleration when using the Iowa Acceleration Scale to make decisions.

Specific Examples of Program Models for Highly Gifted Students

The previous section discusses various programming models and grouping options available to gifted learners and describes benefits and limitations for highly gifted students. In this next section two programs will be discussed in detail. These two program examples were developed, implemented, and supported by the chapter's co-authors, Dr. Dina Brulles (Paradise Valley Unified School District's Self-Contained Gifted Program) and Dr. Kimberly Lansdowne (Herberger Young Scholars Academy [HYSA] at Arizona State University [ASU]). These descriptions provide the reader with a close look at how two practitioners implemented programs designed specifically for highly and profoundly gifted learners in a public school and a private school setting.

Self-Contained Gifted Program

The Self-Contained Gifted Program (grades 1–6) in Paradise Valley Unified School District is designed for highly and profoundly gifted students who are also highly achieving. Students in this program work two or more years beyond grade level with intellectual peers on a daily basis. Classroom instruction expands and accelerates traditional curriculum to accommodate the unique needs and interests of highly gifted students. Students have a rigorous interdisciplinary core curriculum of Language Arts, Social Studies, Science, and Math. Self-contained gifted students participate in special area classes with the other grade-level classes and are also included in non-academic grade-level activities. This district program is housed at five locations.

Students qualifying for this program require scores of 97%+ in two of the three areas: Verbal, Quantitative, Nonverbal, with the third score being 90% or higher, or an IQ of at least 140. They must also demonstrate accelerated learning needs two years beyond their grade level.

Sample curriculum and instructional methods (Paradise Valley Unified Schools, 2021) include:

- Acceleration in the content areas
- Emphasis on critical and creative thinking and problem solving
- Technology integration
- Shared inquiry/Socratic questioning
- Project-based/problem-based learning
- Latin-based vocabulary
- Elements of reasoning
- Junior Great Books
- [College of] William & Mary curriculum
- Continental Math and Math Olympiad

Herberger Young Scholars Academy

Standing on the shoulders of giants like the Davidson Academy and the Robinson Center for Young Scholars, in 2010, Arizona State University developed a unique program for highly gifted secondary students. The program, located directly on an ASU campus, is a learning environment designed for highly gifted students in grades 7–12 who need higher-level options while completing high school. Students may enter the program years earlier than their grade level would indicate. Early entry options such as this private school offers provide highly gifted students with the environment needed to complete high school with fellow gifted students, and also provide opportunities to take college-level classes with college-aged students while still in high school.

> Students may be on grade level in one subject but need radically accelerated curriculum in [other] subjects. Consider a 12-year-old student with difficulty writing a five-paragraph essay, but successful in 300 and 400 level university math classes. The high school instructors in this program are trained in working with highly gifted students allowing students to engage with dedicated instructors in a caring community, and at the same time utilize resources available at a major research university. Students complete high school credits while exploring and pursuing their intellectual interests through high school coursework and college classes.
>
> (Herberger Young Scholars Academy, 2021, n.p.)

Secondary School Programming for Highly Gifted Students

For many highly gifted students, gifted education programs come to an end in middle school. Provided that these students have been accelerated (either in school or at home) throughout their elementary years, it is understandable that by the time they reach secondary school, many will have surpassed the typical coursework offered. Explanation for the lack of gifted programs at the secondary level includes:

- Middle school and high school teachers are seen as content area specialists
- The volume of advanced material available in Honors and Advanced Placement classes
- The organizational design of secondary education
- Challenges that drive master schedules

Although not specifically designed for highly gifted students, some program options available in secondary schools include Cambridge Assessment International Education, International Baccalaureate (IB), Advanced Placement (AP), and Honors classes. These programs can benefit the highly gifted student if they are allowed to take above-grade-level courses and exams. Specific to Cambridge, the ability to sit an exam during the fall semester may provide an opportunity to show mastery of a subject and move on to a higher-level class during the spring semester. For example, if a student is accelerated through the math curriculum during middle school, he or she may take the IGCSE (International General Certificate of Secondary Education) math exam during the October/November test window. By demonstrating mastery on this exam, the student may be able to move to higher-level math classes much earlier than his/her age peers. IB also has fall and spring testing windows. AP's testing window is spring only.

- Cambridge Assessment International Education, www.cambridgeinternational.org/ (Program options: Lower Secondary, Upper Secondary, and Advanced)
- International Baccalaureate, www.ibo.org/ (Program options: Primary Years Program [PYP], Middle Years Program [MYP], and Diploma Programme [DP])
- Advanced Placement, https://ap.collegeboard.org/ (Program options: High school)
- Honors classes

A secondary advantage of taking Advanced Placement, International Baccalaureate, or Cambridge International Assessments is the ability to earn college credit. Commonly referred to as "credit by examination," students may receive credit for a university course by taking an examination in place of the actual course. Some exams may be taken prior to college admission and most universities provide credit.

Early Entry to College Programs

The highly gifted need enrichment and acceleration that is significantly different from their age peers; this can be achieved through early entrance programs. According to Michelle Muratori in her book, *Early Entrance to College: A Guide to Success*,

> students contemplating this option must not only consider their academic readiness to tackle college coursework, but must be prepared for the social and emotional demands of college as well. Those who seem to fare well as early entrants are focused and self-disciplined. Intrinsically motivated, they have the ability to persevere, handle setbacks in a productive way, and demonstrate a strong work ethic. They are goal-oriented

and socially/emotionally mature, and they tend to have supportive relationships with parents, peers, and faculty/university staff.

(Muratori, 2007)

Most universities accept early entry students who are still in high school as non-degree seeking students. Several programs that are associated with universities provide academic, social, and emotional support for young students seeking college- level work. Additional programs listed here have early entrance options available for highly gifted students (Johns Hopkins Center for Talented Youth, 2021). (All programs are residential unless otherwise noted.)

- Arizona State University Herberger Young Scholars Academy (AZ) (commuter)
- Bard College at Simon's Rock (MA)
- Cal State – Los Angeles Early Entrance Program (CA) (commuter)
- The Clarkson School (NY)
- Kansas Academy of Mathematics and Science (KS)
- Mary Baldwin University Early College (VA; for females only)
- Program for the Exceptionally Gifted at Mary Baldwin University (VA; for females only)
- Texas Academy of Leadership in the Humanities (TALH) (Texas residents only)
- Texas Academy of Mathematics and Science (TAMS) (Texas residents only)
- University of Alaska Early Honors Program (AK)
- University of Iowa Bucksbaum Early Entrance Academy (IA)
- University of Washington Academy (WA) (residential and commuter)
- University of Washington Early Entrance Program (WA) (residential and commuter)

Dual Enrollment

Taking college classes while still in high school can be advantageous for students who wish to take higher-level classes in a strength area. Dual enrollment in community colleges and universities is becoming more the norm, and for highly gifted students, it provides an opportunity to take classes of interest before totally committing to a program as a first-time, full-time freshman. Some school districts help defray the cost of tuition for their high school students.

Mentorship Opportunities

It is common for highly gifted students of all ages to have a fixation on a single subject of intense interest. Examples include a deep curiosity about topics such as black holes, animal behavior, dungeons and dragons, astronomy, and artificial intelligence. One way to explore subjects of intense interest is through mentorships with community members, business owners, university professors, and other adults with specific interests or hobbies. Through mentorship opportunities, students enhance their skills in communication, self-advocacy, research, and academics. The following scenario depicts one high school student's experience of working with a mentor from a local university.

Alexa, a highly gifted 16-year-old student, knew from a young age that she wanted to be an astrophysicist. With the help of her science teacher, she participated in a two-year mentorship with a renowned physicist at the School of Earth and Space Exploration. She joined a graduate seminar, and participated in graduate students' research. She was able to examine photographs from the Hubble Telescope looking for black holes and galaxies. What she realized from this experience was that she actually loved science but the math inside the science intrigued her more. When she was ready for university work, she applied and was accepted to a prestigious mathematics program.

Source: Contributed by Clarissa Toupin, Herberger Young Scholars Academy at Arizona State University, AZ.

Effective mentorships should include weekly seminars with the mentor and reflective writing assignments by the mentee. These experiences help mentees process and learn from their experiences and often connect their service to future programs of study and career goals. A mentorship may also fulfill community service hours required by some university programs and scholarships.

Benefits to Mentee (Student):

- Participate in authentic learning while working side by side with experts
- Contributes to building a resumé
- Gain valuable leadership skills
- Explore careers of interest
- Develop professional relationships and interpersonal skills
- Develop critical thinking skills

Benefits to the Mentor/School

- Mentorship experience
- Assistance with research

Benefits to the Community

- High school students making an authentic contribution to real-life research
- Expansion of STEM engagement
- Increase scientific literacy in the future workforce

Emily, a 15-year-old highly gifted student, loved science but she was unsure of the area in science to study at the university level. Together with her high school science teacher, they contacted their local university, the School of Human Evolution and Social Change, where a research scientist was working on an anthropology dig in Sudan. Through a series of emails and one meeting, where Emily met and was interviewed by the research professor, Emily was invited to spend time each week in the university anthropology lab. Her work included scanning 95,000-year-old tools with an electron microscope to see if any of the tools showed evidence of intense heat, indicating the age of the rock (before or after the invention of fire). She concluded her menteeship with a strong letter of recommendation, research experience in a graduate lab, the ability to interact with professors and grad students with confidence, and self-advocacy skills. She was even invited to join the research group on an actual dig in Sudan.

Source: Clarissa Toupin, Herberger Young Scholars Academy, Arizona State University, AZ.

Programs for Multi-Age Students: Online, Summer, and International Opportunities

Other learning environments that are beneficial to highly gifted students include online classes, summer camps, enrichment programs, and homeschooling. Through these programs, students are able to learn at a level appropriate to their academic needs. In this section we showcase a few of the many programs available that have benefited highly gifted students: university-based models, a charter school, and a public-school district example.

ASU Digital Prep – High School and College Classes

One program that allows students to take higher-level courses is ASU Digital Prep at Arizona State University. This personalized learning model integrates high school and university; accelerating the time needed to earn a degree. ASU Digital Prep offers more than 200 curated college pathways, allowing students to take university courses, earn credits in their major while still in high school, and save some time and cost to earn a degree.

ASU Digital Prep's unique teaching model centers students within an intricate web of elevated services and supports. Students routinely interact with highly qualified instructors, professors, and personal learning success coaches. Course design provides choice and pace options. As one student noted, "I've truly never experienced a more welcoming learning environment. I feel as if my learning experience is focused on me as an individual: my goals, strengths, weaknesses, etc."

ASU Digital Prep also proactively searches university resources and assets that will benefit high school students, redesigning and repurposing them as needed for high school learners. For example, Bio Beyond, a state-of-the art, adaptive, media-rich college biology course, developed through the award-winning Education through Exploration Center at ASU, is now offered as a high school biology course. Students enjoy the personalized nature of ASU Digital Prep and the agency it provides, allowing them to make pace and pathway choices, and to get a head start on college.

Source: Contributed by L. Kay Johnson, Director of Strategic Communication, ASU Digital Prep.

PVOnline

PVOnline is a K-12 school that offers students the option of taking courses completely online. Highly accelerated students from within and outside the district may enroll in PVOnline. Students who do not reside within the district's boundaries pay a fee for registration on the online courses. Students who reside in Arizona may attend full-time with PVOnline or part-time while they attend their home school. The curriculum is aligned to district/state standards and resources. Students have flexibility with time, but are required to complete coursework within a semester. The decision to take courses online involves students, parents, and counselors. PVOnline coursework includes the same Honors and AP classes that are offered in the schools.

Source: Paradise Valley Unified School District, 2021

Davidson Academy Online Campus

The Davidson Academy's online campus is a game changer for profoundly gifted students. Open to students living anywhere in the United States, this accredited online option builds off the one-of-a-kind, exceptional framework put in place by the Davidson Academy's Reno day school during the last decade. The result is a robust online community where students thrive. Since 2006, the Davidson Academy's Reno campus has been recognized as the best option for families with profoundly gifted middle and high school students living in the Reno area. Now, for those unable to relocate to Reno, the online campus offers a rigorous academic environment where students can learn and interact with same-age, intellectual peers.

(Davidson Academy, 2021, n.p.)

Johns Hopkins Center for Talented Youth

The world leader in gifted education since 1979, Johns Hopkins Center for Talented Youth (CTY) is a nonprofit dedicated to identifying and developing the talents of academically advanced pre-college students around the world. We serve bright learners and their families through our research, advocacy, and counseling, as well as our signature gifted and talented summer, online, international, and family programs.

CTY students comprise the most promising minds of the next generation. There are more than 165,000 CTY alumni around the world, including the founders of Facebook and Google, Regeneron Science Talent Search winners, Rhodes Scholars, and MacArthur Fellows. At CTY, bright students have the chance to participate in challenging educational opportunities they won't experience anywhere else. Just as important, they'll find a safe, welcoming circle of peers, mentors, and teachers who understand advanced students. And they'll make lifelong friends who share their passion for learning.

(Johns Hopkins Center for Talented Youth, 2021, n.p.)

Centre for Talented Youth, Ireland–Dublin City University

The Centre for Talented Youth, Ireland provides enrichment courses for students with high academic ability. The Centre also offers university style courses for students of all ages and abilities. CTY Ireland aims to allow all talented students to reach their potential both academically and socially by providing relevant and interesting challenges based on ability and interest rather than age.

CTY Ireland was established at Dublin City University in 1992 to meet the needs of high ability students aged 6 to 17 years from Ireland and abroad. Since the first summer program in 1993 over 35,000 students have attended or participated in programs run by CTY Ireland.

(Center for Talented Youth, Ireland, 2021, n.p.)

Duke Talent Identification Program

This program was disbanded at one point, but now seems to be in transition: https://tip.duke.edu/

The Duke University Talent Identification Program (Duke TIP) is a nonprofit organization that has served over three million academically talented students in grades 4–12 since it was founded in 1980. Collaborating with educators and parents, TIP helps gifted students assess the extent of their academic abilities with above-grade-level testing, recognizes them for their achievements, and provides them with a variety of enrichment benefits as well as accelerated face-to-face and online educational programs. In addition, TIP is constantly conducting research into the educational, emotional, and social factors impacting the lives of gifted children, then sharing this research and related advice with our program staff, educators, parents, and the greater gifted community. Our services are designed to augment the efforts of regular schools, not replace them.

(Duke University Talent Identification Program, 2021, n.p.)

Teaching the Highly Gifted Learner

Teaching highly gifted learners requires a special mindset, ongoing professional learning, and motivation to understand these exceptional learners. Teachers who are effective in this role recognize the need for flexibility, for creativity when lesson planning, and for giving students opportunities to pursue their interests and build on their strengths. In her chapter, "Putting Together the Puzzle," Joyce VanTassel-Baska (2015) discusses how Vaille and Quigley (2002) synthesized researchers' conclusions pertaining to desirable qualities of teachers of the gifted:

- Having insights into the cognitive, social, and emotional needs of gifted students;
- Having skills in differentiating the curriculum for gifted students;
- Employing strategies that encourage higher level thinking;

- Providing student-centered learning opportunities;
- Acting as a facilitator or "guide on the side";
- Creating a non-threatening learning environment;
- Being well organized;
- Possessing in-depth knowledge of subject matter;
- Having broad interests, often literary and cultural;
- Having above-average intelligences;
- Being a lifelong learner;
- Thinking creatively;
- Possessing excellent communication skills;
- Being willing to make mistakes;
- Possessing a sense of humor; and
- Being enthusiastic.

(Vaille & Quigley [2002], cited by VanTassel-Baska, 2015, p. 44)

Effective teachers of highly gifted students share a passion for teaching these students that often parallels their students' passion for learning. They think critically, emphasize creativity, and are highly attuned to the sensitivities, quirkiness, and uniqueness of their students. In the next section several experienced teachers of highly gifted learners share their thoughts on, and encouragement for, teaching this special needs' population.

Voices from the Field: Teachers' Reflections

You will find gifted students and their parents take an extra dose of love, patience and caring. Finding an affection for teaching highly gifted children will allow for your teaching career to be challenging, rewarding, and full of fun. Each day the children that enter your classroom will want to learn, need a special kind of support, and think on such a deep level that it will amaze you. With direction, a compassionate heart and flexibility you will be able to plan lessons that go above and beyond standards while differentiating and taking into consideration each student's learning styles. At the end of each school year you will be able to know that you truly made a difference in the lives of these students and families.

(Amy Miller, Sonoran Sky Elementary School, PVSchools, AZ)

It is delightful teaching an entire class of highly gifted fourth grade students because they are free to excel intellectually. They don't have to worry about appearing nerdy or too smart. They find true peers, sometimes for the first time, and realize that there are other people who share their interests and intellectual curiosity. Without a separate program for highly gifted students, these students would be in a classroom where they are always the – or one of the – smartest kids in the class. They might not find intellectual peers until high school or even college. Having a whole class of students who are excited about learning new things and love coming to school every day is not just a pleasure – it's a gift. A big challenge, however, is helping these bright students collaborate with each other. The reality is that many of them could actually produce better work alone, but they need to learn how to work with other people. I spend a lot of time creating situations in which they must collaborate and teaching them strategies for working well with others.

(Deborah Arn, Sonoran Sky Elementary School, PVSchools, AZ)

Giving highly gifted students open-ended objectives to investigate real-world problems provides them opportunities for both critical and creative thinking while learning about important science core ideas. Learning goals that emphasize inquiry and higher-level thinking support gifted students in connecting core ideas with societal issues and needs. Highly gifted students need multiple pathways to use their strengths and find their identities. They need opportunities to collaborate and discuss with intellectual peers, design experiments, use technology, manipulate science concepts in complex ways, and communicate with authentic audiences.

(Pamela Fulk, MEd, 7th/8th Science & 8th Literature,
Digital Learning Center, PVSchools, AZ)

A number of reasons have been presented to explain why highly gifted children require radically different learning structures and approaches from those included in standard curriculum and instruction. As noted previously, they draw upon background information readily and make insightful connections between new knowledge and past experiences. To allow them to thrive intellectually, teachers must create learning situations where the students can access and build on previous knowledge while also having opportunities to direct their current learning, building upon their interests. The following scenario describes a typical unit of study developed by a teacher working in a program for highly gifted middle school students.

Sample Instruction: A Middle School Teaching Scenario

Children in a classroom designated for highly gifted middle school students are embarking on an adventure to the time from the colonies to the American Revolution. By taking on the persona of someone who lived during colonization and their descendants during the American Revolution, the students undergo a simulation where they learn about history from first-person accounts, secondary sources, and a role-playing adventure. In this interdisciplinary social studies unit, the students are embarking on research, writing narratives, letters, laws of governance, treaties, and newspaper articles while also developing economic plans for a successful enterprise within the colonies. As they develop their colony, understand the importance of geography for growth and development, undergo historical events, band together for survival, learn about trade and treaties, undercover spies, and witness battles, the students are asked to make a judgment about biases and the trustworthiness of sources and information. In conjunction with this multidisciplinary unit, students are reading works of literature that correspond with this time period both in [the form of] biographical accounts and in historical fictional narratives that highlight the positions of those citizens who were loyalists, unspecified citizens, or patriots and using these perspectives to help formulate their perspectives in their narrative journals.

As gifted students, they not only enjoy this type of unit of study but are able to grow tremendously as learners, as it plays to many of their strengths. They are able to not only grasp the content contained in primary source documents for the 17th and 18th centuries but make connections between the documents and the secondary source material and apply this understanding to develop a comprehensive plan of action and narrative. As highly gifted students, they perceive these lessons as the actions and events in the undercurrents of our founding civilization and are able to understand the complex structures and patterns found in the relationship between the juxtaposed civilizations and fundamentally their ideas of government, economics, and the world. As this unit has them develop arguments, debate laws and government policies, and evaluate the world and its history, it allows for them to develop their sense of justice and solidify their own thinking in how our country came to be.

In this unit students are working in collaborative groups focusing on the content but are also developing the 4cs[1] in all aspects of the unit, from creating ciphers to using deductive reasoning to uncovering spies [to] creating plans for growth and development of cities. They are able to research real people and develop personas that are a conglomerate of people and events based on historical figures. This unit encourages these highly gifted middle school students to further examine their passions in learning about this time period, whether it is laws, government, medicine, agriculture, espionage, military, people, or even history itself. The students are given opportunities for self-direction, and self-reflection, not only as a character within the simulation pulling from experiences, empathizing with others from history, and working together with others in collaboration for success, but also as a learner as the unit unfolds over time.

Source: Contributed by Rebekkah West-Keur, middle school gifted teacher at the Digital Learning Center in Paradise Valley Unified School District.

Role of Parents and Family

Family Dynamics

Many highly gifted students are either only children or the oldest sibling, and many have parents who are also gifted. Therefore, parents may share many of the intensities that we see in the children. These parents may have experienced great frustration in school themselves and simply do not want their children to share in those experiences. Parents of highly gifted children often tell stories of long-ranging frustrations trying to find educators to consider their child's unique learning needs. As described earlier, the parents of highly gifted children are more likely to pull students completely out of the school system and homeschool, micro-school[2] or un-school.[3]

Home Education

Children who have the opportunity to be effectively home educated can learn in a way that is highly individualized toward their specific needs, interests, and passions. If you then consider gifted children, with their (often) asynchronous development, it is understandable that some parents homeschool their highly gifted children. The advantages of tailoring home education for gifted children include accelerating or slowing the pace of learning; inculcating self-motivation and an owned educational journey; and allowing for other pursuits, especially if the gifted child is talented in other non-academic fields.

The challenges of home educating gifted children cannot be overlooked, and should be carefully considered by parents. Occasionally, having attempted to home educate their gifted children, some parents realize that the best place for their gifted children is not in the home education community, but in a specialized school setting (gifted in-school programs, schools for gifted students, or even online programs). Challenges faced by parents (and teachers of students previously home educated) include the ramifications of a highly individualized approach to learning that becomes part of the home education landscape. This can sometimes make it difficult for gifted home educated children to work within the constraints of institutions, especially if the child goes into school for high school credit classes. Other challenges of home educating gifted children include the support necessary for such an intensive program. The whole family and other support networks (social groups, churches, mentoring programs, and so on) should become part of the gifted children's education: This involves time, money, and organization. The challenge occurs when details, other than the academic program, are not in place for the children's main teacher (usually a parent).

One fellow educator and parent reported,

> I have home educated all four of my children, with a front-row seat to appreciate the individualized educational path that each one has taken. I have also taught profoundly gifted children in a specialized school on a university campus, and some of these children have been previously home educated. I have recognized their highly individualized approach to education as a strength and sometimes a challenge when they have to follow structured school days. These previously home educated gifted children either transition really well into the specialized school, or they realize they still need the freedom of home education. The bottom line, for teachers or parents, is to acknowledge the ways a specialized school or a home education can complement the gifted child in a way that is not practical in a traditional school setting.
>
> (Contributed by Samantha Eddis [Rothermel & Eddis, 2015], Faculty, Herberger Young Scholars Academy, February 3, 2020)

Parents as Advocates

Parents are a powerful force; they can be one's greatest advocate or worst critic. Parents often harness very powerful emotions when advocating for their children. This is not surprising with parents of highly gifted children considering that year after year they need to explain to teachers and school administrators *why* their children may need an alternative learning path, schedule, and/or curriculum. Educators who understand the learning needs of these students also understand the parents' concerns. There is great value in meeting with parents who are advocating for their children to hear their specific concerns. With this input, schools can proactively design processes which ensure that all children are intellectually stimulated throughout their education.

Conclusion

This chapter is intended to help readers develop a broad understanding of who the highly gifted learners are and how educators can support their learning. The beginning of the chapter provided a look at four very distinctive children. All four of these learners are considered highly gifted, but with vastly disparate learning needs. We have attempted to demonstrate why educators and parents are sometimes forced to seek alternative schooling methods when their schools cannot meet these needs. All students deserve to learn every day that they are in school, and to be intellectually inspired by teachers who understand their learning needs. This means that for highly gifted learners, educators and parents must be open and flexible to new ideas, allow the students to have input and pursue areas of interest and strength, and respect and build on what the students bring to the table.

Questions for Discussion

When considering barriers faced by highly gifted students, reflect on the following questions.

1   Do *all* of our students believe that:

   •   schools have their best interests at heart?
   •   getting a good education will benefit everyone in the same way?
   •   they can *each* pursue educational goals with the *same* outcomes in mind?

   Consider each of these questions carefully and individually. Then identify structures that exist in schools which may directly influence these differences and possible outcomes.

2   Reflect and discuss how parental influence, group identity factors, and the impact of the school setting affect highly gifted students. Delve into these three areas by answering the following questions as pertaining to a school or school district.

Parental Influence

   •   How does parental influence differ in regard to highly gifted students in your school or district?
   •   How does parental influence impact the highly gifted student at school?

Group Identity Factors

   •   What is fundamental with all gifted students?
   •   Why is knowing the level of giftedness important?
   •   How do highly gifted students differ among the various demographic groups?
   •   How does the degree of giftedness impact highly gifted students in the learning environment, both socially and cognitively?

Impact of School Setting

- How does the school setting fit with highly gifted students' social experiences?
- What do educators need to know to better support the highly gifted child's education?
- What specific steps can your school take to alter the course of action?

3   Identify three small steps you can take in your professional role to increase others awareness of highly gifted students in your school setting.

Notes

1   The 4cs refer to: critical thinking, creativity, collaboration, and communication.
2   Micro-schools have a small number of students, less than 50, have multi- age classrooms, and emphasize digital and project-based learning.
3   Unschooling is a rejection of the concept of traditional schooling. Curriculum is not used; children pursue what they are interested in learning and are free to not learn things they are not interested in.

Bibliography

Brulles, D., & Winebrenner, S. (2008). *The cluster grouping handbook: A schoolwide model*. Free Spirit Publishing.

Center for Talented Youth, Ireland. (2021). Retrieved from: www.dcu.ie/ctyi/

Cross, T. (2017). *On the social and emotional lives of gifted children*. Prufrock Press.

Davidson Academy. (2020). Retrieved from: www.davidsonacademy.unr.edu/academics/online-campus/

Duke Talent Identification Program. (2021). Retrieved from: https://tip.duke.edu/

Elementary and Secondary Education Act (ESEA). (2002).

Gifted Development Center. (n.d.). Retrieved from: www.gifteddevelopment.com/

Gross, M. (1994). Radical acceleration: Responding to the academic and social needs of extremely gifted adolescents. *Journal of Secondary Gifted Education, 5*(4), 27–34.

Gross, M. (1999). Small poppies: Highly gifted children in the early years. *Roeper Review, 21*(3), 207–214.

Gross, M. (2000). Exceptionally and profoundly gifted students: An underserved population. *Understanding Our Gifted, 12*(2), 3–9. Retrieved September 12, 2008, from: www.hoagiesgifted.org/underserved.htm

Gross, M. (2015). *Applied practice for educators of gifted and able learners*. Sense Publishers, ProQuest Ebook Central.

Hansen, R. (2009). Hollingworth's studies of highly gifted students. In *Encyclopedia of giftedness, creativity, and talent*. SAGE Publications.

Herberger Young Scholars Academy. (2021). Retrieved from: https://herbergeracademy.asu.edu/

Hollingworth, L. S. (1926). *Gifted children, their nature and nurture*. The Macmillan Company.

Hollingworth, L. (1942). *Children above 180 IQ Stanford-Binet: Origin and development*. World Book Company.

Johns Hopkins Center for Talented Youth. (2021). Retrieved from: https://cty.jhu.edu/resources/academic-opportunities/college-entrance/

Lubinski, D., & Benbow, C. (2006) Study of mathematically precocious youth after 35 years: Uncovering antecedents for the development of math-science expertise. *Perspective on Psychological Science, 1*, 316–345.

Muratori, M. (2007). *Early entrance to college: A guide to success*. Prufrock Press.

NAGC. (2019). National Association for Gifted Children. Retrieved from: www.nagc.org

Naglieri, J. A., & Ford, D. (2005). Increasing minority children's participation in gifted classes using the NNAT: A response to Lohman. *Gifted Child Quarterly, 49*(1), 29–36.

Naglieri, J. A., & Otero, T. M. (2017). Essentials of CAS2 assessment. In *Essentials of CAS2 assessment*. John Wiley & Sons, Incorporated.

Natcharian, L. (2017). Why are so many gifted children also highly sensitive? Blog post. Retrieved from: https://educationaladvancement.org/blog-many-gifted-children-also-highly-sensitive/

Ortiz, S. O., Ochoa, S. H., & Dynda, A. M. (2012). Testing with culturally and linguistically diverse populations: Moving beyond the verbal-performance dichotomy into evidence-based practice. In D. P. Flanagan & P. L. Harrison (Eds.), *Contemporary intellectual assessment: Theories, tests, and issues* (pp. 526–552). The Guilford Press.

Padilla, A. M., & Borsato, G. N. (2008). Issues in culturally appropriate psychoeducational assessment. In L. A. Suzuki & J. G. Ponterotto (Eds.), *Handbook of multicultural assessment: Clinical, psychological, and educational applications* (pp. 5–21). Jossey-Bass/Wiley.

Paradise Valley Unified School District. (2021). Retrieved from: www.pvschools.net/academics/academic-programs/gifted-programs

Peters, S. J., & Brulles, D. (2017). *Designing gifted education programs and services: From purpose to implementation*. Prufrock Press.

Potts, J. (2019). Profoundly gifted students' perceptions of virtual classrooms. *Gifted Child Quarterly, 63*(1), 58–80.

Rogers, K. (2006). *A menu of options for grouping gifted students*. Prufrock Press.

Rothermel, P., & Eddis, S. (2015). England, Wales and Florida, USA. In P. Rothermel (Ed.), *International perspectives on home education: Do we still need schools?* (pp. 473–476). Palgrave Macmillan.

Schultz, R. (2018). Recognizing the outliers: Behaviors and tendencies of the profoundly gifted learner in mixed-ability classrooms. *Roeper Review, 40*(3), 191–196.

Siegle, D. (2015). Dr. James Gallagher's concern for gifted learners beyond academics. *Journal for the Education of the Gifted, 38*(1), 58–63.

Shaklee, B. (2009). Highly gifted. In *Encyclopedia of giftedness, creativity, and talent*. SAGE Publications.

Shaughnessy, M., & Fickling, K. (1991). *Testing for giftedness: The pros, cons and concerns*. Distributed by ERIC Clearinghouse.

Tolan, S. (2018). The value and importance of mindfulness for the highly to profoundly gifted child. *Gifted Education International, 34*(2), 193–202

VanTassel-Baska, J. (2015). Putting together the puzzle. In H. A. Vidergor & C. R. Harris (Eds.), *Applied practice for educators of gifted and able learners* (pp. 77–86). Brill.

Webb, J., Gore, J., Amend, E., & DeVries, A. (2007). *Guiding the gifted child*. Great Potential Press, Inc.

Webb, J. T. (2007). *A parent's guide to gifted children*. Great Potential Press.

Winebrenner, S., & Brulles, D. (2018). *Teaching gifted kids in today's classroom: Strategies and techniques every teacher can use*. Free Spirit Publishing.

Chapter 6

Growing Up Gifted in Rural America

Mitigating Challenges Posed by Geography

Kimberley L. Chandler

Vignette

Candace, the younger of two children, has lived in a rural county in Virginia for her entire life. Her school district has just three schools, two of which carry the Title I designation. Candace says that the biggest limitation of attending school there has been the lack of options: only a few clubs, just two Advanced Placement courses and two dual enrollment courses, and a paucity of extra-curricular activities. As she approached her senior year, she worried that the lack of a variety of opportunities for her involvement would be detrimental during the college application process. She also says that a shaky internet connection and a limited public library have sometimes limited her attempts to do in-depth research.

Her older sister was a first-generation college student; Candace will be only the second person on either side of the family to attend college. Although their father was offered a baseball scholarship, he chose not to take it. Their mother's father refused to pay for college, in spite of her desire to attend. Candace's own pathway to college has not been an easy one. Her father believes that "physical work is harder and more meaningful than mental work," (C. Hace, personal communication, November 5, 2020) which gave her the impression that he was not supportive of her aspirations. He also insisted that she try to get loans on her own to pay for tuition. Candace's reaction was to apply for as many scholarships as possible. Additionally, neither parent wanted to pay all of the fees for college applications; like many farm families, Candace's had a low income, but had sizable non-liquid assets because of owning a farm. She was resourceful, though, and was able to get some application fees waived through a special program.

A discussion with Candace about her life and her education reveals several themes: the perceived differences between her and her family, the importance of a regional program for academic and social growth, and the need for self-advocacy. Although Candace believes that living in the country is positive for the most part, she believes that her values are quite different from those of some of her relatives (her father in particular). She describes her father as coming from a farm family that is "very plain and simple" (C. Hace, personal communication, November 5, 2020). She says that her father's family is too conservative and is bigoted; for that reason, she has often rebelled.

Although Candace's father was not convinced that a college education would be necessary for her, he did push her to attend the regional three-year STEM-focused

DOI: 10.4324/9781003265412-11

program (a Governor's School) for the gifted; both he and Candace's mother felt that it would be a program that would be superior to what was available in the district high school. Candace was somewhat uncomfortable with going because she knew it would push her out of her comfort zone. She discovered that she loved biology, and now wants to study genetics. Candace ultimately saw the Governor's School as an important opportunity; she believes that it "gave her a leg up" and "made her a better person" (C. Hace, personal communication, November 5, 2020).

Throughout Candace's description of her educational journey, she referenced the self-advocacy that was needed in various situations. Applying to the Governor's School and then to colleges required that she seek out the teachers who would write the most positive recommendations for her. Attending the Governor's School required that she advocate for assistance when she was struggling to do research because of a lack of a stable internet connection. When she was not accepted into her high school's National Honor Society, she had to make the attempts to get the decision overturned prior to having her mother get involved.

Although Candace considered growing up in a rural setting to be a positive experience overall, especially because of living close to nature, she described her excitement about moving to a different type of setting for college. She looked forward to spending time with people who had more progressive views as she planned to attend an urban university on the East Coast. She sees college as an important opportunity to move beyond her perceived limitations of the place she has lived in her entire life.

Introduction

The United States Census Bureau defines rural as "any population, housing, or territory not in an urban area" (U.S. States Census Bureau, n.d.) Its definition of rural is closely tied to its definition of *urban*. Thier et al. (2020) suggest the need to avoid this current practice of classifying communities dichotomously as either rural or nonrural, arguing that such research which "omits or insufficiently defines geographic locale can impair policy formulation, enactment, and evaluation" (p. 64).

From a practical standpoint, living in a rural setting implies being in a place with a lower population density than in an urban area. There may be limitations on access to certain types of employment and amenities due to lengthy commuting distances or geographical obstacles. In the case of individuals who do not have personal transportation, they may have to rely on regional transit systems that provide limited service times, thus restricting some employment opportunities and access to services. Geographical obstacles include lack of proximity to major highways because of land features, lack of drainage resulting in rough, difficult-to-travel roads, and limited internet connectivity due to infrastructure and the landscape.

From an educational perspective, it is difficult to find an exact definition of what constitutes a rural school setting. According to the Rural School and Community Trust, a school is rural if:

- A majority of its students live in rural places.
- It is located in a district with fewer than 600 students.

- It is located in a town of fewer than 2,500 people, no matter how many students are in the district.
- It is small and located at least five miles from an urbanized area.

(Rural School and Community Trust, 2013, n.p.)

Although there are other definitions of rural schools seen in the literature, this one provides at least a starting point for the context. Individual state departments of education may have their own definitions of what constitutes a rural school. The definition itself is less important than knowing that the characteristics are general and fluid in nature.

According to Mattingly and Schaefer (2015), other considerations about rural settings that are important for schools include information about both diversity and socioeconomics. The poverty level varies widely from state to state and within state; one issue in rural communities is often a lack of jobs generally, but particularly for unskilled workers. The level of diversity also varies greatly, but is often characterized now by an influx of individuals from other countries coming to rural communities through church-based programs or to work in migrant farm settings; one result is the need to accommodate residents with different cultural backgrounds. "Rural school districts reflect a population whose diversity includes cultural, linguistic, economic, and geographic diversity" (Lewis & Boswell, 2020b, p. 122). The sense of place and the rural culture also influence rural school communities and how they operate (Lewis & Boswell, 2020a).

Davis et al. (2020) note that

> challenges faced by rural area students include (a) the multifaceted definitions of rural areas, (b) the complex nature of distance and isolation in rural areas that impact access to higher education opportunities, (c) extreme poverty levels, and (d) a high number of low-performing schools in rural communities across the nation.

(Davis et al., 2020, p. 86)

They indicate that the problems are often even greater for Black students, who may also experience a sense of isolation and of being disconnected from urban areas. Additional potential problems for students living in rural areas include a lack of highly qualified teachers and lack of access to higher-level coursework. "Limited funding, resources, and time are the three core factors affecting rural gifted programs" according to Lewis and Boswell (2020a, p. 184).

Research

Traditionally in gifted education, the research about gifted students from rural settings has been quite limited. Interest in the topic seems to be burgeoning, however. The National Association for Gifted Children (NAGC) recently established a Rural Special Interest Group. In late 2020, *Theory and Practice in Rural Education* devoted an entire special issue to practices in gifted education in rural settings. Actual empirical research is still scarce, however, with most articles relating to ideas about what should be done to serve rural gifted students. Recent empirical studies include ones related to teachers of rural gifted students, place-based instruction, and case studies about rural gifted education programs.

The special issue of *Theory and Practice in Rural Education* provides examples of some of the most recent research about rural gifted education. "*Place* which includes both the geographic surroundings and the local community with whom one shares a common space" plays a strong role in this work (Kuehl et al., 2020, p. 26, italics in the original); this understanding of place as it relates to gifted students from rural settings is important not only for the research, but also warrants a greater level of understanding for those who work with these children in schools. Bass et al. (2020) studied the use of a place-based curriculum with highly able students in a rural setting. This qualitative study provided an examination of the importance of valuing students' lived experiences and their place in their communities. In a study of rural fourth graders' narrative fiction writing, Kuehl et al. (2020) found that the children reflected a sense of place in their writing, including descriptions of the natural world, their communities, and discomfort about being in areas unfamiliar to them.

In a case study of three rural gifted programs in Appalachia, Miller and Brigandi (2020) examined programming, in terms of the teachers' experiences and ideas; place versus a larger worldview was a theme in the findings. Gallagher and Wrenn (2020) examined nonfiction selections about Black historical figures and found place to play a strong role, both in terms of how the figures' giftedness manifested itself in their communities and how they influenced their own worlds. This work can inform practices such as bibliotherapy when working with gifted students from rural settings because it provides the basis for a more in-depth analysis.

It is encouraging to see the growth in research on issues related to rural gifted education. The concerns about a digital divide during the global pandemic have often related to the unmet needs of rural youth. Also, the recent discussions about equity as they relate to access to certain types of resources will, it is hoped, garner continued interest in and dedicated resources to this area of inquiry.

A Focus on Equity

In the rural setting, issues of equity are often exacerbated by the challenges of geography.

For example, during the coronavirus pandemic, when most American schools had to move to fully online instruction, in many cases, rural schools faced the greatest challenge because of the lack of infrastructure and/or geographical barriers to internet access. In the case of Candace's school district, for example, about 40 percent of the households reported that they did not have reliable internet service. In some cases, this meant they might have been able to purchase internet services, but it was unstable; in other cases, there was no possibility of acquiring service because it had not yet been brought to their part of the district. The school district took steps to purchase hotspots to ensure that all students could access online instruction and resources; because of the paucity of towers and high usage, though, students often did not have reliable service.

Geographical location also comes into play with educational programming. Many rural schools are quite small, and thus are unable to offer as many programs and services to students as larger suburban and urban districts. At the high school level, this may mean fewer course and extracurricular options; for highly able students, this means that they may not have as much access to dual enrollment courses and Advanced Placement courses as their peers in more populous districts. Although the proliferation of online courses has helped to provide access for rural students, limited internet access in the homes can often be a barrier.

Transportation concerns may also be a potential contributor to lack of equity for rural students. Often, school bus routes in rural districts are lengthy due to geography and the distance between residences. When coordination with buses traveling to regional programs must be done, there can sometimes be a problem getting students to the home school in time to meet the next bus. In situations where the parents/guardians are unable to provide transportation to the home school, a student may be unable to get to a regional program unless the district personnel intervene and provide alternate transportation.

The equity issues directly related to geography are ones that must be addressed systematically by district leadership and school boards. Although there are sometimes financial and infrastructure-related barriers, it is important for school officials to seek solutions to ensure that all children have the optimal opportunities to achieve their potential. In the case of gifted students, this may mean finding innovative solutions to provide students with the advanced programming that they require for maximum achievement. This includes ensuring that transportation, internet access, and limited course options do not become additional barriers for children.

Identification

Students, children, or youth who give evidence of high achievement capability in areas such as intellectual, creative, artistic, or leadership capacity, or in specific academic fields, and who need services and activities not ordinarily provided by the school in order to fully develop those capabilities

(ESEA, 2002, Title IX, Part A, Definition 22)

is the definition of gifted and talented students provided by the federal Elementary and Secondary Education Act (ESEA). States and localities often use some variation of this definition for their purposes. Besides using the accepted definitions as a starting point, specific practices are suggested by Stambaugh (2015), all of them focusing on context: understanding the nature of gifted students from rural settings, using place-based and contextual tools, using local norms if warranted, and exercising flexibility when developing identification procedures and policies.

An understanding of the nature of gifted students from rural settings is an idea that is repeated through this chapter. As it relates to identification, it is important because the rural context may have in some instances created limitations for students. Due to lack of access to certain resources, they may have underdeveloped skills in some areas. For example, teacher recruitment and retention tend to be problems in rural districts, sometimes resulting in deficits in the quality of the teacher workforce or the availability of advanced options. Another area where the rural context comes into play for these students during identification is when teachers complete the checklists often used; if they do not understand the specific characteristics of these students, they may not complete them accurately. Stambaugh (2015) suggests providing ongoing professional development that focuses on the unique characteristics of these children for all school personnel in rural schools.

Also important is using place-based and contextual tools. This should include the use of multiple measures and possibly some subjective measures. Implementing local norms is another consideration for identification of gifted students in rural settings; this allows for a closer matching of testing profiles to the student population. The emphasis should be less on defining a specific number or percentage of students, but more on finding those students who need differentiated options beyond those found in the regular education classroom.

A final consideration is the need to exercise flexibility when developing identification procedures and policies. The objective is to identify and serve the types of children described in the federal definition. Although much is written in gifted education about identification, strict adherence to a given protocol may not be optimal for a given population. Administrators of gifted education programs must consider their specific contexts and develop appropriate processes that demonstrate best practices, but that also address the learning needs of their students who demonstrate high achievement capability.

Programming and Instruction

Several specific needs from the extant research emerge related to programming and instruction for gifted students from rural settings: the promotion of culturally responsive pedagogy and materials, the creation of more robust distance-learning options, and the development of more regional programs. If deliberate attempts are made to fulfill these needs, programming and instruction for these students may be enhanced.

Culturally responsive pedagogy and materials should look different for different student groups. Culturally relevant teaching is a term created by Gloria Ladson-Billings (1994) to describe "a pedagogy that empowers students intellectually, socially, emotionally, and politically by using cultural referents to impart knowledge, skills, and attitudes." Participating in culturally relevant teaching essentially means that teachers create a bridge between students' home and school lives, while still meeting the expectations of the district and state curricular requirements. Culturally relevant teaching utilizes the backgrounds, knowledge, and experiences of the students to inform the teacher's lessons and methodology.

In the case of rural gifted students, the study by Bass et al. (2020) referenced earlier in this chapter spoke to the need for using a place-based curriculum; in their description, such a curriculum valued students' lived experiences and their place in their communities. This is a relatively new concept for teachers in K-12 settings. It is one that many teachers might argue that they include through making lessons relevant to the real lives of their students; however, it is more complicated and highly developed than that. A place-based curriculum for gifted students should include authentic and meaningful learning experiences that rely on connections to local geography and other community resources. The lived experiences of rural youth differ significantly from those of their urban and suburban peers, so it is essential to capture in instructional experiences what makes their lives unique.

Stambaugh and Chandler (2012) wrote specifically about the curricular needs of underserved gifted students, including students from rural settings and from low-income backgrounds. The intersection of poverty in the lives of many rural gifted students must be considered when discussing culturally responsive pedagogy. Some of their recommendations for teachers could be adapted for this special population:

- Select research-based and place-based curriculum that provides scaffolding through questioning and thinking models, acceleration with support mechanisms, and opportunities for real-world projects and problem solving.

- Model communication techniques and metacognitive skills that will help students to be successful in various settings.
- Ensure that the curriculum intervention matches the identification methods used to admit the gifted learners into special programs.
- On an ongoing basis, provide professional development about gifted rural students' characteristics and effective curriculum and instructional techniques effective with this population to all faculty and paraprofessionals.
- Include rural gifted learners' achievement as a criterion in teacher evaluation and accountability measures.
- Provide targeted course options for rural students in their areas of strength.
- Encourage a welcoming school community that celebrates the individual child.

Another programming and instruction emphasis for rural gifted students that has emerged from the research is the need for more robust distance-learning options. During the years of the coronavirus pandemic, virtual instruction became the major modality of instruction for most students. Its limitations became clear, as students struggled with poor internet connections, instructors' lack of familiarity with distance learning, and poorly designed virtual learning experiences. The increased emphasis globally on virtual instruction has resulted in some initial improvements. For gifted students from rural settings, however, the need for adequate infrastructure is a backdrop to many important requirements moving forward: curriculum designed specifically to address the needs of gifted students; curriculum that is place-based in nature; and providing an orientation to parents/guardians to assist their children in navigating virtual instruction. While the need to assist families in helping their students with distance learning is not restricted only to children from rural backgrounds, the importance of acclimating everyone to what may be a new instructional paradigm is essential so that they can expand their potential options through making distance-learning options viable ones.

The development of more regional programs is another important need for gifted students from rural settings. Some states, like Virginia, are fortunate to have developed numerous "Governor's Schools," which are regional magnet high school and summer programs designed for gifted students; each program focuses on a specific content (such as STEM) and is offered to students within their regions. Although Virginia's students benefit from such programs, the Governor's Schools do not begin to fill the need across the entire state. Other states vary in their offerings of such regional programs, depending on funding and politics. The benefit of regional programs is that various localities can pool funds to develop high-quality programs for gifted students.

To enhance educational programming for gifted students from rural settings, using culturally responsive pedagogy and materials, developing more robust distance-learning options, and planning more regional programs are needed. Those individuals who advocate for this student population should investigate funding sources, possible local and regional resources, and ways to garner additional support for such programs.

Social-Emotional Learning

"Milieu" is defined as "the physical or social setting in which something occurs or develops" (Merriam-Webster, n.d., n.p.). The rural milieu and its impact on the social-emotional development and learning of gifted students from rural settings must be considered. Howley (2007, p. 550) argues that "Rural people have connections to working the land, and to a set of concepts about place, kinship, and community. The associated meanings and purposes are what distinguishes rural education as a field of work and study." Richards and Stambaugh (2015) consider the essence of rural to be the following characteristics: sense of place, family, tradition, spirituality, differing definitions of success, and community. All of these characteristics are part of the rural milieu.

> When individuals bear a special connection to the land they inhabit, they perceive themselves embedded in that place and its history, all its dilemmas, and the possibilities inherent within it. Indeed, fostering such a perception proves promising for the benefit of rural communities.
>
> (Richards & Stambaugh, 2015, p. 4.)

School counselors rarely receive any specific training about gifted education. It is thus even more unlikely that they would have any specialized training related to gifted students from rural settings. A first step in training counselors is ensuring that they understand the impact of the rural milieu on the students' social-emotional development. There are many aspects of this milieu that influence how the children view the world and their place within it. In the case of Candace, as she grew older, she began to see the rural milieu as a place with certain material and philosophical limitations; coupled with her love for her family, this created a conflict for her. She did not work with her school counselor at all when she faced difficulty, as she indicated that he was "from the city and could not possibly understand her life" (C. Hace, personal communication, November 5, 2020).

In the limited research that has been done with this special population of learners, the concept of *place* and its importance are evident. In developing interventions or programming for these students, it is important for school counselors to consider both the opportunities and barriers that these students experience as a result of the place in which they live. Counselors at the high school level must help students who are preparing to get a job, enlist in the military, or attend college to understand that they will bring unique backgrounds to any of these situations; thus, their worldviews will be different. As students start to face these transitions, they may need assistance with various situations, such as application processes, dealing with their achievement orientations, or dealing with their families' responses to their life choices. All of these are the circumstances that counselors assist students with typically, but must be undergirded by a recognition of the unique role of place.

Collaboration

When considering the education of rural gifted learners, there are multiple ways in which collaboration could enhance their experiences. It is essential to leverage various partners to expand academic options for these students. Some of the options include: finding viable options for supplemental and out-of-school programming, building partnerships with parents and the community, and making use of federal grant funds. School district personnel involved in the education of gifted students must be aware of the options and should work to incorporate them in planning and programming.

When considering supplemental and out-of-school programming, an important task is building connections with various entities: other area school districts, colleges and universities, and community members (Olszewski-Kubilius et al., 2015). Many states already have organizing structures in place that put districts within certain geographical regions into groups for the purpose of meetings and collaboration; if this is not already established, a gifted education coordinator could establish a sub-group of colleagues to share resources. The same group could also develop regional enrichment programs. In some parts of Virginia, for example, some school districts have collaborated to form regional summer programs that provide enrichment opportunities for students in rural areas.

Nearby colleges and universities may offer numerous opportunities for gifted students. In some cases, students can attend classes on campus in special enrichment programs targeted specifically to them. There may also be programs that are offered on an occasional basis that may appeal to gifted students' special interests. The proliferation of online programs has begun to eliminate the need to go on campus for special programming, thus enabling gifted students from rural settings to access far more options.

Working with community members through established programming can also allow gifted students to access new experiences. In the high school that Candace attended, for instance, community members worked with students applying to the regional Governor's School on their interview skills. As the students prepared to interview for slots at the school, community members provided an orientation session, followed by conducting mock interviews and giving feedback. This programming could not have been easily facilitated by the already overcommitted school counselors. Through connections made through the Parent–Teacher Organization, this important opportunity was made available to the students.

Building partnerships with the community and with parents is especially important in the rural setting. As in the previous example with the interview sessions, the gifted education coordinator had to work beyond the typical school setting to implement a unique experience for the students. Parents and community members may have resources and skills to share that would otherwise be unavailable through the schools.

Collaboration with other departments in a school district, especially those that have access to federal Title funds, such as Title I and Title V, is important when addressing the needs of rural gifted students.

> Title V, Part B of the *Every Student Succeeds Act* of 2015 (ESSA) is intended to address the unique needs of rural school districts that frequently lack the personnel and resources needed to compete effectively for federal competitive grants and receive formula grant allocations in amounts too small to be effective in meeting their intended purpose.
>
> (Colorado Department of Education, n.d., n.p.)

Although the funding is limited and not guaranteed annually, it can provide additional programming resources for rural districts. Statutory provisions of Title I include specific language about the use of those funds for identifying and serving gifted and talented students; this is typically a greater amount of funding than Title V provides and is available to more districts. The key to collaboration is ensuring that the person in charge of gifted education is aware of these funding streams and has access to using some of the funds for serving the students.

Worldwide Web Connections

Prior to the coronavirus pandemic, there had already been numerous offerings of online courses for gifted students. The Johns Hopkins Center for Talented Youth, for example, offers more than 170 online courses for students "guided by expert instructors who specialize in teaching advanced concepts to bright students" (Johns Hopkins Center for Talented Youth, n.d., n.p.). Other organizations also provide course offerings for gifted students. For gifted children from rural settings, the availability of such online courses can potentially provide options that would never be available for them in their geographic settings.

Post-pandemic, it seems likely that more online programming may be developed for all students. Renzulli Learning, described as "an interactive online system that provides a personalized learning environment for students, which allows teachers to easily differentiate instruction to increase engagement and achieve higher academic performance" (Renzulli Learning, n.d., n.p.) is the type of portal that may be used for enrichment purposes for gifted students. Especially for children from rural settings who have limited access to specialized gifted education programming in their districts or on university campuses, access to such a system could help to address their learning needs.

However, the equity issues related to internet availability discussed earlier in this chapter must be addressed for these students. Related to this, though, is ensuring that teachers of these students have more professional development about how to teach online. In the race to provide some sort of educational programming for children during the unprecedented school shutdowns in 2020 and 2021, in many cases, teachers quickly learned to post materials to learning management systems. Rarely did they receive training about pedagogical practices related to online teaching, however. Also, they often did not learn how to adapt what they were doing specifically for gifted students. The North Carolina Department of Public Instruction (n.d.) was one organization that posted resources for gifted students for remote learning; the activities were designed to help accelerate or enrich units of study. The materials may be found at www.dpi.nc.gov/students-families/enhanced-opportunities/advanced-learning-and-gifted-education/aig-remote-learning-resources. The lesson learned during the pandemic is that teachers of the gifted need continuing training about how to differentiate appropriately for gifted students and they need to learn how to engage their students in an online setting.

Practical Application

As an educator who grew up on a farm and who now serves as an administrator in a rural district, two needs have become apparent as this author works within this population: the importance of a deep understanding of the rural setting and the need for culturally responsive pedagogy and materials. For the educators who work directly with these students and for those who develop policies and procedures at higher levels of administration, these are the most important concerns to be addressed.

A deep understanding of the rural setting is something that is often neglected in schools. The teachers who work in the schools may live in suburban or urban settings and may not fully grasp what the rural lifestyle involves. Simple things, such as a bus tour of the district, may help new teachers and administrators understand in a literal sense from where their students are coming. Putting the rural nature of the district in the forefront is also important; rural education is a specialized area of study at the collegiate level, but its principles are rarely examined in practice in the preK–grade 12 setting. Teachers and administrators need to know what their students are experiencing; the rural setting is a unique one that brings with it specific affordances and constraints relative to education.

The need for culturally responsive pedagogy and materials is another important practical application. Little is written about this, except to a limited extent in some of the studies cited earlier in this chapter. The concept of *place* must be considered in both curriculum and instruction. Just as publishers have sought to provide titles that reflect various other special populations of learners, they also need to seek authors who write about students from rural settings.

Conclusion

This purpose of this chapter is to help readers understand the nature and needs of gifted students from rural settings. The vignette about Candace provided a backdrop to a discussion about this special population of learners. In examining all of the aspects of education related to these children, the concept of *place* has a significant bearing on how they see the world and how they interact in it. In Candace's case, as well as other students like her, *place* has shaped her education, including the types of opportunities she sought for herself. For teachers and administrators to understand them, they must recognize these students' unique characteristics and seek to address them.

Questions for Discussion

1   What is one potential barrier for gifted students from rural settings? How can school personnel and school practices be used to help mitigate these challenges for students?
2   What are some of the difficulties involved in defining the nature of a rural setting?
3   Why is understanding the concept of *place* particularly important in working with gifted students from rural settings? How could an awareness about this concept be shared with all school personnel?
4   What are the major concerns about equity when serving gifted students from rural backgrounds? What types of practices should be implemented to address these concerns?
5   How might an administrator of a gifted education program leverage federal grant funding to improve programming?

References

Bass, E. L., Azano, A. P., & Callahan, C. M. (2020). A place for writing: Examining a place-based curriculum for high-performing rural writers. *Theory & Practice in Rural Education, 10*(2), 11–25.
Colorado Department of Education. (n.d.). Title V, Part B: Rural Education Achievement Program (REAP). Retrieved January 26, 2021, from: www.cde.state.co.us/fedprograms/ov/tvb

Davis, J. L., Ford, D. Y., Moore III, J. L., & Floyd, E. F. (2020). Black and gifted in rural America: Barriers and facilitators to accessing Gifted and Talented education programs. *Theory & Practice in Rural Education, 10*(2), 85–100.

Elementary and Secondary Education Act [ESEA] (2002). Title IX, Part A, Definition 22.

Gallagher, J., & Wrenn, M. (2020). Young, gifted, black ... and country: A community situated approach to analyzing black, rural giftedness in contemporary nonfiction children's literature. *Theory & Practice in Rural Education, 10*(2), 46–62.

Howley, C. B. (2007). Remarks to urban mathematics educators. *Rural Mathematics Educator, 6*(2), 73–85.

Johns Hopkins Center for Talented Youth. (n.d.). Online programs. Retrieved January 26, 2021, from: https://cty.jhu.edu/online/

Kuehl, R., Azano, A. P., & Callahan, C. M. (2020). Gifted rural writers explore place in narrative fiction stories. *Theory & Practice in Rural Education, 10*(2), 26–45.

Ladson-Billings, G. (1994). Who will teach our children? Preparing teachers to successfully teach African American students. In E. R. Hollins, J. E. King, & W. C. Hayman (Eds.), *Teaching diverse populations: Formulating a knowledge base* (pp. 129–142). SUNY Press.

Lewis, K. D., & Boswell, C. (2020a). Perceived challenges for rural gifted education. *Gifted Child Today, 43*(3), 184–198.

Lewis, K. D., & Boswell, C. (2020b). Reflections on rural gifted education in Texas: Then and now. *Theory & Practice in Rural Education, 10*(2), 119–139.

Mattingly, M. J., & Schaefer, A. (2015). Education in rural America: Challenges and opportunities. In T. Stambaugh & S. Wood (Eds.), *Serving gifted students in rural settings* (pp. 53–70). Prufrock Press, Inc.

Merriam-Webster. (n.d.). Milieu. In Merriam-Webster.com dictionary. Retrieved January 27, 2021, from: www.merriam-webster.com/dictionary/milieu

Miller, M., & Brigandi, C. (2020). Exploring gifted education programs and practice in rural Appalachia. *Theory & Practice in Rural Education, 10*(2), 101–118.

North Carolina Department of Public Instruction. (n.d.). AIG Remote Learning Resources. Retrieved January 2, 2021 from: www.dpi.nc.gov/students-families/enhanced-opportunities/advanced-learning-and-gifted-education/aig-remote-learning-resources

Olszewski-Kubilius, P., Corwith, S, & Calvert, E. (2015). Serving rural gifted students through supplemental and out-of school programming. In T. Stambaugh & S. Wood (Eds.), *Serving gifted students in rural settings* (pp. 239–256). Prufrock Press, Inc.

Renzulli Learning. (n.d.). Personalize learning for all students! Retrieved January 24, 2021 from: https://renzullilearning.com/

Richards, Z. J., & Stambaugh, T. (2015). National context of rural schools. In T. Stambaugh & S. Wood (Eds.), *Serving gifted students in rural settings* (pp. 1–21). Prufrock Press, Inc.

Rural School and Community Trust. (2013). It's complicated ... Why what's rural matters. Retrieved January 25, 2021 from: www.ruraledu.org/articles.php?id=3127#:~:text=A%20school%20is%20rural%20if,miles%20from%20an%20urbanized%20area

Stambaugh, T. (2015). Celebrating talent: Identification of rural gifted students. In T. Stambaugh & S. Wood (Eds.), *Serving gifted students in rural settings* (pp. 1–21). Prufrock Press, Inc.

Stambaugh, T., & Chandler, K. L. (2012). *Effective curriculum for underserved gifted students.* Prufrock Press.

Thier, M., Beach, P., Martinez Jr., C. R., & Hollenbeck, K. (2020). Take care when cutting: Five approaches to disaggregating school data as rural and remote. *Theory & Practice in Rural Education, 10*(2), 63–84.

U.S. Census Bureau (n.d.). Rural America. Retrieved from: https://mtgis-portal.geo.census.gov/arcgis/apps/MapSeries/index.html?appid=49cd4bc9c8eb444ab51218c1d5001ef6

Meeting the Needs of American Indian and Alaska Native Youth with Gifts and Talents

Anne Gray

There are more than 600 sovereign Native nations in the United States (Reclaiming Native Truth, 2019). Currently, 574 Native nations are federally recognized, 66 are state recognized (Salazar, 2020), and there are additional nations that, while recognized among other Native nations, are not recognized by state or federal political bodies (Reclaiming Native Truth, 2019). Each of these sovereign nations has a unique culture, an ancestral language, a relationship with the land of their ancestors that predates the formation of the United States, as well as an individual history and relationship with the U.S. federal government. In this chapter the terms *Native*, *Native American*, *Indigenous*, *American Indian* (AI), and *American Indian and Alaska Native* (AIAN) will be used interchangeably when discussing students being educated within the United States who identify themselves by one of these terms. Whenever possible, it is important to identify students by their specific Native nation(s) to distinguish the unique culture and history of those students. Ninety percent of the youth from Native nations attend public schools across all 50 states (U.S. Department of Education, 2008). In 2016, AIAN students were 1.04% of the public-school enrollment with 92% of those concentrated among 27 states (AK, AL, AZ, CA, CO, FL, ID, IL, KS, LA, MI, MN, MT, NC, ND, NE, NM, NV, NY, OK, OR, SD, TX, UT, WA, WI, WY) (Gentry & Gray, 2021).

Students with gifts and talents who identify as American Indian, Alaska Native, or by their tribal membership, are in need of greater consideration in identification and services for gifted education. AIAN students have less access to gifted education and lack equity of identification in schools with gifted education programming. On a daily basis, AIAN students are confronted by barriers directly related to educators who lack cultural competency, yet are responsible for their learning, and do not receive the same level of advocacy as students in other racial groups. In this chapter some barriers experienced by AIAN youth with gifts and talents will be identified and recommendations made for how to remove them or mitigate their impact on students.

The State of Education for AIAN Youth with Gifts and Talents

Underrepresentation of students from culturally and linguistically diverse backgrounds, as well as students from low-income backgrounds, is a familiar issue in gifted education (Ford & Harris, 1999; Gentry & Fugate, 2012; Gentry et al., 2014; Montgomery, 2001; Yoon & Gentry, 2009) with "volumes of literature" (Gentry et al., 2019, p. 11) dedicated to the disparities in educational quality, opportunities, and outcomes experienced by these

DOI: 10.4324/9781003265412-12

students. Yet AIAN students are rarely included in these discussions (Hodges et al., 2018; Gentry et al., 2014; Gentry & Gray, 2021). Gentry et al. (2014) proposed that AIAN youth have been excluded from analyses and receive less advocacy for their needs because they represent a small portion of U.S. students; 1.04% in 2015–2016 (U.S. Office for Civil Rights, 2018). Tuck and Yang (2012) call attention to the common representations of Indigenous peoples when they are included in research:

> Indigenous peoples are rendered visible in mainstream educational research in two main ways: as "at risk" peoples and as asterisk[1] peoples. This comprises a settler move to innocence because it erases and then conceals the erasure of Indigenous peoples within the settler colonial nation-state and moves Indigenous nations as "populations" to the margins of public discourse.
>
> (Tuck & Yang, 2012, p. 22)

As a result, research that reveals the problematic relationship of the U.S. educational system to AIAN peoples and the inequities imbedded within this framework is limited and sometimes dated. Yet the extant literature is necessary for a clearer understanding of the experiences of AIAN youth with gifts and talents in the U.S. educational system.

Limited Access to Gifted Education

Nationally, AIAN students have 8% less access to gifted education than all public-school students in the United States; meaning they are less likely to attend a school that identifies students with gifts and talents (Gentry et al., 2019) than all students. Of the four main categories of school locale (City, Suburb, Town, Rural), rural schools spent the least amount of funds and provided the fewest number of staff for gifted education (Kettler et al., 2015). Among the 27 states where 92% of AIAN students are enrolled, 40% attend rural schools compared to 16% of all students within these same states (Gentry & Gray, 2021).

Additionally, 80% of AIAN students attend Title I schools in comparison to 67% of all students nationally (Gentry & Gray, 2021). In their analysis, Gentry et al. (2019) used school Title I status as an indicator of schools with high concentrations of poverty. High concentrations of poverty in a school has been linked to high teacher turnover, less experienced teachers, less spending on gifted education, low student motivation, poor student academic attitudes, and student academic failure (Battistich et al., 1995; Clotfelter et al., 2007; Myers et al., 2004; Simon & Johnson, 2015; Vanderhaar, 2006). Title I schools were also found to identify a smaller percentage of students with gifts and talents than their Non-Title I counterparts. In fact, in 2015–2016 the identification rates were 7.86% and 13.46%, respectively (Gentry et al., 2019). In 18 of the 27 states analyzed by Gentry and Gray (2021), AIAN youth with gifts and talents were identified in Title I schools at rates less than 80% of the rates of identification in Non-Title I schools. Gentry et al. (2019) estimated that with the lack of access to identification and the lack of equity (underidentification) of identification in schools with identification across the nation, between 48% and 63% of AIAN students, or 24,290 to 44,663 AIAN students with gifts and talents were missing from identification in 2015–2016. In comparison, the rate of all students with gifts and talents missing from identification across the nation this same year was between 39% and 53% (Gentry et al., 2019).

Educational and Instructional Differences

DeVries and Golon (2011) found that a mismatch between the teachers' instructional styles and the learning styles of Navajo students put the students "at a distinct disadvantage" (p. 55). Seventy-one percent of the Navajo students in their study were identified as visual-spatial learners, yet the majority of the textbooks and a bulk of the teachers' instructional time focused on auditory-sequential instructional styles. Indigenous Students Leap Ahead (ISLA Project, 2017) has been successful at increasing the academic success of Native students using a strength-based curriculum which incorporates visual-spatial instructional styles as an important component of their programming.

A mismatch has also been found between the European-American (EA) cultural model of education, which schools generally assume in their design, and the American Indian (AI) cultural model. Both EA and AI cultural models of education view education as an important tool for individual success, but the AI model diverges in that ideas of individual success are held in tandem with community success (Fryberg & Markus, 2007). This finding is also reflected in the mismatch between the EA cultural model, which is present in most schools, that promotes and supports student views of self as independent, whereas the AI cultural model of the self is of the student as individualistic yet interdependent with their family/community (Fryberg et al., 2013).

Belonging and Identity

A discussion of the experiences of AIAN youth in terms of belonging and identity within schools cannot be an honest one unless the abuse and violence to AIAN children in the name of education is recognized and the continuing impact of intergenerational trauma from the *weaponization of education* against AIAN people is admitted. In the 1800s Indian boarding schools were developed with funding from the Indian Civilization Fund Act, Public Law 15–85 (1819), with the express intent to *civilize* Native children and assimilate them into settler society. This was done by isolating them from their families, cultures, and traditions in schools far from their homes where they were instructed in basic academics, agriculture (for boys), and homemaking (for girls). Native children were forced to attend these schools, to conform to settler dress standards, and to speak only English. The last of these boarding schools closed in the 1970s: "Given the substantial number of AIANs with some type of boarding school experience, it is clear that the boarding school experience should be viewed as a context for work with all AIANs" (Evans-Campbell et al., 2012, p. 426).[2]

In spite of these experiences, AIAN families value formal education and recognize its role in future opportunities. Developing a sense of belonging and identity in schools can be difficult for AIAN youth who experience invisibility, relegation to the historic past, and asterisking in American society. Fryberg and Townsend (2008) define invisibility as the "absence of positive or any representations of oppressed groups, particularly those whose voices are typically excluded from the dialogue about what is good or right in America" (p. 173). A national survey of K-12 U.S. History standards found that 87% of the standards pertaining to the cultures, histories, and lives of AIAN people end with the early 1900s (Shear et al., 2015). These representations of AIAN people communicate to students that there are no contemporary AIAN people, and that people who identify as

AIAN must live like those from the history books. There are few societal representations of successful contemporary AIAN people for AIAN youth to model ideas of their future selves on. This absence of representations implies that AIAN people have no belonging in contemporary settings, that people like them do not belong in contemporary life or professions (Fryberg & Townsend, 2008), and specifically, that people like them do not belong in educational settings. "The absence of a social representation is in itself a social representation" (Fryberg & Townsend, 2008, p. 178). The invisibility of AIAN peoples is so prevalent that 62% of Americans living outside of Indian Country (Native nation territories) have no familiarity with Native Americans (Reclaiming Native Truth Project, 2018). Most recently, this absence of representation inspired a former U.S. senator to publicly state that "nothing" was here when colonists arrived and that little Native American culture can be found within American culture (Jiménez, 2021).

In a school on a reservation with students from that Native nation, Jaramillo et al. (2016) analyzed the relationship between ethnic identity and academic achievement among high school students. Students who reported high ethnic identity and low stereotype threat had higher grade point averages than their peers. Additionally, students who reported low ethnic identify and high perceived discrimination had greater hopelessness. In this school where there was greater opportunity for AI students to have a sense of belonging, ethnic identity played a role in the students' academic achievement.

The narrative that AIAN students do not seek individual achievement is a misunderstanding. Fryberg and Markus (2003) found that AI and EA students had similar positive self-understanding and valuing of their individual achievement. Where these students diverged was in their self-concepts of their achievement. EA students viewed their individual achievement as independent or separate from others and social contexts. AI students viewed their individual achievement as interdependent with others and their community. The difficulty here being that within the U.S. education system, the self-concept that is promoted, supported, and expected is individual achievement as an independent autonomous act.

AIAN students with gifts and talents struggle with these same barriers to belonging and identity within educational settings. They experience invisibility and exclusion of their history post-1900 from the curriculum. They struggle to envision their future selves with no AIAN professionals offered as role models. With independent individual achievement as the systemic norm, some AIAN youth with gifts and talents may be perceived as not wanting individual achievement. Although many AIAN students will adapt their behavior to accommodate this expectation, without altering their concept of individual achievement as interdependent (Masta, 2018), sometimes the barriers are just too big for a child.

Vignette (Part I)

Consider the educational experiences of Bri. What are the underlying barriers to her academic success? What could have been done to remove the barriers or mitigate their impact?

Bri had always been at the top of her class in math at her school on the reservation. Not only was she good at it, but she really enjoyed the challenge. Her teacher would lead the whole class through each step of a solution to an example, then assign practice problems for students to work through. Bri and her classmates would work together to solve the problems, recording the processes on their own papers.

When Bri's family moved far from her reservation, things changed. Bri and her sibling were the only AIAN students in the school. The teacher moved more quickly through sample problems, skipping some of the steps of the solution. When Bri tried to work with other students she was told to do her own work. Bri started falling behind and math was not fun anymore.

During parent–teacher conferences, her parents requested that the teacher explain all steps of a solution. Instead, they were told she could ask the teacher for help when she did not understand. Bri could never find the right time to ask the teacher questions and never felt comfortable approaching the non-Native teachers in her new school. Bri's math grade fell to a D in the last semester before her family returned home to her reservation. How could Bri's teacher have responded differently? While Bri's mathematics knowledge was not advanced for this new school, her high achievement at her former school could have been considered as an indicator of high mathematics ability that needed nurturing and remediation in terms of the content she had not had access to. For this to happen, the National Association for Gifted Children (NAGC) (2011) recommends an intentional paradigm shift for educators from a deficit to a strength perspective regarding student abilities. If the school regarded establishing a strong connection with the community as an important value (NAGC, 2011), her teacher, or another staff member, would have taken the time to speak with Bri about the instructional style and content of her previous school. And they would have been more receptive to Bri's parents as they talked about the type of help they believed Bri needed in order to reengage with math learning. If these community ties were in place, perhaps her teacher would have been more culturally sensitive to the struggles of a female student from an invisible racialized group about speaking to an adult male from the cultural majority.

Within the first semester back in school on the reservation, Bri returned to being in the top of the class and math was a fun challenge again.

Identification and Assessment

To better understand the underidentification of AIAN students with gifts and talents in schools that identify, Table 7.1 and Figures 7.1 and 7.2 have been included. Table 7.1 shows the 27 states where 92% of AIAN youth are educated. The first two columns show the percentage of AIAN students identified in Non-Title I schools (column 1) and Title I schools (column 2). The ratio in the last column (column 3) compares the percentage of AIAN students identified in Title I schools (schools with greater concentration of poverty) to Non-Title I schools (schools with greater wealth). A ratio of 1.00 represents equal identification in both types of school. A ratio of less than 1.00 indicates a greater percentage of identification in Non-Title I schools, and a ratio of greater than 1.00 indicates a greater percentage of identification in Title I schools. Following the four-fifths rule adapted by Gentry et al. (2019), ratios less than 0.80 are considered discriminatory and as having "adverse impact" on AIAN students (p. 21). Eighteen of the 27 states have ratios which show that the percentage of AIAN students identified in Title I schools is less than 80% of

Table 7.1 Percentage of AIAN Students, with Access to Identification, Identified as Gifted in Non-Title I and Title I Schools with Ratio Between School Types for 2015–2016 in 27 States.

State	% Students ID as GT in Non-Title I Schools	% Students ID as GT in Title I Schools	Ratio of ID in Title I Schools to Non-Title I Schools
AK	2.75	2.06	**0.75**
AL	12.02	11.51	0.96
AZ	5.26	4.10	**0.78**
CA	8.30	6.78	0.82
CO	4.80	2.81	**0.58**
FL	8.04	4.75	**0.59**
ID	1.75	2.08	1.18
IL	6.58	6.95	1.06
KS	2.30	1.75	**0.76**
LA	7.84	2.65	**0.34**
MI	11.72	5.33	**0.46**
MN	7.47	9.68	1.30
MT	3.82	3.52	0.92
NC	13.80	6.16	**0.45**
ND	4.02	10.99	2.73
NE	7.03	5.42	**0.77**
NM	4.27	3.21	**0.75**
NV	4.40	3.19	**0.73**
NY	12.99	9.56	**0.74**
OK	21.83	14.08	**0.64**
OR	3.68	1.55	**0.42**
SD	2.60	1.59	**0.61**
TX	7.62	5.39	**0.71**
UT	10.64	4.65	**0.44**
WA	2.70	2.60	0.96
WI	3.36	4.63	1.38
WY	11.00	2.21	**0.20**
27 States Average	8.70	7.94	0.91

Note: Ratios in bold font are less than 0.80 and indicate serious inequity in rates of identification in Title I schools.

identification in Non-Title I schools, meaning that attendance at Title I schools has adverse impact on the identification of AIAN students with gifts and talents.

Figures 7.1 and 7.2 use Representation Indices (RI) to show the ratio of the percentage of AIAN youth in a state's enrollment to the percentage of AIAN youth identified with gifts and talents in the state (gifted program AIAN%/enrollment AIAN%). An RI of 1.00 represents equitable identification of AIAN students (e.g., gifted program 20% AIAN/enrollment 20% AIAN = RI of 1.00). An RI of less than 1.00 indicates there is underidentification of AIAN youth with gifts and talents (e.g., gifted program 10% AIAN/ enrollment 20% AIAN = RI of 0.50). RIs of greater than 1.00 indicate AIAN youth are well identified, with a greater percentage identified than in the enrollment (e.g., gifted program 25% AIAN/enrollment 20% AIAN = RI of 1.25). Again, the four-fifths rule is followed and RIs below 0.80 are considered discriminatory.

In both figures, 21 of the 27 states have underidentified AIAN youth with gifts and talents at RIs which show adverse impact to these students. Title I and Non-Title I schools are displayed separately because Gentry et al. (2019) found that although Title I schools identified a smaller percentage of students with gifts and talents, they identified culturally

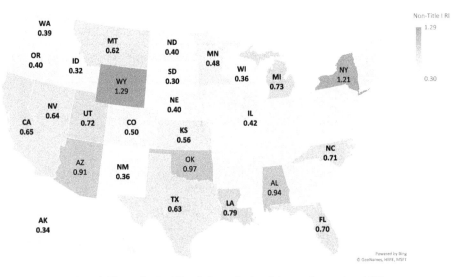

Representation Indices in bold font are less than 0.80 and indicate serious inequity between the percentage of AIAN youth enrolled and the percentage of AIAN youth with gifts and talents identified.

Microsoft product screen shots reprinted with permission from Microsoft Corporation.

www.microsoft.com/en-us/maps/product/print-rights

Figure 7.1 Non-Title I School Representation Indices for AIAN Students in 27 States, 2015–2016

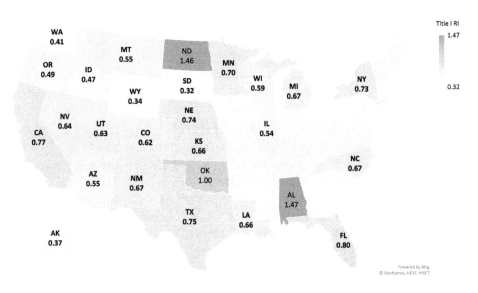

Representation Indices in bold font are less than 0.80 and indicate serious inequity between the percentage of AIAN youth enrolled and the percentage of AIAN youth with gifts and talents identified.

Microsoft product screen shots reprinted with permission from Microsoft Corporation.

www.microsoft.com/en-us/maps/product/print-rights

Figure 7.2 Title I School Representation Indices for AIAN Students in 27 States, 2015–2016

and linguistically diverse students more equitably. In comparing the RIs for each state in Figure 7.1 to Figure 7.2, in 18 states, AIAN youth have greater equity of representation in Title I schools, although 14 of these are still below the 0.80 threshold.

The identification and assessment process must be entered with an understanding of the historical and contemporary experiences of AIAN youth within educational/societal settings. To do otherwise and promote a *colorblind* ideology (Fryberg & Stephens, 2010) in the identification process is to have what Dr. M. L. King, Jr. referred to as "sincere ignorance and conscientious stupidity" (King, 1963, p. 46). In short, equitable identification and assessment of AIAN youth with gifts and talents will require mindful effort.

Lessons from Research-Based Practices

Identification and Local Norms

Just as there are often mismatches between the instructional styles of teachers and the learning styles of AIAN students, mismatches occur in the identification and assessment process. For example, in her work with students with gifts and talents from minority groups, with a focus on Indigenous populations, Bevan-Brown (1999) noted that she often found schools/institutions maintained they identified students with gifts and talents from numerous domains of gifts/talents in an effort to be more inclusive of students from culturally/linguistically/economically diverse backgrounds. But in practice, identification was limited to two, perhaps three, domains. For example, a state definition of giftedness/talent may include the domain of leadership, yet districts rely heavily on assessments of academic achievement and intelligence tests that are fundamentally biased against non-White populations and those from low socioeconomic backgrounds (Gentry et al., in press).

Additionally, ideas of what is a gift/talent/special ability are culturally bound. In some cases what is considered a gift/talent/special ability may be very different; in others, these ideas could be the same yet focus on different aspects of the gift/talent/ability (Bevan-Brown, 1999). This highlights the importance of having culturally competent teachers. Teachers need to be knowledgeable not only of the cultures of their students, but of their own cultures and the influence they exert on the cultures of their students (Bevan-Brown, 1999).

Due to the lack of AIAN social representations and the absence of familiarity with AIAN peoples in the general public, schools are recommended to use the HOPE Teacher Rating Scale (Gentry et al., 2015) as a screening tool. The HOPE Scale was normed on a highly diverse group of students, and Native American students were intentionally included in the norming group. With this screening tool, a pool of students is created for either talent development or further appraisal of potential gifts/talents.

For the same reasons (invisibility), as well as the increased likelihood that AIAN students attend schools with high concentrations of poverty, it is highly recommended that local group norms be used when academic assessments must be used for program qualification. Local norms are the score norms within the building, and local group norms are the score norms of students identified with a specific group using factors such as gender, race, or family income level.

Curriculum and Instruction

Curriculum is where educators can begin to rectify the invisibility and relegation to the historic past experienced by AIAN students within society at large. A starting point for educators is to educate themselves in the history of AIAN peoples in general, and in the history of the Native nations of their students and to share what they learn with their students and colleagues. Also, when engaging students in reviewing the accomplishments of experts, seek out examples of contemporary AIAN experts to present to the class. At the end of the chapter are the names of some individuals and recommended sources of information.

With data indicating a higher percentage of AIAN youth having visual-spatial learning strengths, teachers are advised to ask themselves, "How can I show this?" when designing instruction, and ask, "How can they show me?" when designing formative assessments. For example, rather than exclusively using phonetics for reading instruction, include whole word instruction (DeVries & Golon, 2011). Identify alternative forms of products that display mastery of content. Writing a story is not the only way for a student to show they understand the elements of a story. This can be done through verbal storytelling, dictation of a story, drawing a story board, or even acting the story out as a short play.

As mentioned earlier, individual achievement or success is an educational value held by AIAN students but it is tied to community success/achievement. This value often conflicts with the independent work and individual success focus found in most classrooms. This conflict can lead to AIAN students not having a sense of belonging or feeling they cannot be successful in this type of classroom environment (Fryberg et al., 2013). An instructional strategy for this mismatch is collaborative learning groups, creating small groups for students to work in to develop solutions, answers, or a product.

Role of Family

AIAN families, though not always trusting of educational institutions, are supportive of their students' education and recognize its value in providing future opportunities. As mentioned earlier, ideas of what is a gift/talent/special ability are culturally bound and may vary in focus, importance, or be entirely different (Bevan-Brown, 1999). It is important that teachers be culturally competent to discuss what gifts and talents can be identified and served in the school.

With a cultural model of self as an individual interdependent with family/community, it should not be a surprise that family/community relationships are often prioritized ahead of education for AIAN youth with gifts and talents. As this is the cultural norm for AIAN students and their families, they may not anticipate a school responding out of assumptions of an EA cultural model in which individual academic success is prioritized ahead of family/community. It is the responsibility of the educators and educational institutions to be knowledgeable and respectful of the cultures of their students and to establish policies that reflect this knowledge and respect. Being inclusive of AIAN cultures at the policy level can aid in building relationships with the students, their families, and their communities.

AIAN students in higher education reported persisting through difficult situations to: not disappoint their families, make life better for their families, to give back to their families, to give back to their communities (Guillory & Wolverton, 2008). While these students are older, these same motivations can be found among AIAN youth with gifts and talents. Family and community as a motivation to persist can be tapped into through student passion projects that center on topics students are concerned about or want to support within their families/communities.

Vignette (Part II)

When Bri had her first menstrual cycle, her family immediately began preparations for her to have the traditional ceremony for growing from a child to a young woman. Bri was excited to go back home and to have her ceremony, but she didn't tell anyone at her school. She didn't want to have to explain *everything*.

Bri's parents called the school to arrange for her to get her assignments for the week of school she would miss. They were informed that Bri's absence would not be excused unless they had a letter explaining why the absence was necessary from a healthcare provider, minister/priest, or professional personnel and the reason was accepted by the district. Her parents let the absence be unexcused. They didn't want to have to explain *everything*.

Masta (2018) noted that behavior like Bri's occurred on a regular basis among Native American students attending a mainstream school. The AIAN students displayed pride in their identities as Native people among other Native students, talking about their participation in traditional practices, wearing jewelry or clothing with motifs from Native nations on them. But among mixed groups of peers, their conversations focused on mainstream topics like music, movies, and sports. Bri and her parents engaged in what Brayboy et al. (2007) and Masta (2018) refer to as accommodation. While they took pride in and actively participated in their Native traditions, they did not actively engage with non-Natives at the school around topics that positioned them as *outsiders* in the mainstream school setting (Brayboy et al., 2007; Masta, 2018).

Additional Classroom Strategies

With the mismatch between school cultures which focus on independent achievement and AIAN cultures which focus on interdependent achievement, Fryberg and Markus (2007) recommend creating an educational environment that builds and supports relationships. As mentioned earlier, collaborative learning groups or small group work/projects are an instructional way to build and support relationships between AIAN students and non-AIAN students. It is very important for teachers of AIAN students to build relationships, close and trusting relationships, with their students. For AIAN people it is even considered a "necessary element of the learning process" (Fryberg & Markus, 2007, p. 240). To do this teachers need to have knowledge of the students' culture, history, their personal interests, and even their concerns and then reflect this knowledge of the students by integrating it into the curriculum and instruction (Fryberg & Markus, 2007).

Recommendations

There is no single solution or one way to mitigate the barriers to equity in education experienced by AIAN students with gifts and talents, but there are actionable steps that can be taken. Policies and practices can be implemented, from the classroom to the state, that increase equitable identification, align with the cultural norms of Native communities, and incorporate contemporary Native nations and peoples into the curriculum. All educators at all levels are responsible for creating educational environments which build relationships between Native and non-Native peoples and support Native students in general, and those with gifts and talents, in their educational pursuits.

Being a culturally competent educator with regards to Native students and Native nations takes intentionality. With more than 600 Native nations, it can be difficult to filter available information for what is relevant to your student(s) and/or situation. The U.S. Department of Health and Human Services publication *American Indian and Alaska Native Culture Card: A Guide to Build Awareness* (2009) provides guidance for being culturally respectful, it dispels myths, and gives insight into aspects of these cultures that can be safely generalized. The National Museum of the American Indian website (Smithsonian Institute, n.d.) has curated online exhibitions and other resources that may also be helpful in understanding some historic and contemporary topics among Native nations.

The recommendations made here are of the broad stroke type. They are generalized to AIAN youth rather than specific to youth from individual Native nations and they range from the level of student–teacher interactions to state policies.

- Hire culturally competent teachers: Educators need to be knowledgeable of AIAN cultures and history, both in general and specific to the Native nations of their students, as well as aware of their own cultures and the influence it exerts on the cultures of their students (Bevan-Brown, 1999).
- The HOPE Teacher Rating Scale (Gentry et al., 2015) is a screening tool for identifying students with gifts and talents normed on AIAN students.
- Local group norms should be used when academic assessments must be used for program qualification.
- Educators can help to rectify the invisibility, relegation to the historic past, and asterisking experienced by AIAN students by educating themselves about the history and cultures of their AIAN students and sharing what they learn with their colleagues and students.
- Integrate examples of contemporary AIAN experts into the curriculum.
- Incorporate the literature of AIAN poets and authors into the curriculum.
- Display and discuss the art of AIAN artists.
- When creating lesson plans, teachers should ask themselves, "How can I show this?", and when designing formative assessments ask, "How can they show me?"
- Incorporate collaborative learning groups/small group work into curriculum/lesson plans.
- When establishing classroom/school policies, be inclusive of AIAN cultural norms to aid in building relationships with students, families, and communities.
- Incorporate student passion projects that center on topics students want to address in their families/communities.

Table 7.2 American Indian and Alaska Native Professionals (this list is not exhaustive)

Name	Profession(s)
Sherman Alexie	Author
Lori Alvord	Surgeon, Author
Wilson Aronilth, Jr.	Diné Studies Faculty at Diné College, Philosopher, Educator, Diné Spiritual Leader
Fred Begay	Nuclear Physicist
Bryan Brayboy	Professor of Indigenous Education and Justice at Arizona State University
Gregory Cajete	Author, Professor of Native American Studies and Language, Literacy, and Sociocultural Studies at University of New Mexico
Walter Echo-Hawk	Author, Lawyer, Indigenous Rights Activist
Louise Erdrich	Author of novels and children's books, Poet
Dallas Goldtooth	Environmental Activist, Dakota Language Instructor
Joy Harjo	Poet Laureate, Musician, Author
Sterlin Harjo	Filmmaker
Adrienne J. Keene	Assistant Professor of American Studies and Ethnic Studies at Brown University, Podcast producer, Blogger
Winona LaDuke	Author, Environmentalist, Economist
Terese Marie Mailhot	Author, Journalist, Educator
Stephanie Masta-Zywicki	Assistant Professor of Curriculum Studies at Purdue University
N. Scott Momaday	Author, Poet
Migizi Pensoneau	Television and Film Writer and Producer
Ryan Red Corn	Graphic Artist, Photographer
Luana Ross	Associate Professor Emerita of Gender, Women & Sexuality Studies at University of Washington
Mary Golda Ross	Engineer
Maria Tallchief	Prima Ballerina
James Welch	Author
Matika Wilbur	Educator, Photographer, Podcast producer, Blogger
Bobby Wilson	Visual Artist, Actor
John Baker	Musher
Ron Baker	Basketball player
Ryneldi Becenti	Basketball player
Notah Begay III	Golfer
Sam Bradford	Football player
Jacoby Ellsbury	Basketball player
Ryan Helsley	Basketball player
Kali Reis	Boxer
Shoni Schimmel	Basketball player
Chris and Stephen Wondolowski	Soccer players
Twyla Baker	President, Nueta Hidatsa Sahnish
Tom Cole	Oklahoma U.S. Representative
Sharice Davids	Kansas U.S. Representative
Deb Haaland	U.S. Secretary of the Interior (first Native American cabinet secretary)
Markwayne Mullin	Oklahoma U.S. Representative

Table 7.3 American Indian and Alaska Native Helpful Resources (this list is not exhaustive)

"American Indian College Fund: Education is the Answer." American Indian College Fund. Accessed September 9, 2019. https://collegefund.org

"American Indian Science and Engineering Society." American Indian Science and Engineering Society. Accessed September 9, 2019. www.aises.org

"Center for Native American Youth." The Aspen Institute. Accessed September 9, 2019. www.cnay.org

Dunbar-Ortiz, Roxanne, Jean Mendoza, & Debbie Reese. *An Indigenous Peoples' History of the United States for Young People*. Boston, MA: Beacon Press, 2019.

"562: Changing the Way We See Native America." Project 562. Accessed September 9, 2019. www.project562.com

"For Our Future: An Advocate's Guide to Supporting Indigenous Peoples' Day." Illuminative. Accessed October 17, 2019. https://illuminatives.org/wp-content/uploads/2019/10/Indigenous_Peoples_Day_Toolkit_FINAL_PAGES.pdf

"Honor Native Land: A Guide and Call to Acknowledgement." U.S. Department of Arts and Culture. Accessed September 9, 2019. https://usdac.us/nativeland

"Honor the Earth." Honor the Earth. Accessed September 9, 2019. www.honorearth.org

"Indian Country Today: Digital Indigenous News." News Maven. Accessed September 9, 2019. https://newsmaven.io/indiancountrytoday/

"The ISLA Project: The Missing Link in American Indian Education." ISLA. Accessed September 9, 2019. www.islaproject.org

Keene, Adrienne. *Notable Native People: 50 Indigenous Leaders, Dreamers, and Changemakers from Past and Present.* Berkley, CA: Ten Speed Press, 2021.

Masta, Stephanie. "Strategy and Resistance: How Native American Students Engage in Accommodation in Mainstream Schools." *Anthropology & Education Quarterly, 49*(1) (2018): 21–35. doi:10.1111/aeq.12231

"National Congress of American Indians." National Congress of American Indians. Accessed September 9, 2019. /www.ncai.org/about-tribes

"National Indian Education Association." NIEA. Accessed September 9, 2019. www.niea.org

"Native American and Indigenous Studies Association." NAISA. Accessed September 9, 2019. www.naisa.org

"Nihewan Foundation for Native American Education." Nihewan Foundation. Accessed September 9, 2019. www.nihewan.org

"Reclaiming Native Truth: A Project to Dispel America's Myths and Misconceptions." Reclaiming Native Truth. Accessed September 9, 2019. https://rnt.firstnations.org

"SACNAS: Advancing Chicanos/Hispanic and Native Americans in Science." SACNAS. Accessed September 9, 2019. www.sacnas.org

- Create an educational environment, in the classroom and at the building level, that builds and supports relationships between AIAN students and non-AIAN students.
- Teachers must find ways to develop a close trusting relationship with their AIAN students as it is a "necessary element of the learning process" (Fryberg & Markus, 2007, p. 240) for AIAN students.
- Incorporate knowledge of AIAN students' cultures, history, personal interests, and concerns into the curriculum.

Conclusion

"There's nothing *not* complicated about being Indian" (Masta-Zywicki, 2013, p. 1). In educational settings, many of the complications that arise for AIAN youth with gifts and talents are directly related to their invisibility, relegation to the historic past, and asterisking. AIAN individuals have limited access to gifted education programming and identification because they are more likely to attend schools: without gifted education; in rural areas with less resources devoted to gifted education; that are Title I schools which identify a smaller percentage as gifted than Non-Title I schools; that lack equity in the identification of AIAN youth with gifts and talents.

Additionally, AIAN students experience mismatches between their learning styles and instructional styles, their cultural norms and the cultural norms of educational institutions, and their gifts and talents and the gifts and talents identified and assessed by schools/ districts/states. Good intentions are not enough. It is the impact of actions that makes a difference, trusting relationships cannot be built on "sincere ignorance and conscientious stupidity" (King, 1963, p. 46).

Notes

1 In the majority of educational research, AIAN populations are excluded from analyses and represented through the use of an asterisk or a footnote.
2 For a deeper understanding of Indian Education, see Dunbar-Ortiz (2014) and Adams (1995).

References

Adams, D. (1995). *Education for extinction: American Indians and the boarding school experience, 1875–1928.* Lawrence, KS: University Press of Kansas.

Battistich, V., Solomon, D., Kim, D. I., Watson, M., & Schaps, E. (1995). Schools as communities, poverty levels of student populations, and students' attitudes, motives, and performance: A multilevel analysis. *American Educational Research Journal, 32,* 627– 658. doi: 10.3102/00028312032003627

Bevan-Brown, J. (1999). Special abilities: A Maori perspective, implications for catering for gifted children from minority cultures. *Gifted Education International, 14,* 86–96. doi: 10.1177/026142949901400110

Brayboy, B. M. J., Castagno, A. E., & Maughan, E. (2007). Chapter 6: Equality and justice for all? Examining race in education scholarship. *Review of Research in Education, 31*(1), 159–194. https://doi.org/10.3102/0091732X07300046159

Clotfelter, C., Ladd, H. F., Vigdor, J., & Wheeler, J. (2007). High-poverty schools and the distribution of teachers and principals. *North Carolina Law Review, 85*(5), 1345–1380.

DeVries, M., & Golon, A. S. (2011). Making education relevant for gifted Native Americans: Teaching to their learning style. In J. A. Castellano & A. D. Frazier (Eds.), *Special populations in gifted education: Understanding our most able students from diverse backgrounds* (pp. 47–72). Waco, TX: Prufrock Press Inc.

Dunbar-Ortiz, R. (2014). *An Indigenous peoples' history of the United States.* Boston, MA: Beacon Press.

Evans-Campbell, T., Walters, K. L., Pearson, C. R., & Campbell, C. D. (2012). Indian boarding school experience, substance use, and mental health among urban Two-Spirit American Indian/ Alaska Natives. *The American Journal of Drug and Alcohol Abuse, 38*(5), 421–427. doi: 10.3109/00952990.2012.701358

Ford, D. Y., & Harris, J. J. (1999). *Multicultural gifted education.* New York: Teachers College Press.

Fryberg, S. A., Covarrubias, R., & Burack, J. A. (2013). Cultural models of education and academic performance for Native American and European American students. *School Psychology International, 34*(4), 439–452. doi: 10.1177/0143034312446892

Fryberg, S. A., & Markus, H. R. (2003). On being American Indian: Current and possible selves. *Self and Identity, 2,* 325–344. doi: 10.1080/714050251

Fryberg, S. A., & Markus, H. R. (2007). Cultural models of education in American Indian, Asian American and European American contexts. *Social Psychology of Education, 10,* 213–246. doi: 10.1007/s11218-007-9017-z

Fryberg, S. A., & Stephens, N. M. (2010). When the world is colorblind, American Indians are invisible: A diversity science approach. *Psychological Inquiry, 21*(2), 155–119. doi: 10.1080/1047840X.2010.483847

Fryberg, S. A., & Townsend, S. S. M. (2008). The psychology of invisibility. In G. Adams, M. Biernat, N. R. Branscombe, C. S. Crandall & L. S. Wrightsman (Eds.), *Commemorating Brown: The social psychology of racism and discrimination* (pp. 173–193). Washington, DC: American Psychological Association.

Gentry, M., Desmet, O. A., Karami, S., Lee, H., Green, C., Cress, A., ... Gray, A. (in press). Gifted education's legacy of high stakes ability testing: Using measures for identification that perpetuate inequity. Roeper Review.

Gentry, M., & Fugate, C. M. (2012). Gifted Native American students: Underperforming, under-identified, and overlooked. *Psychology in the Schools, 49,* 631–646. https://doi.org/10.1002/pits.21624

Gentry, M., Fugate, C. M., Wu, J., & Castellano, J. A. (2014). Gifted Native American students: Literature, lessons, and future directions. *Gifted Child Quarterly, 58,* 98–110. https://doi.org/10.1177/0016986214521660

Gentry, M., & Gray, A. (2021) *American Indian and Alaska Native identified as gifted: Access, representation, and missingness.* Manuscript submitted for publication.

Gentry, M., Gray, A., Whiting, G. W., Maeda, Y., & Pereira, N. (2019). *Access denied/system failure: Gifted education in the United States: Laws, access, equity, and missingness across the country by locale, Title I school status, and race* (Report Cards, Technical Report, and Website). West Lafayette, IN: Purdue University; Lansdowne, VA: Jack Kent Cooke Foundation.

Gentry, M., Peters, S. J., Pereira, N., McIntosh, J., & Fugate, C. M. (2015). *HOPE Teacher Rating Scale (manual): Involving teachers in equitable identification of gifted and talented students in K-12.* Waco, TX: Prufrock Press Inc.

Guillory, R. M., & Wolverton, M. (2008). It's about family: Native American student persistence in higher education. *The Journal of Higher Education, 79*(1), 58–87.

Hodges, J., Tay, T., Maeda, Y., & Gentry, M. (2018). A meta-analysis of gifted and talented identification practices. *Gifted Child Quarterly, 62,* 147–174. https://doi.org/10.1177/0016986217752107

Indian Civilization Fund Act (1819). Public Law 15–85. Retrieved from: https://govtrackus.s3.amazonaws.com/legislink/pdf/stat/3/STATUTE-3-Pg516b.pdf

The ISLA Project. (2017). Indigenous students leap ahead: The missing link in American Indian education. Retrieved from: www.islaproject.org/

Jaramillo, J., Mello, Z. R., & Worrell, F. C. (2016). Ethnic identity, stereotype threat, and perceived discrimination among Native American adolescents. *Journal of Research on Adolescence, 26,* 769–775. https://doi.org/10.1111/jora.12228

Jiménez, J. (2021, May 22). CNN drops Rick Santorum after dismissive comments about Native Americans. *The New York Times.* Retrieved from: www.nytimes.com/2021/05/22/business/media/rick-santorum-cnn.html

Kettler, T., Russell, J., & Puryear, J. S. (2015). Inequitable access to gifted education: Variance in funding and staffing based on locale and contextual school variables. *Journal for the Education of the Gifted, 38,* 99–117. https://doi.org/10.1177/0162353215578277

King, M. L., Jr. (1963). *Strength to love.* Minneapolis, MN: Fortress Press.

Masta, S. (2018). Strategy and resistance: How Native American students engage in accommodation in mainstream schools. *Anthropology & Education Quarterly, 49*(1), 21–35. doi: 10.1111/aeq.12231

Masta-Zywicki, S. (2013). *"There's nothing not complicated about being Indian": American Indian student experiences in mainstream middle school* (130130) [Doctoral dissertation, Iowa State University]. Iowa State University Capstones, Theses and Dissertations.

Montgomery, D. (2001). Increasing Native American Indian involvement in gifted programs in rural schools. *Psychology in the Schools, 38,* 467–475. https://doi.org/10.1002/pits.1035

Myers, S. L., Jr., Kim, H., & Mandala, C. (2004). The effect of school poverty on racial gaps in test scores: The case of the Minnesota basic standards tests. *Journal of Negro Education, 73,* 81–98. doi: 10.2307/3211261

National Association for Gifted Children [NAGC]. (2011, November). Identifying and serving culturally and linguistically diverse gifted students. Retrieved from: www.nagc.org/sites/default/files/Position%20Statement/Identifying%20and%20Serving%20Culturally%20and%20Linguistically.pdf

Reclaiming Native Truth. (2018). *Research findings: Compilation of all research.* Retrieved from: www.firstnations.org/publications/compilation-of-all-research-from-the-reclaiming-native-truth-project/

Reclaiming Native Truth. (2019). *Changing the narrative about Native Americans: A guide for allies.* Retrieved from: www.firstnations.org/publications/changing-the-narrative-about-native-americans-a-guide-for-allies/

Salazar, M. (2020, March). Federal and state recognized tribes. Retrieved from: www.ncsl.org/legislators-staff/legislators/quad-caucus/list-of-federal-and-state-recognized-tribes.aspx

Shear, S. B., Knowles, R. T., Soden, G. J., & Castro, A. J. (2015). Manifesting destiny: Re/presentations of Indigenous peoples in K-12 U.S. history standards. *Theory & Research in Social Education, 43*(1), 68–101. doi: 10.1080/00933104.2014.999849

Simon, N. S., & Johnson, S. M. (2015). Teacher turnover in high-poverty schools: What we know and can do. *Teachers College Record, 117,* 1–36. Retrieved from: www.tcrecord.org/Content.asp?ContentId=17810

Smithsonian Institute. (n.d.). National Museum of the American Indian. Retrieved from: https://americanindian.si.edu/.

Tuck, E., & Yang, K. W. (2012). Decolonization is not a metaphor. *Decolonization: Indigeneity, Education & Society, 1*(1), 1–40.

U.S. Department of Education. (2008, September). *Status and trends in the education of American Indians and Alaska Natives: 2008* (NCES 2008–084). Washington, DC: Government Printing Office. Retrieved from: https://nces.ed.gov/pubs2008/2008084.pdf

U.S. Department of Health and Human Services. (2009). *American Indian and Alaska Native culture card: A guide to build cultural awareness.* Substance Abuse and Mental Health Services Administration. Retrieved from: https://store.samhsa.gov/sites/default/files/d7/priv/sma08-4354.pdf

U.S. Office for Civil Rights. (2018). *The civil rights data collection.* Washington, DC: U.S. Department of Education, Author.

Vanderhaar, J. E., Muñoz, M. A., & Rodosky, R. J. (2006). Leadership as accountability for learning: The effects of school poverty, teacher experience, previous achievement, and principal preparation programs on student achievement. *Journal of Personnel Evaluation in Education, 19,* 17–33. https://doi.org/10.1007/s11092-007-9033-8

Yoon, S. Y., & Gentry, M. (2009). Racial and ethnic representation in gifted programs: Current status of and implications for gifted Asian American students. *Gifted Child Quarterly, 53,* 121–136. https://doi.org/10.1177/0016986208330564

Chapter 8

Fostering Cultural Capital and Creativity for Recruitment and Retention

A Holistic Approach to Serving Gifted Black Students in Gifted Education

Kristina Henry Collins and Tiombe Bisa Kendrick-Dunn

More recently in the United States, there has been a renewed focus on social justice, including the creation of the Black Lives Matter movement, and its application to the education of students of color. The call to action has come on the heels of the recent murders of George Floyd, Breonna Taylor, Ahmaud Arbery and Rayshard Brooks – demanding that everyone do more work in promoting social justice, especially for the Black population in the United States. Across the nation, communities including schools are dealing with the negative consequences of social injustice which include economic marginalization, structural racism, systematic racism, discrimination, inequity, violence, and isolation. The capacity and well-being of our nation's children are undermined as a result of these decades-long challenges. For far too long, similar inequities have been the status quo in Gifted Education and continue to be experienced by many students of color across this nation. Teachers and school-based mental health professionals responsible for nurturing and educating and guiding Black gifted students can begin this process by fiercely advocating for their well-being and access to high-quality and culturally responsive educational opportunities and experiences that will become a catalyst to their success. All educational professionals at all levels must be held accountable for the educational and social-emotional development and wellness of these students. They must ensure that social-emotional development and overall health and wellness are priorities integrated in curriculum planning and implementation. Educators must dedicate themselves to become advocates for systems and services that reduce barriers and create genuine, sustained, and equitable opportunities for each and every student. As a case and point, meet Gizelle:

Vignette: Gizelle

Gizelle, an unidentified gifted Black female, exhibited a strong sense of self that included a dual-identity as a student scholar and creative performer. In addition to these identities she exhibited other commonly accepted cognitive, creative, affective, and behavioral traits of giftedness (e.g., unusual alertness, rapid learning, pronounced attention to linguistic and nonverbal nuances, advanced comprehension of abstract ideas, keen sense of humor, independence in attitude and social behavior, insatiable curiosity, leadership, and an eager spirit, to name just a few). Yet Gizelle entered 10th grade as an unidentified gifted student who had been accepted, with a special waiver, into a high school magnet school-within-a-school program designed for gifted and

---

DOI: 10.4324/9781003265412-13

highly talented students. When questioned about her unidentified gifted status, she declared, "I was never referred by my teachers even though I made the highest grades in all of my classes. My friends weren't in EXCEL [district's gifted program name] so I didn't care. I knew I was smart". Gizelle graduated high school in the Top 10 of her class, and went on to earn several college scholarships including the highly competitive, half-million-dollar, Bill and Melinda Gates Millennium Scholarship. By all measures, she fared well without the gifted label. However, this does not pardon the ineffectual policies, practices, and programming systems that failed her.

Stories similar to Gizelle's are far too common without schools' accountability for institutional and systemic change – the level of significant change that is necessary to be considered social justice.

Any discussion of identification and assessment of giftedness must begin with a definition of giftedness. Added to the problem of varied definitions is the interpretation, alignment, and validity of items within an assessment that are designed to measure the construct (Mayes et al., 2018). For the purpose of this chapter, the authors identify and use as a frame for common understanding, the 1993 U.S. federal definition of gifted students as being the most inclusive:

> Children and youth with outstanding talent perform or show the potential for performing at remarkably high levels of accomplishment when compared with others of their age, experience, or environment. These children and youth exhibit high performance capacity in intellectual, creative, and/or artistic areas, and unusual leadership capacity, or excel in specific academic fields. They require services or activities not ordinarily provided by the schools. Outstanding talents are present in children and youth from all cultural groups, across all economic strata, and in all areas of human endeavor.
> (Ross & Office of Educational Research and Improvement, 1994, p.11)

Although the role of creativity has been established as a gifted student characteristic and essential domain in gifted education policies and practices (National Association for Gifted Children & The Council for State Directors for Programs for the Gifted [NAGC & CSDPG], 2015), its positive impact on equity in gifted education for culturally and linguistically different (CLD) and low-income students has been neglected. Despite the browning of the United States' (U.S.) K-12 student population, the teaching force has not kept pace with the ethnic and racial make-up of children in America's classrooms. Today, fewer than 20% of teachers in the United States identify themselves as ethnically and culturally diverse. In fact, approximately 80% of the individuals in the teaching force are White females (Fay, 2018; Office for Civil Rights, n.d.). Given the difference in demographics, paying attention to the cultural capital and experiences of students is critically important.

Traditional Recruitment and Identification Methods for GATE

As with the case of Gizelle, traditional recruitment and identification of gifted students often start with teachers' referrals (Collins et al., 2019). During the process of identification, the referring teacher typically completes some type of rating scale designed to identify culture-neutral characteristics of gifted children. However, it has been well documented that such "colorblind" assessments emulate sameness standardized by the dominant culture, dismissing others (Bostick, 2016; Collins, 2018; Ford et al., 2018). These, as initial steps for identification and selection, create initial barriers and contribute to the underrepresentation of Black students in gifted and advanced academic programs (Grissom et al., 2017).

Use of Intelligence (IQ) and Academic Achievement Tests

The use of IQ and/or academic achievement tests to identify gifted students is the norm in many public-school districts and within the fields of school and clinical psychology. The selection and use of intelligence (IQ) and academic achievement tests in the identification process of culturally and linguistically diverse (CLD) students for special education programs are fraught with controversy, limit consequential validity, and diminish fairness in the assessment process (Graves & Mitchell, 2011). From a historical perspective, IQ tests have been solicited to legitimize claims that Black people are both intellectually and racially inferior to those of European descent and to defend the segregation of students based on race (Shealey et al., 2011). The administration of culturally biased instruments has created decades-long consequences which have resulted in the overrepresentation of Black children in special education and underrepresentation in gifted education programs (Kearns et al., 2005; Proctor et al., 2012). Results of the infamous Larry P. court case in the State of California is worth mentioning and relevant to this issue.

In 1979, the United States District Court for the Northern District of California issued a decision in Larry P. *v* Riles against a public-school superintendent (Riles). The court found that the San Francisco Unified School District failed to provide Larry P. and students in a similar situation with equitable education opportunities and thus violated the equal protection clause of the 14th amendment of the U.S. Constitution. The court accepted the argument that Larry P. was treated unfairly because standardized IQ tests, normed on White students from middle-class backgrounds and not Black students, were used to place him in "dead end" special education classes (Wade, 1980).

The plaintiffs in the case charged that IQ tests used in the placement of Black students in special education contained racial and cultural biases, discriminated against Black children, and resulted in placing them in classes that subjected them to "stigma, inadequate education, and failure to develop the skills necessary to productive success in society" (Wade, 1980, p. 1196). Most importantly, the plaintiffs charged that the gross overrepresentation of Black children in Educable Mentally Retarded (EMR) classes in proportion to their numbers in the general student population confirmed the racial bias of IQ tests. Although Larry P. and his fellow plaintiffs were not the first group of people to suggest discrimination in special education placement, they were the first to succeed in obtaining a permanent injunction against the use of IQ tests in special education assessment (Wade, 1980).

Ironically, Sattler (2018) conducted a review of several studies examining test bias in IQ tests. His examination of the psychometric properties of IQ tests revealed that these tests were not culturally biased according to the majority of definitions of test bias. Despite these findings, the fact still remains that IQ tests yield differences in mean scores among different groups of people along racial and ethnic lines. This "outcome bias" has undoubtedly contributed to the gross underrepresentation of Black students in gifted education.

Therefore, while extant evidence exists which suggests that IQ tests are psychometrically sound, there is little doubt that these tests are unfair in their assessment of Black individuals (Gregory, 2004).

Implications of Underrepresentation for Black Students

Others factors negatively impact the performance of CLD children on IQ tests, including how intelligence is defined, the relationship between measured IQ and group differences in terms of access to quality education, cultural differences, and cultural influences on test administration and test interpretation (Ogbu, 1978; Washington et al., 2016). Documented concerns about the assessment of intellectual giftedness in Black students date as far back as Jenkins' (1936) study that focused on dispelling the myth that Black children lacked intellectual giftedness due to their racial background as posited by Lewis Terman, creator of IQ testing and gifted education in America (Mansfield, 2007). Jenkins showed that some Black children who obtained high scores on (IQ) tests did not receive similar IQ scores when assessed by other examiners. To combat the issues of cultural bias with the use of traditional IQ tests, test publishers and authors created nonverbal and culturally responsive tests and assessments. Table 8.1 highlights some of the most used and recognized instruments.

Table 8.1 Most Common Nonverbal and Culturally Responsive Tests and Assessments

Individually Administered IQ Tests	Individually Administered Achievement Tests	Group Administered Abilities Tests
Wechsler Intelligence Scale for Children-Fifth Edition (WISC-V)	Wechsler Individual Achievement Test-Fourth Edition (WIAT-4)	*Naglieri Nonverbal Ability Test (NNAT)
*Wechsler Intelligence Scale for Children-Fifth Edition Spanish (WISC-V Spanish)	Kaufman Test of Educational Achievement-Third Edition (KTEA-3)	Cognitive Abilities Test (CogAT)
Stanford-Binet Intelligence Scales-Fifth Edition (SB-5)	Woodcock-Johnson Tests of Achievement-Fourth Edition (WJ-IV-ACH)	Otis-Lennon School Ability Test (OLSAT)
*Kaufman Assessment Battery for Children-Second Edition Normative Update (KABC-II NU)	*Bateria-IV Pruebas de aprovechamiento (Tests of Achievement)	
*Differential Ability Scales-Second Edition (DAS-2)		
*Differential Ability Scales-Second Edition Early Years Spanish Supplement (DAS-II)		
Reynolds Intellectual Assessment Scales-Second Edition (RIAS-2)		
Woodcock-Johnson Tests of Cognitive Abilities-Fourth Edition (WJ-IV COG)		
*Bateria IV Woodcock-Muñoz (Bateria IV) (WJ-IV COG in Spanish)		
* Leiter International Performance Scale-Third Edition (Leiter-3) (nonverbal test)		
*Universal Nonverbal Intelligence Test (Unit-2)		
*Cognitive Assessment System-Second Edition (CAS-2)		

Note: *Denotes instruments designed to be more culturally fair.

As an example, the KABC-II NU includes three different global indexes to ensure a fairer measure of intelligence of children from ethnically diverse backgrounds. According to the test publishers, the KABC-II NU was designed to provide a more culturally fair assessment of cognitive abilities in traditionally marginalized populations. It includes the Fluid Crystallized Index (FCI); the Mental Processing Index (MPI), which excludes subtests that measure crystallized knowledge; and the Nonverbal Index (NVI), which excludes any subtest that requires verbal expression. The test authors of the KABC-II NU encourage psychologists to interpret the assessment using the MPI for culturally diverse children and the NVI for assessing children who are linguistically diverse. The information obtained from individually administered tests are more accurate than group assessments. The examiners of these assessments usually have advanced training in assessing students from diverse backgrounds and the examiner has more time to build rapport with students. (Schreiber & Kaufman, 2015)

Nonverbal ability assessments are typically utilized with CLD student populations and students from economically marginalized backgrounds. Many public-school districts have turned to the administration of nonverbal group-based assessments such as the NNAT-3 to screen groups of children for gifted programs (Naglieri & Ford, 2003). While many school districts report increases in the identification of gifted and talented CLD students with the use of nonverbal abilities tests as screeners, this option has not fully resolved the problem of under-identification of Black students in GATE programs.

Recommendations for a Holistic Assessment Approach for Gifted and Talent Development

Although it is not possible to accurately estimate the number of unidentified students from underrepresented groups, researchers in the field suggest that the enrollment in gifted and advanced programs should reflect the overall pool of students from the school population (Ford, 2013; Ford et al., 2021; Pauley & Johnstone, 2009). Accepting this equitable suggestion as a way to neutralize underrepresentation, we offer more fitting methods to address issues of recruitment and retention.

Adopt a Comprehensive Approach to Assessment

The terms "testing" and "assessment" are often used interchangeably in the literature. However, there is a fundamental difference between the two terms that has implications for the recruitment and identification of Black students for gifted programs. Tests refer to a single assessment tool that utilizes an objective and systematic way to identify children who may meet eligibility for gifted programs. Students who are "tested" are typically administered an IQ and/or academic achievement test that produces standardized scores used to describe their intellectual and/or academic performance in comparison to their peers. The exclusive use of tests to qualify or disqualify a child for gifted services is highly discouraged as they appear to contribute significantly to the underrepresentation of Black students in gifted programs. This was the case for Gizelle.

Methods of gifted identification for Black students like Gizelle should include a whole-child approach to assessment and use of multiple methods (Cao et al., 2017). Each instrument administered to these children and youth should provide information that can be useful in guiding school teams in understanding the unique needs of Gifted Black students and more importantly should inform educational planning! The first step of a comprehensive evaluation of gifted Black students should include the gathering of a full developmental history. All children are members of families and communities and any assessment data gathered about them should be interpreted and understood in the context of who they are as individuals. This information can be gathered from interviews conducted with parents/legal guardians and should include the child's history in the areas of general development, cultural background, language background, education, social and emotional development, health, and family background. The thorough collection of information from parents through the use of report forms, checklists, rating scales, and most importantly direct interviewing, becomes the foundation on which the individual evaluation is conceptualized. When evaluating Black students for gifted programming, it's critical to also evaluate these students in multiple areas of development. The latter ensures that the needs of these children are addressed once they enter gifted programs. The evaluation should include an assessment of general ability, academic functioning (reading, writing, and mathematics), social-emotional functioning, and a survey of academic and non-academic interests. In addition, once the student enters middle school, the arduous process of concentrating on talent development should become a major focus (Collins, 2017). This manner of assessing students will be more inclusive and culturally responsive in its nature. As an example, recognition and valuing of Gizelle's strong interest and ability not only in dancing but in choreographing entire dance performances should have been documented and assessed for its transferability into the academic classroom.

Conduct Ongoing and Culturally Responsive Assessment

Because potential for academic success is a latent factor that refers to "possibility and promise" (Grantham et al., 2011, p. 81), there is limited research that addresses measurement of potential academic success in GATE. In addition, the loss of potential among unidentified and underserved gifted youth is inadequately addressed. Noble and Morton (2013) urged that the focus of assessment "must shift away from achievement gaps to the realization of these students' academic potential" (p. 35). Frequent, formative assessment (i.e., in-class discussions, progress tests, group-work, portfolio assessment, etc.) are more beneficial for improved teacher and student development alike.

It is equally important that school-based mental health practitioners (school psychologists, school counselors, and school social workers) also be involved in the ongoing assessment of students' academic and social-emotional functioning and offer culturally responsive provision of services. To do so, these practitioners must understand the concepts of giftedness so they can assist students with discovering their emerging strengths and developing their talents (Chung, 2017). The vast majority of schools in the United States employ these "education specialists" who are trained mental health providers. These school-based mental health practitioners play a critical role in the support and development of Gifted Black students as well as their educational outcomes. These students can benefit from a variety of services that impact program retention, social and emotional development and functioning, academic functioning, and overall wellness. School counselors can conduct whole- group lessons in gifted classrooms about a variety of topic areas that are relevant to Black gifted students. For example, these students can learn about methods to engage in self-care or how to advocate for causes they are passionate about. School counselors can also conduct whole-group lessons about character development. These students may also benefit from group and individual counseling services. Each school-based practitioner mentioned can offer a series of group counseling services to address topics such as time-management skills, improving interpersonal relationships, cultural diversity, ways to handle injustice, increasing resilience, and addressing academic challenges, etc. Students with more individualized and personal needs that may include experiencing feelings of sadness, anxiety, or family issues may benefit more from individual counseling. School-based mental health practitioners have the power to equip gifted Black students with the tools they need to successfully navigate their environments and increase their overall wellness! School-based practitioners should also consider partnering with the families of gifted Black students to increase awareness of their unique needs. They can provide support to families in the form of parent/family workshops, family counseling, consultation, and resource linkage in the community as needed. For example, they can provide direct support to gifted students through individual or group counseling that focuses on navigating home and school cultural differences, academic success plans, and understanding their individual giftedness.

Utilize Equity Goals

Ford (2013) suggested that a discrepancy (i.e., beyond statistical chance and influenced by some systemic barrier) is significant when underrepresentation or overrepresentation exceeds an equitable threshold, determined legally and/or by local decision makers). It is recommended that gifted enrollment for any subgroup should be within a 20% threshold, or equitable allowance, of the total enrollment of that subgroup. For example, according to the 2015–2016 OCR Civil Rights Data Collection (OCR, n.d.), Black students represent 10% of the total student population served in gifted programs. Based on a total K-12 student population of 19%, the gifted representation index (GRI) for gifted Black students in gifted programs, nationally, is then 53%; that is an underrepresentation of 47%. According to the equity allowance, an equitable goal for Black students' representation of the national gifted student population should be between 15.2% and 22% (within 3.8 percentage points which represents 20% of the total 19% population). Anything beyond this percentage range illuminates potential discrepancies in recruitment and/or retention.

Once districts determine their local GRI, it is imperative that they study the magnitude and underlying causes of any representation discrepancies and set equity goals for their overall gifted and talented programs (Lamb et al., 2019). The equity goals should reflect an adopted definition for giftedness, their philosophy of diversity and inclusion, and goals for academic achievement for all students. The allowance, or equity index (EI), unlike a cutoff score, alerts districts to potential discrepancies and offers a solution for setting local, equitable representation goals.

Fostering Cultural Capital and Creativity for Recruitment and Retention

The policies and practices by which we educate *all* students must be creatively implemented to identify and nurture the students enrolled. This can be done by identifying, recognizing, and embedding cultural capital (Collins & Fields-Smith, n.d.; Hegemin, 2017) into the formal educational structures. Utilizing the cultural capital of Black students includes applications of common cultural structures as determined by the values of that culture to aid in developing the strengths of these students. For example, E. Paul Torrance, the author of the Torrance Test for Creative Thinking (TTCT) asserted that Black students demonstrated unusual and distinct characteristics of creativity, in addition to unique problem-solving skills, that were not manifested in the same manner as with other ethnic groups (Baldwin, 2003); he understood that skills and talents which are culturally developed can serve as strengths to be used to foster success and achievement in academic areas. Collins and Grantham (2014) further posited that creative giftedness (unique perspective, approach, and problem solving) is indicative of cognitive abilities and critical thinking, suggesting that the burden of maximizing the potential of creatively gifted Black students rests on the educational system in which they are enrolled. The development and use of measures that allow students to respond in terms of their own experiences, common cultural values, and unique talents allows for culturally responsive assessment as well as opportunities for growth and development of the student (Collins, 2017).

Revisiting Torrance's Creative Positives as a Cultural and Formative Assessment Tool

Torrance (1970) conceptualized the idea of creative strengths, suggesting that a set of "creative positives," present to a high degree among disadvantaged students, primarily Blacks, could be used to build educational programs to effectively shape their gifted potential and talent development. His work represented one of the earliest promising works that guided educators in their understanding of strengths exhibited by culturally different and low-income students. Torrance's *Creative Positives* (see Table 8.2) provide a general sampling of the strengths and creative abilities of CLD students that can be used to build confidence, background knowledge, and capacity to aid in the development of academic strengths. *Creative Positives* describes behaviors associated with the mental action of using existing knowledge to generate new knowledge. We assert that understanding them as gifted behavior in assessment for students like Gizelle would greatly decrease underrepresentation of Black students in GATE.

Creative Positives encompass cognitive processes and functions that are exhibited in ways that are culturally intuitive and often habitual in nature. They exemplify creative memory schemas, active and physical engagement, human connectedness to language, and responsive comprehension of information in a culturally responsive manner. Students that exhibit creative strengths to problem solving, for instance, possess a level of divergent thinking that is also present in the other intelligences. These attributes are readily manifested and more observable in an environment that is grounded with trust, freedom, opportunity for challenging engagement, and an open-minded practitioner who is sensitive to these traits. For example, Torrance, as a high school teacher in the 1940s, was able to use the creative positives of students who others considered unreachable to help them to overcome their obstructing attitudes about academic subject matter, to learn at an accelerated pace, and to excel on standardized tests well beyond other high-achieving students.

Table 8.2 Torrance's (1973) Checklist of Creative Positives

Creative Positive	Sample Observable Behaviors
1. Ability to express feelings and emotions	____ Expresses feelings and emotions in dance and/or creative movement ____ Expresses feelings and emotions in music and rhythm
2. Ability to improvise with commonplace materials	____ Uses commonplace materials to make or modify toys ____ Makes games from commonplace materials
3. Articulateness in role playing and storytelling	____ Responds at empathic level toward others in role playing ____ Engages in fantasy in storytelling
4. Enjoyment of and ability in visual art	____ Experiences real joy in drawing ____ Understands subject matter by "drawing it" (illustrating stories, making maps, etc.) ____ Communicates skillfully through drawings
5. Enjoyment of and ability in creative movement, dance, dramatics	____ Experiences deep enjoyment in dance and/or creative movement ____ Can interpret songs, poems, stories through creative movement ____ Creates own style of movement, dance, etc.
6. Enjoyment of and ability in music, rhythm	____ Writes, moves, works, walks with rhythm ____ Rhythm facilitates learning of skills and understanding ideas, events, concepts ____ Creates songs, music ____ Can interpret ideas, events, feelings, etc. through rhythm or music
7. Expressive speech	____ Speech is colorful, picturesque (suggests a picture, etc.) ____ Speech includes powerful analogies, metaphors, etc. ____ Invents words to express concepts new to him
8. Fluency and flexibility in non-verbal media	____ Produces large number of different ideas through drawings, play situations ____ Produces large number of ideas with common objects, creative movement/dance ____ Produces large variety of ideas through drawings, dance, music
9. Enjoyment of and skills in small group activities, problem-solving.	____ Tries harder in small groups; Produces ideas in small groups ____ Highly aware of feelings and skills of others in small groups ____ Supports other members of small group, high group loyalty and involvement
10. Responsiveness to the concrete	____ Ideas start flowing when concrete objects and materials are involved ____ Uses concrete objects and materials to generate ideas, solutions, etc.
11. Responsiveness to the kinesthetic	____ Movement stimulates ideas ____ Movement communicates ideas ____ Skillful in interpreting meaning of movement
12. Expressiveness of gestures, "body language"	____ Expresses ideas powerfully through gestures, "body language" ____ Body says the things his words do not say
13. Humor	____ Portrays comical, funny, amusing [things] in writing, role playing, drawings ____ Makes humorous cartoon strips (original), humorous jokes ____ Makes people laugh (not make fun of) in discussion
14. Richness of imagery in informal language	____ Makes others see pictures when he tells a story or relates personal experiences ____ Makes people see a picture when he describes something in a conversation ____ Makes people see pictures in role playing and dramatics

Table 8.2 Cont.

Creative Positive	Sample Observable Behaviors
15. Originality of ideas in problem-solving	___ Produces solutions that others do not think of or when no one else can ___ Solutions are unusual, unconventional ___ Stories have unusual endings, unusual plots
16. Problem-centeredness	___ Shows concern about the problems of others and tries to solve them ___ Is hard to distract when s/he is concerned about a problem ___ Keeps seeing relevance of new information to problems of group
17. Emotional responsiveness	___ Responds emotionally to stories, events, needs of group members
18. Quickness of warm-up	___ Always ready to go; may get tired of waiting and become "turned off"

Credit: Reoriented and printed with permission by E. Paul Torrance (1973) as noted in his article published in *Gifted Child Quarterly* entitled "Non-Test Indicators of Creative Talent among Disadvantaged Children."

Research Implications and Practical Applications

What is the impact of creativity assessment on the identification and placement of underrepresented students from culturally, economically, or linguistically diverse backgrounds? This is a question that deserves greater attention, as a lens for looking at children differently, by current scholars and practitioners in GATE. It also affirms a need for a resurgence of research in the areas of creativity and equity to realize the full impact of creativity, and specifically creative positives, on underrepresentation and other inequities in GATE.

Culturally Responsive Curriculum Development

Creativity and *Creative Positives* serve as ideal frameworks that can be integrated into curriculum development, program planning, and implementation with promise as culturally responsive solutions. Observation, assessment, and academic translation of students' creative positives serve as an effective guide to inform this approach to address growth for exceptional academic performance and productivity of gifted Black students. Collins and Grantham (2017) posited that the integration of authentic, cultural-valued, and practical activities (e.g., scholarship applications, academic competitions, problem-based learning, etc.) provide a high standard of rigor, depth, and challenge that can further develop cognitive and affective skills especially when aligned with domain-specific curriculums. Ford (2013) further asserted that recruitment and retention require providing academic, cultural, and social support.

Social and Emotional Growth and Development of Black Gifted Students

Ford et al. (2020) wrote that educators, particularly school counselors and mental health professionals, understand how social and emotional needs significantly influence achievement. When social and emotional needs and development (SEND) is positive, students tend to do well; when SEND is negative, student achievement can be compromised, resulting in underachievement. When it comes to the SEND of gifted Black students, a critical topic must be racial identity (Collins, 2018). It is imperative that counselors (including school psychologists and social workers) and teachers are formally trained in the social and emotional needs and development (SEND) of students of color, particularly Black students, who are gifted and talented. They should be aware and fully familiar with resources that are available to support the SEND of students of color including strategies for teachers and families to nurture pride in Black students' race and ethnicity.

In evaluating gifted education programs using an equity-based and culturally responsive lens, Ford et al. (2020) offered the following guiding principles, among others, for the social and emotional needs and development of gifted students of color:

- Our students have access to supportive services and programs by school counselors trained in multicultural counseling (e.g., theories, methods, strategies).
- Our students have access to counselors familiar with and skilled in racial identity theories.
- Our students have access to counselors who understand and promote racial identity development, as well as the relationship between racial identity and achievement.
- Our students have access to counselors and teachers who understand the unique challenges of being gifted students of color.
- Our students have access to preservice educators, current educators, and counselors formally trained in the social and emotional needs of gifted students of color.

Situated within the community that it serves, it is also important that the school is positively connected to its community. Partnerships and collaborations with community-based mental health agencies/professionals, including private entities, can serve as a resource for school-based professionals in their professional development. As recommended in the case for Gizelle, positive working relationships with the parents also serve as a benefit to educators when they are collecting information about the students; this information will more than likely be presented within a cultural context that can further provide cultural knowledge to the educators.

Conclusion

Methods used for the identification of gifted Black students must include a whole- child approach to assessment and use of varied methods. Comprehensive evaluation of potentially gifted Black students should include the gathering of their full developmental history, assessment of cognitive levels, assessment of academic levels, and assessment of social and emotional functioning. Comprehensive evaluations help to determine the specific and unique needs of gifted students. In essence, the information learned from comprehensive evaluations is also important for the purpose of future academic planning.

Ford et al. (2018) warned that the lenses by which educators within gifted education view students have profound implications to include, but not be limited to, recruitment, preferred measures, screening processes, and programming. The potential to be academically successful in gifted and advanced programs exists within every population, including Black students and other special populations such as twice-exceptional (2e) students. Whenever possible, their cultural and creative attributes should be considered as motivators when developing programming goals, curriculum implementation, and choosing instruments used in the evaluation of culturally diverse students, especially those underrepresented and/or underserved in gifted education. The principles that Torrance (1984, pp. 155–156) developed for identification of giftedness based on his experiences and research more than 80 years ago hold true today as much as they did. They are:

1   Creativity should almost always be one of the identification criteria, though not the sole criteria.
2   Different kinds of excellence (multiple talents) should be evaluated.
3   Where disabilities and sensory handicaps are involved and where young children (3–6 years) are involved, attention must be given to procedures that permit responses in appropriate modalities.
4   Where historically marginalized and culturally different children are involved, attention must be given to the selection of test tasks that assess the kinds of excellence that are valued by the particular culture or subculture.
5   Even in using creative tests, select one that considers a wide variety of indictors rather than a single one.

These principles offer a framework for practical applications that can be situated within a comprehensive identification process. In addition, creative positives are indicative of behaviors to inform effective ways to support the social, emotional, and cultural needs of Black students for a holistic approach to identity and talent development (Frasier, 1997; Hodges et al., 2018). Considerations of creative positives offer a "voice" for Black students to negotiate their own learning process in such a way that fosters ownership and enables growth in terms of cultural and social identity.

Bibliography

Baldwin, A. Y. (2003). Understanding the challenge of creativity among African Americans. *Inquiry: Critical Thinking Across the Disciplines, 22*(3), 13–18.

Bostick, D. (2016, July 12). How colorblindness is actually racist. *The Huffington Post*. Retrieved from: www.huffingtonpost.com/dani-bostick/how-colorblindness-isact_b_10886176.html

Cao, T. H., Jung, J. Y., & Lee, J. (2017). Assessment in gifted education: A review of the literature from 2005–2016. *Journal of Advanced Academics, 28*(3), 163–203.

Chung, E. Y. (2017). School counselling for the gifted: Responding to the social-emotional needs of gifted students. In M. Hue (Ed.), *School counselling in a Chinese context: Supporting students in need in Hong Kong* (pp. 94–105). Routledge.

Collins, K. H. (2017). From identification to Ivy League: Nurturing multiple interests and multi-potentiality in gifted students. *Parenting for High Potential, 6*(4), 19–22.

Collins, K. H. (2018). Confronting colorblind STEM talent development: Toward a contextual model for Black student STEM identity. *Journal of Advanced Academics, 29*(2), 143–168. doi:10.1177/1932202X18757958

Collins, K. H., & Fields-Smith, C. A. (n.d.). *Understanding the cultural capital of Black parent engagement in STEM talent development among gifted Black students*. Manuscript under review.

Collins, K. H., & Grantham, T. (2014). Creative mindfulness in STEM talent development. *Gifted Education Press Quarterly, 2*(3), 10–14.

Collins, K. H., & Grantham, T. C. (2017). Develop scholar identity: Dr. Martin Jenkins scholars program. *Teaching for High Potential*, November, 6–9.

Collins, K. H., Joseph, N., & Ford, D. Y. (2019). Missing in action: Gifted, Black girls in science, technology, engineering, and mathematics (STEM). *Gifted Child Today*, 43(1), 55–63. https://doi.org/10.1177/1076217519880593

Fay, L. (2018, August 14). The state of America's student-teacher racial gap: Our public school system has been majority-minority for years, but 80 percent of teachers are still White. *The 74*. Retrieved from: www.the74million.org/article/the-state-of-americas-student-teacher-racial-gap-our-public-school-system-has-been-majority-minority-for-years-but-80-percent-of-teachers-are-still-white/

Ford, D. Y. (2013). *Recruiting and retaining culturally different students in gifted education.* Prufrock Press.

Ford, D. Y., Collins, K. H., Grantham, T., & Moore III, J. L. (2021). Equity-based gifted and talented education to increase the recruitment and retention of underrepresented students. In D. Ambrose & R. Sternberg (Eds.), *Conceptions of giftedness and talent* (pp. 141–161). Palgrave-Macmillan.

Ford, D. Y., Grantham, T. C., & Collins, K. H. (2018). Giftedness, racial identity, and social-emotional learning: Challenges and recommendations for culturally responsive practice. In F. Hellen & R. Piske (Eds.), *Emoção e Criatividade na Educação de Superdotados e Talentosos (Emotion and Creativity in Gifted Education)* (pp. 87–102). Jurua Editor.

Ford, D. Y., Lawson Davis, J., Dickson, K. T., Frazier Trotman Scott, M., Grantham, T. C., Moore III, J. L., & Taradash, G. D. (2020). Evaluating gifted education programs using an equity-based and culturally responsive checklist to recruit and retain under-represented students of color. *Journal of Minority Achievement, Creativity, and Leadership, 1*(1), 119–146.

Frasier, M. (1997). Gifted minority students: Reframing approaches to their identification and education. In N. Colangelo & G. A. Davis (Eds.), *Handbook of gifted education* (2nd ed., pp. 498–515). Allyn & Bacon.

Grantham, T., Ford, D. Y., Henfield, M., Trotman Scott, M., Harmon, D., Porchér, S., & Price, C. (Eds.) (2011). *Gifted and advanced Black students in school: An anthology of critical works.* Prufrock Press.

Graves, S., & Mitchell, A. (2011). Is the moratorium over? African American psychology professionals' views on intelligence testing in response to changes to federal policy. *Journal of Black Psychology, 37*(4), 407–425. doi:10.1177/0095798410394177

Gregory, R. J. (2004). *Psychological testing: History, principles and applications* (3rd ed.). Allyn and Bacon.

Grissom, J. A., Rodriguez, L. A., & Kern, E. C. (2017). Teacher and principal diversity and the representation of students of color in gifted programs: Evidence from national data. *The Elementary School Journal, 117*(3), 396–422.

Hegemin, T. C. (2017). "We don't need no creative writing": Black cultural capital, social (in)justice, and the devaluing of creativity in higher education. In S. Vanderslice & R. Manery (Eds.), *Can creative writing really be taught? Resisting lore in creative writing pedagogy* (pp. 123–134). Bloomsbury Academic.

Hodges, J., Tay, J., Maeda, Y., & Gentry, M. (2018). A meta-analysis of gifted and talented identification practices. *Gifted Child Quarterly*, 62(2), 147–174.

Jenkins, M. D. (1936). A socio-psychological study of Negro children of superior intelligence. *Journal of Negro Education, 5*(2), 175–190.

Kearns, T., Ford, L., & Linney, J. A. (2005). African American student representation in special education programs. *Journal of Negro Education, 74*(2), 297–310.

Lamb, K. N., Boedeker, P., & Kettler, T. (2019). Inequities of enrollment in gifted education: A statewide application of the 20% equity allowance formula. *Gifted Child Quarterly, 63*(4), 205–224. https://doi.org/10.1177/0016986219830768

Mansfield, K. C. (2007). "Just the way things were" or malicious intent? One professor's effort to facilitate truth – A JRLE student voices essay. *Journal of Research on Leadership Education, 2*(2). https://doi.org/10.1177/194277510700200202

Mayes, R. D., Jones, S. G., & Hines, E. M. (2018). Diverse gifted students: Intersectionality of cultures. In S. M. Wood & J. S. Peterson (Eds.), *Counseling gifted students: A guide for school counselors* (pp. 47–64). Springer Publishing Company.

Naglieri, J. A., & Ford, D. Y. (2003). Addressing underrepresentation of gifted minority children using the Naglieri nonverbal ability test (NNAT). *Gifted Child Quarterly, 47*(2), 155–160.

National Association for Gifted Children & The Council of State Directors for Programs for the Gifted [NAGC & CSDPG]. (2015). *2014–2015 State of the states in gifted education: Policy and practice data.* Retrieved from: www.nagc.org/sites/default/files/key%20reports/2014-2015%20State%20of%20the%20States%20%28final%29.pdf

Noble, R., & Morton, C. (2013). African Americans and mathematics outcomes on national assessment of educational progress: Parental and individual influences. *Journal of Child and Family Studies, 22*(1), 30–37. doi:10.1007/s10826-012-9640-y.

Office for Civil Rights. (n.d.). Civil Rights Data Collection. Retrieved from: https://ocrdata.ed.gov

Ogbu, J. U. (1978). *Minority education and caste: The American system in cross-cultural perspective.* Academic Press.

Pauley, G., & Johnstone, K. (2009). *Addressing under-representation of student populations in gifted programs: Best practices for student selection, service delivery models, and support structures.* Office of Superintendent of Public Instruction. Retrieved from: www.k12.wa.us/sites/default/files/public/highlycapable/pubdocs/2010/underrepresentationgiftedprograms.pdf

Powell, R. G., & Powell, D. L. (2010.). *Classroom communication and diversity: Enhancing instructional practice* (2nd ed.). Routledge.

Proctor, S. L., Graves, S. L., & Esch, R. C. (2012). Assessing African American students for specific learning disabilities: The promises and perils of response to intervention. *Journal of Negro Education, 81*(3), 268–282.

Ross, P. O., & Office of Educational Research and Improvement (Eds.). (1994). *National excellence: A case for developing America's talent. An anthology of readings.* Author.

Sattler, J. M. (2018). *Assessment of children: Cognitive foundations* (6th ed.). Sattler.

Schreiber, C., & Kaufman, A. S. (2015). Which of the KABC-II global scores is the least biased? *Journal of Pediatric Neuropsychology, 1*(1–4), 21–35.

Shealey, M. W., McHatton, P. A., & Wilson, V. (2011). Moving beyond disproportionality: The role of culturally responsive teaching in special education. *Teaching Education, 22*(4), 377–396. doi:10.1080/10476210.2011.591376

Steele, C. (2003). Race and the schooling of Black Americans. In S. Plous (Ed.), *Understanding prejudice and discrimination* (pp. 98–107). McGraw-Hill.

Torrance, E. P. (1969). Creative positives of disadvantaged children and youth. *Gifted Child Quarterly, 13*(2), 71–81.

Torrance, E. P. (1970). Broadening concepts of giftedness in the 70's. *Gifted Child Quarterly, 14*(4), 199–208. https://doi.org/10.1177/001698627001400401

Torrance, E. P. (1973). Checklist of creative positives. *Gifted Child Quarterly, 17*(1), 5–8.

Torrance, E. P. (1984). The role of creativity in identification of the gifted and talented. *Gifted Child Quarterly, 28*(4), 153–156. doi:10.1177/001698628402800403

Wade, D. L. (1980). Racial discrimination in IQ testing: Larry P. v. Riles. *DePaul Law Review, 29*(4), Article 12.

Washington, K., Malone, C., Briggs, C., & Reed II, G. (2016). Testing and African Americans: Testing monograph from the Association of Black Psychologists. In Council of National Psychological Associations for the Advancement of Ethnic Minority Interests (Eds.), *Testing and assessment with persons & communities of color* (pp. 3–11). American Psychological Association. Retrieved from: www.apa.org/pi/oema/resources/testing-assessment-monograph.pdf

Chapter 9

Gifted Identification and Services for Asian Americans

Rachel U. Mun and Glorry Yeung

Introduction

Asian American Diversity and Need to Focus on Equity

Asian Americans comprised 20 million or about 5% of the total U.S. population in 2018 (U.S. Census, 2018) and represented the fastest growing racial or ethnic group between 2000 and 2010 with a growth rate of 72% between 2000 and 2015 alone (Hoeffel et al., 2012; Lopez et al., 2017). At this current growth rate, Asian Americans are projected to surpass Hispanics and become the largest immigrant group by 2055 (Lopez et al., 2017). Asian Americans have highly diverse cultures, languages, histories and sociopolitical conditions with ancestral roots traceable to countries in East (China, Japan, and Korea), South (Bangladesh, Bhutan, India, Nepal, Pakistan, and Sri Lanka), and Southeast Asia (Cambodia, Indonesia, Laos, Malaysia, Myanmar, the Philippines, Singapore, Thailand, and Vietnam) (U.S. Census, 2018; Wu et al., 2019). Globally, member states of the United Nations are formed into five regional groups. The Group of Asia-Pacific states (see Figure 9.1), officially titled *Group of Asia and the Pacific Small Island Developing States*, comprises 54 member states (Aeschlimann et al., 2017). To the U.S. Census, and within the American school systems, Asian Americans are often compressed into a homogeneous group and stereotyped as *model minorities* (Museus & Kiang, 2009; Poon et al., 2016) or generally successful in academics and careers, overrepresented in gifted and talented programs, elite high schools and universities (Lee & Zhou, 2015; Worrell et al., 2019; Yoon & Gentry, 2009), and mentally healthy, despite contrary evidence.

Equity, while still a concern in this population, is not typically discussed due in part to the model minority stereotype. Contemporary views of Asian Americans as model minorities may seem positive on the surface, but these stereotypes are both misleading and damaging, and can negatively affect equitable opportunities for students. These stereotypes mask inequalities and disparities in achievement and socioeconomic outcomes across sub-groups (e.g., Cambodians, Laotians, and Hmongs) (Lee, 2015; Lee & Zhou, 2015), create additional social pressure on students to achieve, dismiss the significance and impact of racial discrimination, pit Asian Americans against other ethnic groups (e.g., African Americans and Latinx Americans), create a "bamboo ceiling" or barriers encountered in achieving leadership positions at work, and result in potential neglect of salient academic, professional, and mental health needs (Kiang et al., 2017; Lee, 2015; Lee & Zhou, 2015; Mun & Hertzog, 2019; Museus & Kiang, 2009; Zhou & Lee, 2017). This also means that Asian

DOI: 10.4324/9781003265412-14

Figure 9.1 Countries with Membership in Network on Education Quality Monitoring in the Asia-Pacific (NEQMAP).

Note: Immigrants from some of these member states (e.g., Islamic Republic of Iran, Papua New Guinea) are likely to adopt a different race/ethnic group than Asian as their self-identifies.

Source: Figure adapted from "Who Are We?" [image] by UNESCO Office Bangkok and Regional Bureau for Education in Asia and the Pacific, 2021 (https://neqmap.bangkok.unesco.org/wp-content/uploads/2021/03/NEQMAP-Brochure_FINAL.pdf) CC-BY-SA 3.0.

American students with high academic potential and other talents can be overlooked for gifted services and programs.

Also, there are other Asian American stereotypes that are less positive. In the last two decades, South Asians have been racially targeted due to the post 9/11 War on Terror's focus on "Muslim, Arab, and Muslim-looking peoples" (Lee, 2015, p. 374), reflecting both an "acceptance and rejection of Asian Americans" (p. 374) and their complex place in America today. More recently, in the spring of 2020, the global COVID-19 pandemic ushered in a new wave of anti-Asian racism in America with "an alarming rise of xenophobic backlash and racial harassment and violence against Asians globally, blaming China and the Chinese for the spread of the COVID-19 virus" (Okazaki, n.d., para. 2). According to the Center for the Study of Hate & Extremism (2021), there was a historic increase of 146% in Anti-Asian hate crime in 2020 across 26 of America's largest jurisdictions.

Scholars in the field of gifted education are bringing more attention to the problem of traditionally underrepresented students and equity (Connery et al., 2019; Crawford et al., 2019; Morgan, 2020). However, rarely are any of this complexity with Asian Americans – cultural, historical, linguistic, or religious – and potential issues of equity addressed within the corpus of gifted education (Yeung & Mun, 2021). The discourse on identification, services, and assessment of Asian Americans tends to treat gifted students from such diverse cultures and political structures as China, India, South Korea, Pakistan, or Cambodia as a singular community (Yeung & Mun, 2021). Furthermore, when Asian Americans are mentioned in recent gifted education literature, they are noted for their *overrepresentation* in gifted programs and typically grouped with White students (Hodges et al., 2018; Shaughnessy & Cordova, 2019; Worrell et al., 2019) with only a few articles focused on student needs and experiences (Mun & Hertzog, 2019; Paik et al., 2018; Park et al., 2018; Siegle et al., 2016). Homogenization of Asian Americans has been adopted into normative narrative when the discourse is centered upon disproportionality in enrollment figures (Ecker-Lyster & Niileksela, 2017; Grissom & Redding, 2016) with few exceptions (Siegle et al., 2016).

In contrast, researchers outside of our field continue to counter this misrepresentation, and advocate for the need for disambiguation of the Asian American label. For example, Poon et al. (2016) reviewed the literature on Asian American Pacific Islanders (AAPI) and the model minority myth through the lens of critical race theory. They found that "the great majority (more than 63%) of the reviewed publication[s] cited the model minority myth, but presented incomplete and uncritical definitions of the myth…" (p. 479). Studies have been conducted on ethnic Asian American groups and within-group disparity. In a study of the decentralized concentration of "Koreangelos" (Koreans who resided in Orange county in California), Sharma and Koh (2019) found that educational attainment varied between suburban clusters. The researchers reported that 85% of the southern Orange county population had achieved an associate or higher degree. In comparison, 61% of the Koreatown residents had attained high school or lower education (Sharma & Koh, 2019).

Yoon and Gentry (2009) succinctly pointed out that demographic changes may impact the representation index (RI) of Asian Americans in gifted programs. In their investigation into the lowering RI in Wisconsin between 2002 and 2006, they found that Hmong refugees congregated around three states including Wisconsin. The influx of the sub-group led to an increase of the total number of Hmong to exceed the entire existing population of Asian Americans in Wisconsin. This change in demographic profile may explain the lowering of the RI for Asian Americans' participation in GT programs in Wisconsin (Yoon & Gentry, 2009).

In an earlier study, Konstantopoulos et al. (2001) examined Asian American gifted students by ethnic group. When racial data were disaggregated, the researcher asserted that Southeast Asian American students were significantly underrepresented at a 0.3 RI (Konstantopoulos et al., 2001). These findings exemplify some of the inequities in gifted programming that continue to be obfuscated by aggregated ethnic data. It is generally agreed (Grissom & Redding, 2016; Peters et al., 2019) that Asian American students are among the largest groups of enrollees in GT programs. However, critical examination of the data used to substantiate such broad claims is likely to expose notable disparities that exist for sub-groups aggregated under the Asian American label (Konstantopoulos et al., 2001; Sharma & Koh, 2019; Yoon & Gentry, 2009).

Chapter Purpose and Organization

In this chapter, our goal is to broaden the understanding of Asian Americans in gifted education and present a more nuanced view of the complexity of identifying and serving these students in American schools. We also consider their wide diversity and the human and social capital (Coleman, 1988) they bring with them into gifted and advanced academic classrooms. Because educational systems, didactic material, and assessments differ among countries of origin, it is no surprise that Asian American students, particularly recent immigrants, are *uneven* in their subject mastery within the same classrooms. These gaps are likely to present a challenging instructional environment for educators to navigate. Finally, we examine issues necessary to a successful learning environment for this group of heterogeneous learners including the importance of individualized assessment that considers prior education, instructional strategies, and culturally responsive pedagogy to meet diverse student needs. We use vignettes and a case study to portray "lived experiences" or individual interpretations and experiences of events based on the phenomenological approach (Merriam & Tisdell, 2016) as an instructional example. We may refer to these stories throughout this text to put theories into context when appropriate. Further, we draw upon information available outside the field of gifted literature to enhance the understanding of issues presented.

Review of Literature

While Asian Americans have often been portrayed at par with European Americans in academics, their history in America indicates that the population experienced discrimination, exclusion, and racism similar to other minoritized groups (Lee, 2015; 2019). As a group, Asian American children are also considered overrepresented in gifted programming (Worrell et al., 2019; Yoon & Gentry, 2009) despite contrary evidence. For example, there are data that some Southeast Asian Americans (e.g., Cambodian, Hmong, Laotian) are underrepresented in gifted programs when compared to East and South Asian counterparts (Erwin & Worrell, 2012; Siegle et al., 2016; Yoon & Gentry, 2009).

Our discourse becomes more complex when we consider student needs based on immigrant generationality. Immigrants who came to the United States at 18 or older are considered first (1.0) generation immigrants and their U.S.-born children are considered second (2.0) generation immigrants (Rumbaut, 2004). Finally, third generation immigrants represent children of second-generation immigrant parents, and so forth. Immigration timing can be viewed along an "arrival age continuum" (Roberge, 2002, p. 107) with differences in acculturation and educational outcomes based on timing. Sociological literature has made a finer distinction between first and second generation immigrants, with children who immigrated at middle childhood (ages 6–12) considered "the classic 1.5 generation" (Rumbaut, 2004, p. 1167).

In a recent meta-analysis, 53 studies were examined for generational differences in educational achievement for immigrant youth (Duong et al., 2016). Duong et al. (2016) found that first and second generation immigrants, including those of Asian descent, tend to perform well academically as measured by scores on tests and grades, with a slight advantage for second generation students. Interestingly, this achievement may not be sustained in third or later generations (Duong et al., 2016; Özek & Figlio, 2016; Yang, 2004). Yang (2004) used the term "third-generation flattening" (p. 51) to describe this trend where the achievement of third generation immigrants begins to decline. Özek and Figlio (2016) examined Asian (more than half comprising Filipino, Chinese, Indian, South Korean, and Vietnamese origin) and Hispanic youth in Florida. They found similar declines in achievement in third generation immigrants and noted that this was an important area to explore further. In this chapter, we focus mainly on identifying and serving the needs of gifted first and second generation immigrant Asian American students. However, educators must be aware of the individual variability in this population and show care not to generalize students based on prior assumptions.

Role of Parents/Families

Research on talent development suggests that parents play vital roles in the cultivation and fulfillment of student gifts and potential. Parents can help to build social networks and model personality traits such as resilience, despite setbacks (Garn et al., 2012), and encourage the development of students' academic motivation through high expectations and academic support (Olszewski-Kubilius, 2016). Bronfenbrenner's (1979; 2004) bioecological model of human development underscores the importance of parents in promoting healthy development and academic achievement of students (Crawford et al., 2019; Galindo & Sheldon, 2012; Garces-Bacsal & Yeo, 2017).

The role of parents in affecting student learning and outcomes has been investigated at length in the Asian American community, and much of this applies to gifted Asian American students. In contemporary Asian American families, a majority of parents are immigrants with 73% of adults identified as foreign-born (Lopez et al., 2017). Asian American parents have been found to have higher educational expectations, defined as "realistic beliefs or judgments that parents have about their children's future achievement" (Yamamoto & Holloway, 2010, p. 191), than other ethnic groups for reasons related to financial security and increased social mobility, which can become internalized in their children (Mun & Hertzog, 2019; Samura, 2015). High expectations are associated with higher achievement, as often seen in East Asian and Indian American students. High levels of academic achievement can also be attributed to cultural values of hard work and prioritization of education, as well as structural factors of immigration self-selectivity (Lee, 2015; Lee & Zhou, 2015).

Parental support for the gifted population varies across Asian cultures. While Asian American parents in the United States have access to well-funded, professional organizations (e.g., National Association for Gifted Children [NAGC], Supporting Emotional Needs of the Gifted [SENG]) dedicated to support the needs of or provide networking for parents with gifted children, many more parents do not have the same type or level of professional resources available in their home countries. For example, in India where parents with gifted children are considered "lucky," this perception of "better offness" tends to negatively impact the allocation of resources to gifted education and ancillary services (Roy & Kurup, 2016). Indian parents with fewer financial resources face challenges from social stigmatization of giftedness, convoluted understanding of the nature of being gifted, and in accessing appropriate education for their gifted children (Roy & Kurup, 2016). In contrast, Hong Kong has had an organized support organization by parents since 1992. Further, the government has been funding a robust gifted program including a resource center, school-based gifted educational programs, and the Hong Kong Academy for Gifted Education (HKAGE) (Tommis, 2016). The roles of parental support for the gifted child are more likely to be coherent between parents from India's affluent and their counterparts from Hong Kong in terms of access to information, leverage of private and governmental resources, and conceptualization of giftedness than between parents of lower socio-economic status (SES).

Cultural Influences

Cultural differences can influence the conceptualization of giftedness, programming needs, and the repertoire of psychosocial skills in Asian American gifted learners. Psychosocial skills, in terms of an internal characteristic and from the family environmental perspective, have long piqued the interest of gifted education researchers. Silverman examined emotional sensitivity and intensity in gifted children as integral traits within the construct of asynchronous development (Silverman, 1997). From the talent development paradigm perspective, Olszewski-Kubilius et al. (2015) argued for acquisition of psychosocial skills being requisite for achievement in talent domains. Garn et al. (2010) investigated academic motivation of gifted children using the self-determination theory. Other researchers, Marsh et al. (2008) and Seaton et al. (2009), studied the big-fish–little-pond effect (BFLPE) and its implications for student motivation, gifted learning, and programs. Findings from these studies underscore the importance of motivation to academic self-concept and school success for gifted students. Most importantly, the findings from Marsh et al. (2008) and Seaton et al. (2009) suggested BFLPE to be cross-culturally applicable. However, there are also unique cultural influences to consider for gifted Asian American students.

In many Asian immigrant households, the goals and needs of the family take precedence above the individual's goals and needs, reflecting the cultural values of collectivism and filial piety (Md-Yunus et al., 2017; Yee et al., 2009). Filial piety can be understood as "loving one's parents, being respectful, polite, considerate, loyal, helpful, dutiful, and obedient" (Md-Yunus et al., 2017, p. 84) and has roots in Confucian philosophy, an ethical and philosophical system of thought that originally developed in China in the second century BC and spread to Hong Kong, Korea, Japan, and Singapore (Lee & Kennedy, 2017; Mun & Hertzog, 2019; Phillipson & Phillipson, 2016; Stankov, 2010). Scholars have suggested that Confucianism had a profound influence upon the educational dispositions of Asians (Lee & Kennedy, 2017; Stankov, 2010) as education and effort are particularly valued according to this philosophy. In Korea the saying *sugo haseyo* is translated as *keep working hard* and is often used in academic settings after a student has worked diligently on a task and succeeded due to his or her effort (Grant & Dweck, 2001; Mun & Hertzog, 2019). Within this phrase is the idea that a student or individual can always work harder to improve. It is common to find students attending cram schools, or extracurricular academies, in East Asian countries like China, Japan, and Korea and increasingly in America (Byun & Park, 2012; Lin, 2019). Parents are willing to take on the additional and often heavy financial burden for tutors and cram schools to help their children succeed in a highly competitive educational and economic environment.

Other philosophies and religious views have been impactful to cultures across Asia. Historically, Buddhism spread from India to central Asia and beyond; though the introduction of Islam brought to some of the East and South Asian cultures a transformative presence in philosophical and religious teachings. The tenets of Buddhism, Confucianism, Daoism, and Islam can be found across many Asian countries (Lee & Kennedy, 2017). There are also exceptions where Catholicism dominates the national culture. For example, the Philippines is a country with over 80% Roman Catholics (Central Intelligence Agency, 2020). These philosophical and religious factors often inform cultural values in countries of origin and guide the development of didactic material and pedagogy in educational settings. A study of 94 Taiwanese and 140 U.S. teachers' views of moral education topics found low agreement between the Taiwanese and U.S. teachers regarding moral topics taught to sixth grade students (Lin et al., 1998). Exemplifying this divergence, while American teachers and Taiwanese teachers were in general agreement on the importance of an AIDS (acquired immunodeficiency syndrome) curriculum in university settings, only 54% of Taiwanese teachers believed the topic was suitable in sixth grade classrooms as compared with 93% of American teachers (Lin et al., 1998).

Indian Americans in the United States represent one of the most highly educated groups with 70% of adults aged 25 or older holding a college degree in 2014 (Desilver, 2014). According to this research, about half of Indian Americans in America are Hindu, 18% are Christians, and 10% are Muslim, and many immigrants come with professional qualifications. Similar to many East Asian cultures, collectivistic dispositions are prized over the self, and children are expected to obey, exhibit appropriate behavior, perform well academically, and contribute to the overall well-being of the family (Farver et al., 2002). The influence of culture on educational attainment is more mixed for Southeast Asian immigrants, many of whom initially arrived as refugees and children of refugees after 1975.

As a group, Southeast Asian Americans have found less overall success compared with their East and South Asian peers and have been beset with challenges such as socioeconomic disadvantages, higher drop-out rates, and higher rates of violence as compared to East and South Asian counterparts (Bui, 2017; Lee et al., 2017). However, there is some evidence to suggest that Vietnamese Americans who comprise the majority of the Southeast Asian American population are excelling academically (Bui, 2017; Kim, 2002; Lee et al., 2017). Lee et al. (2017) compared the reading and math performance of Cambodian, Laotian, and Vietnamese students on the CAT/6 assessment and found that Cambodian and Laotian American students scored lower than European Americans and similarly with African Americans on the test. Notwithstanding, Vietnamese American students performed significantly better than Cambodian and Laotian peers (Lee et al., 2017). Culturally based values of hard work, achievement, education, as well as the mix of Buddhism and Confucian values in Vietnamese families may explain their educational achievement (Ngo & Lee, 2007). Also, the more connected the students were to the culture of their family and ethnic networks, the more likely they were to experience academic success. The roots of Cambodian culture stem from Theravada Buddhism, a doctrine which includes a strong belief in destiny. This may lead to a "laissez-faire approach to children's education" (Ngo &

Lee, 2007, p. 433) and less parental involvement in the child's education. This is quite different from the conceptualization of effort and ability in East Asian cultures, where there is more belief in the ability to change the future.

Structural Influences

The structural perspective provides a lens to examine Asian Americans within the broader context of American society and the economic and social forces at play (Lee & Zhou, 2015; Xie & Goyette, 2003). Immigrant scholars have noted the high educational aspirations and expectations of immigrant parents for their children, involvement in education, and the value placed on achievement (Chung, 2015; Feliciano & Lanuza, 2017; Lee & Zhou, 2015; Suarez-Orozco et al., 2008). Children of immigrants also tend to perform better academically than their peers with native-born parents from similar socioeconomic backgrounds, a curious phenomenon described as the *immigrant paradox* (Feliciano & Lanuza, 2017).

Lee and Zhou (2015) used the term *hyper-selectivity* to describe how Asian immigrants commonly have the dual features of being highly selected, in that they are more highly educated than those who remain in their countries of origin and more highly educated than average Americans "despite the tremendous heterogeneity in their countries of origin" (p. 6). After analyzing interviews with 162 mostly Chinese and Vietnamese American samples in Los Angeles, Lee and Zhou (2017) found that this hyper-selectivity imported "class specific cultural frames, institutions, and mindsets from their countries of origin, including a strict 'success frame'" (p. 2321). These success frames included earning straight As in school, graduating at the top of the class, and admittance to top schools such as an Ivy League school and "then working in one of four professions – medicine, law, science, or engineering" (Lee & Zhou, 2017, p. 2321). In a separate paper, Zhou and Lee (2017) observed that Asian immigrant families tended to have more access to human and ethnic capital (for example, test prep and advanced tutoring services in ethnic communities) as compared to other immigrant groups which could also contribute to successful outcomes.

In the Filipino culture, the immediate family is extended to third-degree levels of kinship in accordance with the *kapwa* framework of family relationships (Garces-Bacsal, 2011). This extended familial network has implications for programming support for gifted Filipino students. Educators may seek to better understand and leverage the degree and the extent of structural influences and cultural capital at the disposal of the gifted Filipino student. According to Garces-Bacsal (2011), in contrast to the propensity to camouflage one's own intellectual prowess, exceptionalities of gifted Filipino children are celebrated by the entire *kapwa* framework.

Vignettes on Cultural and Structural Influences for Gifted Asian Americans

Several gifted Asian American individuals who entered college two or more years early were interviewed by the first author about the influence of culture and immigration on their academic and career decision-making growing up in America (Chung, 2015; Mun & Hertzog, 2019).

Jaya

Jaya, an Indian American young woman, was 27 years old at the time of interview (Mun & Hertzog, 2019). She reflected on the influence of culture and immigration on her career development and noted that in India, there were more specific job categories that defined success such as doctor, professor, and lawyer. She shared how, "In India, there is a conception of career tiers and when I chose international studies that was a real source of concern for my mom because it's very open-ended … and there's no clear-cut career path" (Mun & Hertzog, 2019, p. 132).

Steven

Steven, who was 29 years old at the time of interview, was a child of Korean immigrants. He mentioned how the Korean culture partly influenced his parental expectations for him. His parents gave up more prestigious jobs as a teacher and banker in South Korea to become small-business owners in America. Their sacrifice was intended to ensure a better and brighter future for him and his younger brother. Steven acknowledged that "they're dramatically turning over their lives and they're giving up their professional credentials in their home country" (Chung, 2015, p. 90) for the promise of upward mobility.

Timothy

Timothy, a gifted 26-year-old man at the time of interview and first-born son of Indonesian immigrants, shared similar sentiments about this idea of sacrifice. The value of education was very important in his family as both parents had immigrated to America to improve the family's educational outcomes. His parents had very high expectations for him and his two younger sisters, not just in academics but also in music. One of the messages his parents shared was about not wasting the opportunity and the sacrifice which is consistent with the immigrant narrative. Timothy observed that, "Immigrants have this value that in this new context we have to achieve and we should be near the top … in music, sports and academics" (Chung, 2015, p. 91).

Belonging and Ethnic Identity

Acculturation (U.S. culture assimilation), enculturation (ethnic culture orientation), and ethnic identity vary among Asian Americans depending on culture and immigrant generationality, with levels varying among sub-groups (Le & Raposa, 2019). In a study of 56 Asian Americans (Chinese and Asian Pacific/Pacific Islander most commonly reported) and 38 European Americans who reported information about enculturation, acculturation, social stress, and social support, Le and Raposa (2019) found that higher enculturation may contribute to "fewer stressful social experiences for Asian Americans" (p. 11) while higher mainstream acculturation may contribute to "increased social support for

European Americans" (p. 11). According to Oyserman & Destin's (2010) Identity-Based Motivation (IBM) model, individuals are motivated to act and make sense of the world in ways that are consistent with perceived personal and social identities. These identities are not fixed but "situated" and may shift depending on context. Children of Asian immigrants, who navigate various cultural contexts, may face multiple barriers (i.e., language, cultural, and socioeconomic) in accessing high-quality curriculum and instruction (Siegle et al., 2016). The development of a strong scholarly and ethnic identity may act as a protective factor in their academic and mental health outcomes. Ethnic identity is derived partly from social group membership. Wu et al. (2019) noted that "[an] individual's retention and knowledge of his/her ethnic culture creates a sense of belonging that strengthens the identity formation process, which, in the United States, is a significant factor to the self-esteem and self-confidence of minority adolescents" (p. 169). A strong ethnic identity is associated with feelings of belonging and commitment and can lead to overall more positive mental health outcomes (Wu et al., 2019).

Kitano (2011) noted the extreme heterogeneity within the Asian American cultural context and cautioned regarding the potential for bias when familial factors are not well understood. In a study of the lived experiences of ten Asian American parents (Chinese, Korean, Taiwanese, Japanese, Indian, and Filipino) whose children were diagnosed as twice-exceptional, Park et al. (2018) found that most parents actively advocated for their children's special needs and more than half changed their children's schooling to improve the learning environment. Notably, three of the parents in this sample were 1.5 and second generation immigrants and their educational levels ranged from bachelor's degree to doctorate. Fifty percent of the parents had also experienced pressure to excel academically in their childhood. However, most shared that they themselves did not "push their children to perform well academically" (Park et al., 2018, p. 314) which may imply acculturation to Western values of parenting for some.

Case Study of Ryan

Educators should strive to learn more about the richness, diversity, and different learning experiences of the Asian American students in their district and schools depending on their immigrant generationality and country of origin. We present the case of Ryan, a ten-year-old foreign-born Chinese American born to 1.5 generation parents. He was educated from kindergarten to third grade at public schools in Hong Kong before returning to the United States. Ryan also sat for the School and College Ability Test (SCAT) and was admitted to the Talent Search program of the Johns Hopkins Center for Talented Youth. Additionally, he was admitted to and attended the Gifted and Talented Program administered by The Chinese University of Hong Kong. Currently, Ryan is attending a public elementary school located in a Southwest Central region in the United States. The independent school district reports an enrollment size of 30,000 students. We will discuss the experience of Ryan within the context of assessment and program intervention later in this chapter.

Identification and Assessment

There is a dearth of literature specific to gifted identification for Asian Americans, perhaps due to the pervasive belief that Asian American children are already overrepresented in gifted programming (Worrell et al., 2019; Yoon & Gentry, 2009) and that current systems are working fine. However, this is simply not the case and students may be overlooked, particularly if they are also English learners, from low-income households, and children of refugees (Hamilton et al., 2018; Mun et al., 2016; Mun et al., 2020, 2021; Siegle et al., 2016). Furthermore, depending on immigrant generation, prior education in country of origin, language ability, and access to resources, which can all be considered a form of family capital (Coleman, 1988; Ngo & Lee, 2007; Noguera, 2004; Zhou & Lee, 2017), recommended strategies for identification, assessment, and services may look different for each student.

According to a meta-analysis conducted by Hodges et al. (2018), gifted program referrals vary across states. Because policies and programs relating to education are administered at state levels, each state is free to adopt its own definition of giftedness. Increasingly, states and districts are using a broader definition of giftedness that takes talents and potentiality into consideration with a mix of traditional assessments (e.g., intelligence scores, achievement scores) and additional criteria such as parent rating scales and portfolio assessment (Borland, 2014; Hodges et al., 2018). Authors in gifted literature have often raised the concern of fairness when intelligence assessments are used to identify giftedness in minoritized groups (Castellano, 2011; DeVries & Golon, 2011; Mun et al., 2021; Siegle et al., 2016) with English language fluency being a noted concern (Mun et al., 2016).

The question remains how professionals in our field can approach assessment of Asian American children when traditional methods are not always appropriate. Based on best practices in gifted identification practices, we recommend a holistic approach that considers multiple criteria and students' unique backgrounds (Borland, 2014; Mun, 2016). To do this, educators must first closely review the Asian American students they serve in their district and schools, looking beyond the monolithic marker. For example, are there students from East, South, or Southeast Asian countries of origin? If so, which countries? Are there specific ethnic groups represented with unique characteristics to consider for gifted identification or services? Where are students on the spectrum of immigrant generations and are there special considerations here related to family and individual capital? Equitable gifted programs should promote inclusion, not exclusion, and aim to meet individualized, educational needs. For first and 1.5 generation Asian Americans, their prior experiences with schooling, testing, and tutoring may lead to differential performances.

Taking Inventory of Prior Academics/Didactics of Home Countries

American students continue to underperform in terms of academic skills when compared with their international peers in two globally recognized assessments. In 2015, the average scores in math, science, and reading placed U.S. students at the ranking of 31 despite our educational expenditures being the second highest in elementary and secondary education among Organisation for Economic Co-operation and Development (OECD) countries. Furthermore, our spending for the same year was 93% higher than the average expenditures of OECD countries (NCES, n.d.). Many authors have cautioned against straitened interpretation of these results (Baird et al., 2016; Feniger & Lefstein, 2014; Rubinstein-Avila, 2016). For newly immigrant children from one of the 30 countries with PISA (Programme for International Student Assessment) scores ranking above the United

Table 9.1 Result of CBE Acceleration Assessment and Academic Readiness Tests Results

Subject	Elementary 4	Elementary 5	STAAR 4
English Language Arts and Reading	84	57	n/a
Mathematics	86	87	2040
Reading			1676
Science	87	74	n/a
Social Studies	74	51	n/a
Writing			5038

Note: Ryan met mastery level in all three academic readiness tests and achieved the percentile rankings of Mathematics (100th), Reading (90th), and Writing (98th) within the state.

States, the resultant achievement gap creates a conundrum for intervention. The apparent advance in mathematical skills may mask deficiencies in other subject areas.

For example, near the end of Ryan's first fourth-grade term, his parents requested his elementary school to administer credit by examination (CBE) under the current state education code which provides for one-level acceleration for primary school students based on examination results (see Table 9.1). According to the parents, a noticeable decline in Ryan's learning trajectory, particularly in mathematics, was their impetus to seek intervention. Because the threshold for grade acceleration is 80 in all subjects being tested, Ryan was denied acceleration. The student sat for the statewide academic readiness assessment administered to all fourth- grade students and results from the examination placed him at or above 90% of his peers in all three subjects tested. How should school districts service a student who meets or exceeds grade expectations except for content that is geographically and culturally specific such as social studies. More importantly, what can educators at the front line do to provide a suitable learning experience for students like Ryan? This is an important issue critical to the success of an Asian American student participating in the American educational system for the first time.

The case of Ryan may be difficult to resolve within a school district, yet it is a mere glimpse into the diversity of academic abilities observed at the front line of classrooms. Because educators and professionals are likely to encounter a much more complex spectrum of uneven academic performances in their classrooms, professionals in the field must take inventory of the prior academics and didactics of their gifted students to better understand extant content depth from home countries.

While there are purported cultural- and language-neutral intelligence tests such as the Naglieri Nonverbal Ability Test (NNAT) and Raven's Standard Progressive Matrices, scholars remain concerned that nonverbal intelligence assessments may not measure the constructs aligned to the abilities of some Asian American children (Cao et al., 2017). One possibility is the use of localized versions of intelligence tests. For example, not only are there translated versions of the Wechsler Intelligence Scale for Children (WISC) (Cao et al., 2017), local norms may also be available through the publisher of the instrument. Another possibility is testing children in their native language if they have demonstrated high fluency in that language (Mun et al., 2016).

Finally, there is considerable evidence from the literature to support disaggregating demographic data for Asian American sub-groups (Teranishi et al., 2014; Yeung & Mun, 2021). For example, a group of first generation Myanmar refugee students who are

English Learners will typically underperform on standardized cognitive assessments as compared with third generation immigrant Asian American students with parents from professional working backgrounds, despite the Asian demographic classification that both groups would fall under. In making decisions of identification, assessments, and services, educators must also carefully consider family capital and assess for prior education if the child is a recent immigrant.

Curriculum and Instruction

Knowing our students, understanding their interests, and teaching to their levels are basic ingredients for good pedagogy. In a 2018 interview, Julia Link Roberts said that, "Teachers must know that effective differentiation is more than doing something different; instead, it is matching learning experiences to learners' interests or readiness levels" (Henshon, 2018, p. 4). These principles are important when considering curriculum and instructional techniques for gifted Asian American students.

Researchers have offered diverse views of what are important characteristics of gifted curriculum during the past century. Hollingworth (1926) introduced the concept of rapid progress (acceleration), teachers' qualifications (with emphasis on the positionality of teachers – their judgement, bias, and speculations in relation to giftedness and students' intelligence), modification of method (project-based learning), segregation (pull out), curriculum enrichment (inquiry-based learning), equipment of the classroom (resources and artifacts), and special classes in chapter XI of her seminal work – *Gifted Children: Their Nature and Nurture*. Housand (2017) proposes that gifted curriculum design must take into consideration the characteristics of connected, curious, creative, capable, and conscientious leaders as commonly found in gifted learners. NAGC includes critical thinking strategies, creative thinking strategies, problem-solving models, and inquiry models in their recommended instructional strategies (NAGC, 2020). Using the Actiotope model of giftedness, curriculum is a component of didactic educational capital which is defined as one of five exogenous learning resources (Ziegler et al., 2017).

According to Lim et al. (2019), students' experiences and learning interests are framed by their prior experiences, home knowledge, and cultural resources. Thus, culturally responsive pedagogy could be used to better serve Asian American students in the classroom. Ladson-Billings' (1995) theory of culturally relevant pedagogy has often been cited in educational literature (Chang & Qin, 2017; Lim et al., 2019) as a promising approach with students of color, and has been found to support academics and cultural identity. Culturally relevant pedagogy (CRP), as defined by Ladson-Billings (1995), is a "theoretical model that not only addresses student achievement but also helps students to accept and affirm their cultural identity while developing critical perspectives that challenge inequities that schools (and other institutions) perpetuate" (p. 469). A cultural mismatch between school and home tends to impose conformity upon students. The use of culturally responsive pedagogy in the classroom can honor the inherent qualities of the students' culture and identity.

Classroom Strategies

Gifted and talented (GT) programming is often different across states and school districts. Contemporary gifted curricula are largely built upon differentiation frameworks and subject-specific models (Dimitriadis, 2016). Service options are aligned to two mega-models; acceleration and enrichment (Robinson & Tabler, 2016) which can both be used effectively with Asian American students. In order to meet the uneven prior contents and the varying levels of English language proficiency commonly found within the Asian American gifted student population, we further recommend the use of service options such as cluster grouping and mentoring.

One strategy for a diverse gifted classroom is a selective implementation of front loading. The front-loading strategy is an instructional approach designed to advance the achievement of students who are near the threshold for enrollment in gifted intervention (Olszewski-Kubilius & Steenbergen-Hu, 2017). Results have been positively related to narrowing achievement gaps for students from groups traditionally underrepresented in gifted programs who demonstrated high potential (Olszewski-Kubilius & Steenbergen-Hu, 2017). We speak of partial implementation of this strategy to reflect the reality of uneven prior academics and linguistic abilities that are common to the Asian American gifted population. Conceptually, the strategy is modeled after a talent development schema. While the strategy entails modification of identification thresholds, and supplemental and pull-out programs (Olszewski-Kubilius & Steenbergen-Hu, 2017), it can be implemented selectively as an intensive intervention for Asian American students exhibiting a deficit in particular subjects.

Again, with Ryan, while his math and science scores would have supported promotion to two grades above his current level, his results in English and Social Science subjects were marginal when tested at two levels above his current grade. Because science was taught in a local language from Kindergarten to third grade, it is conceivable that technical understanding of scientific concepts had been retained in a foreign language. The lack of practical use and academic exposure may also explain his low achievement in English. Intensive intervention using front-loading strategy is likely to accommodate a student's unique needs for subject-focused remediation.

Curriculum compacting, grouping, mentoring, and other research-based classroom strategies are available to gifted specialists when working with this diverse group of Asian Americans (NAGC, 2020). For best results, teachers should be aware of practices familiar to the Asian American gifted learners. For example, grouping is one of the three common practices employed in gifted classrooms across Taiwan (Ibata-Arens, 2012). Another characteristic that practitioners in gifted education should be aware of is how to provide challenges that can address the disparity in intellectual giftedness of the students. Some Asian countries (e.g., Singapore, Korea, or Vietnam) rely either solely or heavily on intelligence tests or achievement tests when selecting students for gifted programs (Aljughaiman et al., 2016; Y. Dương, personal communication, January 20, 2020; Neihart & Tan, 2016). Other Southeast Asian nations adopt an entirely different approach to gifted programming. Anuruthwong (2017) pointed out that the identification process for gifted intervention in Thailand relies upon preponderance of evidence from academic achievement, intelligence tests, and teacher nomination. Disparities from prior gifted programming can be expected to manifest themselves as differences in abilities and ease of assimilation between first generation cohorts of diverse Asian ethnicities within the same gifted classrooms. Inquiry-based instructional methods involve learners in their own knowledge acquisition processes and allow students to pursue questions or subjects of personal interest. Research suggests that inquiry based methods are beneficial to achievement outcomes (Hariyanto et al.,

2019; Maxwell et al., 2015), enhance students' engagement (Hariyanto et al., 2019), and promote science and language development differentially for both incipient and ascendant English learners (Lyon et al., 2012) and gifted students (Chen et al., 2020). We recommend the integration of inquiry-based learning methods in classroom practices for gifted Asian American students.

Recommendations

In this chapter, we have explained the many differences in Asian sub-groups related to culture, varying degrees of capital, prior academics, and learning needs. Our aim is to illustrate that there is no "one size fits all" solution that can meet the varying aptitudes of Asian American gifted students. Perhaps the first and most important step is for practitioners in the field to look beyond the "Asian American" label when working with students from an Asian heritage. Disaggregating data into sub-groups is highly recommended. The wide diversity between sub-groups of gifted Asian American students also calls for flexibility in gifted identification and services. Based on a review of the literature, we provide a list of recommendations for educators working with this special population.

1   **Understand that equity and access are also issues that need to be addressed in the Asian American population**
    Due to the model minority stereotype and the pervasive perception that Asian Americans are overrepresented in gifted programs, students (particularly those belonging to sub-groups of Asian Americans that have not traditionally achieved as well) may be overlooked for advanced academic services. It is important to look beyond proportionality of enrollment numbers and see who constitutes the sub-groups of Asian Americans. For example, is the overrepresentation data masking the underidentification of sub-groups of Asian American students who are English Learners, students classified as low-income, or students who are children of refugees?

2   **Disaggregate racial and ethnic data in the district and school to better identify and serve specific gifted Asian American sub-groups**
    Aggregated racial or ethnic labels tend to mask distinctive linguistic, religious, and cultural orientations of the particular gifted student's heritage. Conversely, ethnic data that have been disaggregated offer clarity to administrators and practitioners in how best to match services to needs. There is also an implication for funding, recruitment, resources management, and in-service training needs. In-service training that includes programs on the Asian American diaspora serves to enrich teachers' knowledge and enhance their understanding of the diversity represented by an Asian American label in their districts.

3   **Avoid broad generalizations and stereotyping by learning about country of origin, culture, ethnic membership, immigrant generationality, and student needs**
    Generalization of racial or ethnic groups can negatively impact service delivery. More importantly, administrators and practitioners must maintain high levels of sensitivity to the disparate skill sets present in the same learning space. For example, the English proficiency level of gifted Asian American students who self-identify in the same ethnicity may range from initially fluent English proficient (IEEP), redesignated fluent English proficient (RFEP), or limited English proficient (LEP). However, the

unevenness in language skills may not be indicative of the students' abilities or potential in mastering subjects; thus, reliance upon this performance as a determinant of aptitudes in a diagnostic manner should be avoided.

4   **Provide acceleration and remediation: subject, grade, or both**
Due to the wide disparity of skills amongst gifted Asian American students, whenever feasible, administrators, counselors, and educators should consider the implementation of service regimes composed of acceleration for subjects where students have demonstrated mastery at the required level or above, and remedial instruction for areas where the students are performing below district standards.

The case of our fourth grader, Ryan, exemplifies the rationale for this recommendation. While it is true that Ryan's application for acceleration was declined, his quantitative skills were clearly above his fourth grade level. Further, his scores in fifth grade (Math = 87, Science = 74) would likely pass school district standards for promotion to sixth grade. Conversely, his Social Studies score of 74 would not have been the reason for grade retention. Subject acceleration would have been the appropriate intervention. For the combined subjects of English language, arts, and reading (ELAR) and for Social Studies (SS), Ryan achieved passing scores for Grade 4 level (ELAR = 84, SS = 74), but failed at the Grade 5 level (ELAR = 57, SS = 51); see Table 9.1. Naturally, a remedial program targeting these areas would help to narrow the asynchrony between his quantitative subjects and his English language/Social Sciences achievement.

5   **Differentiation may be carried out within class and within grade when deemed appropriate**
VanTassel-Baska (2017) explained that "using any curriculum development model effectively will require schools to implement different aspects of curriculum simultaneously" (p. 62). In the case of Ryan, curriculum differentiation is arguably the most appropriate choice for intervention under the circumstances. Specifically, Ryan would likely benefit from a differentiated social science curriculum with emphasis on local and regional knowledge that were not part of the curricula in schools outside of the region. Additionally, a differentiated curriculum targeting mathematics and science should be implemented for Ryan concurrently.

6   **Practice culturally relevant pedagogy (CRP) in classrooms**
We use CRP (Ladson-Billings, 1995) as our foundation in lobbying for a closer connection between theory and practice of culturally relevant education. CRP arose out of the scholarship of Ladson-Billings (1995) in the critical examination of gains in academic achievement at the expense of cultural competence. Similarly, our population of gifted Asian American students brings with them diverse cultural capital to the classrooms that may be vastly different from the norms of the dominant culture. Participation in gifted education should not be detrimental to these students' cultural competence. Rather, because cultural capital is an important element of their structural influences, it should be capitalized upon to enhance the student's knowledge acquisition process (Lim et al., 2019).

Since Ladson-Billings first introduced CRP, researchers have promoted variations and refinements. Authors Lim et al. (2019) and others (e.g., Seidl, 2007; Sleeter, 2012; Young, 2010) were particularly concerned with superficial and simplistic application of CRP in the field. Conceptually, CRP advocates the leveraging of cultural knowledge, prior experiences, frames of reference, and performance styles of students from diverse backgrounds. Practitioners operationalize this through practices that affirm the cultural diversity of students in the classroom. For starters, we urge educators to recognize how students with a collectivistic cultural orientation may behave differently from their peers from an individualistic culture that is dominant in the West. What may be observed as disinterest in classroom participation may just be a manifestation of a more revered trait of humility in Asian cultures.

7   **Provide professional development on identification, assessment, and services for gifted Asian Americans**

Cross-cultural studies have found that learning styles may differ not only between gifted and non-gifted students, but also across cultures (de Hahn, 2001). The time that these gifted students spend with the regular teachers who may be less informed of their learning needs when compared to GT specialists is substantive. Our recommendation for professional development and in-service training is that these programs are reflective of the myriad factors informing the knowledge acquisition processes of gifted Asian American students. To put a context on our recommendations, we have included relevant examples of gifted populations with each item:

- Understanding academic performance – A seven hours gap per week on academics exists between academically talented students from India and their American peers (Makel et al., 2015).
- Cognizant of cultural orientation – Asian American parents with twice-exceptional (2e) children were found to be adaptive in their parenting styles in contrast to the perception of a performance-oriented and controlling disposition typified in prevalent discourse on the Asian American parenting style (Park et al., 2018).
- Mindful of the three capitals: educational capital, learning capital, and cultural capital – Vialle & Ziegler (2015) proposed five forms each of exogenous and endogenous resources impactful to gifted education across Asia, unlike those proposed in the original work on the Actiotope Model of Giftedness (Ziegler & Phillipson, 2012).

Conclusion

It has been our intent to provide as many relevant examples, drawn from various nations and territories across Asia, as is reasonable to help improve identification and services for gifted Asian American students. To achieve this goal, we consulted gifted scholarship from the past (e.g., Hollingworth, 1926) and present (e.g., Le & Raposa, 2019) and examined literature across disciplines (e.g., psychology, sociology). To ensure that our chapter is reflective of native perspectives of learning needs unique to students from Asia, we drew upon the authorship of researchers from the region (e.g., Anuruthwong from Thailand, Garces-Bacsal of Singapore) and communicated with incumbent educators and administrators in Asia. From time to time, we relied upon literature outside of gifted education to gain a better understanding of the *funds of knowledge* (Moll et al., 1992) typical to a locale.

In conclusion, the number of Asian Americans is growing rapidly in U.S. schools, meaning that there will be a commensurate rise in students being identified for gifted services. At the same time, the number of misdiagnoses and under-identification will likely increase. Underrepresentation of some of these students will be masked by the overrepresentation rhetoric of the Asian American gifted population, leading to loss of equitable opportunities. Disaggregation of racial and ethnic data in districts and schools will be a helpful step forward to better serve sub-groups of gifted Asian Americans. We must acknowledge the special assessment and learning needs within these various sub-groups and ensure that our colleagues in the field understand the idiosyncrasies and cultural nuances within this population. We know that the timing and nature of immigration matter to the acculturation, SES, and family capital of Asian American students. Professionals in the field are best positioned to mitigate issues relating to acculturation and iatrogenic effects from within the social environment of the gifted Asian American population. Finally, there is a need for more research as the literature on identifying and serving these students is scant – particularly research published in the last decade. By considering the unique and diverse needs of gifted Asian American students in the classroom and permitting their understanding to guide dispositions, educators can better nurture their development and maximize individual potential.

References

Aeschlimann, J., Ruder, N., Nakano, K., & Aeschlimann, J. (2017). *The PGA handbook: A practical guide to the United Nations General Assembly* (M. Regan, Ed.; 2nd ed.). Permanent Mission of Switzerland to the United Nations.

Aljughaiman, A., Nofal, M., & Hein, S. (2016). Gifted education in Saudi Arabia: A review. In D. Y. Dai & C.-C. Kuo (Eds.), *A critical assessment of gifted education in India* (pp. 191–212). Information Age Publishing.

Anuruthwong, U. (2017). Education for the gifted/talented in Thailand. *Cogent Education, 4*(1). https://doi.org/10.1080/2331186X.2017.1332825

Baird, J.-A., Johnson, S., Hopfenbeck, T. N., Isaacs, T., Sprague, T., Stobart, G., & Yu, G. (2016). On the supranational spell of PISA in policy. *Educational Research, 58*(2), 121–138. https://doi.org/10.1080/00131881.2016.1165410

Borland, J. H. (2014). Identification of gifted students. In J. A. Plucker & C. M. Callahan (Eds.), *Critical issues and practices in gifted education* (2nd ed., pp. 323–342). Prufrock Press.

Bronfenbrenner, U. (1979). *The ecology of human development: Experiments by nature and design.* Harvard University Press.

Bronfenbrenner, U. (2004). *Making human beings human.* Sage.

Bui, L. (2017). Examining the academic achievement–delinquency relationship among Southeast Asian Americans. *International Journal of Offender Therapy and Comparative Criminology, 62*(6), 1556–1572. https://doi.org/10.1177/0306624X17699896

Byun, S., & Park, H. (2012). The academic success of East Asian American youth: The role of shadow education. *Sociology of Education, 85*(1), 40–60. https://doi.org/10.1177/0038040711417009

Cao, T. H., Jung, J. Y., & Lee, J. (2017). Assessment in gifted education: A review of the literature from 2005 to 2016. *Journal of Advanced Academics, 28*(3), 163–203. https://doi.org/10.1177/1932202X17714572

Castellano, J. A. (2011). Hispanic students and gifted education: New outlooks, perspectives, and paradigms. In A. D. Frazier & J. A. Castellano (Eds.), *Special populations in gifted education: Understanding our most able students from diverse backgrounds* (pp. 249–269). Prufrock Press.

Center for the Study of Hate & Extremism. (2021). *Report to the nation: Anti-Asian prejudice & hate crime.* Retrieved from: www.csusb.edu/sites/default/files/Report%20to%20the%20Nation%20-%20Anti-Asian%20Hate%202020%20Final%20Draft%20-%20As%20of%20Apr%2030%202021%206%20PM%20corrected.pdf

Central Intelligence Agency. (2020, January 16). *East Asia/Southeast Asia: Philippines.* The World Factbook. Retrieved from: www.cia.gov/the-world-factbook/countries/philippines/

Chang, T.-F., & Qin, D. B. (2017). Relations between academic adjustment and parental psychological control of academically gifted Chinese American and European American students. *Child Indicators Research, 10*(3), 715–734. https://doi.org/10.1007/s12187-016-9403-1

Chen, Y.-C., Pan, Y.-T., Hong, Z.-R., Weng, X.-F., & Lin, H.-S. (2020). Exploring the pedagogical features of integrating essential competencies of scientific inquiry in classroom teaching. *Research in Science & Technological Education, 38*(2), 185–207.

Chung, R. U. (2015). *Parental expectations for Asian American men who entered college early: Influences on their academic, career, and interpersonal decision-making* [PhD thesis, University of Washington]. Available at: https://digital.lib.washington.edu/researchworks/handle/1773/33756

Coleman, J. S. (1988). Social capital in the creation of human capital. *American Journal of Sociology, 94*, S95–S120. Available at: www.jstor.org/stable/2780243

Connery, C. E., Green III, P. C., & Kaufman, J. C. (2019). The underrepresentation of CLD students in gifted and talented programs: Implications for law and practice. *University of Mary Law Journal of Race, Religion, Gender and Class, 19*(1), 80–101.

Crawford, B. F., Snyder, K. E., & Adelson, J. L. (2019). Exploring obstacles faced by gifted minority students through Bronfenbrenner's bioecological systems theory. *High Ability Studies, 31*(1), 43–74. https://doi.org/10.1080/13598139.2019.1568231

de Hahn, E. L. H. (2001). Cross-cultural studies in gifted education. In K. A. Heller, J. Franz, R. J. Sternberg, & R. F. Subotnik (Eds.), *International handbook of giftedness and talent* (2nd ed., pp. 549–561). Elsevier.

Desilver, D. (2014, September 30). 5 facts about Indian Americans. Pew Research Center. Retrieved from: www.pewresearch.org/fact-tank/2014/09/30/5-facts-about-indian-americans/

DeVries, M., & Golon, A. S. (2011). Making education relevant for gifted Native Americans: Teaching to their learning style. In J. A. Castellano & A. D. Frazier (Eds.), *Special populations in gifted education: Understanding our most able students from diverse backgrounds* (pp. 47–71). Prufrock Press.

Dimitriadis, C. (2016). Gifted programs cannot be successful without gifted research and theory: Evidence from practice with gifted students of mathematics. *Journal for the Education of the Gifted, 39*(3), 221–236. https://doi.org/10.1177/0162353216657185

Duong, M. T., Badaly, D., Liu, F. F., Schwartz, D., & McCarty, C. A. (2016). Generational differences in academic achievement among immigrant youths: A meta-analytic review. *Review of Educational Research, 86*(1), 3–41. https://doi:10.3102/0034654315577680

Ecker-Lyster, M., & Niileksela, C. (2017). Enhancing gifted education for underrepresented students: Promising recruitment and programming strategies. *Journal for the Education of the Gifted, 40*(1), 79–95. https://doi.org/10.1177/0162353216686216

Erwin, J. O., & Worrell, F. C. (2012). Assessment practices and the underrepresentation of minority students in gifted and talented education. *Journal of Psychoeducational Assessment, 30*(1), 74–87. https://doi: 10.1177/0734282911428197

Farver, J. M., Narang, S. K., & Bhada, B. R. (2002). East meets West: Ethnic identity, acculturation, and conflict in Asian Indian families. *Journal of Family Psychology, 16*(3), 338–350. https://doi.org/10.1037/0893-3200.16.3.338

Feliciano, C., & Lanuza, Y. R. (2017). An immigrant paradox? Contextual attainment and intergenerational educational mobility. *American Sociological Review, 82*(1), 211–241. https://doi:10.1177/0003122416684777

Feniger, Y., & Lefstein, A. (2014). How *not* to reason with PISA data: An ironic investigation. *Journal of Education Policy, 29*(6), 845–855. https://doi.org/10.1080/02680939.2014.892156

Galindo, C., & Sheldon, S. B. (2012). School and home connections and children's kindergarten achievement gains: The mediating role of family involvement. *Early Childhood Research Quarterly, 27*(1), 90–103. https://doi.org/10.1016/j.ecresq.2011.05.004

Garces-Bacsal, R. M., & Yeo, S. D. (2017). Why and what they read when they don't have to: Factors influencing the recreational reading habits of gifted students in Singapore. *Journal for the Education of the Gifted, 40*(3), 247–265. https://doi.org/10.1177/0162353217717035

Garn, A. C., Matthews, M. S., & Jolly, J. L. (2012). Parents' role in the academic motivation of students with gifts and talents. *Psychology in the Schools, 49*(7), 656–667. https://doi.org/10.1002/pits.21626

Grant, H., & Dweck, C. S. (2001). Cross-cultural response to failure: Considering outcome attributions with different goals. In F. Salili, C. Chiu, & Y. Hong (Eds.), *Student motivation: The culture and context of learning* (pp. 203–219). Kluwer Academic/Plenum.

Grissom, J. A., & Redding, C. (2016). Discretion and disproportionality: Explaining the under-representation of high-achieving students of color in gifted programs. *AERA Open, 2*(1), 2332858415622175. https://doi.org/10.1177/2332858415622175

Hamilton, R., McCoach, D. B., Tutwiler, S. M., Siegle, D., Gubbins, E. J., Callahan, C. M., … Mun, R. U. (2018). Disentangling the roles of institutional and individual poverty in the identification of gifted students. *Gifted Child Quarterly, 62*(1), 6–24. https://doi.org/10.1177/0016986217738053

Hariyanto, Joyoatmojo, S., Nurkamto, J., & Gunarhadi. (2019). The influence of inquiry-based learning materials towards students' achievement. *Journal of Physics: Conference Series, 1339,* 012067. https://doi.org/10.1088/1742-6596/1339/1/012067

Henshon, S. E. (2018). Serving the needs of gifted learners around the globe: An interview with Julia Link Roberts. *Roeper Review, 40*(1), 4–6. https://doi.org/10.1080/02783193.2018.1393740

Hodges, J., Tay, J., Maeda, Y., & Gentry, M. (2018). A meta-analysis of gifted and talented identification practices. *Gifted Child Quarterly, 62*(2), 147–174. https://doi.org/10.1177/0016986217752107

Hoeffel, E. M., Rastogi, S., Kim, M. O., & Shahid, H. (2012). The Asian population: 2010. United States Census Bureau. Retrieved from: www.census.gov/prod/cen2010/briefs/c2010br-11.pdf

Hollingworth, L. (1926). *Gifted children: Their nature and nurture* (1st ed.). The MacMillan Company.

Housand, A. M. (2017). In context: Gifted characteristics and the implications for curriculum. In K. R. Stephens & F. A. Karnes (Eds.), *Introduction to curriculum design in gifted education.* Prufrock Press.

Ibata-Arens, K. C. (2012). Race to the future: Innovations in gifted and enrichment education in Asia, and implications for the United States. *Administrative Sciences, 2*(1), 1–25. https://doi.org/10.3390/admsci2010001

Kiang, L., Huynh, V. W., Cheah, C. S. L., Wang, Y., & Yoshikawa, H. (2017). Moving beyond the model minority. *Asian American Journal of Psychology, 8*(1), 1–6. http://dx.doi.org/10.1037/aap0000070

Kim, R. Y. (2002). Ethnic differences in academic achievement between Vietnamese and Cambodian children: Cultural and structural explanations. *Sociological Quarterly, 43*(2), 213–235. https://doi.org/10.1111/j.1533-8525.2002.tb00047.x

Kitano, M. K. (2011). Issues in research on Asian American gifted students. In A. D. Frazier & J. A. Castellano (Eds.), *Special populations in gifted education: Understanding our most able students from diverse backgrounds* (pp. 3–25). Prufrock Press.

Konstantopoulos, S., Modi, M., & Hedges, L. V. (2001). Who are America's gifted? *American Journal of Education, 109*(3), 344–382. https://doi.org/10.1086/444275

Ladson-Billings, G. (1995). Toward a theory of culturally relevant pedagogy. *American Educational Research Journal, 32*(3), 465–491. https://doi.org/10.3102/00028312032003465

Le, T. P., & Raposa, E. B. (2019). The role of enculturation and acculturation in Asian and European American college students' daily social stress and support. *Asian American Journal of Psychology, 10*(1), 11–21. https://doi.org/10.1037/aap0000114

Lee, D. M., Duesbery, L., Han, P. P., Tashi, T., Her, C. S., & Pang, V. O. (2017). Academic needs and family factors in the education of Southeast Asian American students: Dismantling the model minority myth. *Journal of Southeast Asian American Education and Advancement, 12*(2), 1–31. https://doi:10.7771/2153-8999.1154

Lee, E. (2015). *The making of Asian America: A history.* Simon & Schuster.

Lee, E. (2019). *America for Americans: A history of xenophobia in the United States.* Basic Books.

Lee, J., & Zhou, M. (2015). *The Asian American achievement paradox.* Russell Sage Foundation.

Lee, J., & Zhou, M. (2017). Why class matters less for Asian-American academic achievement. *Journal of Ethnic and Migration Studies, 43*(14), 2316–2330. https://doi.org/10.1080/1369183X.2017.1315851

Lee, J. C.-K., & Kennedy, K. J. (Eds.). (2017). *Theorizing teaching and learning in Asia and Europe: A conversation between Chinese curriculum and European didactics.* Routledge.

Lim, L., Tan, M., & Saito, E. (2019). Culturally relevant pedagogy: Developing principles of description and analysis. *Teaching and Teacher Education, 77*, 43–52. https://doi.org/10.1016/j.tate.2018.09.011

Lin, H. Y., Davidman, P., Petersen, G., & Thomas, R. M. (1998). Teachers' views of moral education topics – Taiwan and the USA. *International Review of Education, 44*(1), 65–85. https://doi.org/10.1023/A:1003331212351

Lin, L. (2019). The visible hand behind study-abroad waves: Cram schools, organizational framing and the international mobility of Chinese students. *Higher Education, 79*, 259–274. https://doi.org/10.1007/s10734-019-00408-1

Lopez, G., Ruiz, N. G., & Patten, E. (2017, September 8). Key facts about Asian Americans, a diverse and growing population. Pew Research. Retrieved from: www.pewresearch.org/fact-tank/2017/09/08/key-facts-about-asian-americans/

Lyon, E. G., Bunch, G. C., & Shaw, J. M. (2012). Navigating the language demands of an inquiry-based science performance assessment: Classroom challenges and opportunities for English learners. *Science Education, 96*(4), 631–651. https://doi.org/10.1002/sce.21008

Makel, M. C., Wai, J., Putallaz, M., & Malone, P. S. (2015). The academic gap: An international comparison of the time allocation of academically talented students. *Gifted Child Quarterly, 59*(3), 177–189. https://doi.org/10.1177/0016986215578746

Marsh, H. W., Trautwein, U., Lüdtke, O., & Köller, O. (2008). Social comparison and big-fish-little-pond effects on self-concept and other self-belief constructs: Role of generalized and specific others. *Journal of Educational Psychology, 100*(3), 510–524. https://doi.org/10.1037/0022-0663.100.3.510

Maxwell, D. O., Lambeth, D. T., & Cox, J. T. (2015). Effects of using inquiry-based learning on science achievement for fifth-grade students. *Asia – Pacific Forum on Science Learning and Teaching, 16*(1), 1–31.

Md-Yunus, S., Li, M., Mullins, F., & Gong, R. (2017). The Pygmalion effect of the filial piety on immigrant children: The influence on Asian American students. *Journal of Cultural Diversity, 24*, 84–90.

Merriam, S. B., & Tisdell, E. J. (2016). *Qualitative research.* Jossey-Bass.

Moll, L. C., Amanti, C., Neff, D., & Gonzalez, N. (1992). Funds of knowledge for teaching: Using a qualitative approach to connect homes and classrooms. *Theory into Practice, 31*(2), 132–141. https://doi.org/10.1080/00405849209543534

Morgan, H. (2020). The gap in gifted education: Can universal screening narrow it? *Education, 140*(4), 207–214.

Mun, R. U. (2016). Identifying and assessing highly capable students. *Washington Educational Research Association Educational Journal (WEJ), 8*(2), 14–17.

Mun, R. U., Ezzani, M. D., Lee, L. E., & Ottwein, J. K. (2021). Building systemic capacity to improve identification and services in gifted education: A case study of one district. *Gifted Child Quarterly, 65*(2), 132–152. https://doi.org/10.1177%2F0016986220967376

Mun, R. U., Hemmler, V., Langley, S. D., Ware, S., Gubbins, E. J., Callahan, C. M., ... Siegle, D. (2020). Identifying and serving English learners in gifted education: Looking back and moving forward. *Journal for the Education of the Gifted, 43*(4), 297–335. https://doi.org/10.1177/0162353220955230

Mun, R. U., & Hertzog, N. B. (2019). The influence of parental and self-expectations on Asian American women who entered college early. *Gifted Child Quarterly, 63*(2), 120–140. https://doi: 10.1177/0016986218823559

Mun, R. U., Langley, S. D., Ware, S., Gubbins, E. J., Siegle, D., Callahan, C. M., ... Hamilton, R. (2016, December). *Effective practices for identifying and serving English learners in gifted education: A systematic review of the literature.* National Center for Research on Gifted Education (NCRGE).

Museus, S. D., & Kiang, P. N. (2009). Deconstructing the model minority myth and how it contributes to the invisible minority reality in higher education research. *New Directions for Institutional Research, 142*, 5–15. https://doi.org/10.1002/ir.292

National Association for Gifted Children [NAGC]. (2020, January 22). Gifted education strategies. National Association for Gifted Children. Retrieved from: www.nagc.org/resources-publications/gifted-education-practices

National Center for Education Statistics [NCES]. (n.d.). *The condition of education—International comparisons—Finances—Education expenditures by country—Indicator May (2019)*. The Condition of Education. Retrieved October 28, 2019 from: https://nces.ed.gov/programs/coe/indicator_cmd.asp

Neihart, M., & Tan, L. S. (2016). Gifted education in Singapore. In D. Y. Dai & C.-C. Kuo (Eds.), *Gifted education in Asia: Problems and prospects* (pp. 77–96). Information Age Publishing.

Ngo, B., & Lee, S. J. (2007). Complicating the image of model minority success: A review of Southeast Asian American education. *Review of Educational Research, 77*(4), 415–453. https://doi:10.3102/0034654307309918

Noguera, P. (2004). Social capital and the education of immigrant students: Categories and generalizations. *Sociology of Education, 77*(2), 180–183. https://doi.org/10.1177/003804070407700206

Okazaki, S. (n.d.). *Asian American experiences of racism during COVID-19*. New York University, The Institute of Human Development and Social Change. Retrieved from: https://steinhardt.nyu.edu/ihdsc/on-the-ground/asian-american-experiences-racism-during-covid-19

Olszewski-Kubilius, P. (2016). Optimal parenting and family environments for talent development. In M. Neihart, S. I. Pfeiffer, & T. L. Cross (Eds.), *The social and emotional development of gifted children: What do we know?* (2nd ed., pp. 205–215). The National Association for Gifted Children and Prufrock Press.

Olszewski-Kubilius, P., & Steenbergen-Hu, S. (2017). Blending research-based practices and practice-embedded research: Project Excite closes achievement and excellence gaps for underrepresented gifted minority students. *Gifted Child Quarterly, 61*(3), 202–209. https://doi.org/10.1177/0016986217701836

Olszewski-Kubilius, P., Subotnik, R. F., & Worrell, F. C. (2015). Conceptualizations of giftedness and the development of talent: Implications for counselors. *Journal of Counseling & Development, 93*(2), 143–152. https://doi.org/10.1002/j.1556-6676.2015.00190.x

Oyserman, D., & Destin, M. (2010). Identity-based motivation: Implications for intervention. *The Counseling Psychologist, 38*(7), 1001–1043. https://doi.org/10.1177/0011000010374775

Özek, U., & Figlio, D. N. (2016). Cross-generational differences in educational outcomes in the second great wave of immigration (NBER Working Paper No. 22262). National Bureau of Economic Research. Retrieved from: www.nber.org/papers/w22262

Paik, S. J., Choe Shirlie, M. M., Otto, W. J., & Zaynah, R. (2018). Learning about the lives and early experiences of notable Asian American women: Productive giftedness, childhood traits, and supportive conditions. *Journal for the Education of the Gifted, 41*(2), 160–192. https://doi.org/10.1177/0162353218763927

Park, S., Foley-Nicpon, M., Choate, A., & Bolenbaugh, M. (2018). "Nothing fits exactly": Experiences of Asian American parents of twice-exceptional children. *Gifted Child Quarterly, 62*(3), 306–319. https://doi.org/10.1177/0016986218758442

Peters, S. J., Rambo-Hernandez, K., Makel, M. C., Matthews, M. S., & Plucker, J. A. (2019). Effect of local norms on racial and ethnic representation in gifted education. *AERA Open, 5*(2). https://doi.org/10.1177/2332858419848446

Phillipson, S. N., & Phillipson, S. (2016). Lessons in gifted education from Asia. In D. Y. Dai & C.-C. Kuo (Eds.), *Gifted education in Asia: Problems and prospects* (pp. 97–119). Information Age Publishing.

Poon, O., Squire, D., Kodama, C., Byrd, A., Chan, J., Manzano, L., … Bishundat, D. (2016). A critical review of the model minority myth in selected literature on Asian Americans and Pacific Islanders in higher education. *Review of Educational Research, 86*(2), 469–502. https://doi.org/10.3102/0034654315612205

Roberge, M. M. (2002). California's generation 1.5 immigrants: What experiences, characteristics, and needs do they bring to our English classes? *The CATESOL Journal, 14*(1), 107–109. Retrieved from: www.catesoljournal.org/wp-content/uploads/2014/07/CJ14_roberge.pdf

Robinson, A., & Tabler, A. (2016). Survey of curriculum models in gifted education. In F. A. Karnes & K. Stephens (Eds.), *Introduction to curriculum design in gifted education* (pp. 23–40). Prufrock Press. Available at: www.overdrive.com/search?q=838B7AF4-89C4-4FED-BCFA-5C53F6D5607A

Roy, P., & Kurup, A. (2016). A critical assessment of gifted education in India. In D. Y. Dai & C.-C. Kuo (Eds.), *Gifted education in Asia: Problems and prospects* (pp. 147–165). Information Age Publishing.

Rubinstein-Avila, E. (2016). Immigrant and refugee students across "receiving" nations: To what extent can educators rely on PISA for answers? *Clearing House, 89*(3), 79–84. https://doi.org/10.1080/00098655.2016.1168350

Rumbaut, R. G. (2004). Ages, life stages, and generational cohorts: Decomposing the immigrant first and second generations in the United States. *International Migration Review, 38*, 1160–1205.

Samura, M. (2015). Wrestling with expectations: An examination of how Asian American college students negotiate personal, parental, and societal expectations. *Journal of College Student Development, 56*(6), 602–618. https://doi.org/10.1353/csd.2015.0065

Seaton, M., Marsh, H. W., & Craven, R. G. (2009). Earning its place as a pan-human theory: Universality of the big-fish-little-pond effect across 41 culturally and economically diverse countries. *Journal of Educational Psychology, 101*(2), 403. https://doi.org/10.1037/a0013838

Seidl, B. (2007). Working with communities to explore and personalize culturally relevant pedagogies: Push, double images, and raced talk. *Journal of Teacher Education, 58*(2), 168–183. https://doi.org/10.1177/0022487106297845

Sharma, M., & Koh, D. (2019). Korean Americans in Los Angeles: Decentralized concentration and socio-spatial disparity. *Geographical Review, 109*(3), 356–381. https://doi.org/10.1111/gere.12358

Shaughnessy, M. F., & Cordova, M. (2019). An interview with Jonathan Plucker: Reducing and eliminating excellence gaps. *North American Journal of Psychology; Winter Garden, 21*(2), 349–359.

Siegle, D., Gubbins, E. J., O'Rourke, P., Langley, S. D., Mun, R. U., Luria, S. R., ... Plucker, J. A. (2016). Barriers to underserved students' participation in gifted programs and possible solutions. *Journal for the Education of the Gifted, 39*(2), 103–131. https://doi.org/10.1177/0162353216640930

Silverman, L. K. (1997). The construct of asynchronous development. *Peabody Journal of Education, 72*(3, 4), 36–58.

Sleeter, C. E. (1996). Multicultural education as a social movement. *Theory Into Practice, 35*(4), 239–247. https://doi.org/10.1080/00405849609543730

Stankov, L. (2010). Unforgiving Confucian culture: A breeding ground for high academic achievement, test anxiety and self-doubt? *Learning and Individual Differences, 20*(6), 555–563. https://doi.org/10.1016/j.lindif.2010.05.003

Suarez-Orozco, C., Suarez-Orozco, M. M., & Todorova, I. (2008). *Learning a new land: Immigrant students in American society*. The Belknap Press of Harvard University Press.

Teranishi, R. T., Nguyen, B. M. D., & Alcantar, C. M. (2014). The Asian American and Pacific Islander data disaggregation movement: The convergence of community activism and policy reform. *Asian American Policy Review, 25*, 26–36.

Tommis, S. D. (2016). The long view of gifted education in Hong Kong: 1990–2015 and beyond. In D. Y. Dai & C.-C. Kuo (Eds.), *Gifted education in Asia: Problems and prospects* (pp. 3–32). Information Age Publishing.

UNESCO Office Bangkok and Regional Bureau for Education in Asia and the Pacific. (2021). *NEQMAP: Network on Education Quality Monitoring in the Asia-Pacific*. UNESCO. Retrieved from: https://neqmap.bangkok.unesco.org/wp-content/uploads/2021/03/NEQMAP-Brochure_FINAL.pdf

U.S. Census Bureau. (2018). About race. Retrieved from: www.census.gov/topics/population/race/about.html

VanTassel-Baska, J. (2017). Curriculum issues: What makes differentiated curriculum work? *Gifted Child Today, 40*(1), 62–63. https://doi.org/10.1177/1076217516675905

Vialle, W., & Ziegler, A. (2015). Gifted education in modern Asia: Analysis from a systemic perspective. In D. Y. Dai & C. K. Ching (Eds.), *Gifted education in Asia: Problems and prospects*. IAP. Available at: www.infoagepub.com/products/Gifted-Education-in-Asia

Worrell, F. C., Subotnik, R. F., Olszewski-Kubilius, P., & Dixson, D. D. (2019). Gifted students. *Annual Review of Psychology, 70*(1), 551–576. https://doi.org/10.1146/annurev-psych-010418-102846

Wu, Y., Outley, C., & Matarrita-Cascante, D. (2019). Cultural immersion camps and development of ethnic identity in Asian American Youth. *Journal of Youth Development, 14*(2), 166–182. https://doi:10.5195/jyd.2019.708

Xie, Y., & Goyette, K. (2003). Social mobility and the educational choices of Asian Americans. *Social Science Research, 32*(3), 467–498. https://doi.org/10.1016/S0049-089X(03)00018-8

Yamamoto, Y., & Holloway, S. D. (2010). Parental expectations and children's academic performance in sociocultural context. *Educational Psychology Review, 22*(3), 189–214. https://doi.org/10.1007/s10648-010-9121-z

Yang, P. Q. (2004). Generational differences in educational attainment among Asian Americans. *Journal of Asian American Studies, 7*(1), 51–71. https://doi.org/10.1353/jaas.2005.0009

Yee, B. W., Su, J., Kim, S. Y., & Yancura, L. (2009). Asian American and Pacific Islander families. In N. Tewari & A. N. Alvarez (Eds.), *Asian American psychology: Current perspectives* (pp. 317–336). Psychology Press.

Yeung, G., & Mun, R. (2021). *A renewed call for disaggregation of racial and ethnic data to advance equity in gifted and talented education research*. Manuscript in preparation.

Yoon, S. Y., & Gentry, M. (2009). Racial and ethnic representation in gifted programs: Current status of and implications for gifted Asian American students. *The Gifted Child Quarterly, 53*(2), 121–136. https://doi.org/10.1177/0016986208330564

Young, E. (2010). Challenges to conceptualizing and actualizing culturally relevant pedagogy: How viable is the theory in classroom practice? *Journal of Teacher Education, 61*(3), 248–260. https://doi.org/10.1177/0022487109359775

Zhou, M., & Lee, J. (2017). Hyper-selectivity and the remaking of culture: Understanding the Asian American achievement paradox. *Asian American Journal of Psychology, 8*(1), 7–15. http://dx.doi.org/10.1037/aap0000069

Ziegler, A., Chandler, K. L., Vialle, W., & Stoeger, H. (2017). Exogenous and endogenous learning resources in the actiotope model of giftedness and its significance for gifted education. *Journal for the Education of the Gifted, 40*(4), 310–333. https://doi.org/10.1177/0162353217734376

Ziegler, A., & Phillipson, S. N. (2012). Towards a systemic theory of gifted education. *High Ability Studies, 23*(1), 3–30. https://doi.org/10.1080/13598139.2012.679085

Identifying and Providing Instructional Services for Twice-Exceptional Students

Megan Foley-Nicpon and Ching-Lan Rosaline Lin

Vignette

Jonny entered fourth grade with excitement and trepidation. He had heard Mr. Alverez was a nice, but strict teacher, and he was ready to enjoy school for a change. In third grade, he began to read faster and more easily, which opened his world to cool topics like space, time, trains, and the history of superheroes. Yet he was also typically in trouble, the last one done with all his assignments, and teased by most of his classmates. He hoped fourth grade would be more of the former and less of the latter; unfortunately, fourth grade started out worse than third. His friends quickly tired of hearing about his interests. He couldn't understand why they did not want to learn about his latest discoveries or play the same games at recess. Math became more challenging; he often got lost in the numbers or made small errors that threw off his answer. School was boring and tedious. All he wanted to do was sit outside during recess, read, and escape the reality of fourth grade.

Later that year, Mr. Alverez suggested to Jonny's parents that they consult with someone regarding Attention-Deficit Hyperactivity Disorder (ADHD). His parents also wondered if this diagnosis would explain some of Jonny's quirks and challenges and provide a vehicle for them to obtain services at school. However, private evaluations were expensive, and one of Jonny's parents had just lost his job. They learned through their pediatrician about a community mental health center that provided low-cost services for children struggling in school. After waiting several months, Jonny and his parents completed a battery of tests and interviews with a psychologist from the center. The psychologist confirmed Jonny's diagnosis of ADHD, but also mentioned he had symptoms of anxiety, which sometimes can be present among children with high ability and a disability who feel misunderstood. Jonny's parents were shocked – their son was "gifted?" They always thought he was smart, but no one ever talked about that – they solely focused on his difficulties. The psychologist told them Jonny was "twice-exceptional" and that he would benefit from accelerative opportunities in reading and writing, as well as accommodations for his impulsivity, distractibility, slow processing, and math challenges. Jonny's parents felt fortunate to have found help for their son, but worried about all the other families who could not afford the services needed to find answers for their child.

Fourth grade ended on a high note. Jonny's school principal scheduled a professional development session for teachers about twice-exceptionality. Mr. Alverez

DOI: 10.4324/9781003265412-15

arranged for Jonny to join the sixth graders for reading and writing, after which he won second place in his district's creative writing contest. He started working on math with the resource teacher, who taught him to slow down and outline the steps needed to complete word problems. Jonny began taking tests separately from his classmates, which increased his focus and performance. He learned some strategies for making friends from the school counselor. Through his pediatrician, he started taking medication, which made it easier to concentrate on longer assignments or those he did not really want to complete. Things were not perfect, but he had more academic success and friends who appreciated his interests, spent less time in the principal's office, and, for the first time, felt understood.

Twice-Exceptionality

The presence of co-existing high ability and disability within a student, often referred to as twice-exceptionality, has been recognized and researched for the past two to three decades. These students possess high ability and potential in one or more talent domains while simultaneously identifying with one or more disabilities as defined by state or federal eligibility criteria (Reis et al., 2014). Specifically, talent domains refer to any structured area (e.g., mathematics, music, language) and/or sensorimotor skills (e.g., painting, sports, dance; Subotnik et al., 2011), whereas disabilities may include ADHD, Autism Spectrum Disorder (ASD), Specific Learning Disabilities (SLD), emotional and/or behavioral disorders, speech and language disorders, and/or physical and sensory disabilities (National Education Association, 2006; Reis et al., 2014). Although no federal agency or organization collects empirical prevalence data on twice-exceptional students, it is estimated there are approximately 360,000 to 385,000 twice-exceptional students in the U.S. school system (National Center for Education Statistics, 2016; National Education Association, 2006). However, these prevalence rates likely are inaccurate as they exclude individuals served under 504 accommodation plans and those who are not identified (Foley-Nicpon et al., 2011).

Twice-exceptional students often experience unique learning, social, emotional, and/or behavioral difficulties (Robinson et al., 2007). The combination of high ability and disability may result in a masking phenomenon, where students' high ability may hide their disability, or their disability may hide their high ability (Assouline et al., 2010). As a result of such masking effects, students' high ability and disability may not be recognized or addressed. Thus, it is important that educators are exposed to empirically informed identification processes and educational programming through training programs and professional development opportunities (Baldwin et al., 2015).

Even though co-existing learning difficulties among high-ability students are variable, the previous literature on twice-exceptionality mostly focused on ADHD, ASD, SLD, emotional and/or behavioral disorders, and speech and language disorders (Foley-Nicpon et al., 2013). Thus, we will review the current research on best practice identification and assessment of these diagnostic categories among high-ability students, as well as potential co-existing mental health concerns. We also will discuss recommended curriculum and instructional strategies for educators as well as the role parents and family play as both advocates and supports. We will conclude with overall recommendations for identification, intervention, and advocacy for twice-exceptional students that are applicable for educators and parents.

Equity, Belonging, and Identity

Twice-exceptional students are challenged by a discrepancy between their strengths (i.e., high ability) and vulnerabilities (i.e., difficulties associated with their disabilities; Assouline et al., 2010; National Education Association, 2006). Imagine being a child who lives with two seemingly very different identities. They may participate in their school's gifted and talented program because they have a "gifted" label, but also have an Individualized Education Plan (IEP) because they have a disability label. In this scenario, neither identity captures the full experience of the student; at the same time, neither gifted and talent education nor student disability services alone can address their needs. The discrepancy between high ability and disability may result in social-emotional distress, such as depression and anxiety, or behavioral problems, such as aggression and hyperactivity (Doobay, 2010; Foley-Nicpon et al., 2012).

To address the complexity of twice-exceptionality, some researchers have examined the intersectionality of high ability and disability. Among all the variations of twice-exceptionality, high-ability students with SLD have received the most attention from research studies (Foley-Nicpon et al., 2011), followed by high-ability students with ADHD and ASD (Pfeiffer & Foley-Nicpon, 2018). Overall, findings identified the general characteristics of twice-exceptional students to include both vulnerabilities and strengths. Specifically, high-ability students with SLDs tend to struggle with academic domains and are more sensitive to failures (Ruban & Reis, 2005); high-ability students with ADHD report lower self-esteem, behavioral self-concept, and overall happiness (Foley-Nicpon et al., 2012) and greater academic concerns (Antshel, 2008; Antshel et al., 2007); high-ability students with SLDs or ASD can experience lower self-esteem and self-efficacy, as well as feelings of inadequacy (Barber & Mueller, 2011; Foley-Nicpon et al., 2010).

Although these findings tend to focus on the vulnerabilities of twice-exceptional students, current scholarship, particularly strengths-based studies, also have recognized the distinct aptitudes of this population. Generally, high-ability students with SLDs demonstrate exceptional abilities in the areas of verbal and nonverbal reasoning, analytical thinking, and creativity (Assouline et al., 2010); high-ability students with ADHD may have accelerated creativity and higher levels of creative thinking than high-ability students without ADHD (Fugate et al., 2013); and high-ability students with ASD display social creativity, or the ability to generate novel and creative responses in social situations (Lerner & Girard, 2018).

Little is known about how twice-exceptional students' intersecting identities may manifest uniquely among students of color because previous research has been conducted primarily with White families and children. This is a glaring hole in a body of research that already has quantity and quality problems. For example, the sole study examining the parental experiences of Asian American parents of twice-exceptional children concluded that parents reported experiences like those from other studies (e.g., Besnoy et al., 2015; Speirs Neumeister et al., 2013), suggesting this phenomenon exists across races and ethnicities (Park et al., 2018). Similarly, Mayes and Moore (2016) worked with Black twice-exceptional students and their parents and discovered the students primarily identified with their disability and not their talent domain. Whether this was because the students' talents were not fostered, or whether it had to do with internalized racism or stereotyped threat (Ford & Helms, 2012) is unclear and needs further investigation.

Like other high-ability students, twice-exceptional students are bright and creative and have a wide range of interests and expertise; like other students with disabilities, twice-exceptional students may be limited by their learning, social/emotional, and/or behavioral difficulties. Because of these discrepancies and despite their exceptional cognitive ability and potential, these students may display inconsistent academic performance, frustration, and lack of motivation (National Education Association, 2006). Therefore, as educators and professionals working together to address students' vulnerabilities, it is critical to recognize students' strengths and engagement in the learning process (Pfeiffer, 2016).

Identification and Assessment

Despite increased attention to the urgent need to diversify gifted education and the use of identification methods targeting underrepresented groups (McClain & Pfeiffer, 2012), inequity persists (Hamilton et al., 2017; Peters et al., 2016; Yoon & Gentry, 2009). This is true for students with Latinx, Black/African American, and/or American Indian racial/ethnic identities, students who are English Language Learners, as well as students with disabilities. In their analysis of who gets identified for gifted and talented programming, Peters and colleagues revealed that students served under the Individuals with Disabilities Education Act (IDEA) (Pub.L. 101-476) represent 13% of American students (NCES, 2016), yet their representation in states' gifted and talented programs is almost always below that percentage. The lowest percentage is in Louisiana, with 0.13% of students with disabilities participating in gifted/talented programming. Having a mandate for gifted education services seems not to matter, either; students with disabilities make up 3% of the gifted and talented population in states with service mandates and 5% in states with no service mandate; these rates mirror those of students who are English Language Learners (Peters et al., 2019).

The masking effect may contribute to this underrepresentation. For example, McCoach and colleagues (2020) found teacher-rated ADHD inattentive symptoms among high-ability underachieving students were over five times as high as those from the normative sample used to create the ADHD measure. In fact, 19% of the gifted underachievers had elevated parent and teacher scores on the inattention subscale, again far higher than expected in the general population of students. In these cases, it is possible some students' diagnoses of ADHD were missed even though their high ability was identified. In other cases, the student's disability is identified, but not the high ability. In a separate, recent investigation of high-ability students with ASD identified through analysis of secondary data from the U.S. Department of Education, most did not participate in their school's gifted and talented program, despite having one or more scores above the 90th percentile on a standardized test of achievement (Cain et al., 2019). In other cases, students may not be identified as gifted or as having a disability, because their composite scores wash out the differences among the index scores used to create the composite. For those students with high ability and SLD, the variability of their testing profiles necessitates examining achievement and ability score discrepancies along with test scores that are below age/

grade expectations, rather than composite scores alone, to prevent missing students who would benefit from services for their gifts/talents and their disabilities (Foley-Nicpon & Assouline, 2020; Maddocks, 2020).

The goal of identification for gifted programming in schools should be to broaden opportunity for all who need it, not restrict it to a few, globally gifted individuals from over-represented groups (McBee et al., 2014; Silverman & Gilman, 2020). This may mean altering the way gifted education is perceived in schools, which is a necessary first step to increasing inclusivity. Methods such as teacher nomination or screening part of the student population likely will perpetuate the problem (McBee et al., 2016). As has been noted by multiple scholars (e.g., McBee et al., 2016), multiple assessments are recommended to identify all high-ability students for gifted and talented programming, but special considerations may be needed for the twice-exceptional (Foley Nicpon et al., 2011), such as more individualized approaches or examining index score distributions (as noted above). As Silverman and Gilman (2020) note, flexibility in assessment is key, and it may be beneficial to reduce the number of markers required for programming identification. Understanding the necessity for and providing access to comprehensive assessment that accurately captures the variability in performance among the twice-exceptional is essential (Foley-Nicpon & Assouline, 2020: Foley-Nicpon et al., 2011).

Curriculum and Intervention

Although twice-exceptional research continues to be in the nascent stage and is often not very empirically solid (Pfeiffer & Foley-Nicpon, 2018), there are some recommended strategies for working with twice-exceptional students in school. In all circumstances and educational environments, we recommend strengths-based approaches (Baum & Owen, 2004; Baum et al., 2014; Baum & Schader, 2018; Crepeau-Hobson & Bianco, 2011) which are grounded in positive psychology tenets. When school policies and procedures place a greater emphasis on remediating students' disabilities, many twice-exceptional students who receive IEPs or 504 Plans may be excluded from participating in talent development programming (Barnard-Brak et al., 2015). As Foley-Nicpon and Kim (2018) stated, by utilizing a strengths-based approach, "students benefit from exposure to advanced material within their talent domains while receiving accommodations for their identified disability domain" (p. 357). All people, especially children and adolescents who are developing their identities, need to know where they excel and have chances to foster their talent domains.

Second, it is important to consider psychosocial factors that impact academic performance (Foley-Nicpon, 2015). Increased attention is being played to the psychosocial factors inherent in talent development (Subotnik et al., 2011), and some of these skills may need extra attention among twice-exceptional children (Beckmann & Minnaert, 2018). For example, Subotnik and colleagues (2011) discussed the importance of providing "psychosocial coaching" to students as they transition from an educational to a professional environment. They may need help developing resilience and the stress-management skills necessary for them to thrive in their careers. A twice-exceptional individual who has depression and/or anxiety may require extra attention and support to develop coping strategies. Interventions that include these components acknowledge the need to attend not only to students' cognitive and academic development, but also their social, emotional, and behavioral development in school.

Third, consider multimodal approaches to intervention (Baum et al., 2005; Busi & Berman, 2018). When using multimodal approaches to teach academic content, students are given the option to learn material through diverse pathways, such as hands-on activities and creative arts (Baum et al., 2005). Busi and Berman (2018) provide an example of utilizing multiple media to facilitate the writing process for students who struggle with writing and composing. In this approach, students are encouraged to first express their ideas in a different format other than writing and then explore various ways to organize their thoughts and ideas. Additionally, students could receive feedback and credit on drafts incrementally rather than obtaining a sole grade on a finished product. They could demonstrate their knowledge using a different medium, such as creating a video or giving an oral presentation.

Fourth, just as multiple measures are required for identification, a team approach is required for intervention implementation (Coleman et al., 2018; Wormald et al., 2015). This team of professionals could consist of those in gifted education and special education, a school counselor, and parents, all those who recognize and respect the student's abilities and learning difficulties and are willing to advocate for their unique identities. Outcomes of this team approach could include establishing formal accommodations for school personnel as well as continual development and modification of the student's educational and career goals (Coleman & Gallagher, 2015).

There are various private school models of teaching twice-exceptional youth from which educators can learn strategies they can modify in their own classroom. One is the Bridges Academy, which is described as a "dynamic educational ecostructure" designed for highly gifted students with different learning needs who may not succeed in traditional educational settings (Sabatino & Wiebe, 2018, p. 301). Individuals with diagnoses such as ADHD, ASD, SLD, and/or anxiety and depression may attend the academy. In addition to these diagnoses, students often present with sensory-integration or self-regulation challenges. Founders note they respond less to a child's diagnosis and more to their symptom presentation to meet their needs. The program also takes a strengths-based approach to intervention to identify and foster talent development and accommodate for students' difficulties. A second example is the Quad Preparatory School, where they report synthesizing evidence-based practices from multiple disciplines into a model that provides academic excellence and psychosocial support to facilitate students' growth and development (Busi & Berman, 2018). By incorporating community resources into the model, students acquire knowledge and skills in different disciplines and establish relationships with professionals in the community. The philosophy is that their acquired knowledge and skills may turn into lifetime interests and potentially jumpstart their career trajectory, as outlined in the Schoolwide Enrichment Model (Renzulli & Reis, 2014). A third example is the Lang School (www.thelangschool.org/mission), an independent school that focuses on talent development in high-ability and twice-exceptional students. Their curriculum is based on the equal integration of math, engineering, science, and the humanities to teach students complex problem-solving skills. Educators focus on social and emotional learning at the same time as they develop students' cognitive strengths. While these three independent and/or private schools are challenging to replicate across variably resourced schools, the philosophy of fostering strengths while remediating weaknesses is one that can be implemented universally.

Roles of Parents and Family

Most of the extant literature regarding twice-exceptionality focuses on identification and intervention, but some also highlights the critical role of parents in advocating and supporting the development of twice-exceptional students (Assouline et al., 2006; Giovacco-Johnson, 2007; King, 2005; Yssel, 2011). Although more and more people have become aware of the concept of twice-exceptionality, the needs of these students remain unfamiliar for many teachers and school officials (Foley-Nicpon et al., 2013). As a result, the responsibility of advocating for twice-exceptional students often lies with parents (Besnoy et al., 2015; Speirs Neumeister et al., 2013). Speirs Neumeister et al. (2013) interviewed ten primary caregivers (who were all mothers) of twice-exceptional students; their findings revealed that primary caregivers not only took on the responsibility of nurturing the success of their children, but also their involvement was a critical factor to their children's academic success. In their study, the primary caregivers recognized their children's strengths (i.e., high ability) and challenges (i.e., disabilities) early on, but were able to advocate for their children's needs despite facing resistant teachers and school officials. To ensure their children had equal opportunity to reach their potential, these parents dedicated time, energy, and financial resources to seek professional evaluations and recommendations. The parents understood the importance of helping their children establish healthy beliefs and expectations while considering their disabilities. They normalized the difficulties associated with their disabilities, while simultaneously holding high expectations. On the one hand, they validated their children's social-emotional challenges; and on the other hand, they encouraged their children to explore strategies and secure appropriate accommodations that would help them overcome these challenges. While it was difficult, these parents recognized that it was important for their children to develop independence and advocacy skills.

To learn more about parents' experience of advocating for their twice-exceptional children, Besnoy and colleagues (2015) conducted individual interviews and focus group sessions with eight parents of six twice-exceptional elementary school students. The results indicated that parents of twice-exceptional children were driven by "their fear that their child's disability would stunt her or his seemingly limitless potential" (p. 119). As a result, a common experience of these parents was to "advocate for their child's disability, while simultaneously protecting their child's giftedness" (pp. 113–114). Moreover, the findings indicated that these parents often were challenged to navigate their local school systems; all reported at one point losing confidence. Thus, Besnoy et al. (2015) highlighted the importance of establishing collaborative, positive relationships between home and school as well as parents acquiring twice-exceptional-specific knowledge (i.e., educational terminology, policies) to aid with advocacy efforts. They noted this process can be challenging and emotionally burdensome. Positive collaborations often were more facilitative than what was achieved through a more combative approach. A conclusion from the focus group data was that parents may benefit from sharing their successes and challenges with other parents of twice-exceptional youth.

While these studies' findings offer meaningful insights into the role of parents in advocating for and supporting their twice-exceptional children's success, it is important to note that they did not include students and parents from underserved backgrounds. As having financial resources to seek professional evaluations and acquire professional knowledge seems to be a key ingredient to the success of twice-exceptional students, we, as educators and psychologists, need not only to facilitate increased awareness of twice-exceptionality, but also to lead advocacy efforts (Dare & Nowicki, 2015). Moreover, these findings highlight the importance of encouraging and helping twice-exceptional students develop independence and ultimately acquire self-advocacy skills.

Recommendations

In this chapter, we have outlined the research foundation for the following recommendations for identifying and providing instructional services for twice-exceptional students:

1 Twice-exceptional children are more complex than their labels. Diagnostic categories and educational classifications have benefits, but it is important not to reduce a person to their identities alone. Instead, educators and clinicians are called to understand the individual differences and intersecting identities of the person sitting before them and be reflective of the systems in which they live (Bronfenbrenner, 1977).
2 Identification of talent development in schools should follow a consistent model across states and be ongoing given developmental and task-specific differences in talent acquisition (McClain & Pfeiffer, 2012). Children grow and develop at different rates and a child should not be penalized if they do not qualify for a gifted or talent development program at one window in time.
3 The goal of gifted and talented identification should be to create opportunities for the largest number of students who need it, not to restrict access to a select few. This latter model perpetuates the inequities inherent in gifted education and must be stopped. Models of identification now should follow the National Association for Gifted Children's (NAGC) most recent definition of talented and gifted that is more inclusive to all children who would benefit (NAGC, 2020).
4 To help reduce the class divides between who is and is not identified as twice-exceptional, the term needs to be understood more universally so that systems can correctly refer students who are best described educationally by this identity. Colleges and universities should make courses in gifted and special education required for preservice teachers (Wormald et al., 2015). Additionally, clinical training programs should consider high ability as a contextual factor as they conceptualize clients' presenting concerns.
5 Exposure to twice-exceptionality should not stop at graduation. All licensed professionals need to participate in ongoing professional development, which should include opportunities for educators to learn more about twice-exceptional students.
6 Identification and intervention strategies should comprise multiple informants from multiple pathways and consider an individual's social-emotional issues, cultural and family background, strengths and interests, and vulnerabilities and areas for growth in their conceptualization (National Education Association, 2006; Pfeiffer, 2013).

7   Make sure to incorporate intervention for students' strengths, not just their disability, and remember individual differences. For example, while high-ability students with ASD may benefit from whole-grade, single-subject acceleration, the same intervention may not be appropriate for high-ability students with SLD (Foley-Nicpon & Cederberg, 2015).

8   Maintain high expectations for children's overall performance (Speirs Neumeister et al., 2013). Just because a student requires accommodations for their specific disability does not mean they do not need to be challenged. As noted by Siegle and McCoach (2005), engagement is directly tied to material that is "optimally challenging" (p. 23); thus, decreasing challenge introduces a risk of disengagement and apathy toward learning.

9   At some point in one's development, advocacy for needs shifts from parents to the children themselves (Speirs Neumeister et al., 2013, p. 271). While frightening for some parents, this shift is a necessary part of parenting. Practice, trial and error, and modeling these techniques are all potentially useful, as well as consulting with a therapist about the challenges inherent in this transition.

10 Parents and educators would benefit from establishing collaborative partnerships. Through this network of support, successes and challenges can be shared among those who are dealing with similar issues. Professionals, parents, and those with twice-exceptionality would subsequently stay informed of national trends and local resources available (Besnoy et al., 2015).

11 Employ strengths-based approaches to communication between parents and educators. Starting with what is going right in school and/or at home may make hearing what is not working more palatable. Advocacy efforts must not solely focus on remediating weaknesses. Collaborative, positive partnerships between school and home are more advantageous in the long run (Besnoy et al., 2015)

Conclusion

It is long past due for gifted and talented programs nationwide to be representative of the population of students who reside in our schools. This includes students with disabilities. Twice-exceptional students may need individualized approaches to identification that involve taking a closer look at the multiple datapoints gathered by schools throughout the year. Intervention should assume a strengths-based approach to talent development where accommodations and/or remediation of areas for growth are included. Working together, parents and school personnel can create the best possible environment for twice-exceptional children to thrive in their talent domains, as well as rise to the challenges they face.

References

Antshel, K. M. (2008). Attention-deficit hyperactivity disorder in the context of a high intellectual quotient/giftedness. *Developmental Disabilities Research Reviews, 14*(4), 293–299. doi:10.1002/ddrr.v14:4

Antshel, K. M., Faraone, S. V., Stallone, K., Nave, A., Kaufmann, F. A., Doyle, A., … Biederman, J. (2007). Is attention deficit hyperactivity disorder a valid diagnosis in the presence of high IQ? Results from the MGH longitudinal family studies of ADHD. *Journal of Child Psychology and Psychiatry, 48*(7), 687–694. doi:10.1111/jcpp.2007.48.issue-7

Assouline, S. G., Foley Nicpon, M., & Whiteman, C. (2010). Cognitive and psychosocial characteristics of gifted students with specific learning disabilities. *Gifted Child Quarterly, 54*, 102–115.

Assouline, S. G., Nicpon, M. F., & Huber, D. H. (2006). The impact of vulnerabilities and strengths on the academic experiences of twice-exceptional students: A message to school counselors. *Professional School Counseling, 10*(1 Suppl.). https://doi.org/10.1177/2156759X0601001S03

Baldwin, L., Baum, S., Pereles, D., & Hughes, C. (2015). Twice-exceptional learners: The journey toward a shared vision. *Gifted Child Today, 38*, 206–214. http://dx.doi.org/10.1177/1076217515597277

Barber, C., & Mueller, C. T. (2011). Social and self-perceptions of adolescents identified as gifted, learning disabled, and twice-exceptional. *Roeper Review, 33*(2), 109–120. doi:10.1080/02783193.2011.554158

Barnard-Brak, L., Johnsen, S. K., Hannig, A. P., & Wei, T. (2015). The incidence of potentially gifted students within a special education population. *Roeper Review: A Journal on Gifted Education, 37*(2), 74–83.

Baum, S. M., & Owen, S. V. (2004). *To be gifted and learning disabled: Strategies for helping bright students with LD, ADHD, and more.* Mansfield Center, CT: Creative Learning Press.

Baum, S., & Schader, R. (2018). Using a positive lens: Engaging twice exceptional learners. In S. B. Kaufman (Ed.), *Twice exceptional: Supporting and educating bright and creative students with learning difficulties* (pp. 48–65). New York, NY: Oxford University Press.

Baum, S. M., Schader, R. M., & Hébert, T. P. (2014). Through a different lens: Reflecting on a strengths-based, talent-focused approach for twice-exceptional learners. *Gifted Child Quarterly, 58*(4), 311–327. http://doi.org/10.1177/0016986214547632

Baum, S. M., Viens, J., & Slatin, B. (2005). *Multiple intelligences in the elementary classroom: A teacher's toolkit.* Teachers College Press.

Beckmann, E., & Minnaert, A. (2018). Non-cognitive characteristics of gifted students with learning disabilities: An in-depth systematic review. *Frontiers in Psychology, 9*(504), 1–20. https://doi.org/10.3389/fpsyg.2018.00504

Besnoy, K. D., Swoszowski, N. C., Newman, J. L., Floyd, A., Jones, P., & Byrne, C. (2015). The advocacy experiences of parents of elementary age, twice-exceptional children. *Gifted Child Quarterly, 59*(2), 108–123. https://doi.org/10.1177/0016986215569275

Bronfenbrenner, U. (1977). Toward an experimental ecology of human development. *American Psychologist, 37*(7), 513–531. https://doi.org/10.1037/0003-066X.32.7.513

Busi, K., & Berman, K. (2018) Integration and dynamic adaptation in the formation of a novel 2e school model. In S. B. Kaufman (Ed.), *Twice exceptional: Supporting and educating bright and creative students with learning difficulties* (pp. 323–339). Oxford University Press.

Cain, M. K., Kaboski, J. R., & Gilger, J. W. (2019). Profiles and academic trajectories of cognitively gifted children with autism spectrum disorder. *Autism, 23*(7), 1663–1674. http://doi.org/10.1177/1362361318804019

Coleman, M. R., Baldwin, L., & Pereles, D. (2018). It takes a team. In S. B. Kaufman (Ed.), *Twice-exceptional: Supporting and educating bright and creative students with learning difficulties.* (pp. 156–176). New York, NY: Oxford University Press.

Coleman, M. R., & Gallagher, S. (2015). Meeting the needs of students with 2e: It takes a team. *Gifted Child Today, 38*(4), 252–254. doi:10.1177/1076217515597274

Crepeau-Hobson, F., & Bianco, M. (2011). Identification of gifted students with learning disabilities in a response-to-intervention era. *Psychology in the Schools, 48*(2), 102–109.

Dare, L., & Nowicki, E. A. (2015). Twice-exceptionality: Parents' perspectives on 2e identification. *Roeper Review, 37*(4), 208–218.

Doobay, A. F. (2010). Comparison of cognitive, psychosocial, and adaptive behavior profiles among gifted children with and without autism spectrum disorder (Order No. 3439177). Available from ProQuest Dissertations & Theses Global (851540191).

Foley-Nicpon, M. (2015). The social and emotional development of twice-exceptional children. In M. Neihart, S. I. Pfeiffer, & T. L Cross (Eds.), *Social and emotional development of gifted children: What do we know?* (pp. 103–118). Waco, TX: Prufrock.

Foley-Nicpon, M., Allmon, A., Sieck, B., & Stinson, R. D. (2011). Empirical investigation of twice-exceptionality: Where have we been and where are we going? *Gifted Child Quarterly*, *55*, 3–17. https:// doi.org/10.1177/0016986210382575

Foley-Nicpon, M., & Assouline, S. G. (2020). High ability students with co-existing disabilities: Implications for school psychological practice. *Psychology in the Schools*, *57*(10), 1615–1626. https://doi.org/10.1002/pits.22342

Foley-Nicpon, M., Assouline, S. G., & Colangelo, N. (2013). Twice-exceptional learners: Who needs to know what? *Gifted Child Quarterly*, *57*(3), 169–180. https://doi.org/10.1177/0016986213490021

Foley-Nicpon, M., & Cederberg, C. (2015). Acceleration practices with twice-exceptional students. In S. G. Assouline, N. Colangelo, J. VanTassel-Baska, & A. Lupkowski-Shoplik (Eds.), *A nation empowered: Evidence trumps the excuses holding back America's brightest students* (Vol. 2, pp. 189–198). Iowa City: The University of Iowa, The Connie Belin & Jacqueline N. Blank International Center for Gifted Education and Talent Development.

Foley-Nicpon, M., Doobay, A. F., & Assouline, S. G. (2010). Parent, teacher, and self perceptions of psychosocial functioning in intellectually gifted children and adolescents with autism spectrum disorder. *Journal of Autism and Developmental Disorders*, *40*(8), 1028–1038. https://doi.org/10.1007/s10803-010-0952-8

Foley-Nicpon, M., & Kim, J. Y. C. (2018). Identifying and providing evidence-based services for twice-exceptional students. In S. Pfeiffer (Ed.), *Handbook of giftedness in children* (pp. 349–362). New York, NY: Springer.

Foley-Nicpon, M., Rickels, H., Assouline, S. G., & Richards, A. (2012). Self-esteem and self-concept examination among gifted students with ADHD. *Journal for the Education of the Gifted*, *35*, 220–240.

Ford, D. Y., & Helms, J. E. (2012). Overview and introduction: Testing and assessing African Americans: "Unbiased" tests are still unfair. *Journal of Negro Education*, *81*, 186–189.

Fugate, C. M., Zentall, S. S., & Gentry, M. (2013). Working memory and creativity in gifted students with and without characteristics of ADHD: Lifting the mask. *Gifted Child Quarterly*, *57*, 234–246.

Giovacco-Johnson, T. (2007). Twice-exceptional children: Paradoxes and parenting. *Childhood Education*, *83*, 175–177.

Hamilton, R., McCoach, D. B., Tutwiler, M. S., Siegle, D., Gubbins, E. J., Callahan, C. M., … Mun, R. U. (2017). Disentangling the roles on institutional and individual poverty in the identification of gifted students. *Gifted Child Quarterly*, *62*, 6–24. http://doi.org/10.1177/0016986217738053

King, E. W. (2005). Addressing the social and emotional needs of twice-exceptional students. *Teaching Exceptional Children*, *38*, 16–20.

Lerner, M. D., & Girard, R. M. (2018). Appreciating and promoting social creativity in youth with Asperger's syndrome. In S. B. Kaufman (Ed.), *Twice exceptional: Supporting and educating bright and creative students with learning difficulties* (pp. 201–212). New York, NY: Oxford University Press.

Maddocks, D. L. S. (2020). Cognitive and achievement characteristics of students from a national sample identified as potentially twice exceptional (gifted with a learning disability). *Gifted Child Quarterly*, *64*(1), 3–18. https://doi.org/10.1177/0016986219886668

Mayes, R. D., & Moore, J. L. III (2016). The intersection of race, disability, and giftedness: Understanding the education needs of twice-exceptional, African American students. *Gifted Child Today*, *39*, 98–104

McBee, M. T., Peters, S. J., & Miller, E. M. (2016). The impact of the nomination stage on gifted program identification: A comprehensive psychometric analysis. *Gifted Child Quarterly*, *60*, 258–278. https://doi.org/10.1177/0016986216656256

McBee, M. T., Peters, S. J., & Waterman, C. (2014). Combining scores in multiple criteria assessment systems: The impact of combination rule. *Gifted Child Quarterly*, *58*, 69–89.

McClain, M. C., & Pfeiffer, S. (2012). Identification of gifted students in the United States today: A look at state definitions, policies, and practices. *Journal of Applied School Psychology, 28*, 59–88. https://doi.org/10.1080/15377903.2012.643757

McCoach, D. B., Siegle, D., & Rubenstein, L. D. (2020). Pay attention to inattention: Exploring ADHD symptoms in a sample of underachieving gifted students. *Gifted Child Quarterly, 64*(2), 100–116. https://doi.org/10.1177/0016986219901320

National Association for Gifted Children [NAGC]. (2020). A definition of giftedness that guides best practice. Position Statement. Retrieved from: www.nagc.org/sites/default/files/Position%20 Statement/Definition%20of%20Giftedness%20%282019%29.pdf

National Center for Education Statistics [NCES]. (2016). *Children 3 to 21 years old served under Individuals with Disabilities Education Act (IDEA), Part B, by type of disability: Selected years, 1976–77 through 2014–15*. Retrieved from: https://nces.ed.gov/programs/digest/d16/tables/dt16_ 204.30.asp

National Education Association. (2006). *The twice-exceptional dilemma*. Washington, DC: Author.

Park, S., Foley-Nicpon, M., Choate, A., & Bolenbaugh, M. (2018). "Nothing fits exactly": Experiences of Asian American parents of twice-exceptional children. *Gifted Child Quarterly, 62*(3), 306–319. https://doi.org/10.1177/0016986218758442

Peters, S. J., Gentry, M., Whiting, G. W., & McBee, M. T. (2019). Who gets served in gifted education? Demographic representation and a call for action. *Gifted Child Quarterly, 63*(4), 273–287. http://doi.org/10.1177/0016986219833738

Pfeiffer, S. I. (2013). *Serving the gifted: Evidence-based clinical and psychoeducational practice*. New York, NY: Routledge.

Pfeiffer, S. I. (2016). Success in the classroom and in life: Focusing on strengths of the head and strengths of the heart. *Gifted Education International, 33*(2), 95–101. https://doi.org/10.1177/ 0261429416640337

Pfeiffer, S. I., & Foley-Nicpon, M. (2018). Knowns and unknowns about students with disabilities who also happen to be intellectually gifted. In S. B. Kaufman (Ed.), *Twice exceptional: Supporting and educating bright and creative students with learning difficulties* (pp. 104–119). New York, NY: Oxford University Press.

Reis, S. M., Baum, S. M., & Burke, E. (2014). An operational definition of twice-exceptional learners: Implications and applications. *Gifted Child Quarterly, 58*(3), 217–230. https://doi.org/ 10.1177/0016986214534976

Renzulli, J. S., & Reis, S.M. (2014). *Schoolwide enrichment model* (3rd ed.). Waco, TX: Prufrock Press.

Robinson, A., Shore, B. M., & Enersen, D. L. (2007). *Best practices in gifted education: An evidence-based guide*. Waco, TX: Prufrock Press.

Ruban, L. M., & Reis, S. M. (2005). Identification and assessment of gifted students with learning disabilities. *Gifted Education, 44*(2), 115–124.

Sabatino, C. A., & Wiebe, C. R. (2018). Bridges Academy: A strengths-based model for 2e. In S. B. Kaufman (Ed.), *Twice-exceptional: Supporting and educating bright and creative students with learning difficulties* (pp. 301–321). New York, NY: Oxford University Press.

Siegle, D., & McCoach, D. B. (2005). Making a difference: Motivating gifted students who are not achieving. *Teaching Exceptional Children, 38*(1), 22–27. https://doi.org/10.1177/ 004005990503800104

Silverman, L. K., & Gilman, B. J. (2020). Best practices in gifted identification and assessment: Lessons from the WISC-V. *Psychology in the Schools*, advance online publication. http://dx.doi.org./ 10.1002/pits.22361

Speirs Neumeister, K., Yssel, N., & Burney, V. H. (2013). The influence of primary caregivers in fostering success in twice-exceptional children. *Gifted Child Quarterly, 57*(4), 263–274.

Subotnik, R. F., Olszewski-Kubilius, P., & Worrell, F. C. (2011). Rethinking giftedness and gifted education: A proposed direction forward based on psychological science. *Psychological Science in the Public Interest, 12*(1), 3–54.

Wormald, C., Rogers, K. B., & Vialle, W. (2015). A case study of giftedness and specific learning disabilities: Bridging the two exceptionalities. *Roeper Review: A Journal on Gifted Education, 37*(3), 124–138.

Yoon, S., & Gentry, M. (2009). Racial and ethnic representation in gifted programs: Current status of and implications for gifted Asian American students. *Gifted Child Quarterly, 53*, 121–136. https://doi.org/10.1177/0016986208330564

Yssel, N. (2011). Twice-exceptional students. In T. L. Cross & J. R. Cross (Eds.), *Handbook for counselors serving students with gifts and talents* (pp. 245–257). Austin, TX: Prufrock Press.

Chapter 11

Young, Curious, and Resilient
The Population of Early Learners

Nancy B. Hertzog

Vignette

Maria and Pedro enter the kindergarten classroom – think for a minute what your own image is of these children. Suppose I said Jia and Mark enter the kindergarten classroom. As a white teacher you may have different images of what these children bring with them into your classroom. You might worry whether Maria or Pedro speak English well enough or have the ability to follow your directions, sit long enough to listen to a story in English, or have the ability to take home work and have parent support to complete it. Although both children are fluent in Spanish, know how to collaborate and show leadership in small groups with other Spanish-speaking children, you might choose to give them worksheets that make them copy the English alphabet or provide them with flashcards with sight words for them to memorize rather than engage them in open-ended tasks where they seek answers to their own questions about toads, flowers, or architects. Would you allow them to write stories in their own language and have it translated for you? Would you engage their parents to share what their children are doing at home so that you could find ways to connect their interests from home to your classroom? Would you talk to their parents about the gifted program in your school district? Or would you plan to give them remedial instruction because you fear that they do not have the skills they need to pass literacy or math assessments required for them to be successful in kindergarten. What is driving your curricular and instructional choices?

Before you get to know the children, what differences do you anticipate in your teaching of Maria, Pedro, Jia, or Mark?

Introduction

There is no more vulnerable a population than that of young children – they are living lives they have not chosen. They may be living in poverty. They may be hungry, misplaced, mistreated, or misunderstood – or they may be living with families that have a high income and can indulge them in travel, music, dance, and the fine arts. There is no more essential a need for young children than that of belonging. How they are welcomed into the educational community in preschool or kindergarten may impact their future identities

DOI: 10.4324/9781003265412-16

as successful students, scholars, or contributors to society. Early childhood educators are empowered to create warm, welcoming, rich learning contexts for young children to grow and develop their potential – the potential to excel academically, to lead, to collaborate, to problem solve, to create, to design, to develop, and to innovate. The population of early learners will live in a future that their teachers can only imagine. Information technology is changing society in ways that impact what we know about the jobs and skills that our young children will need in the future. Young students present the ultimate challenge for their teachers:

- How do early childhood educators nurture the talents and potential of all young children that enter their classrooms?
- How do they identify their unique learning needs that result from the influence of intersectionality of their identities: race, religion, cultural ethnicity, gender, and economic status?

In this chapter, the young child (PreK – Grade 3) will be the focus of discussion. In particular, we will focus on the young child from populations of students that do not have equitable access to advanced learning opportunities. Students of color, students from low socioeconomic backgrounds, and English Language Learners (ELL) are consistently underrepresented in U.S. gifted programs (Borland, 2008; Ford, 2013; Lamb et al., 2019; Peters & Engerrand, 2016; Peters et al., 2019; Yoon & Gentry, 2009).

A Focus on Equity

This chapter will focus on equity as it relates to early childhood gifted education. However, equity in gifted education cannot be seen as separate from educational and societal structures that impact learning, especially in the early years. Equity means that we cannot predict educational achievement outcomes of children by the color of their skin, the language that they speak, the income of their family, or their family heritage.

It must be understood that the young child is vulnerable to systems of inequity in many areas that impact learning, including health care, immigration policies, welfare, and access to high-quality early childcare. All of these systems impact future educational outcomes (Tout et al., 2013). For example, Ryan et al. (2011) showed that families who accessed Federal subsidies for day care selected higher-quality care on average than comparable families without subsidies. Children who are undocumented, or whose parents are undocumented, may not have access to Federal subsidized programs, limiting their access to high-quality early childhood programs. The quality of early education matters – and young children who are exposed to high-quality programs fare better in later life, including lower rates of crime, higher lifetime earnings, and better health outcomes (NIEER, 2019).

To advance equity in early childhood gifted education, we must first acknowledge that the "professional research and knowledge bases [are] largely grounded in a dominant Western scientific-cultural model" (NAEYC, 2019, p. 14). According to the National Association for the Education of Young Children (NAEYC),

> Whiteness, for example, confers privilege, as does being male. Other aspects of identity that society tends to favor with easier access to power structures include being

able-bodied, US born, Christian, heterosexual, cisgender, thin, educated, and economically advantaged. Conversely, other aspects of identity tend to be associated with societal oppression, experienced, for example, by those who are members of indigenous societies and those who do not speak fluent, standard English.

(NAEYC, 2019, p. 14)

Understanding that our schools and our structures of education, including gifted education, have historically privileged specific groups of people and have oppressed other groups is critical to understanding why we must change our current practices in gifted education.

In the special issue of the *Kappan* (December 2020/January 2021) which focused on gifted education, several authors posed suggestions for reframing gifted education and for increasing access to traditionally underserved populations of students. However, all of the authors continued to pose suggestions for including underserved students in a "top" percentage of students who could be served. Their suggestions of more equitable identification systems often included a universal screening using a standardized cognitive ability test, multiple measures such as achievement tests or teacher rating scales, and using a portfolio or strength-based profile approach to help identify the top proportion of diverse populations of students. However, none of these ideas question why we are sorting or comparing children to each other. Their ideas do not change established inequities of drawing an arbitrary line between groups of students – those who receive, and those who will not receive the rich educational curriculum and instruction that defines gifted education. Using standardized tests for decision making for young children and comparing them to their peers does not value the unique rich and diverse knowledge, skills, and dispositions that they bring to their learning environment from their own social and cultural backgrounds.

Young children need ongoing assessment, opportunities for rich learning environments, and teachers who take an individualized strengths-based approach to their teaching. With an equity lens, I suggest we think differently about gifted education, especially for young children. Gifted education need not be comparative to address the needs of learners who benefit from advanced content or inquiry-based instructional strategies. Gifted education need not be defined by serving an arbitrary "top" percentage of students. In this chapter, critical perspectives on what is currently offered and practiced will be shared to raise new questions and solutions for how to address the strengths of young children as we move the field of early childhood gifted education forward.

Belonging and Identity

The concept of belonging to a school environment must start with a critical look at our preconceptions about the meaning and policies of school readiness. For decades, the national discourse to close achievement gaps, or opportunity gaps, has focused on what our young children are *not* doing – what their deficits are before they enter our schools. Programs such as Head Start were developed to catch up children from poverty to having the same academic skills as their white middle-class peers have when they enter kindergarten. To qualify to attend Head Start programs, families had to document inherent risk factors (e.g., poverty, single parent, speaking English as a second language, disability, homelessness), and teachers in those programs had to make sure their students met *readiness goals*. This focus on what these children did *not* bring to school has created an historical framing of early education to focus on their academic deficits, implicitly (or explicitly) privileging the academic skills that higher-income and predominantly white children already brought to their early learning environment. Government accountability to Federal funding programs has mandated assessments that measure growth in discrete skills, which in turn have defined school readiness, as well as the type of curriculum and instruction offered especially to children living in poverty. Most Federally funded Head Start programs use the Teaching Strategies Gold Assessment System (GOLD®, n.d.) which defines kindergarten readiness by accomplishing 38 teaching objectives, two of which relate to understanding and using the English language:

37. Demonstrates progress in listening to and understanding English
38. Demonstrates progress in speaking English

(GOLD®, n.d., n.p.)

With the emphasis on these specific readiness goals, it is easy to see how teachers are trained to teach from a deficit approach. For their students to measure growth on assessments, teachers need to focus their students on mastering the discrete skills on the assessment tools (e.g., identifying and naming the letters of the English alphabet, counting in English, following directions). Students who do not perform well on these tasks, or students who have difficulty meeting these objectives are then labeled "not ready" for kindergarten, and not ready for the next educational environment in which they will struggle to belong and be successful.

The concept and definition of readiness as discrete skills students need to know to be ready for kindergarten has been challenged. More than 30 years ago, Kagan (1990) distinguished the difference between readiness for learning and readiness for school. She stated,

> Not surprisingly, readiness to learn and readiness for school – representing different conceptual constructs and having different definitions – have yielded very different orientations. The former applies to students of all ages; the latter, to young children, primarily at the prekindergarten or kindergarten level. In the former readiness is fostered; in the latter, it is expected. The former views the content of early education as fluid and evolving; the latter, as more static and fixed. The former has been considered a 'gate opener'; the latter, a gatekeeper.
>
> (Kagan, 1990, p. 273)

To her point, *all* children are ready to learn – but to be ready for school implies a whole different mindset. It implies conforming to expectations that are arbitrary and more related to the school environment itself than to the children who will be entering into that environment.

To be oriented to fostering learning, teachers would have to start from a strengths-based or asset-based approach. This would mean that teachers valued what their students brought with them to the new learning environment, not what they did not accomplish before coming to school. In this approach, teachers would value the multi-lingual knowledge that the children may have, or the ability to switch their understanding of cultural expectations that they flow in and out of on a daily basis coming from home to school and back to their home again. Teachers would appreciate the specific talents children have when they make friends with other children who do not speak the same language at home as they do. Families might feel more comfortable sharing what their children love to do at home with educators, and students who spoke English would get daily lessons on other languages that are present in the classroom as a demonstration that all languages and cultures are valued in the classroom. Young children might feel a stronger sense of belonging to a classroom where many languages are spoken, and everyone is learning a language. These are just some examples of how educators can create a more welcoming environment for their diverse students. This is especially critical in the field of early childhood education, because in order for young children to feel a sense of belonging and a sense of affiliation to their class and school, they must feel successful and welcome. Their "scholarly identity" starts the moment they enter the school setting.

We know the important relationship that the sense of belonging has with a child's identity as a learner. We also know that young children are living in a complex world of multiple identities, feeling the impact of those identities from the people around them. It may be useful here to review briefly Bronfenbrenner's bioecological systems theory that emphasized the importance of the interactions between children and the spheres of influence around them. His theory included five spheres of influence beginning with what is closest to the child, the microsystem (e.g., parents, home life, day care, peers), leading all the way to the macrosystem which included the wider attitudes and cultural ideologies that influence families. Bronfenbrenner's work significantly acknowledged the importance of understanding that relationships do not exist "in a social vacuum but were embedded in the larger social structures of community, society, economics and politics" (Woo, 2005, n.p.).

Students of color, students who are learning English as a second language, and especially students from low-income homes, must be seen as competent learners not only by their parents and teachers, but also within the societal and political context in which they live. The image of the child as competent and someone with rights is a cornerstone of the Reggio Emilia Approach (Edwards et al., 1993) to early childhood education. Educators following the Reggio Emilia Approach view the child as the future of their country and society, and they provide instruction that assumes children are ready to learn and inquire about the world around them. Rethinking the concept of readiness with a critical lens is essential in moving toward strengths-based pedagogies. Durden (2015) described how

> teachers who espouse a critical theoretical lens consciously and constantly question: a) whether the children's voices and experiences are being respected and affirmed, b) how the teachers and school's culture can create dissonance for students and their families, c) how power is exerted by the teacher, curriculum, schools, and policies to perpetuate oppressive systems in society, and d) how he or she can transmit a dominant ideology or belief that is detrimental to students.
>
> (Durden, 2015, p. 80)

The last point made by Durden requires that teachers be aware of the way they may be impacting students and families by conforming to and teaching the prescribed curriculum and instruction that is found in typical early childhood classrooms. It may be difficult to shift the national narrative related to what young children need to be ready for school because policies and funding influence curriculum and instruction. Rather than believe that students need academic skills they don't already have – instead, young children should be valued and respected for all of the skills, dispositions, and knowledge that they do have. Focused on an asset-based education, families and educators need to work together. "Rather than assuming that there is a common set of expectations for starting school, and agreed intervention strategies to ensure all children meet these, alternative approaches consider children's strengths, instead of attending to their perceived deficits" (Docket & Perry, 2016, p. 141).

The National Association for the Education of Young Children (NAEYC) recently published a position statement entitled, *Advancing Equity in Early Childhood Education* (2019), in which they acknowledged the important ways that teacher bias influences the classroom environment and the children in it.

> Implicit biases also result in differential judgments of children's play, aggressiveness, compliance, initiative, and abilities. These biases are associated with lower rates of achievement and assignment to "gifted" services and disproportionately higher rates of suspension and expulsion, beginning in preschool, for African American children, especially boys.
>
> (NAEYC, 2019, p. 5)

Bias is internal to the educator, and to change this requires providing teachers with opportunities for professional development on culturally responsive teaching strategies, self-reflection, and more understanding of one's own relationship to power and privilege. But other work to create welcoming environments for young people to identify as scholars requires understanding of structural and historical barriers that should be studied through critical pedagogies and equity lenses. According to Wells, "The sting of privilege, bias, and racism has restricted and continues to limit achievement opportunities in education for children of color. There is an urgent need for educators to view diverse learners as academically capable and worthy" (Wells, 2020, p. 10). One such area in which we need to take a critical stance is in how we identify young children for advanced learning opportunities, including enrichment and gifted education programs.

Identification and Assessment

To disrupt inequitable systems, racism, and structural barriers in gifted education, we need to start early. Understanding that belonging and identity are critical to achievement, we should not label young children as "gifted." Period. The practice of labeling some young children as gifted also labels the others as *not gifted*. Obviously, young children who are identified as gifted using cognitive ability tests have had significant advantages in their environment. Peters et. al. (2019) in their examination of inequality, stated "higher family income comes with greater access and opportunities before formal schooling starts within and outside of school" (p. 274). Income discrepancies reflected in the results of standardized testing have been widely acknowledged. Therefore, we should not perpetuate the practice of seeking a culture-free test, a nonverbal test, or an in-depth test of cognitive ability. Instead, we should advocate against any formal or standardized measures of intelligence or cognitive ability testing that serve to separate children from their peers, or label some children as inherently smarter than others. Are there children who come to school with more academic skills? Yes. Are there some children who need above-grade-level curriculum and instruction – especially in literacy and math? Yes, but we must see those skills for what they are – advanced accomplishments from the practice and experiences that the children had to acquire them. We must not use the advanced learning of some children to label the others as "not ready, not competent, or not successful." All young children are curious, resilient, and *ready* to learn.

In many previous articles, I have advocated against using standardized tests to make high-stakes decisions about young children that would serve to initiate tracking. (Hertzog, 2013; Hertzog, 2017a; Hertzog, 2017b; Hertzog & Gadzikowski, 2017; Hertzog & Mammadov, 2018). Standardized tests, and in particular tests of cognitive ability, do not measure inherent ability in young children. Quite the contrary, they are developed and skewed for children who come from homes where they have had more experience doing tasks like those on the test to achieve a higher score. Cole in his seminal chapter (1985) argued that one cannot even create a test of intellectual ability without it having a cultural bias. He stated, "culture free intelligence testing is a contradiction in terms" (p. 218). Cole refuted the major assertation from psychologists who seek the bias of inequality on the individual and not the society, and he argued that "the only way to obtain a culture free test is to construct items that are equally a part of the experience of all cultures" (p. 236).

Thus, with an equity lens, I question the numerous attempts to make a culture- fair or culture-free test to identify giftedness. Districts all over the country have engaged in creating alternative ways to identify students as gifted, but most always they rely on tests of cognitive ability or use of standardized tests that do not relate to young children's strengths, particularly if these young children come from low-income homes, families of color, or speak English as a second language. Even a call for universal screening, when it involves only test-taking, is not in and of itself, an equitable way to increase the identification of young children from diverse backgrounds.

In a recent study with a non-profit community organization that supported students of color, families we interviewed confirmed that they felt assessments used to identify children in their public schools for gifted education were racially biased. One parent shared,

> They make it as isolating, they make it as we're not smart, and that is what the system is made for; it wasn't made for us, even the testing wasn't made for us. So, I feel like the fight has to continue, and if a child is benefitting you have to remember there are a lot of kids that are left out and it's not fair. (Hertzog et al. 2020, Focus Group B, 12/ 05/2019)

A common theme among the families that we interviewed revolved around the lack of communication between the schools and the communities of color. They spoke frequently about not getting enough information about how access to the gifted program works, how the gifted program may benefit their child, and most importantly, what they need to access the system. In particular, one parent shared,

> I said is there anything we can prepare our child for this kind of stuff, and he actually told me there wasn't, but then I found out later from other parents you can actually buy the CogAT® online and prepare your child!
> (Hertzog et al. 2020, Focus Group A, 11/23/2019)

In fact, families "in the know" or those who have resources may buy practice materials. All one would have to do is Google "gifted testing preparation" and there is a plethora of materials one can buy to practice for tests that districts use to determine giftedness. Sites like Testingmom.com have all types of materials, including practice questions of many common tests such as the CogAT®, NNAT®, and the Gifted and Talented Test. Testingmom.com advertises on its website, "If your child goes into the test without any idea of what to expect, the many children who have prepared and DO know what to expect will have an advantage, fair or not" (TestingMom.com, n.d.). Clearly, that statement alone refutes the idea that the knowledge on the tests is somehow inherent to the child. Instead, these types of preparation programs demonstrate that the tests are heavily influenced by children's prior experiences, not only with the content, but also with test-taking strategies. Therefore, districts that continue to use standardized tests to determine who is in or out of a gifted program, or who deserves to receive advanced instruction are holding on to the status quo that perpetuates structural barriers and culture biases. These biases are particularly felt by families whose children are young and may be having their *first* experiences with test-taking. Nowhere has there been more public concern about these biases than in regard to the testing that surrounds entrance into special schools and gifted education programs in New York City. Falchi and Friedman (2015) reiterated this point:

> Being gifted in NYC, is greatly influenced by social and cultural experiences and highly subject to modification with expensive tutoring, training, and courses of preparation, rather than potential capabilities. Children are selected based on skills practiced prior to their testing date rather than their capacity to learn. As one parent commented, 'it's not testing for who you are, it's for how much you have prepared.' Those who can afford the time and resources to prepare their children are disproportionately labeled as gifted.
> (Falchi & Friedman, 2015, p. 115)

Even with public calls for changing the way districts identify children for gifted programs, statistics still indicate that our current identification systems leave many children out of advanced learning opportunities (Peters et al., 2019; Siegle et al., 2016). Listening to the voices of families who have been interviewed about what they see as structural barriers for their children to enter into gifted programs (Hertzog et al., 2020), we know that we must start doing something different with families of young children. They must be welcomed into their children's learning environment and valued as equal partners in the learning process. Their children must not be "tested for giftedness" to gain access to enriching and challenging learning experiences. These types of experiences should be *created and accessible* to all students in all early learning classrooms.

Designing Curriculum and Instruction to Identify Strengths and Talents

Developing and identifying strengths and talents in young children requires curriculum and instruction that elicit children's expressions of ideas, and application of skills, knowledge, and dispositions. In a special issue of *Gifted Child Today*, Kaplan and I articulated the need to shift one's thinking from identifying gifted or advanced academic achievement that is already present to using the curriculum and instruction to illuminate and develop the student's academic growth and prowess. Most importantly, we said that there needs to be, "Transitions from educators 'waiting for potential to be displayed' to setting the conditions and situations that require, and possibly demand the expression of a young child's potential, talent, and/or emerging aptitude" (Kaplan & Hertzog, 2016, p. 136). We advocated ongoing "informal identification that *recognizes the development of strengths and abilities as an ongoing goal of early childhood education*" (p. 135, italics in the original). Rather than focusing on discrete skills through paper and pencil tasks, we argued instead for curriculum and instruction that emphasized student autonomy and experiential learning that "creates a difference between socializing students into school and socializing them on *how to learn*" (p. 135, italics in the original).

Formative and ongoing assessment, as opposed to evaluative and static assessment, is essential in early childhood education simply because young children's skills are never static. Their growth in language and literacy may grow exponentially when they begin to apply phonemic awareness or when they begin to acquire vocabulary in the English language. Best practices for ongoing assessment include gathering data within authentic activities, rather than having children take "tests" or perform learning tasks out of context. According to NAEYC, best practice in assessment requires that "Assessment evidence is gathered from realistic settings and situations that reflect children's actual performance" (NAEYC, 2003, p. 3). Therefore, to provide these activities to children coming from all backgrounds, we need to alter ways in which we document, assess, and plan differentiated instruction that addresses students' strengths. Identification of students' strengths in early childhood requires capturing student work samples, conversations (in English or home languages), processes of problem solving and thinking, and products of self-initiated learning activities. Creating student portfolios is fairly common among early childhood educators – but focusing on students' strengths through portfolios to plan enrichment or acceleration for students is generally not the focus when accountability systems include mastery of discreet basic literacy and math skills.

In summary, identification and assessment for children to access advanced learning opportunities in early childhood classrooms should look very different from what is currently the mode of operating in gifted education today. Educators should strive to develop early childhood classrooms that meet the unique needs and foster the talents of individual young children within an inclusive setting. Educators in gifted education should recognize the inequitable systems and barriers that start early and should stop trying to find the "right" test of cognitive ability to identify giftedness or the right formulas or procedures that sort children by scores on standardized tests. Instead, they should disrupt the status quo of the identification and labeling process, and instead design more equitable and respectful ways to work with families to identify and initiate culturally responsive instruction that builds upon their children's unique strengths and talents upon entering school.

By valuing educator/family partnerships as pathways to learning about their students, educators will more easily be able to prepare curriculum and instruction that is culturally responsive and also adaptive to meet individual and unique learning needs.

Roles of Parents and Families

Plucker and his colleagues (2017) proposed the importance of context in talent development approaches to gifted education, and in particular, using the sociocultural theory of learning to establish that what is valued as strengths, talents, or intelligence is often culturally and community driven. Therefore, it is important to understand what is valued in the young children's family culture and community in order to establish relationships with families when designing instruction to maximize the growth of students' unique strengths and talents. Early educators know that "developing a working relationship with families is key" (Arndt & McGuire-Schwartz, 2008, p. 283). The authors stated the importance of communicating, learning about parents' goals and preferences for their children, and being respectful of cultural and family differences. It is also important to acknowledge that there are differences in expectations about school and parent/educator relationships across families and cultures, and to understand when a dominant U.S. cultural expectation or value may be in contrast to what families may believe, value, or understand.

In its recommendations for educators, the NAEYC *Advancing Equity in Early Childhood Education* Position Statement listed this strategy to create a caring, equitable community of engaged learners:

> Involve children, families, and the community in the design and implementation of learning activities. Doing this builds on the funds of knowledge that children and families bring as members of their cultures and communities while also sparking children's interest and engagement. Recognizing the community as a context for learning can model citizen engagement.
>
> (NAEYC, 2019, p. 7)

There are numerous concrete and practical ways in which families may be welcomed as partners and become part of the context of the child's early learning environment at schools. Photographs of children and their families prominent on the classroom walls and displays that include all of the teachers and other workers in the school – the chefs, the janitorial staff, the office workers, etc. – represent a learning community that values all who work on behalf of the child.

Educators following the tenets of the Reggio Emilia Approach consider the environment as the "Third Teacher." The classroom teachers in Reggio Emilia intentionally prepare the learning environment to extend possibilities for the students to interact with their environment in ways that provoke critical and creative thinking. For example, classrooms may be designed to have learning spaces that have materials, books, musical instruments, or artistic representations that come from different cultures. They encourage families to be a part of the project investigations that they work on at school. Parents are key resources for sharing expertise and experiences related to the projects that they study. This is also true when teachers are using the Project Approach (Katz et al., 2014).

Positive relationships begin with the first contact with families. Teachers are encouraged to begin the year with conversations and meetings with families to ask questions to learn about their students, and to hear about the experiences that the children have had and are having at home on a daily basis. School districts are encouraged to hire and support cultural mediators to work with families as they enter into the school system and provide access to interpreters to help mitigate any language barriers. Written materials, when possible, should be translated for parents and sent home by mail so as not to assume that families have access to Internet or are always capable of receiving electronic messages. When arranging meetings with families, it might be advisable to use community spaces that are close to the children's homes such as churches, public libraries, or community centers.

Most importantly, when communicating with parents about what their children are learning, growth should be framed in positive ways – invite conversations about growth and ask questions about the types of things the child is doing and sharing at home. Teachers need to have many opportunities where they invite families to share with them their perspectives on their children's learning experiences, and their suggestions for helping their children grow. Although families are different, research shows that there is commonality in their hopes and dreams for their children. Families want their children to do well academically and be successful (Arndt & McGuire-Schwartz, 2008).

Classroom Strategies

There are specific strategies and pedagogical approaches that help teachers create warm, welcoming, inclusive, and challenging early learning environments. I have with colleagues (Hertzog & Gadzikowski, 2017; Kaplan & Hertzog 2016) provided the rationale for using approaches to curriculum that are emergent rather than overly prescriptive so that teachers may differentiate instruction according to interests, learning preferences, and readiness skills. In particular, inquiry-based approaches allow students the ability to follow their passions and interests, and to apply academic skills within authentic contexts. For example, they may be learning about 3-dimensional shapes at the same time they are investigating different styles of architecture in the homes and businesses that are in their neighborhood.

Pinedo-Burns (2015) wrote from her perspective as the director of the Hollingworth Preschool at Teachers' College about the importance of wonder:

> I focus on three vital pedagogical stances teachers can take in order to reestablish wonder at the center of the realm of early childhood: (1) invite children's sense of wonder; (2) listen to the wonderings of children; and (3) make room for wonder.
>
> (Pinedo-Burns, 2015, p. 166)

Pinedo-Burns said that wonder offers children opportunities for engagement, observation, exploration, and inquiry. These are the same components of project work that could be found following the Project Approach or the Reggio Emilia Approach. (The articulation of these approaches is not the focus here, but for more information see Katz et al., 2014 and Edwards et al., 1993).

Language and literacy have always been important parts of early childhood curriculum and instruction. But from a critical perspective, the way language has been traditionally taught misses authentic opportunities and meaningful contexts to build vocabulary and provide meaningful contexts for learning. Gramling (2015) argued for language instruction to go beyond the standards and assessment practices that give children only opportunities to demonstrate if they have or have not mastered the objectives. In his words,

> Standards-driven early childhood education is not only that it reduces complex human behavior such as communication and critical thinking to observable microsteps, thereby rendering it useless, but that it reduces the child to nothing more than a set of objectives, a collection of deficits, a problem.
>
> (Gramling, 2015, p. 93)

In order to create more authentic opportunities for students to develop their language and literacy skills, Gramling recommends changing the behaviors of the teachers and interactions with their students. Gramling suggests that teachers need to have the following objectives:

> Objective 1: The teacher will use words in meaningful contexts.
> Objective 2: The teacher will ask questions to promote problem solving and critical thinking.
> Objective 3: The teacher will share personal stories with the child that draw the child into extended conversations.
> Objective 4: The adult will use complex sentence structure and a rich vocabulary.
> Objective 5: The teacher will provide opportunities for children to use print and numeracy in ways that are personally meaningful.
>
> (Gramling, 2015, p. 96–97)

All of these objectives can be accomplished when early childhood educators focus on providing integrated and meaningful activities for their students. For example, for children to learn and understand different colors, teachers may provide opportunities for children to explore colors in nature (e.g., shades of green, oranges, yellows, or browns) as they start to observe seasonal changes. When teaching letters, it might be meaningful to teach them in the context of what students are interested in such as animals or insects around them. To teach about measurement or measurement vocabulary, students may observe what people measure every day in cooking, feeding animals, or grocery shopping. In other words, to maximize the growth of students, teachers need to start with the everyday experiences that children already know and have experienced and build onto their prior schemas for new learning to occur.

In their textbook on early childhood curriculum, Jackman et al. (2015) created checklists of questions to help guide teachers for what to put into the environment to foster growth in each learning domain. To enhance culturally responsive teaching of literacy, some of their questions for teachers to reflect upon include:

1. Does the literacy center include written materials in English and all other languages spoken by the children in the class?
2. Do the books represent a variety of cultures and families?
3. Is an author's chair available?

4. Is there a variety of writing materials such as wipe-off boards, notepads, envelopes, chalkboards, appointment books, and receipts?
5. Is there a computer with writing software and a printer?

(Jackman et al., 2015, p. 113)

These types of questions guide teachers into thinking about the authenticity of the literacy experiences for students, and the importance of children seeing themselves within the literacy environment as active agents of print and producers of knowledge. They are encouraged to be readers, writers, and story tellers, and their own literacy and language skills are valued as starting points for their growth in communication skills.

In order for classrooms to be contexts for talent development, instruction should be focused on enriching and extending children's experiences, as opposed to remediating their deficits. Students' interests and ideas should be valued and extended. This would require early childhood teachers pushing back on what has been termed a "reductionist" approach to teaching early childhood curriculum (focusing on mastery of discrete readiness skills), and instead providing instructional practices that engage children in personally, culturally relevant and meaningful learning. If all early childhood classrooms focused on enrichment and became places for talent development, rather than emphasizing isolated basic academic skills, early childhood gifted education would be available and accessible to all young children. Enrichment, starting with the earliest school experiences, could play a major role in changing inequitable access to advanced learning opportunities throughout the educational system.

Recommendations for Educators

1 Take action: Take an equity perspective.
   The most important recommendation for educators in the field of early childhood gifted education is to change the narrative. The label and rhetoric of the "gifted child" should not be used when you welcome children into your kindergarten classrooms. Change the premise that there are "gifted children" as distinct from non-gifted – most especially at the early childhood level. "Recognize that the professional knowledge base is changing" (NAEYC, 2019, p. 5), and start changing recommendations and standards for developing gifted programs. Stop trying to manipulate identification criteria to find equal percentages of children from all populations to label as gifted. The focus in the field about who is on top, or who is *more qualified than whom* to receive gifted services is wrong! We now know what contributes to inequitable systems – and it's more than just faulty identification systems. From the very beginning, teacher bias, teaching from a deficit approach, and not acknowledging the strengths that young children bring to their learning environments impact differences in achievement outcomes. Start developing learning profiles to showcase the strengths of all students, and to identify the educational needs of students.
   This is not a new idea – some scholars have been advocating this for years (Borland, 2003; Hertzog, 2009). Dai (2019) wrote, "I advocate a system that is service-oriented, defining the goal of gifted education as serving the *excellence needs* of students with a diverse range of talent potential who are underserved in the current education system" (p. 5). But the field has not changed, even though it has

been labeled the most segregated of our educational systems that we have in the United States today.

2   **Provide professional development for early childhood educators that includes self-reflection on privilege, power, and implicit bias.**

It is important to expose teachers to the historical context of systematic racism and oppression in the United States. Teachers need to see examples of how the media portrays families and children of color, or how social media has been a source of microaggressions. Explicit acts of racism are unfortunately present all around us – and teachers need to be sensitive to how families are impacted by what they see and feel every day. The NAEYC *Advancing Equity in Early Childhood Education* Position Statement includes six recommendations for pre-service and in-service programs for teachers:

1. Build awareness and understanding of your culture, personal beliefs, values, and biases.
2. Recognize the power and benefits of diversity and inclusivity.
3. Take responsibility for biased actions, even if unintended, and actively work to repair the harm.
4. Acknowledge and seek to understand structural inequities and their impact over time.
5. View your commitment to cultural responsiveness as an ongoing process.
6. Recognize that the professional knowledge base is changing

(NAEYC, 2019, p. 5)

3   **Educate classroom teachers to design environments that maximize the use of emergent curriculum and instruction.**

To combat the reductionist approach to early childhood education where teaching objectives focus on discrete and disparate readiness goals, the system of accountability and the skills that are valued in early learning need to be changed. Instead of looking for growth in discrete academic minutiae, develop greater emphasis on growth in learning dispositions – disposition to inquire, to seek resources, to express ideas, and to engage in self-initiated learning. By valuing these growth measures, classrooms will become rich contexts for young children to develop and exhibit their strengths and talents. Professional development should focus on helping teachers to create opportunities for children to extend their learning, explore their wonderings, and apply their skills at levels commensurate with their abilities.

4   **Partner and collaborate with families.**

The most important way to learn about the young children that we teach is to show respect and value the contributions of our students' families. Get to know the students' families and extend ways to collaborate and share growth goals for their children. Parents of young children know them better than their teachers, and teachers need to fully appreciate the family values and circumstances that impact their students.

Conclusion

The recommendations here require massive rethinking and redesigning of the field of gifted education, particularly as it relates to early childhood gifted education. These suggestions also target reshaping the concept of readiness in the field of early childhood education – a concept that has driven educators to focus on what can be measured, not necessarily on what should be valued and developed. To break down the structural barriers for young children to enter into advanced learning opportunities, there must be an enormous effort to change systems of accountability on a Federal level, and to change how early educators are taught to provide curriculum and instruction in their preservice programs. More emphasis needs to be placed on valuing their classrooms as contexts for talent development, and on their young students as having the curiosity, the skills, and the resilience to develop their talents. The call to action (Peters et al., 2019) needs to start with our youngest, most vulnerable population. We need to apply these recommendations now.

References

Arndt, J. S., & McGuire-Schwartz, M. E. (2008). Early childhood school success: Recognizing families as integral partners. *Childhood Education, 84*(5), 281–285. www.tandfonline.com/doi/abs/10.1080/00094056.2008.10523025

Borland, J. H. (Ed.). (2003). *Rethinking gifted education.* Teacher's College Press.

Borland, J. H. (2008). Identification. In J. A. Plucker & C. M. Callahan (Eds.), *Critical issues and practices in gifted education* (pp. 261–280). Prufrock Press.

Cole, M. (1985). Mind as a cultural achievement: Implications for IQ testing. In E. Eisner (Ed)., *Learning and teaching the ways of knowing* (pp. 218–249). NSSE.

Dai, D. Y. (2019). Toward a new era of gifted education: Principles, policies, and strategies. *Turkish Journal of Giftedness and Education, 9*(1), 2–15.

Dockett, S., & Perry, B. (2016). Imagining children's strengths as they start school. In W. Parnell, & J. M. Iorio (Eds.), *Early childhood education research* (pp. 139–153). Routledge.

Durden, T. R. (2015). Cracking the walls of the education matrix: Are you ready to educate culturally and linguistically diverse students? In W. Parnell & J. M. Iorio (Eds), *Rethinking readiness in early childhood education* (pp. 77–91). Palgrave MacMillan.

Edwards, C., Gandini, L., & Forman, G. (1993). *The hundred languages of children: The Reggio Emilia approach to early childhood education.* Ablex.

Falchi, L., & Friedman, J. W. (2015). Rethinking the discourse of readiness in preschool. In W. Parnell & J. M. Iorio (Eds.), *Disrupting early childhood education research* (pp. 109–121). Routledge.

Ford, D. Y. (2013). *Recruiting and retaining culturally different students in gifted education.* Prufrock Press.

GOLD® (n.d.). TeachingStrategies. Bethesda, MD: Teaching Strategies, LLC. Retrieved from: https://teachingstrategies.com

Gramling, M. G. (2015). *The great disconnect in early childhood education: What we know vs. what we do.* Redleaf Press.

Hertzog, N. B. (2009). The arbitrary nature of giftedness. In L. Shavinina (Ed.), *Handbook on giftedness* (pp. 205–214). Springer Science.

Hertzog, N. B. (2013). Critical issues in early childhood education. In J. Plucker, & C. M. Callahan (Eds.), *Critical issues and practices in gifted education* (2nd ed., pp. 195– 206). Prufrock Press.

Hertzog, N. B. (2017a). Designing the learning context in school for talent development. *Gifted Child Quarterly, 61*(3), 219–228.

Hertzog, N. B. (2017b). Provisions for young advanced learners. In J. R. Cross, C. O'Reilly, & T. Cross (Eds.), *Providing for the special needs of students with gifts and talents* (pp. 153–172). CTYI Press.

Hertzog, N. B., & Gadzikowski, A. (2017). *Early childhood gifted education – Fostering talent development.* (Series Ed. Adams, C. M.). NAGC Select. National Association for Gifted Children.

Hertzog, N. B., Lamb, K. N., & Lamon, J. (2020). *Exploring how families of color experience advanced learning opportunities.* Interim Report (Unpublished). Unite:Ed Research + Practice Seed Grant.

Hertzog, N. B., & Mammadov, S. (2018). Young learners and specialized preschools in practice. In B. MacFarlane (Ed.), *Specialized schools for high ability learners: Designing and delivering schoolwide educational change* (pp 149–164). Prufrock Press.

Jackman, H., Beaver, N. H., & Wyatt, S. S. (2015). *Early education curriculum* (6th ed.). Cengage Learning.

Kagan. S. L. (1990, December). Readiness 2000: Rethinking rhetoric and responsibility. *Phi Delta Kappan, 72(4)*, 272–279.

Kaplan, S., & Hertzog, N. B. (2016). Pedagogy for early childhood gifted education. *Gifted Child Today, 39*(3), 134–139.

Kappan. (December 2020/January 2021). Finding and developing talented youth. PDK International.

Katz, L., Chard, S. C., & Kogan, Y. (2014). *Engaging children's minds: The project approach* (3rd ed.). Praeger.

Lamb, K. N., Boedeker, P., & Kettler, T. (2019). Inequities of enrollment in gifted education: A state-wide application of the 20% equity allowance formula. *Gifted Child Quarterly*, *63*, 205–224. https://journals.sagepub.com/doi/10.1177/0016986219830768

National Association for the Education of Young Children [NAEYC]. (2003). *Early childhood curriculum, assessment, and program evaluation.* Position Statement. Retrieved from: www.naeyc.org/sites/default/files/globally-shared/downloads/PDFs/resources/position-statements/pscape.pdf

National Association for the Education of Young Children [NAEYC]. (2019, April). *Advancing equity in early childhood education.* Position Statement. Retrieved from: www.naeyc.org/sites/default/files/globally-shared/downloads/PDFs/resources/position-statements/naeycadvancingequityposition statement.pdf

NIEER. (2019). *Pre-K in American cities.* City Health.

Peters, S. J., & Engerrand, K. G. (2016). Equity and excellence: Proactive efforts in the identification of underrepresented students for gifted and talented services. *Gifted Child Quarterly*, *60*, 159–171. https://journals.sagepub.com/doi/10.1177/0016986216643165

Peters, S., Gentry, M., Whiting, G., & McBee, M. T. (2019). Who gets served in gifted education? Demographic representation and a call to action. *Gifted Child Quarterly, 63*(4), 273–287.

Pinedo-Burns, H. J. (2015). Puffins, butterflies and clouds in the preschool: The importance of wonder. In W. Parnell & J. M. Iorio (Eds), *Rethinking readiness in early childhood education* (pp. 165–178). Palgrave MacMillan.

Plucker, J. A., McWilliams, J., & Guo, J. (2017). Smart contexts for 21st-century talent development. In J. Plucker, A. Rinn, & M. Makel (Eds.), *From giftedness to gifted education* (pp. 227–248). Prufrock Press.

Ryan, R., Johnson, A., Rigby, E., & Brooks-Gunn, J. (2011). The impact of child care subsidy use on child care quality. *Early Childhood Research Quarterly, 27*(3), 320–331.

Siegle, D., Gubbins, E. J., Rourke, P. O., Langley, S. D., Mun, R. U., & Plucker, J. A. (2016). Barriers to underserved students' participation in gifted programs and possible solutions. *Journal for the Education of the Gifted*, *39*, 103–131. https://journals.sagepub.com/doi/abs/10.1177/0162353216640930

TestingMom.com. (n.d.). CogAT Test prep. Retrieved from: www.testingmom.com/tests/cogat-test/cogat-test-prep/

Tout, K., Halle, T., Daily, S., Albertson-Junkans, L., & Moodie, S. (2013). *The research base for a birth through age eight state policy framework.* Child Trends. Alliance for Early Success.

Wells, A. (2020). *Achieving equity in gifted programming.* Prufrock Press.

Woo, E. (2005, September 27). Urie Bronfenbrenner, 88; Co-founder of Head Start urged closer family ties. Los Angeles Times. Retrieved from: www.latimes.com/archives/la-xpm-2005-sep-27-me-bronfen27-story.html)

Yoon, S. Y., & Gentry, M. (2009). Racial and ethnic representation in gifted programs: Current status of and implications for gifted Asian American students. *Gifted Child Quarterly, 53*(2), 121–136. https://journals.sagepub.com/doi/abs/10.1177/0016986208330564

Chapter 12

Identifying and Educating Gifted English Language Learners (ELLs)

Jaime A. Castellano and Erik M. Francis

School-aged English language learners (ELLs) positively add to the fabric of the American school system. They come to the United States from all corners of the world with their language, customs, heritage, life experiences, and dreams for a better life that make their schools and communities a better place. Some arrive wealthy and educated; most do not. They enroll in our public schools, charter schools, and private schools. Hispanics are by far the largest ELL group and represent one territory and 19 countries where Spanish is identified as the official language. ELLs from these locations may be called Hispanic, Latino, Chicano, or Latinx. Academic achievement data at the local, state, national, and international levels all confirm that as a group they are performing below expectation. But there are those among them that are gifted, advanced, and high-ability. The purpose of this chapter is to inform readers on the identification, assessment, nature and needs, programming, and instruction of gifted ELLs.

Throughout my professional career (Jaime A. Castellano) as a teacher of the gifted, assistant principal and principal supervising gifted programs, district level coordinator and director of gifted education, and as a state department of education expert in the field, I have supported the identification and education of gifted English language learners (ELLs). The following snapshots over the years (see Table 12.1) in part support my efforts at equity and access for this unique subset of students.

Saul Ramirez, a teacher and chess coach at Henderson Middle School in El Paso, Texas, states in an interview with John Seidlitz (2018):

> I encourage teachers to focus on what English language learners are capable of and the linguistic and cultural assets they bring to our schools and communities. ... I strive to be radically available to my students. I try to be fully present with all my strengths to help build up theirs. I bring who I am and, in the spirit of love, put all my talents, stories, and every resource I have into serving them. I make a commitment every day to be as present to the students as I possibly can.
>
> (Ramirez, quoted by Seidlitz, 2018, p. 25)

In 2015, his team of 12 middle school ELLs from El Paso, Texas, most of whom had never previously heard of chess, went on to become national chess champions. Are these ELL national chess champions gifted? What cognitive ability did they employ to become champions of a game that requires intensive critical thinking and problem solving? Abstract reasoning, creative thinking, pattern recognition, and strategic thinking are some of the

DOI: 10.4324/9781003265412-17

Table 12.1 Identifying Gifted ELLs: Snapshots of Success

Year	Professional Position	Number of Gifted ELLs Identified	Achievement
1995–1996	As Principal	5	Created one of the first programs for gifted ELLs in the state of Florida and in the nation
2000–2004	As District Specialist/Expert	56	Result of OCR lawsuit
2006	As Javits Consultant	>50	Groundbreaking research (**NNAT, CogAT, Ravens SPM**)
2008	As State Specialist	>100	Working with districts throughout state
2009–2012	As Principal	42	Native Americans on reservation
2013	As Executive Director	8	Dual Language Charter School
2014–2018	As Assistant Director	30	Head Start Program

skills associated with playing chess at a highly competitive level; and coincidently, these same skills are also found on tests of intelligence that students must demonstrate in order to gain eligibility for advanced academic programs like gifted education.

How students demonstrate these skills and ability often dictate access and opportunity. Students who demonstrate these skills on a traditional intelligence test and are formally identified as gifted may not necessarily be able to apply them to a game of competitive chess at the national level; and those who demonstrate them on a chess board and are identified as national champions may not necessarily be able to apply them on a verbally intensive test of intelligence. In the traditional school context, which student is most likely to gain access to gifted education? What is important to note is that the cultural, ethnic, and linguistic diversity that gifted ELLs bring to their schools is an asset, not a hindrance or burden. For example, the Seal of Biliteracy (n.d.) is an award given by a school, district, or state in recognition of students who have studied and attained proficiency in two or more languages by high school graduation. It encourages students to pursue biliteracy, honors the skills our students attain, and can be evidence of skills that are attractive to future employers and college admissions offices. Currently, 44 states and Washington DC have approved a statewide Seal of Biliteracy (sealofbiliteracy.org).

According to the National Center for Educational Statistics (NCES, 2018), ELLs accounted for approximately 10% of the total number of students enrolled in U.S. public schools in SY 2014–2015, or about five million students. The United States Department of Education, Office for Civil Rights (2014), reported that 2% of ELLs, (or 100,000), are enrolled in gifted and talented programs. Historically, there is an underrepresentation of students from racially, culturally, and linguistically diverse backgrounds in gifted and talented programs (Castellano, 2018; Castellano & Frazier, 2011).

ELLs with gifts, talent, and potential represent a great untapped national resource of intelligence, energy, and creativity. They deserve an opportunity to demonstrate what they know and are able to do. Their individual perspectives are to be validated and respected in their schools and communities. Despite this truth, they are disproportionately underserved in programs serving gifted, advanced, and high-ability students. As school-aged ELLs continue to grow in numbers, it would behoove educators across the United States to develop processes and strategies; rules, regulations, and policies that help them to realize that among them are students deserving of a gifted education.

Gifted ELLs: Belonging and Identity

Given their rich linguistic and cultural diversity – more than 400 languages are spoken by ELLs nationwide – the dramatic leap in the number of language minority students presents great possibilities and great challenges for America's school systems. Unfortunately, these demographic changes haven't seen parallel changes in the way schools perceive and educate those among them who are gifted. Consider the following points:

- Most educators are unaware of the characteristics of gifted ELLs, and many lack the professional development to deal with this diverse group of students.
- Identifying gifted ELLs may not be a priority for schools and districts.
- Lack of a national movement to identify and serve gifted ELLs has led to inconsistencies in supporting them.
- The programmatic support that gifted ELLs receive varies widely from school to school, district to district, and state to state.
- Gifted ELLs are expected to accommodate the conventional, status quo programs they are placed in, and as a result, struggle without the skills they need for academic success. Issues of identity will continue to manifest with the growth that exists in this population.

Park et al. (2018) write in their report for the Migration Policy Institute that diversity is on the rise across the United States, where Dual Language Learners (DLLs) – young children who have at least one parent who speaks a language other than English in the home – now make up nearly one-third of all young children between the ages of 0 and 8. Far from being a homogeneous group, differences within the DLL population are both considerable and increasing. Their families speak many different languages, identify with many races and ethnicities, and have widely varied countries of origin, socioeconomic statuses, level of education, and migration histories – all important characteristics that influence DLL children's development. This *superdiversity* has important implications for schools and other systems that face the challenge of building the capacity to effectively serve children with unique learning strengths and needs; in this case, gifted ELLs. Belonging and identity inform who we are. For gifted ELLs, this is critical to their success, growth, and development. The implications of superdiversity for those who serve gifted ELLs, in whatever capacity, are equally important. For example, from FY 2008–2017, the top native languages (Park et al., 2018) for refugee arrivals were:

- Arabic 21%
- Nepali 14%
- Somali 8%
- S'gaw Karen 7% (Myanmar and Thailand)
- Spanish 5%
- Other 45%

For local school districts that serve these emerging language communities, belonging and identity have expanded their view of diversity and whom to identify and serve as gifted. As a nation, certainly in the field of gifted education, we have an inherent responsibility to embrace this superdiversity. The current focus, however, is on ELLs with a

Spanish-speaking heritage as they represent approximately 73% of all ELLs in the United States(Migration Policy Institute, 2015). In our search for ways to honor the identity and belonging of gifted ELLs, one strategy is to celebrate their voices; their stories. Capitalizing on their home language, knowledge, and cultural assets, gifted ELLs celebrate who they are while demonstrating and mastering important cognitive and academic skills found in the standards and benchmarks used by their teachers.

Vignette: Pamela's Story

Every day, I remember the importance of my family history, how it constantly motivates me, and how it greatly defines the person that I have become today. Being Hispanic, raised in a Spanish-speaking home, has not only affected my personal life, but it has also affected me academically. I come from a background of proud Hispanics who came here to the United States to seek opportunity. My mother is Dominican, and my father, who is Peruvian, never got a chance to attend college in America. Not only am I the first generation to be born in America, but I will also be a first-generation college student.

As a Latina, I have carried myself with great pride to represent the cultures throughout all my years of public education. As I have grown older, I have understood the great effects both my parents have had on my academic life. For example, my mother only speaks Spanish, and although she has gone above and beyond for me when it comes to my education, she can only do so much. Also, my mother is unemployed, which leads to my father working multiple jobs and still receiving little income. Daily, I appreciate everything my parents have given up for me. Yet, because of my family's circumstances it has made me not only extremely responsible but also very self-reliant.

Alone, I have proudly accomplished many achievements during my high school years. The variety of Advanced Placement and Honors classes my public high school has offered to me has allowed me [to] grow and flourish as a student. In addition, these upper-level classes have taught me to surround myself with other creative, intelligent, and well-rounded classmates and friends. I am in the top 10 percent of my graduating class, have made the honor roll each year, am a member of the National Honor Society, and have received a plethora of other awards and recognitions.

As a first-generation Latin-American, I have recognized many things as the years go by. Watching my parents struggle financially has not only affected my family, but also the academic lives of me and my two younger sisters. Watching my parents sacrifice many things for us has given me hope and ambition to achieve greatly beyond my high school education. I have a duty as a Latina to not only make my parents and my family in the Dominican Republic and Peru proud, but to make every Hispanic young adult with the same struggles as mine ever prouder. I have a great desire to be a role model for my little sisters, for the children at my local church, for my peers, and especially for myself. As the years go by, and my successes materialize, I will always remember to celebrate my beautiful Hispanic culture.

This was Pamela's response when asked how her Hispanic ethnicity affected her academic achievement, and how it influenced her aspirations. Students like Pamela abound in our nation's schools. The following information on identification, assessment, and sensibility will assist educators in reaching students like Pamela and other gifted ELLs to fulfill their potential and realize their dreams.

Identification, Assessment, and Sensibility

The identification of ELLs as gifted continues to confound regular classroom teachers, bilingual teachers, ESL teachers, and any other educator who serves them. The proof is their skeletal representation in programs serving gifted students; only 2% of ELLs nationwide (or 100,000) are enrolled in gifted and talented programs. What these numbers imply, in part, is that professional development in the identification of giftedness and how it is manifested by ELLs is required. To begin, Table 12.2 provides a historical review of the characteristics of gifted ELLs by scholars who have studied this population, both qualitatively and quantitatively.

The characteristics presented in the historical review reflect the importance of qualitative behaviors that should be taken into account in the identification process. This level of knowledge is the result of relationship-building and acknowledging the idiosyncratic behaviors of individual students. This qualitative data point should be part of a larger identification process that includes multiple criteria. Brulles and Weinbrenner (2019) also highlight the need to help teachers understand that the behaviors and traits listed above are characteristics of giftedness, even though they may not be correlated with achievement. They state that many characteristics are present among gifted students consistently and intensely over time. To be considered gifted, it is not necessary for an ELL to exhibit all

Table 12.2 Historical Review of the Characteristics of Gifted ELLs

Bernal (1974)	Aguirre and Hernandez (1999)	Project Bright Horizons (2006)	Brulles and Weinbrenner (2019)
Enjoys intelligent risk-taking behavior	Eagerly shares culture	Strong desire to learn in their language and in English	Persistent
Has older playmates and can easily engage adults in lively conversations	Interprets at very high levels	High interest in certain topics	Takes on leadership roles
Is "street wise" and recognized by others as possessing ability to "make it" in the "White" society	Possesses advanced knowledge of idioms	Quickly grasps new information	Independent
	Possesses cross-cultural flexibility	Evidence of creative ability in thinking and problem solving	Ability to carry responsibilities well
Rapidly acquires English language skills	Learns a second language at an accelerated rate	Ability to see relationships and make connections	Keen power of observation
Accepts adult-like responsibilities at home	Ability to code-switch	May have exceptional talent in areas valued by their culture	Originality and imagination
		Hold high standards for themselves	Self-directed
		Curiosity	Ability to express emotions and feelings
		May have exceptional ability in the visual or performing arts; kinesthetic preference	Tendency to find and correct their own or other's mistakes
			Articulates in role-playing & storytelling
			Has a command of informal language
			Ease in adapting to new situations

these characteristics; some gifted students also exhibit characteristics not on these lists. However, ELLs who consistently demonstrate a good portion of these characteristics are likely to be gifted. Quantitatively, and typically in the form of test scores on tests of intelligence and achievement, gifted ELLs must meet the program criteria set by the local school district and/or state department of education. Written in policy, these cutoff scores are the standard for eligibility. Even when school districts initiate local norms, a certain percentage must be achieved to access gifted education programs.

According to Carmen et al. (2018), the use of school-normed or group-normed cutoff scores to ensure equality of representation in gifted education could have major effects on the performance and retention of students in gifted programs. Using school-normed or group-normed cutoff scores should result in an influx of students being identified as gifted who would otherwise not have been selected for participation in those programs. However, the inclusion of students to achieve greater equity, without proper planning, resources, and support systems, could result in a decrease in program performance. It is vitally important to ensure that schools using these norming methods are prepared for the differing educational needs that some of these students may bring to the gifted program that the district may not have needed to address previously. Students whom the district would not have identified based on their scores – affected by their lack of opportunity to learn – will bring those gaps in learning with them to their new programs. Gifted programs will need to prepare to address these gaps to increase student success and retention. Gifted ELLs are one of the student groups that may present districts with this challenge.

National Survey

In the spring of 2019, the Education Week Research Center (2019) conducted a survey of more than 1,200 K-12 gifted and talented teachers and coordinators to learn more about how districts and schools define, identify, serve, and instruct students in gifted and talented programs. A major objective was to gain a better understanding of the extent to which districts are experiencing and addressing issues related to the overrepresentation or underrepresentation of specific student groups in gifted education. The findings suggest that gifted programs are likely to face serious equity-related challenges. The following data is specific to ELLs.

Definitions and Screening

Gifted education is largely defined as intellectual or academic giftedness. Relatively few educators say that their districts' definitions account for the fact that certain groups (e.g., English language learners) have historically been underrepresented in gifted education. The population of English learners is unevenly distributed across the United States, with some districts enrolling substantial numbers and many others enrolling none. Roughly 800 educators report that their districts do enroll students learning English. Of that 800, a majority (63%) perceive that English language learners are underrepresented in gifted education; while 34% state that they are neither overrepresented nor underrepresented. Just 3% say they are overrepresented.

Urban educators are significantly more likely to say that definitions of giftedness account for cultural or ethnic diversity, socioeconomic status, or English proficiency. When asked if

ELLs are addressed in their district's definition of gifted/talented, 31% of urban educators answered that definitions of giftedness account for cultural or ethnic diversity, socio-economic status, or English proficiency; compared to 17% of suburban educators and 18% of rural/town educators.

Uneven Equity

Most educators say that their district's screening process identifies all or almost all of the students who should be in the gifted education program. However, a majority of educators also say that Black, Hispanic, Native American, low-income, and emerging bilingual students are underrepresented in their district's gifted programs. Despite this widespread perception of underrepresentation, fewer than one in three educators say that their district has made a big effort in the past five years to address this issue. Compared to those who work in lower-poverty districts, gifted education personnel in high-poverty school districts are more likely to say that English learners are underrepresented.

- When the district is majority low-income, 62% of educators surveyed say that ELLs are underrepresented in gifted education.
- When the district is 50% or less low-income, 27% of educators surveyed say that ELLs are underrepresented in gifted education.

Educators from "majority-minority" districts are significantly more likely to say that English learners and whites are underrepresented in gifted education. Those from majority-white districts are more likely to report that ELLs are underrepresented in gifted education.

- 71% of educators from majority-minority school districts say that these student groups (English learners and whites) are under-represented in gifted education.
- 61% of educators from majority-white school districts say that these student groups (ELLs) are underrepresented in gifted education.

The percentage of educators who say that gifted ELLs are underrepresented in gifted education varied by location, in that:

- 75% of educators from urban school districts say that gifted ELLs are underrepresented in gifted education.
- 68% of educators from suburban school districts say that gifted ELLs are underrepresented in gifted education.
- 51% of educators from rural school districts say that gifted ELLs are underrepresented in gifted education.

Finally, compared to their colleagues elsewhere in the United States, Western educators are more likely to perceive that ELLs are underrepresented in gifted education.

- 78% of educators from the Western region of the United States perceive that ELLs are underrepresented in gifted education.

- 64% of educators from the Southern region of the United States perceive that ELLs are underrepresented in gifted education.
- 57% of educators from the Midwest region of the United States perceive that ELLs are underrepresented in gifted education.
- 50% of educators from the Northeast region of the United States perceive that ELLs are underrepresented in gifted education.

This survey of 1,200 K-12 gifted and talented teachers and coordinators validates that as a nation we have a long way to go to achieve equity in gifted education for special populations of students like ELLs.

Assessment

Brulles and Weinbrenner (2019) write that schools should adopt assessments that appropriately identify all gifted students. Nonverbal assessments or batteries are essential in this process. Many ELLs are identified as gifted on nonverbal assessments, which require students to rely on the advanced reasoning and problem-solving skills that clearly define giftedness in any population. To see how effective a school's identification methods are in recognizing and serving giftedness across cultures, look at the percentage of gifted-identified students from each demographic group, and compare this to the percentage of all students from that demographic group in the school. For example, if 45% of the students in the school are Hispanic, approximately 45% of the students identified as gifted should be Hispanic. If this is not the case, it may be necessary to look at alternatives for identifying and assessing ELL gifted students.

In their report titled *Exploratory Study on the Identification of English Learners for Gifted and Talented Programs*, the University of Connecticut's National Center for Research in Gifted Education (Gubbins et al., 2018) cites multiple scholars and researchers (p. 3) who support the practice of using multiple measures and alternative assessments – to include, but not limited to, nonverbal ability tests, intelligence tests in the students' own languages, dynamic and authentic procedures, classroom observations, checklists and rating scales, portfolios, parental input, and self-identification. How and when multiple measures and alternative assessments are used are important considerations in the overall identification process for gifted and talented programs. Universal screening of all students in one or more grade levels may include standardized tests of IQ, ability or aptitude, and achievement. For ELLs, these cognitive assessments represent one of the greatest barriers to gifted identification if they are not culturally sensitive. Researchers have long asserted that ELLs will not perform as well on cognitive assessments with verbal components in English due to linguistic and cultural factors.

Building a Sensible Identification and Assessment System

Teachers have become more aware of the possibilities of bias in assessing students who live in poverty, speak a language other than English, and come from culturally diverse backgrounds. Nonetheless, bias and exclusion continue to exist. When it comes to identifying and assessing ELLs as gifted, the following challenges, adapted from the work of Friend and Bursuck (2019), should be addressed by school and district personnel:

- ELL students may exhibit test anxiety due to lack of familiarity with the assessment process.
- ELLs may not be proficient in the language used for the test.
- ELLs may speak with a dialect that differs from that of the assessor.
- ELLs may lack exposure to the test content.
- ELLs may have different communication styles; for example, they may not feel comfortable asking for help with directions or may respond using fewer words.
- ELL test scores may be depressed because the assessor is unfamiliar or speaks a different language.
- ELLs may lack motivation to perform well on tests because of differing cultural considerations.

Strategies for assessing and interpreting their performance more accurately should include:

- Give ELLs practice tests.
- Qualify test performance with class performance.
- Allow more time for assessors to establish rapport and gain trust.
- Check for understanding of test directions; avoid automatically penalizing ELLs for not saying enough or not giving details.
- Eliminate unfamiliar content.
- Assess students using both English and the student's native language.
- Do not count dialectical differences as errors; examine your attitudes about using alternative measures of intelligence and achievement.

Sensible identification and assessment systems are inclusive, modify the language of the test items (but not the content) by reducing low-frequency vocabulary and complex language structures, and provide ELLs with definitions or simple paraphrases of potentially unfamiliar or difficult words on tests. These sensible accommodations have the potential to boost the ELL's test-related self-efficacy and motivation.

A Focus on Equity

Effective teachers of gifted ELLs form an important backbone of equity for this special population of learners. Some of the observable characteristics of equity include familiarity with their students as individuals (including their linguistic and cultural backgrounds), knowledge of the corresponding pedagogical approaches that are effective based on this familiarity, expectations for learning that are rigorous, and a collaborative and advocacy-based focus. They also teach their students to understand their own goals, talents, and learning behaviors.

Title VI of the Civil Rights Act of 1964 prohibits discrimination on the grounds of race, color, or national origin by recipients of federal financial assistance. The Title VI regulatory requirements have been interpreted by the court system to prohibit denial of equal access to education because of a student's limited proficiency in English. Other high-profile court cases that address issues of equity for ELLs include:

- *Lau v. Nichols*: This 1974 Supreme Court case involved parents who petitioned against the failure of the San Francisco United School District to provide English language instruction to approximately 1,800 students of Chinese heritage who did not speak English. The schools they attended had provided inadequate instructional programs, thereby denying students a meaningful opportunity to participate in the public educational program. The Supreme Court found a violation of the equal education opportunities provision of the Civil Rights Act of 1964.

- *Castañeda v. Pickard* (1981): Through this case, the Fifth Circuit Court ruled that schools must take "appropriate action" regarding students learning English and that such action must be based on sound educational theory, produce results, and provide adequate resources, teachers, and materials.
- *Plyler v. Doe*: In 1982, the Supreme Court ruled in *Plyler v. Doe* that public schools were prohibited from denying immigrant students access to public education, stating that undocumented children have the same right to a free public education as U.S. citizens and permanent residents. Undocumented immigrant students are obliged, as are all other students, to attend school until they reach the age mandated by law.

These landmark cases set the foundation for ELLs to access any of the educational programs that are offered through a public school system, like gifted education. Today, the inclusion of gifted ELLs is found in programs like Title I and the Jacob K. Javits program. In addition, a special issue of the *Journal of the Education of the Gifted* (43(4), December 2020) focuses on "Identifying and Serving Gifted English Learners." In one article, Gubbins et al. (2020) identified emergent themes related to the identification of gifted ELLs that conceivably serve as "equity markers." They include adopting universal screening procedures, creating alternative pathways to identification, establishing a web of communication, and viewing professional learning as a lever for change. Finally, they emphasize that these four themes are presented for review and reflection by state and local decision-makers responsible for the screening, nomination/referral, identification, and placement of ELLs in gifted and talented programs.

Communicating and Collaborating with Parents and Families of Gifted ELLs

Castellano (2018) maintains that culturally and historically, the reverence that many Hispanic/Latino parents have toward their children's school and teachers prevents them from asserting themselves in the education process. Those with a gifted (ELL) child often believe that their teacher will do the right thing for their child. Despite this mindset by parents, communicating and collaborating with them is our collective responsibility. We must provide them with the tools to help their children succeed.

As a Spanish-speaking scholar in the field of gifted education for more than 25 years, I (Jaime A. Castellano) have been invited by schools and school districts from every region of the United States to speak with their primarily Hispanic/Latino parents and families about their gifted children. In this capacity I have worked with thousands of parents and families. The vast majority of parents whom I have encountered are Spanish-speakers; often undocumented. The norm is that they are low-income, uneducated, and often face literacy issues in English and Spanish. Hence, the need to use comprehensible Spanish instead of the jargon often associated with gifted education. They prefer to share their stories in a small-group format and acknowledge that they want their children to be educated so that they can have a better life. Despite these challenges, they are committed to their children and are willing to make sacrifices that benefit them. They want information. They prefer, however, to partner with their gifted child's teachers and schools in their advocacy efforts.

Just as schools have an inherent responsibility to educate the students they serve, parents and families with a gifted child have an equal, if not greater, responsibility to ensure their children are prepared to be successful. Raising resilient children who are able to persevere in today's complex society is no easy task. Parents must compete with the latest technology, social media, the child's peer group, and the demands placed on them at work and home. Despite the challenges that often present themselves, parents are bound to engage and interact as their child's first teacher. A gifted ELL who is able to exhibit self-regulation, effort, and discipline will most likely do well in school. Teachers and other educators will attest that these skills are not only important for school but also in life. So then, how can parents and families, working with teachers and schools, advocate for their children? This open-ended question has an infinite number of responses, but here are some ideas that I have shared with them.

- Parent modeling
  - Trying difficult tasks and discussing the process with their children
  - Enrolling in an adult ESL class or other lifelong learning class
  - When possible, being an active participant in the child's homework while remaining calm and focused
- Extracurricular participation
  - Child enrollment in sports, arts, or music clubs and teams (in school or in the community) where the student learns to be reliable
  - Playdates/get-togethers with other gifted students (also an excellent time for parents to convene)
  - Child participating in community service projects sponsored by the school or a local agency
- Emotional availability
  - Encouraging and supporting their gifted child's feelings
  - Listening and keeping lines of communication open; not responding in anger
  - Sharing family meals on a regular basis.

Here is some additional information I provide to them in Spanish.

- Essential questions to ask teachers and administrators about the gifted education program
- Essential questions to ask teachers and administrators about their student using a whole child framework
- Open-ended discussion questions about hope, effort, discipline, and expectations
- A Bill of Rights as patrons of their respective school district.

Murphey et al. (2014) document that for most Latinos there are few things that are more important than family. School personnel who understand this about Hispanic/Latino parents and families have an easier time engaging and collaborating with them. By creating an environment of trust through dialogue, schools can engage the whole family to promote student success.

Educating Gifted ELLs about Self-Advocacy: Teachers and Parents Working Together

Castellano and Robertson (2021) propose that although it may appear contradictory, the journey of self-advocacy often begins with collaboration, most typically between the home and school personnel. Teaching gifted ELLs to advocate for themselves gives them a voice in their education, beyond lip-service. It empowers them to ask questions and make decisions that are unique to who they are and their local context. Teaching gifted ELLs to ask key questions of the right person allows for accessing information that influences their decision-making. Reflection is part of the self-advocacy process. Through reflection and self-assessment, gifted ELLs are able to identify and understand their own needs and beliefs. In turn, they communicate these thoughts to others they trust and respect (teachers, parents) with an expectation of feedback that is authentic. This is, in part, the journey to self-advocacy.

For adults who are part of the gifted ELL self-advocacy experience, cross-cultural perspectives on gifted education are important. In my work (Jaime A. Castellano), I write that culturally competent adult educators who "get it" when working with gifted ELL students put themselves in a position to make a difference based on their ability to use relational pedagogy. This means the use of empowerment strategies and activities that promote both increased academic achievement and mastery of learning, as well as having a connection that encourages students to advocate for themselves. Gifted ELLs who self-advocate put themselves in a position to take control of their own narrative and demonstrate the ability to persevere, to be resilient, and to rise above any challenge that may stand in their way; often with the assistance of key adult collaborators.

Here are some key points for consideration:

1   It is generally recognized by today's educational and instructional leaders in the field of gifted education that in order to develop the gifts, talents, and self-advocacy skills of ELLs, stakeholder groups must follow a collaborative and collegial approach rooted in clear communication and respect for the challenges faced by ELL students.
2   Improved parental awareness is critical to gifted ELL self-advocacy. Support for parents is as important as it is for the student; as is sensitivity to English language proficiency. Through collaborative efforts, parents receive one collective message rather than multiple and possibly conflicting messages.
3   Self-advocacy is a process that involves personal reflection and self-assessment. It requires identifying needs and beliefs, being respectful yet assertive, and understanding rights and responsibilities.
4   Using schools and classrooms to promote gifted ELL self-advocacy is fundamental to changing the status quo for them, their parents, families, and communities. This advances a culture of influence in the form of advocacy, participation, and shared decision-making that informs equity, access, and opportunity.

5   Self-advocacy may involve making difficult decisions that impact family dynamics, friendships, and other such relationships. This is not selfish behavior. Rather, self-advocacy is an attempt to actualize the gifts, talents, and potential that one possesses; and taking control of one's educational future.

6   In promoting student self-advocacy, teachers and administrators develop positive relationships with students, reinforcing qualities that are key to resilience. They also share personal examples of resilience, perseverance, and advocacy. They become models and mentors for gifted ELLs.

Curriculum and Instruction

Questioning and inquiry are two of the most effective methods for strengthening and supporting language development and communication of learning – especially for gifted students and English language learners who both struggle to express and share their knowledge, thinking, and reasoning in a language that's both clear and comprehensible to others. These methods also increase the cognitive rigor of learning experiences by challenging students to demonstrate different levels of thinking and communicate their depth of knowledge (Francis, 2016, 2017, 2021; Hess, 2018; Hess et al., 2009a, 2009b).

Questioning and inquiry encourages both intellectual and language development. A good question that fosters and promotes both cognitive rigor and communication (Francis, 2016, 2021) does the following:

- Stimulates deeper thinking
- Deepens knowledge, understanding, and awareness
- Expands knowledge and extends thinking
- Piques curiosity, interest, imagination, and wonder
- Prompts students to reflect as well as respond
- Phrases the instructional focus and purpose as an interrogative statement
- Expresses and shares learning in its own unique way.

The last three characteristics are most essential for both language development and communication of learning. With English language learners, the challenge is for students to express and share their learning using the conventions of a language – be it their primary home or country's language or the language of the country or culture in which they live. With gifted students, the challenge is for them to express and share their knowledge and ideas in a language that's clear and understandable. Both English language learners and gifted students must also understand how questions can be used as a means to deepen and extend their learning, not just assess it.

Questioning and inquiry can also foster and promote social development and expression. This approach encourages ELLs to express themselves and interact with diverse audiences and groups, not just with their peers. Learning the language of others or how they communicate also engages and encourages students to be aware of their audience. This not only ensures clear communication between the individual gifted English language learner and their audience, but also establishes a connection with the audience and expresses a feeling of respect. The student is presenting the message that they not only want to be understood but are also willing to learn the language of their audience to ensure they understand as well.

Questioning

Questioning is a strategy. It's what we educators do and use to have students demonstrate and communicate what they know, understand, think, or can do. We mostly use questions to assess the depth and extent of students' learning. However, questioning can also be used not only to develop and deepen students' learning, but also to deliver and drive instruction from the teacher or the text.

Francis (2016) identifies seven kinds of good questions that will not only challenge students to demonstrate higher levels of thinking, but also to communicate their depth of knowledge.

1   **Factual Questions:** These good questions prompt students to develop and demonstrate foundational knowledge and functional understanding. Students must answer correctly *who, what, where, when,* or *how* and *why* according to the information presented in texts or by credible sources. Students demonstrate and communicate their learning by restating or retelling, quoting the source or text, or by paraphrasing and summarizing in their own words. These questions may be challenging for English language learners who are acquiring and developing their language skills. Gifted students may be abrupt or dismissive with these questions because they only require them to provide just the facts. However, we can support our gifted and ELL students by using sentence frames or formulas that will help them express themselves using complete sentences in the proper grammatical form. We can also challenge our gifted and ELL students to express and share their knowledge and understanding in their own words, rather than simply restating or retelling the answers literally or verbatim from a text or source.

2   **Analytical Questions:** These good questions challenge students to demonstrate and communicate conceptual and procedural understanding. Students must establish and explain with examples *how* or *why; what categorizes; what classifies;* or *what determines, distinguishes,* or *indicates.* Students express and share their learning by providing explanations and interpretations, making generalizations and inferences, or paraphrasing and summarizing ideas and information in their own words. Both gifted students and English language learners may struggle with these questions because they demand longer-form responses. They also focus more on explaining ideas and processes than restating information and procedures. However, we can strengthen and support our gifted ELL students' language development by providing them with formulaic sentence and paragraph structures that will allow them to communicate their learning clearly and comprehensively. We can also use graphic organizers that sequence events or procedures, classify ideas and information, or define in context. The challenge will be for students not only to complete these visuals but also explain how and why they organized the details, information, and procedures.

3   **Reflective Questions:** Questions that ask students to express and share their deeper awareness of causes, comparisons, connections, and consequences. These good questions demand that students establish and explain with examples or examine and

explain with evidence: *what is the cause(s) and/or effect(s); what are the similarities and differences; what is the connection or relationship; or what are the reasons.* Students demonstrate and communicate their learning by expressing and sharing their thinking and reasoning in their own words supported by specific examples and credible evidence. Gifted ELL students may struggle to explain the connections between ideas and information or how the examples and evidence support reasons, relationships, or results. However, we can strengthen and support our gifted ELL students' language development by using graphic organizers such as compare-contrast graphics, flow charts, or analogy bridges.

4   **Hypothetical Questions:** These good questions encourage students to think creatively about possibilities and potential. They foster and promote both creative thinking and creative expression. They also pique students' curiosity, imagination, interest, and wonder by asking *what if, what could happen,* or *what would happen?* Students are encouraged to explore and explain their original ideas and imagination. They also form conclusions or make predictions based on evidence, examples, and their own experience. Gifted ELLs may struggle with these questions, not only from a language aspect but also a socio-emotional perspective. Some students may be more literal or logical and find it difficult to envision, imagine, or predict more figurative ideas. Other gifted ELLs may be highly imaginative or visionary but unable to express or support their ideas clearly. However, we can support our gifted ELLs by having them demonstrate and communicate their ideas and imagination figuratively or literally through creative expression. For example, we encourage students to use sequential art or storyboarding to express their vision. We can also encourage students to express themselves through creative writing or design or explore their ideas through creative genres such as alternative history, historical fiction, or science fiction based on facts, hypotheses, and theories. We can also encourage students to produce texts that are multisensory such as audio recordings or visual productions such as videos or slide presentations using PowerPoint or Keynote. The goal here is for gifted ELL students to express and share their ideas and imagination not only in a language but also a form that's clear, comprehensive, and even creative.

5   **Argumentative Questions:** These good questions engage students in thinking critically and require them to defend, justify, or refute actions, answers, or arguments – be it their own or those written by others. These are true multiple-choice questions in that students are provided with multiple claims or options and must decide which one is the best, most effective, or most rational given the circumstance or context. They should be phrased to provide choice or options (i.e., *Is... or...? Should... or...? Which one(s)...?*) rather than lead students to respond with "yes" or "no." Like hypothetical questions, addressing and responding to these good questions may be difficult from both a language and socio-emotional standpoint. These questions require evidentiary support, which means students must understand the nuances of fact versus opinion. They can also be highly emotionally charged as students share their feelings as well as the facts that they believe strengthen and support them. We can support our gifted ELLs by providing them with a structured format that will help them not only share but also support their claims and conclusions clearly with credible evidence. We can also teach them how to persuade others, using not only evidence but also by phrasing their statements as declarations, demands, and rhetorical questions that make logical,

ethical, and emotional appeals using rhetorical questions. To increase the strength of the student voice, have students begin every sentence with a first-person referent (e.g., *I think…, I feel…, In my opinion…, In my reading or research…*). Then, have students cross out all first-person references. The result will be sentences that are not only stronger in their tone, but also more powerful in their convictions and more focused on the idea or issue than the individual.

6   **Affective Questions:** Affective questions emphasize the pronoun referent "you" to stress that students' responses should reflect not only their knowledge and thinking but also their disposition or feelings. These questions address the Affective Domain of Bloom's Taxonomy, encouraging students to consider and communicate their attitudes, beliefs, feelings, thoughts, values, or ways they see or do things (Francis, 2016; Krathwohl et al., 1964). These questions prompt and encourage personal expression and investment by asking *what do **you** think, feel, or believe; how could or would **you**;* or *what would **you*** do? They are also effective in addressing the socio-emotional needs of students, providing them opportunities to be reflective with and responsive to their thinking and feelings. Students who struggle with or are hesitant about expressing and sharing their attitudes, feelings, or thoughts may find these questions difficult to address. From a language standpoint, we can support students by having them use sentence frames that utilize first-person pronouns such as the subjective *I,* the objective *me,* and the possessive *my* or *mine.* From a socio-emotional standpoint, we can support students by establishing a learning environment in which students can feel safe and secure with expressing their attitudes, feelings, and thoughts. We can also use affective questions and their responses as a starting point for responding to good questions that focus more on explaining conceptual or procedural understanding (analytical); examining causes, comparisons, or connections (reflective); thinking creatively or making predictions (hypothetical); or defending, justifying, or refuting actions, answers, or arguments (argumentative).

7   **Personal Questions:** Personal questions ask students to come up with their own questions about what else or what they individually want to learn about the text, topic, or technique taught in class. These are the students' questions – the ones they personally want to answer. We can use these questions not only to tap into students' natural curiosity but also to teach them how to phrase their questions clearly or properly in their primary or second language. In fact, we can teach students how to ask any of the six types of questions listed above using the specific interrogative sentence frames and question stems associated with them. Table 12.3 shows the question stems and interrogative sentence frames for each of type of good question.

Inquiry

Inquiry is not only an instructional method and a learning process. It is also a mindset and an experience. Mitchell (2019) describes inquiry as "a way of being (a disposition) and a way of teaching (a pedagogy) that gets the students to do most of the question asking and answer seeking" (p. 3). It is how we acquire and process bits and bytes of information into deeper knowledge, understanding, awareness, expertise, and how we can understand and use the acquired information in different contexts. It is also how we look at learning and life – with a sense of curiosity, interest, imagination, and wonder. Both teachers and

Table 12.3 Cognitive Rigor Questioning (CRQ) Framework

Type of good question	Question stem	Interrogative sentence frame
Factual	Who is/are? What is/are? Where is/are? When is/are?	What does it mean to? What does___mean?
Analytical	How does? Why does? What categorizes? What characterizes? What classifies?	What determines? What indicates? What distinguishes? What does___infer? What does___suggest?
Reflective	How did? Why did? What is the cause(s)/effect(s)? What is the connection between?	What are the consequences? What are the similarities/differences? What is the reason(s)? What is the relationship between?
Hypothetical	What if? What would happen? What could happen	How may? How might? How will?
Argumentative	Is/Was___or? Does/Did___or? Should___or?	Will___or? Which one(s)?
Affective	What do you think? How do you feel? What do you believe? How can you? How do you?	How could you? How would you? What is your opinion? What is your perspective? What are your thoughts?

students use the good questions we develop and rephrase from the performance objective of academic standards and learning targets to do the following:

- Assess and build background knowledge
- Deepen understanding and awareness
- Develop and demonstrate personal expertise

The overall inquiry learning experience should be driven by good essential questions that set the instructional focus and tone of the learning experience. Francis (2016) identifies four different types of good essential questions:

1   **Universal Question:** What are the grand or global ideas, issues, themes, or topics? These good questions are highly existential or philosophical, prompting and encouraging students to reflect and connect between school and life. They also address the central ideas, messages, or themes explored and expressed in literature.

2   **Overarching Question:** What are the core ideas or enduring understandings of a subject area? These questions are derived from the anchor standards or subject-specific practices of a content area (e.g., mathematical practices, science and engineering practices, historical thinking skills). They can be asked at any grade level within a content area. They can also serve as summative assessment questions that require students to use examples and evidence from the units and lessons they learned over the course of the year.

3   **Topical Question:** What is the instructional focus and purpose of the unit of a lesson? These questions are addressed to a specific unit or lesson. They can also be derived from the performance objectives of grade-level or subject-specific standards.

4   **Driving Question:** What could you create, design, develop, or do with what you have learned? These questions prompt and encourage students to develop and demonstrate their talent and thinking by asking *how could you?* In fact, you could put this question stem in front of any performance objective and turn it into a driving good question that will encourage critical or creative thinking and talent development.

The inquiry process should begin by asking a good question that will not only set the learning expectation, but also "hook" students' curiosity, interest, imagination, and wonder. This is the good question that introduces the lesson and the learning. It's meant to be addressed initially, not answered immediately. It could be as simple as asking a seemingly easy or basic question that seems obvious to answer but actually prompts deeper thinking and discussion. For example, we can ask, "Who was the first President of the United States?" or, "What is 2 + 2?" Once the student gives their response, ask them, "What do you mean?" or, "How do you know?" This challenges students not only to explain themselves further but also to question their own knowledge and understanding. That's the goal of the good question that "hooks 'em" into the inquiry experience. Once the inquiry experience is initiated, teaching and learning focus on four areas.

1   **Foundation:** These learning experiences expect students to ask for and acquire the information they need to develop and demonstrate their foundational knowledge and functional understanding of content, concepts, and procedures. These questions are most factual, asking *who, what, where,* or *when.* However, they can also be analytical or reflective as students process information from sources and texts as examples and evidence. Most of these questions will come from the teacher or the text. They are also used primarily for the purpose of assessment. However, we can teach gifted ELLs how to ask good foundational questions to advocate for themselves and communicate what they don't know or understand but need to learn. For example, we can present students with a segment of text or a learning objective of a standard and ask them, "What are the words, terms, or details you don't know or understand? How would you express this as a question?" We then can have students generate their own questions they can use to build and develop their foundational knowledge and functional understanding of the text, topic, or technique they are learning. This not only makes the learning experience more student-driven, but also helps identify potential gaps in learning that need to be addressed or filled.

2   **Understanding:** These learning experiences focus on students demonstrating and communicating their conceptual and procedural understanding. The good questions are mostly analytical or reflective. They are also rephrased directly from the learning objectives of grade- level and content-area standards. They set the instructional focus and serve as the assessment for a learning experience. Inquiry for understanding is highly student-centered. They are also focused more on showing and telling their understanding of how concepts and procedures can be used to answer questions, address problems, accomplish tasks, or analyze the ideas and information presented

in texts or pertaining to topics. Inquiry for understanding is generally driven by the topical good question of a unit or individual lesson.

3 **Depth:** These learning experiences engage gifted ELLs in delving deep into the text, topics, techniques, and theories they are learning. The goal of these inquiry experiences is to think deeply and express and share the depth and extent of their understanding and awareness of how their knowledge could be used in different contexts. Students are posed and prompted to respond to analytical and reflective questions. However, their responses must be supported with evidence as well as examples. Inquiry for depth also encourages students to ponder hypothetical questions. It also requires students to defend, justify, or refute claims and conclusions made in response to argumentative questions. Inquiry for depth can also be driven by an overarching good question that addresses the core ideas or enduring understandings of a content area.

4 **Expertise:** These learning experiences encourage gifted ELLs to develop their learning and talent into personal expertise they can use in different contexts, new situations, or to address and respond to real- world scenarios or situations. The questions posed here are affective, prompting students to think critically or creatively as to what they personally can do with what they have learned. They also engage students in authentic learning experiences through in-depth research and investigations, creative design, or problem-based and project-based learning. The goal is for students to recognize and realize what they personally can do with what they have learned and how their personal talent and thinking – or expertise – makes them unique and special.

Figure 12.1 shows how to use the DOK (Depth of Knowledge) Levels as a multi-tiered system of support to develop and deliver inquiry-based learning experiences for gifted English language learners (Francis, 2021). Each DOK Block describes a different and deeper way in which students can demonstrate their learning in a certain context. The four core DOK Levels designate the level of cognitive demand of grade-level academic standards and activities, based on the complexity of the content knowledge and the context in which students must understand and use the knowledge. The Extended Depth of Knowledge (EDOK) Stages and Gifted and Talented Depth of Knowledge (GDOK) Supports are layers, not levels, that supplement the depth of knowledge demanded by grade-level standards. They support grade-level instruction by providing students with the specialized support they need to achieve and surpass the learning expectations set by both the standards and the students themselves. For example, if the grade-level standard requires an English language learner to demonstrate their learning at a DOK-3, both the teacher and student can use the EDOK to help students comprehend the proficiency expectations set by the standard in the target language. The GDOKs can also be used to serve gifted ELL students who possess both the academic and innate ability to have their learning accelerated or enriched, but not the language skills to comprehend or communicate their learning in the target language.

The questions within the DOK Block set the instructional focus and serve as the assessment for an inquiry-based learning experience that requires students to demonstrate and communicate their learning. The inverted pyramid within the DOK Block shows how the delivery and intensity of the instruction is tiered based on the demand of the standard and the needs of the students. The goal and expectation are that all students – no matter

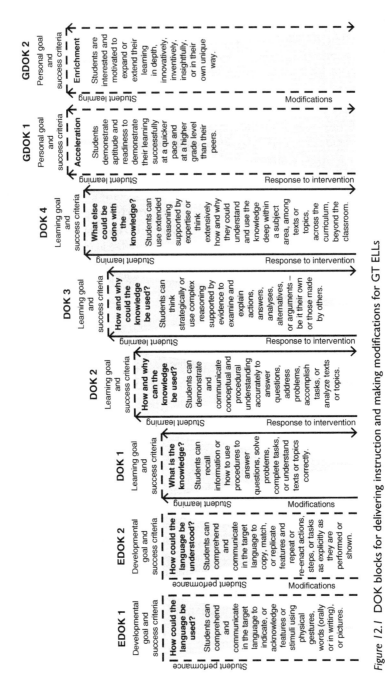

Figure 12.1 DOK blocks for delivering instruction and making modifications for GT ELLs

Source: Adapted with permission. From *Deconstructing Depth of Knowledge: A Method and Model for Deeper Teaching and Learning* by Erik M. Francis. Copyright 2021 by Solution Tree Press, 555 North Morton Street, Bloomington, IN 47404, 800.733.6786, SolutionTree.com. All rights reserved.

their level of learning or language ability – will achieve and surpass both proficiency and personal expectations. This can be accomplished by using the EDOKs and GDOKs to supplement and support grade-level instruction for second language learners – specifically, those with high ability, motivation, and potential. The EDOKs supplement language development and the GDOKs support acceleration or enrichment for gifted and talented (GT) ELLs.

Questioning and inquiry are often referred to synonymously. However, they both have a specific focus and purpose. Questioning is the strategy we use to prompt and promote critical or creative thinking and language development. Inquiry is the experience in which students use questions to develop, demonstrate, deepen, and discuss their learning. Both can be used not only to increase the cognitive rigor of learning experiences for our students, but also develop their communication and language skills.

Strategies for the Classroom

Successful classrooms and schools are defined by a commitment to a common purpose – the increased academic achievement of all students. Fostering shared beliefs and a sense of community and cooperation promotes continuity among staff and allows them to focus on developing the talent and potential of the gifted ELLs they serve. Castellano (2014) asserts that successful classrooms are defined by four categories of instructional strategies that directly impact student achievement, and thus, the individual skill and ability of gifted ELLs.

1   The first category addresses the monitoring of progress, balancing individual work with group work, reinforcing effort, and celebrating success. In promoting talent and language development in two languages, teachers must provide the explicit feedback necessary for continuous improvement.
2   The second category speaks to identifying individual goals; for ELLs, this may mean, for example, that in the area of writing they will be able to use the mechanics of written language in different genres. For the teacher, this means providing students with clear evaluations of their progress and allowing them time to reflect on their own growth, evaluating themselves in order to compare their own perceptions with those of the teacher.
3   The third category requires teachers use engaging, motivating, focused, and culturally responsive instruction in order to help students understand and assimilate content knowledge.
4   The fourth and last category expects that teachers will help gifted ELLs to review, practice, and apply content through problem-solving tasks requiring critical thinking, inquiry-based tasks, and decision-making opportunities. These practices facilitate skill, talent, and potential.

When these four practices are effectively applied, the result is not only increased student achievement, but also the development of individual student talent. For gifted ELLs acquiring a new language, these expectations are essential to their success.

Conclusion

ELLs continue to be underrepresented in programs serving gifted students. When they are identified, supporting their talent development requires the same fundamental commitment pledged to those special needs students found on the opposite end of the bell curve. Success comes in many forms. When programs, products, and services are part of a programmatic infrastructure designed to meet the individual needs of gifted ELLs, opportunities for experiencing success know no boundaries. Collaboration and communication among stakeholder groups that directly impact the education of gifted ELLs share a vision that ensures the capacity of the school and school district to support the development and potential of its most able students. In every school where ELLs attend, there are gifted ELLs; in urban, suburban, and rural America. They come from culturally and linguistically diverse backgrounds and their families sometimes have values that differ from those represented in U.S. schools. As such, teachers, principals, and other educators who serve gifted ELLs need to learn about students' cultures, teach in a manner that is responsive to those cultures, and acknowledge and value their classroom and school diversity.

References

Aguirre, N., & Hernandez, N. (1999). *Characteristics of students who are linguistically and culturally diverse*. Modern Language Services.

Bernal, E. (1974, April). *Gifted Mexican-American children: An ethnico-scientific perspective*. Paper presented at the Annual Meeting of the American Education Research Association, Chicago, IL.

Brulles, D., & Weinbrenner, S. (2019). *The cluster grouping handbook: How to challenge gifted students and improve achievement for all*. Free Spirit Publishing.

Carmen, C. A., Walther, C. R. P, & Bartsch, R. A. (2018). Using the cognitive ability test (CogAT) 7 nonverbal battery to identify the gifted/talented: An investigation of demographic effects and norming plans. *Gifted Child Quarterly, 62*(2), 193–209.

Castañeda v. Pickard, 648 F.2D 989 (5th Cir. 1981).

Castellano, J. A. (2014). Talent development, language development, and writing skills. In M. S. Matthews & J. A. Castellano (Eds.), *Talent development for English language learners: Identifying and developing potential* (pp. 15–45). Prufrock Press.

Castellano, J. A. (2018). *Educating Hispanic and Latino students: Opening the doors to hope, promise, and possibility*. Learning Sciences International.

Castellano, J. A., & Frazier, A. D. (2011). *Special populations in gifted education: Understanding our most able students from diverse backgrounds*. Prufrock Press.

Castellano, J. A., & Robertson, R. (2021). Opening the doors for gifted English language learners through self-advocacy. In J. L. Davis & D. Douglas (Eds.), *Empowering underrepresented gifted students* (pp. 77–91). Free Spirit.

Civil Rights Act of 1964 § 7, 42 U.S.C. § 2000e et seq. (1964).

Education Week Research Center (2019). *Gifted education: Results of a national survey*. Author.

Friend, M., & Bursuck, W. D. (2019). *Including students with special needs: A practical guide for classroom teachers* (8th ed.). Pearson.

Francis, E. M. (2016). *Now that's a good question! How to promote cognitive rigor through classroom questioning*. ASCD.

Francis, E. M. (2017). What exactly is depth of knowledge? (Hint: It's not a wheel). ASCD Blog post (no longer available online).

Francis, E. M. (2021). Deconstructing depth of knowledge: A method and model for deeper teaching and learning. Solution Tree International.

Gubbins, E. J., Siegle, D., Hamilton, R., Peters, P., Carpenter, A. Y., O'Rourke, P., … EsteparGarcia, W. (2018, June). *Exploratory study on the identification of English learners for gifted and talented programs*. University of Connecticut, National Center for Research on Gifted Education.

Gubbins, E. J, Siegle, D., Peters, P. M., Carpenter, A. Y., Hamilton, R., McCoach, D. B., … Long, D. (2020). Promising practices for improving identification of English learners for gifted and talented programs. *Journal for the Education of the Gifted, 43*(4), 336–369.

Hess, K. J. (2018). *A local assessment toolkit to promote deeper learning: Transforming research into practice.* SAGE Publications.

Hess, K. K., Carlock, D., Jones, B. S., & Walkup, J. R. (2009a). Cognitive rigor: Blending the strengths of Bloom's Taxonomy and Webb's Depth of Knowledge to enhance classroom-level processes. White paper. Retrieved from: https://files.eric.ed.gov/fulltext/ED517804.pdf

Hess, K., Carlock, D., Jones, B., & Walkup, J. (2009b). What exactly do "fewer, clearer, and higher standards" really look like in the classroom? Using a cognitive rigor matrix to analyze curriculum, plan lessons, and implement assessments. White paper. Retrieved from: https://01fd4346-c1b0-45d9-899e-3654cb2c37d5.filesusr.com/ugd/5e86bd_2f72d4acd00a4494b0677adecafd119f.pdf (from www.karin-hess.com/free-resources).

Krathwohl, D. R., Bloom, B. S., & Masia, B. B. (1964). *Taxonomy of educational objectives. Handbook II: Affective domain.* David McKay.

Lau *v.* Nichols, 414 U.S.563 (1974).

Migration Policy Institute. (2015). *Top languages spoken by English language learners nationally and by state.* Author.

Mitchell, K. L. (2019). *Experience inquiry: 5 powerful strategies, 50 practical experiences.* Corwin/SAGE Publications. Kindle Edition.

Murphey, D., Guzman, L., & Torres, A. (2014). *America's Hispanic children: Gaining ground, looking forward.* Child Trends Hispanic Institute.

Park, M., Zong, J., & Batalova, J. (2018). *Growing superdiversity among young U.S. dual language learners and its implications.* Migration Policy Institute.

Plyler *v.* Doe, 457 U.S. 202 (1982).

Project Bright Horizons. (2006). Retrieved from: www.azed.gov/gifted-education/project-bright-horizon

Seal of Biliteracy. (n. d). Frequently asked questions: What is a seal of biliteracy? Retrieved from: https://sealofbiliteracy.org/faq/

Seidlitz, J. (2018). Border-school champions: Chess and English language learners. *American Educator, 42*(3), 24–26, 40.

United States Department of Education: National Center for Education Statistics [NCES]. (2018). *The condition of education: English language learners in public schools.* Author.

United States Department of Education: Office for Civil Rights. (2014). *Civil rights data collection, data snapshot: College and career readiness.* Retrieved June 13, 2019 from: www2.ed.gov/about/offices/list/ocr/docs/crdc-college-and-career-readiness-snapshot.pdf

Chapter 13

Gifted Hispanic/Latino Students

Jaime A. Castellano

Historically speaking, Hispanic/Latino students have been disproportionately under-represented in educational programs serving gifted students. As presenting evidence, the United States Department of Education's Office for Civil Rights (2016), through their Civil Rights Data Collection, reported that during the 2015–2016 school year, Hispanic/Latino students accounted for about 25% of the public school enrollment, but their participation rate in programs for gifted students was 16%. Clearly there is an equity discrepancy. Furthermore, according to a report from the National Center for Educational Statistics (2017), 13% of Asian American students; 8% of white students; 5% of Hispanic students; and 4% of Black students are enrolled in gifted and talented programs. Castellano (2020) states that gifted Hispanic/Latino students who demonstrate high levels of general intellectual ability, most typically on IQ tests, or who score highly on tests of academic achievement, often participate in advanced academic programs in their schools. Gifted Hispanic/Latino students are the focus of this chapter; its purpose is to magnify how to identify and educate them; and to explain why it is important to acknowledge and promote their sense of belonging and identity. Strategies for the classroom and recommendations for inclusion will also be presented.

The significance of this chapter lies in the need to identify the success factors that facilitate the inclusion of Hispanic/Latino students in programs for the gifted and talented. The education of this group of students is of paramount importance to the future of the United States. Relatedly, the economic or national competitiveness argument, whose goal is the development and utilization of mental resources for the benefit of this country, and for humanity in general (Dixon et al., 2016), also recognizes the importance of capitalizing on the contributions of talented Hispanic/Latino students.

So, then, why do educators consistently fail to recommend them for gifted education? For Hispanic/Latino students living here undocumented, in poverty, who experience adverse childhood experiences (ACEs), and who face conflicting notions of identity, there are often limits on equity, access, and opportunity. Educators who fail to involve family in the child's learning, or to care for the whole child, and who do not incorporate Hispanic/Latino culture in their classrooms are failing to take into account the sheer perseverance a gifted Hispanic/Latino student must have to be recognized. These circumstances should be no excuse. It is imperative that educators should raise the ceiling and expect the most from them. Part of this acknowledgement is recognizing that students on the high end of a school's achievement continuum also require specialized instruction through challenging programs, products, and services. Raising the ceiling must also apply to our expectations

DOI: 10.4324/9781003265412-18

for ourselves as educators. It isn't enough for us to only raise the floor for students who struggle; as educators, we need to raise the ceiling for those Hispanic/Latino students whom we consider gifted and talented.

Belonging and Identity

Interviewed by Evie Blad (2017), Dena Simmons, the director of education at the Yale Center for Emotional Intelligence, and a former middle school teacher, said that

> if students don't feel like they belong in their school environment, they can feel like impostors. … That feeling can create fear and anxiety that hijack students' learning experiences or lead them to believe they are not capable of success. … Your teachers very rarely, if you're a student of color, look like you. Or, if you're a student with a disability, you rarely see teachers who look like you as well. Constantly you're getting all these messages where your experience, or your identity, isn't present. …
>
> In some ways, your experience, your identity, is erased; it's invisible. You start to look around and try to find pictures of you and you can't, and so you start to panic. You start to say, "Do I belong here?" That's why I think it's crucial for educators to, if they don't represent their students' backgrounds or can't relate, make a concerted effort in inviting those experiences into the classroom through expanding the curricular experience of students and inviting mentors in that can speak to their own experiences, and many times those are experiences that are marginalized. We have a status quo in this country, and if you don't fit it … you will feel like an impostor.
>
> (Simmons, quoted by Blad, 2017, n.p.)

For gifted Hispanic/Latino students, belonging and identity can be a very complicated issue. Reconciling who you are personally with who you want to be, where you come from, and how other people see you can be distressing under the best of circumstances; factoring in the effects of immigration and poverty can be absolutely overwhelming. Many gifted Hispanic/Latino students are not only held responsible for overcoming their own trauma and family history of hardships; but also for juggling the complications of belonging and identity. Educators who are better informed on the particular difficulties that many gifted Hispanic/Latino students face in understanding who they are and their place in the world will be able to serve this unique population more effectively. Part of this overwhelming feeling resides in the socio-cultural history of Hispanics in that the preservation of the group, the community, the family, takes priority over the individual.

Vignette: JAC's Story

In reflection, belonging and identity was always on his mind. As a boy, he knew he did not quite fit with his childhood friends. They were all Hispanic, poor, and came from dysfunctional households. He knew them all through the K-8 elementary school they attended together on the south side of Chicago. They were into sports; he was into books and studying. They were athletes, he was not. Even when they went to high school, they had classes in the old buildings, receiving a remedial or compensatory education; his classes were in the new buildings for students enrolled in the Honors program. Often, he was the only Hispanic male in his advanced academic program. He chose to go to college, they decided to stay in the neighborhood and work in the steel mills and factories.

At the university he attended, belonging and identity took on a different form. He was Hispanic, and the other 49 guys who were on his dorm floor were white. He was made to feel inferior; he sometimes felt inferior. He arrived at the university with one suitcase and an allowance of $25 per month via financial aid. They came with stereos, televisions, cars, and a checking account provided by their parents. They went home on weekends to see family and friends. He stayed on campus at the weekends, not being able to afford the price of a Greyhound Bus ticket. Belonging and identity was constantly on his mind. Was he good enough to attend a major Midwest university? Could he tolerate the racial and ethnic slurs? Why was it difficult for his white classmates to accept him as he was? Was he smart enough to get good grades?

Because of his traumatic childhood experiences, he learned to persevere and become resilient. And combined with being both street smart and book smart, he knew he would be successful. The doubtfulness that sometimes entered his mind was simply temporary. He accepted the challenge of being a poor Hispanic university student. He knew how to survive. He sought out a support network by joining the Organization of Latin American Students (OLAS). Here, the members shared similar backgrounds, faced the same challenges and stereotypes, and were committed to being successful in higher education. Finally, he discovered others who were like him. He became friends with many, they supported and counted on each other, and they often ate, played, and prayed together. He graduated in four years and was accepted to graduate school with an assistantship to work in the Special Education Department of the College of Education.

After graduate school, he secured his first job as a teacher working with learning-disabled, behavior-disordered, and emotionally disturbed middle school students. Belonging and identity, again, became an issue. This time, he saw the Hispanic/Latino students of the school struggling with issues of belonging and identity. Many were monolingual Spanish-speakers in an English-speaking school environment. The vast majority of them were poor, undocumented, and their families were disenfranchised. He vowed he would not let them slip through the cracks. Along with the only other Hispanic teacher in the school they paired up to support these students as best they could. It was because he saw how they were being treated by other teachers and school administrators that he decided to become a school principal.

He worked full-time as a special education teacher while he pursued his second master's degree and a doctorate degree in Educational Leadership. It was while he was enrolled in his doctoral program that he had his first Hispanic professor. He was in awe of him. He knew that one day he, too, would become a professor. In the meantime, the challenges of identity and belonging once again presented themselves. He was the only Hispanic student enrolled in the university's doctoral program in Educational Administration and Leadership. He felt different, he looked different from the other doctoral students. Could he compete at the highest academic level? What did the professors think of him? In the end, he received his doctorate degree and was very proud of his accomplishment.

He aspired to be a school administrator after seven years of teaching. That meant applying for assistant principal's jobs. He completed more than 30 applications and was interviewed about 13 times in his search for a position. He was denied several times, he is convinced, because of the color of his skin and because of his strong stance on diversity and inclusion. There were at least two separate occasions when, as soon as they saw him, they canceled the interview claiming the position had been filled. It had not. Eventually he secured an assistant principal's position in a barrio school filled with Hispanic/Latino students. It was a dream come true. Following this position, he had a long and successful career as a school administrator, university professor, scholar, researcher, and author. His work is not quite done yet.

Belonging and Identity and the Mixed Messages Gifted Hispanic/Latino Students Receive

When one looks at the complex cross-section of gifted Hispanic/Latino students attending our nation's public schools, academic achievement data help us identify how students are performing in core content areas. These assessments do not account for how students feel, if they have been fed, or the fact that many Hispanic/Latino students live in a world of conflict and contradiction and are put in situations where navigating their lives is difficult and demanding. This conflicting world in which these students live is accompanied by a range of social and emotional behaviors that can manipulate, or influence, how they react in school. Even those identified as gifted may be overwhelmed by the mixed messages they are given by those individuals and institutions that are a part of their daily reality. Table 13.1 gives some examples:

The institutional culture of the school, the conflict with the socialized environment (street life and peer group) that many of our gifted Hispanic/Latino students face on a daily basis, and the expectations of the home with parents wanting their children to honor and respect tradition, culture, religion, and language pulls them in multiple directions where they are caught in a socio-cultural tug-of-war. Combined with social angst, educational anxiety, and the mixed messages of school and political leaders, students may feel

Table 13.1 Mixed Messages…

In an Age of Social Angst	In an Age of Educational Anxiety	From School and Political Leaders
• Trolling, bullying • Body image • Sexuality/relationships • "No one understands me" • "Life is unfair" • Feelings of isolation, loneliness, and unhappiness • Angry at basically everything	• High-stakes tests • School violence • Expectations • Unqualified teachers • Relevance • "Fitting In"/perfection • Diversity in gifted education	• **From teachers:** "It's just a test. Do your best; but if you don't, there will be consequences." • **From politicians:** "Make America great again; but we don't want your kind here." • **From administrators:** "I don't see poverty or color in our students. We love them all. But will they water down our advanced programs?"

they are a different person when in different groups. Belonging and identity is critical to their well-being. Rather than fracture an individual's identity, our purpose, our goal, is to increase our collective understanding about gifted Hispanic/Latino students and discover how this knowledge of their unique characteristics, life experiences, and cultural backgrounds can be made a part of classroom culture.

VanTassel-Baska (2018) writes that while much can be accomplished in educational environments to assist the gifted poor, the desire to persevere and prevail in challenging circumstances must come from within an individual. This will is related to the belief in self, belief in one's own power to personally change and to control and overcome circumstances, resiliency, and optimism. In the dark hours of the night and early morning, it is the individual spirit that must be motivated to accomplish what no one has done before. Just as sports figures prove their mettle in the Olympics and beyond, so too must all promising learners from adverse circumstances find their own idiosyncratic pathway to success. While nurturance from multiple sources at key stages of life may help, in the end it is an individual decision to delay gratification, to develop self-discipline, to continue with education, to resist temptation, to rebound from setbacks, and to find and make a commitment to a niche area. Consider JAC's story as an example; or perhaps that of Mark who had to make some difficult decisions to achieve his dream.

Mark's Story

Born in Ecuador to parents of little means and education, Mark has been the perpetual underdog. His modest roots provided a wonderful moral foundation, but in the absence of certain professional and academic role models, Mark has had to chart his own course. Navigating the path between integrating into his new community in the United States and staying true to his heritage and family under the duress of poverty, his high school AP chemistry teacher marvels at his ability to get to where he is today with such incredible grace and dignity. "Mark hasn't just survived the trials and tribulations of circumstance, he has conquered them unequivocally." (AP Chemistry Teacher, 2018, p. 3).

> Notwithstanding, the most courageous thing about Mark is his decision to go to college at all. Mark is a Jehovah's Witness. Despite the love he has for his congregation and their undeniable part of his personal growth and development, they do not support his continuing education. The fact that he is already capable of providing for himself and his family is sufficient enough in their eyes, and all other time and energy should be expected [to be spent] in the service of Jehovah and spreading His word. The decision to go to college may very well drive a wedge between himself, his family, and his entire religious community. It is redefining who he is and it is testing the strength and understanding of those he holds most dear. With all that is at stake, he still wants to go to college. He wants to get better, smarter, and more capable.
>
> (AP Chemistry Teacher, 2018, p. 3)

His AP English teacher writes,

> Mark is a naturally intelligent person who couples his intellectual capabilities with a strong work ethic. He is a good writer who scored a 5 on his national AP English Language and Composition exam; nationally, fewer than 8 percent of students who take the exam score as well. There is no doubt that Mark will be successful at Stanford.
>
> (AP English Teacher, 2018, p. 5)

When asked to describe a personal or academic challenge that he has faced and how he was able to overcome that challenge, Mark states,

> Life is a labyrinth of choices with walls just tall enough to stop us from peeking at the consequences. In my junior year, I saw my choices, many paths that I could take and I thought I had to take one. Should I take a left and continue as one of Jehovah's Witnesses like my parents and community wanted? Or should I take a right towards the fulfillment of my dreams in college like my peers? The two seemed contradictory in values and virtues. For months I harbored doubts about God and my religion and felt like a hypocrite because I still preached. One of my teachers helped me realize that what mattered most was my intent, not just my conviction. I preached because I felt that people deserved the opportunity to cultivate a relationship with God. As I gained a sense of security in who I was, I looked back to determine who I wanted to become. In examining my past, I saw that being a student has become an integral part of me and that dreaming of opportunity and pursuing it had helped me to get where I was. I now realize that I cannot take a path that has been laid out for me by others, I must define my own. The freedom to define my own past and identity matters to me. I will not take a left or right, I will go forward and if a wall is in my way, I will knock it down.
>
> (Rivera, 2018, p. 1)

Mark hasn't just persevered through the pressures and temptations of financial hardship, he's conquered it. He has used his natural, entrepreneurial spirit to take control of his family's business and lifted them from financial ruin to relative stability. While many teens worry about the latest fashions, the newest and coolest gym shoes, and going to the mall, Mark is focused on his future; a future that holds untold promise and possibilities for a Hispanic teen raised in poverty, but filled with love and devotion. There is no doubt that he is ready to succeed, academically, socially, and emotionally, in college, and will make a positive contribution in whatever he decides to become professionally.

Promising learners from poverty must understand that they are in charge of their lives and must chart their own course, whatever it may be. Promising learners from poverty must also carefully consider how family may both facilitate and impede their progress on the road to talent development. More critical, however, is the lack of understanding in most families, particularly where the child will be a first-generation college student, that academic success requires the development of skills and attitudes associated with a professional world of which parents are not a part (VanTassel-Baska, 2018).

Hispanic, Latino, or Latinx?

"Ask several people with Latin American roots what term best describes us collectively, and you'll certainly receive a variety of answers." According to Simón (2018, n.p.), some will say we're Latinos or Latinxs, while others will opt for Hispanic, and still there are some who will criticize these words for promoting a pan-ethnic identity that erases their countries and doesn't necessarily result in real camaraderie among people of Latin American descent. Having a word that groups us into one category has been used as a political tool in the past, and this line of thinking certainly inspired the emergence of "Hispanic" and "Latino" in the United States.

While the word Hispanic has helped bring some progress, it has also been heavily criticized, even decades ago. Hispanic refers to anyone from Spain or Spanish-speaking parts of Latin America. It therefore promotes Spanish heritage, something many oppose because of the violent ways in which the Spanish colonized our countries and the erasure of Afro-Latinos and Indigenous people. Today, some dismiss the word Hispanic and call it a government creation. This is something that Grace Flores-Hughes, the government official credited with coining the term, has spoken out against.

Latino refers to people from the Spanish- and Portuguese-speaking countries of Latin America, but it does not include those from Spain or Portugal. This word, however, typically doesn't make room for people from Latin America whose countries were not colonized by Spain or Portugal, leaving out Belizeans and Haitians. (There are some people with ties to these countries who do self-identify as Latino.) Across various age groups in our community, about 50% of people say they do not have a preference between Latino and Hispanic, according to Lopez et al. (2021). However, those who did have a preference veered toward Hispanic in larger numbers. But with Latino seen as a more inclusive word, it's become necessary to describe our communities. Places like Chicago – which had and have a large Mexican and Puerto Rican population – helped bring about this change. Since then, the term Latino has been adapted to become even more specific. For groups often excluded from the discourse, words like Afro-Latino, Muslim Latinos, and Asian Latinos have helped to center their experiences. It's an example of the malleability of the words we use to describe ourselves. That's why Latinx, a new(ish) word is now taking center stage.

Latinx – which has existed online since at least 2004 – arose as a gender-neutral alternative to Latino and Latina. However, some believe that Latino already effectively groups a large number of men and women with Latin American origins and that substituting the x for the o unnecessarily complicates the language. The conversation of Latinx has mostly revolved around whether this word makes sense and how to pronounce it. It has even sparked a host of think pieces arguing both sides of the equation. And while Latinx comes with heavy scrutiny, for those who are non-binary, it helps them feel seen. But regardless of the very compelling arguments made for Latinx, there are still many who remain reticent – or outright resistant – to the word. Through conversations and research into the background of these terms, it became clear that the origins and evolution of what we call ourselves is as complicated as our history in the United States. We'll probably never find a perfect term, especially as some prefer to identify as their (or their family's) country of origin.

How do gifted students with a Spanish-speaking ancestry choose to be identified? Are they Hispanic, Latino, Latinx; or perhaps Chicano? Or do they prefer to be associated with their family's country of origin, i.e., Mexican-American or Dominican-American? For teachers working with this population of students, the most logical response is simply to ask them. Engage them in a conversation about who they are and where they come from. Hear their stories; share yours. The benefits will present themselves in the classroom with these students demonstrating the skills and abilities that helped them gain access to gifted education in the first place.

Reflection

Castellano writes (2018) that part of our collective journey to leveling the playing field involves engaging ourselves in a process of self-reflection, self-assessment, and understanding how we perceive others who are different from ourselves. This self-examination will help us gain a clearer understanding of our own experiences, boundaries, and challenges. Any educator who has contact with gifted Hispanic/Latino students will benefit from this self-review process. As a result of the self-assessment and evaluation of their own cultural identity, educators begin not only to understand how they themselves influence teaching and learning, but also recognize the importance of identity and belonging of the students they serve. The following example is a testament when gifted students' identity, strengths, and culture are considered. The website of Okeeheelee Middle School (2017), located in Greenacres, Florida, documents that in May that year, 14 gifted students in the International Spanish Academy (ISA) were given the opportunity to take the Advanced Placement (AP) exam in Spanish Language and Culture, and all 14 of the 8th graders passed. Of the 14 students, one scored a 3, eight scored a 4, and five scored a 5 on the college-level exam that allows students to earn college credit or receive Advanced Placement in college courses. The students were able to pass the test with less than a semester of AP-focused preparation.

Identifying and Assessing Hispanic/Latino Students for Gifted Education Programming

Identification for gifted education programming typically begins at the classroom level and includes an analysis of how the student demonstrates the need for advanced academic services. Whether teachers have been trained to identify gifted behavior in Hispanic/Latino students influences the rate of nomination and referrals. This is of particular importance because in a document titled *The State of Racial Diversity in the Educator Workforce*, the U.S. Department of Education's Office of Planning, Evaluation, and Policy Development (2016) reports that while Hispanic students are expected to make up almost 30% of the student population by 2024, the elementary and secondary workforce within schools is still overwhelmingly white. In fact, the most recent United States Department of Education (Office of Planning, Evaluation, and Policy Development 2016) School and Staffing Survey (SASS), a nationally representative survey of teachers and principals, shows the following racial diversity of teachers during 2015–2016:

- 80% of public school teachers were white
- 9% of public school teachers were Hispanic
- 7% of public school teachers were Black
- 1% of public school teachers were American Indian or Alaska Native
- 77% of teachers were women
- 90% of elementary school teachers were women

Generally speaking, Hispanic/Latino students, including those in gifted programs, are being taught by white females. Providing them with the professional development training needed to identify giftedness in this population makes complete sense. Professional development means that teachers recognize that receiving their degree is only the beginning of the learning process. With regards to gifted education, their training will create a more diverse program where the gifts and talents of Hispanic/Latino students can be actualized. Empowering teachers with the tools they need to identify gifted Hispanic/Latino students leads them to improved student performance and connectedness. In addition, with improving cultural competency in mind, professional learning opportunities can focus on gaining greater understanding about the history, values, beliefs, and perspectives of students from different cultural backgrounds. An understanding and acknowledgement of local demographics should inform which of the 20 Hispanic/Latino ethnicities should be targeted.

Gifted Hispanic/Latino Students and Issues of Equity

Ford et al. (2020) write that Hispanic students are consistently underrepresented in gifted and talented education and related academic programs. Attitudes, philosophies, tests and other instruments, and policies and procedures are often the fundamental barriers. Equity for this special population, then, becomes problematic. In addition, Ricciardi et al. (2020) document that students who identified as white/Asian were identified for gifted education at a rate of 28.8%, while Latinx students were identified at a rate of 14.8%. The fact remains that even when controlling for early school performance, school-entry readiness skills, and poverty status, ethnic differences in identification were still present. In order to achieve a greater commitment to equity, more work is needed to understand the selection factors currently used by school districts. The importance of identifying and serving greater numbers of Hispanics/Latinos in gifted education is critically important. Cohn (2020) states that Latino students are everywhere in this nation. They are no longer confined to large urban districts or border-states, but are an emerging majority in many rural and some suburban school districts throughout the United States. Figuring out what contributes to their academic success and their access to advanced academic programs and higher education becomes an important part of the nation's quest to improve its economic standing and productivity on the world stage. To promote equity, Castellano (2018) presents the following four policy action worksheets that set a vision for educating Hispanic/Latino students, including those identified as gifted.

Policy Action Worksheet 1: Setting a Vision for Educating Gifted Hispanic/Latino Students
Given the sheer numbers of Hispanic students enrolled in our nation's public schools, state and district boards have an opportunity to drive reform efforts in the education of these students through identifying issues facing state and/or local districts and developing an approach to address these challenges. Therefore, it is important from the beginning that state and/or district boards develop a vision and strategy for educating gifted Hispanic/Latino students. This worksheet provides some initial questions that state and/or district boards should consider asking and the information they need to gather to have a complete picture.

	Questions to Ask When Considering Policy Action
Setting a Vision for Educating Gifted Hispanic/Latino Students	• What challenges exist in educating gifted Hispanic/Latino students in the state and/or district? Does the state or district have information from surveys or questionnaires that helps answer the question? • What challenges does the state or district currently face in its efforts to educate gifted Hispanic/Latino students as well as the issues faced by teachers and administrators? • Has the state and/or district board interacted with and received input from stakeholder groups (teachers, administrators, parents and families, students, and members of the community) to provide additional perspectives on the challenges surrounding the education of gifted Hispanic/Latino students? • Does the state or district board require any induction or mentoring support for teachers and administrators serving gifted Hispanic/Latino students? • Does the state or district collect information about what schools are doing to address issues in educating gifted Hispanic/Latino students? • What state or district supports are in place and made available for gifted Hispanic/Latino students and the teachers and administrators serving them? • How are teacher preparation programs, professional development opportunities, and teacher induction programs aligned to support teachers and administrators serving gifted Hispanic/Latino students?

Policy Action Worksheet 2: Identifying Standards for Educating Gifted Hispanic/Latino Students	
Standards are an important tool available to state and district boards of education. Moving forward, state and district boards need to provide schools with goals and expectations for educating gifted Hispanic/Latino students so that all teachers and administrators receive the support they need to be effective. This policy worksheet provides some of the key considerations when crafting standards designed to assist teachers and administrators.	
	Questions to Ask When Considering Policy Action
Identifying Standards for Educating Gifted Hispanic/Latino Students	• What challenges in educating gifted Hispanic/Latino students does the state and/or district board want to address through program standards? • Are there specific statewide or districtwide supports that teachers and administrators need in order to be successful in serving gifted Hispanic/Latino students? • What foundational, structural, and instructional standards should state and district boards consider in their efforts in educating gifted Hispanic/Latino students? • How do current state or district standards emphasize the education of gifted Hispanic/Latino students and the role of comprehensive support for teachers and administrators? • Is there non-instructional time set aside for teachers and administrators to interact with mentors and experts about educating gifted Hispanic/Latino students? • What role do local, state, and national experts have, if any, in the programs, products, and services used by teachers and administrators in educating gifted Hispanic/Latino students to achieve the goals linked to the standards? • How could effective completion of a teacher and administrator induction program help them demonstrate competency and growth in educating gifted Hispanic/Latino students? • How might the standards be used to communicate a vision for educating gifted Hispanic/Latino students, identify research-based program elements, and hold states and districts accountable for implementing these elements?

Policy Action Worksheet 3: Ensuring Quality for Educating Gifted Hispanic/Latino Students	
Teachers and administrators are at the heart of quality programming that addresses the education of gifted Hispanic/Latino students. Given their importance, teachers and administrators are a vital component of an overall comprehensive program. As such, training and professional development are key elements of ensuring that they have the skill, ability, and desire to serve gifted Hispanic/Latino students.	
	Questions to Ask When Considering Policy Action
Teacher and Administrator Selection	• What challenges do states and districts face when trying to innovate, train, and provide quality programs to teachers and administrators serving gifted Hispanic/Latino students? • What skills do teachers and administrators need to support gifted Hispanic/Latino students, and do state and district leadership identify these skills prior to selection and hiring? • What are the benchmarks or progress indicators that make a teacher or administrator effective in serving gifted Hispanic/Latino students? • What requirements could be added to provide states and districts with additional information or perspectives when selecting teachers and administrators to work directly with gifted Hispanic/Latino students? • What kinds of compensation and recognition exist for teachers and administrators to ensure that enough quality candidates apply to work directly with gifted Hispanic/Latino students?
Training and Professional Development	• What training do teachers and administrators receive in educating gifted Hispanic/Latino students prior to the start of the school year? • What support do teachers and administrators receive during the school year? • What tools are available to teachers and administrators to assess progress in the related standards of the state or district? • How do teachers and administrators serving gifted Hispanic/Latino students integrate the work they do into their own learning and professional development?

Policy Action Worksheet 4: Evaluating Progress in Educating Gifted Hispanic/Latino Students	
The overarching goals of program evaluations should be both to assess the quality of programs involving gifted Hispanic/Latino students and to inform discussions on improving such programs across the state or district. No program is perfect and no program is without merit. An effective evaluation system for serving and educating gifted Hispanic/Latino students ensures that programs at both ends of the quality spectrum can identify strengths and areas of improvement and offer direction for how teachers and administrators can continuously improve their practice.	
	Questions to Ask When Considering Policy Action
Evaluating Progress in Educating Gifted Hispanic/Latino Students	• What should be the role of the state and district in evaluating teachers and administrators serving gifted Hispanic/Latino students (e.g., defining major elements to include in the assessment; disseminating information about what states and districts are doing to assess progress)? • How are various standards integrated into evaluations to ensure that all teachers and administrators demonstrate competency in these standards? • Does the state or district collect outcome data on teacher and administrator evaluations and link the information back to training and professional development programs that target the education of gifted Hispanic/Latino students? • How do teacher and administrator evaluations inform and/or impact school-wide improvement and reform efforts that target gifted Hispanic/Latino students? • How do teacher and administrator evaluations account for school culture? • What supports and follow-up are in place for teachers and administrators who receive unsatisfactory evaluations for their work with gifted Hispanic/Latino students? • What is the role of program standards in evaluating program implementation and outcomes?

Building equity through a culture of achievement, promoting academic capacity, and sustaining gifted programs, products, and services for moving gifted Hispanic/Latino students forward involves active communication, collaboration, and collegiality of key stakeholder groups – among them teachers, administrators, parents, family, and community.

Peters and Engerrand (2016) report that a major barrier to greater equity in the identification of students for gifted and talented programs is that, on average, students from
Hispanic/Latino and low-income backgrounds, among others, receive lower scores on tests
of academic achievement and ability than do their Caucasian, Asian, and higher-income
peers. English language learners (ELLs) also have lower observed scores, though differences
in ability are confounded to some extent by the specific language demands of the test. In
the past, the field of gifted education has approached these observed score differences, and
the underrepresentation that is the result, using two perceived solutions: Use different tests
and use tests differently (Peters & Engerrand, 2016).

Use Different Tests

Under the "use different tests" perspective, culture-neutral or bias-free tests and assessment
methods are recommended for identification. Frequently mentioned is the use of a nonverbal test of cognitive ability or achievement protocols that include a nonverbal subtest
of some sort. Peters and Engerrand (2016) go on to add that even if culture-neutral
tests exist, they are not likely to align well with the most common types of gifted programming – a problem of content validity – where Hispanic/Latino students and other
underrepresented groups gain access through these nonverbal, culture-neutral measures,
but where programs are verbally rich and language-intensive. What matters is that the
measure or measures used for identification are closely aligned to the intervention (gifted
education) for which the student is identified. This criterion is the single most important
characteristic of a strong, equitable identification system.

Use Tests Differently

In this perspective, a school district uses instruments already in place but in a different
way – specifically by using different norm samples. In using local norms, a school focuses
on the question of which students are the most advanced and therefore most likely to be
under-challenged and in need of additional services, compared to other students in the
same grade, school, or district. Local norms, especially at the building level, make the most
sense for gifted identification because they identify the students who would most likely
benefit from additional advanced intervention – following the logic that those students
who are farthest from typical in a given school are the most likely to be under-challenged.
Such decisions should also be made locally because it is locally that a child is or is not
appropriately challenged; and it will be locally, within a particular school, that any intervention will be provided.

In the spring of 2019, the Education Week Research Center (2019) conducted a survey
of more than 1,200 K-12 gifted and talented teachers and coordinators to learn more
about how districts and schools define, identify, serve, and instruct students in gifted and
talented programs. A major objective was to gain a better understanding of the extent to
which districts are experiencing and addressing issues related to the overrepresentation or
underrepresentation of specific student groups in gifted education. The findings suggest
that gifted programs likely face serious equity-related challenges.

Uneven Equity

Most educators say that their district's screening process identifies all or almost all of the students who should be in the gifted education program. However, a majority of educators also say that Black, Hispanic, Native American, low-income, and emerging bilingual students are underrepresented in their district's gifted programs. Despite this widespread perception of underrepresentation, fewer than one in three educators say their district has made a big effort in the past five years to address this issue. Among districts that are making an effort, the most commonly reported remedy is the adoption of new or additional screening assessments. Among those whose districts are not addressing under-representation, the most common reason is that this is not considered a priority by school or district educators. Here are some of the questions and response data from the survey specific to identification and assessment.

1   Are schools required to use specific criteria/methods for identification of gifted students? Select all that apply.
   • (66%): Yes, determined at the local level
   • (49%): Yes, determined at the state level
   Ninety-six percent of educators say their districts' schools are required to use specific criteria or methods to identify gifted students. Most report that these criteria are determined at the local – not the state level.

2   Which of the following indicators does your district use when identifying gifted students? Select all that apply.
   • (79%): Test scores other than IQ scores
   • (71%): Nominations/referrals
   • (66%): IQ scores
   • (64%): Multiple criteria model
   • (50%): Range of approved assessments
   • (32%): Grades
   Non-IQ tests are the most common method of screening gifted students, followed by nominations or referrals. IQ scores are the third most common factor – two-thirds of educators report their use. Most educators say their districts use multiple criteria to screen for giftedness.

3   Which of the following assessments does your district use to identify gifted students? Select all that apply.
   • (54%): Cognitive Abilities Test (CogAT)
   • (40%): Weschler Intelligence Scale for Children
   • (34%): Naglieri Nonverbal Ability Test
   • (26%): Woodcock–Johnson
   • (22%): ITBS
   • (19%): Otis–Lennon
   • (17%): Screening Assessment for Gifted Elementary Students
   • (13%): Stanford–Binet L-M
   • (11%): Test of Nonverbal Ability
   • (10%): District Created Assessment

- (9%): ACT
- (7%): Raven's Progressive Matrices

The Cognitive Abilities Test or CogAT is the assessment most frequently used to screen for gifted education. The assessment, produced by Riverside Publishing, a Houghton Mifflin Company, assesses verbal, quantitative, and nonverbal reasoning. Forty-two percent used an assessment other than the exams mentioned on the survey.

4 To what extent do you agree or disagree with the following statement? My district's procedure for screening gifted and talented students identifies all or almost all the students who should be in the program.
- (17%): Completely Agree
- (47%): Somewhat Agree
- (24%): Somewhat Disagree
- (12%): Disagree

Most educators (64%) agree that their district's screening process identifies all or almost all of the students who should be in the gifted education program. However, of that 64%, just 17% completely agree. And a substantial minority (36%) disagree.

5 How would educators describe the representation of students of different races/ethnicities in gifted education in their districts?
- Black: 61% Underrepresented
- Hispanic: 57% Underrepresented
- Native Americans: 53% Underrepresented
- Asian: 24% Overrepresented
- White: 46% Overrepresented

Most educators whose districts enroll Black, Hispanic, or Native American students perceive that each of these groups is underrepresented in gifted education. Educators are more likely to perceive that Black students are underrepresented than to perceive that students of other ethnicities or races are underrepresented. Most say that Asians and whites are neither overrepresented nor underrepresented. However, they are twice as likely to perceive that Asians are overrepresented than to say they're underrepresented. And they are more than 20 times more likely to say that whites are overrepresented than to say whites are underrepresented.

The queries listed above represent five of the 31 questions contained in the survey. They were selected to provide information on how the respondents answered questions specific to identification and assessment. Overall, the Education Week Research Center (2019) states that the results suggest that equity-related challenges remain alive and well today even as America's schools have grown ever more diverse.

The College Board's Adversity Score

Gewertz (2019) reports that the College Board's plan to expand a program that's designed to help colleges assess students' SAT performance more fairly, by scoring students' high schools and neighborhoods by "level of disadvantage" has failed. The "disadvantage level" scores are based on federal education and census data about income, education, family structure, jobs, and housing; and on College Board data about enrollment. Factors that make up the "disadvantage scores" include:

- Income (median family income, percentage of households in poverty or getting food stamps)
- Education attainment (percentage of adults with less than a four-year degree or high-school diploma)
- Family structure (percentage of single parents with children)
- Employment (percentage of adults unemployed; in "nonprofessional" jobs or agriculture jobs)
- Housing (percentage of rental, vacant, or owned homes; mobility/housing turnover, vacancy rate)
- College-going behavior (likelihood that students will attend a four-year college)
- Crime rate (factored only into a neighborhood score)

This attempt was a failure because "The idea of a single score is wrong. It was confusing and created the misperception that the indicators are specific to an individual student," said David Coleman, the College Board's chief executive (quoted by Gewertz, 2019, p. 21). Persistent underrepresentation of Hispanic/Latino students on elite campuses continues to be a source of debate, just as the underrepresentation of Hispanic/Latino students in K-12 gifted education, Honors, and Advanced Placement continues to exist. Ironically, the same factors that the College Board has identified as the reasons why Hispanic/Latino college-bound students are not found on elite campuses are the same as those explaining why they are not found in advanced academic programs in the public schools they attend. In gifted education, the use of multiple criteria is often a nonnegotiable in identification processes. Unlike the College Board's "clumping" of data into a single score, in gifted education, particularly when it comes to special populations of students, each component found in a multiple-criteria approach to identification carries its own relevance and importance.

Empowering Gifted Hispanic/Latino Students through Curriculum and Instruction

Once identified as gifted, Hispanic/Latino students receive differentiated curriculum and instruction in any one of the program models that are part of a district's continuum of gifted education services. Carefully designed lessons emphasize combinations of critical thinking, problem solving, rigor, complexity, and/or attention to analyzing, synthesizing, and evaluating information and data. In addition, to become more culturally competent and effective in the classroom, teachers providing curriculum and instruction should infuse meaningful learning experiences that address multiple perspectives, helping students move to a deeper knowledge of personal validation by emphasizing cross-cultural communication and understanding, acceptance, and the celebration of diversity.

Culturally competent teachers and administrators who "get it" when working with gifted Hispanic/Latino students put themselves in a position to make a difference based on their ability to use *relational pedagogy*. Castellano (2018) defined this as the use of instructional processes, strategies, and activities that promote both increased academic achievement and mastery of learning, as well as having a connection that empowers and encourages students to include any element of their culture, ethnicity, or language in demonstrating what they know and are able to do. For example:

- Connecting students' prior knowledge and cultural experiences with new concepts by constructing and designing relevant cultural metaphors and images
- Understanding students' cultural knowledge and experiences and selecting appropriate instructional materials
- Helping students to find meaning and purpose in what is to be learned
- Using interactive teaching strategies
- Helping learners construct meaning by organizing, elaborating, and representing knowledge in their own way.

To create a supportive, caring environment, teachers of the gifted should translate their attitudes into the following actions (Derman-Sparks & Edwards, 2010):

1   **Celebrate diversity:** There is great diversity among gifted Hispanic/Latino students. They don't want to be criticized because they have some characteristic that is different from others. Through your actions, recognize that each student contributes to the rich variety of ideas and actions in the classroom. Show that you appreciate and value the diversity that is reflected among your Hispanic/Latino students. In turn, they will feel appreciated rather than feeling different, and this will make them feel more comfortable in the classroom.

2   **Have high expectations for students, and believe all students can succeed:** Teachers may sometimes consider certain sources of student diversity – -cognitive ability, language, disabilities, socioeconomic status (SES), for example – as having a negative effect on student performance. Thus, teachers may have lower expectations and adjust the content and activities accordingly. However, this is a disservice to the students when they are not given the opportunity to address meaningful and challenging content and to develop their knowledge and skills. It is important to hold high expectations for all students and to believe all students can succeed. Students appreciate the challenge and will find the classroom more stimulating and worthwhile than a classroom with lowered expectations.

3   **Give encouragement to all students:** Students who perform well academically often receive words of praise, reinforcement, and encouragement from teachers. Encouraging words and guiding suggestions will help students feel that they are being supported in their efforts.

4   **Respond to all students enthusiastically:** When students see their teacher is welcoming and enthusiastic about each student, they feel more comfortable in the classroom and are more willing to participate fully. Warm greetings when students enter the classroom, conversations with individual students, and positive reactions when students contribute to classroom discussions are just a few ways that enthusiasm might be expressed. The main point is that students need to feel valued, and they see this through enthusiastic teacher responses.

5   **Show students that you care about them:** When students know you care for them and that you are looking out for them, it makes all the difference in the world. Students

then feel valued, regardless of their characteristics, and are more likely to participate actively in the classroom.

6   **Create an anti-bias educational environment:** Sometimes when students interact with others who are different from them, they may talk or act in ways that express disapproval. Teachers need to take steps to overcome this bias. In an anti-bias classroom children learn to be proud of themselves and of their families, to respect human differences, to recognize bias, and to speak up for what is right.

Castellano (2018) adds that quantitatively, and historically, there are benchmarks for professionalism in the form of earned degrees, teaching licenses, transcripts, and acquired certifications that serve as documentation stating one is qualified. Caring, on the other hand, is a qualitative construct that means different things to different people. Ideally, teachers of the gifted working with Hispanic/Latino students nurture, support, challenge, engage, inspire, and motivate them. They collaborate with parents and families, and they are intentional in their efforts to make a positive difference in the lives of the students they serve. The challenge for any principal and human resources department is to identify and hire teachers who are both qualified and caring. A caring educator embraces diversity by being respectful, inquisitive, and authentic. Educators who are both qualified and caring have the best chance to be successful when working with gifted Hispanic/Latino students. Most of these high-ability students attend public schools, live in poverty, and qualify for free or reduced-priced lunch. Teachers who care enough to put in the work needed to help this intra-ethnically diverse group of students reach their greatest chance of success must be better able to adjust the teaching and learning process to promote academic, social, and emotional growth and development in their students than their counterparts who do not have the same passion and empathy.

Engaging the Parents and Families of Gifted Hispanic/Latino Students

Engaging the parents and families of gifted Hispanic/Latino students requires a differentiated approach based on need. Simply put, different parents and families require different forms of engagement. In working directly with parents and families of gifted Hispanic/Latino students throughout the United States, I have had to make adjustments based on the demographics of the parents I would be engaging. With some audiences, the presentation was in Spanish and included basic information about gifted education; what it is, why it is important, and what it mean for parents and families. With other audiences, also presented in Spanish, the focus was on how to advocate for your child and what questions needed to be asked to hold teachers and schools accountable; with an additional focus on their rights as parents. Yet, for other Hispanic/Latino parents and families, the presentation was in English and it was they who asked the questions, sought out suggestions and recommendations, and who were already actively involved in their child's gifted education. I have presented to Hispanic/Latino parents and families who were monolingual Spanish-speakers, uneducated, undocumented, who lived in poverty, and were fearful of many governmental and community entities. And yes, they had gifted and talented children. I worked with bilingual parents and families who understood that information was power, that they had rights, and that their children were "special" and needed to participate in advanced academic programs. And I worked with monolingual English-speaking Hispanic/Latino parents and families who had high expectations for their children, the school, and the gifted education programs of their children. They were actively involved in their child's education and could be referred to as "helicopter parents."

Local relevancy and context determined what the parent engagement looked like. I had to modify my approach, the materials presented, including the need to give tailored, specific feedback. One of the most important empowerment strategies that I include in my work as a trainer, consultant, parent educator, and scholar working directly with Hispanic/Latino parents and families with gifted children is the opportunity for them to tell their story and share their experiences. This collaboration is powerful because it is the parents who are now educating teachers and administrators; helping them to become more culturally competent, empathetic, and responsive. Bernal (2002) suggested that when parents of high-ability Latino students collaborate with others, gifted education programs and services are improved. In this model, similar to what I have presented above, teachers and administrators learn more about the students and families served in their community while simultaneously providing contextually relevant information about advanced academic programs like gifted education.

Developing and engaging their child's talents, strengths, and potential may call for assessing internal and external support systems that instill a sense of passion where children learn discipline toward something that is important to them. Relatedly, by providing an environment for learning and by providing the necessary materials, supplies, and resources; as well as encouragement, motivation, and social and emotional support, high expectations are being promoted. This is especially important to building resiliency and perseverance. By helping their children to "stick with it," parents and families promote grit and a growth mindset. Building capacity and sustaining a child's gifts, talents, and potential takes time and often involves a collaboration with other stakeholder groups. Collaboration and communication are powerful tools that any parent and family can engage with regardless of language proficiency, immigrant status, socioeconomic level, or geography.

Strategies for the Classroom

Castellano (2018, 2020) states that from an instructional perspective, teachers and administrators who are culturally competent and use culturally responsive pedagogy ensure that students feel physiologically, socially, and emotionally safe and secure, in part by using textbooks, resources, and materials in which students see themselves represented. Furthermore, part of becoming a culturally competent teacher is understanding the impact of poverty on students and accepting those facts. Culturally competent teachers recognize the great diversity within the Latino diaspora, embrace it, and find ways in teaching and learning that allow their students to feel pride about who they are and where they come from.

The role of the teacher in programming for success, promoting academic capacity, and sustaining programs and services involves honoring and respecting the abilities of students and acknowledging their contributions on a daily basis. This student validation through cultural competence and integration empowers students to use their personal and unique gifts and talents in various learning contexts. For some students, opportunities to participate in community-based service projects is one such context. Allowing them to make meaningful connections beyond the classroom and to apply the lifelong learning skills promoted in their advanced academic classes is another form of student validation.

Adapted from the work of the Council for Exceptional Children (CEC) and their book on *High-Leverage Practices in Special Education* (2017), teaching gifted Hispanic/Latino students is a strategic, flexible, and recursive process as effective teachers of the gifted use content knowledge, pedagogical awareness (including evidence-based practice), and data on student learning to design, deliver, and evaluate the effectiveness of instruction. This process begins with well-designed instruction. Effective teachers of gifted Hispanic/Latino students are well versed in contextually relevant curricula and use appropriate standards, learning progressions, and evidence-based practices to prioritize long- and short-term learning goals and to plan instruction. This instruction, when delivered with fidelity, is designed to maximize academic learning time, actively engage learners in meaningful activities, and emphasize proactive and positive approaches across tiers of instructional intensity.

Teachers value diverse perspectives and incorporate knowledge about students' backgrounds, cultures, and language in their instructional decisions. Their decisions result in improved student outcomes across varied curriculum areas and in multiple educational settings. They use teacher-led, peer-assisted, student-regulated, and technology-assisted practices fluently, and know when and where to apply them. Analyzing instruction in this way allows teachers to improve student learning and their own professional practice. Student choice is part of this practice.

Ten Ways to Incorporate Student Choice

Spencer (2016) writes that student choice is more than simply choosing a topic. It is about empowering students through the entire learning process. This is especially true in classrooms that embrace creativity, design thinking, and project-based learning. Here are a few of the ways we can incorporate student choice:

1 **Let students choose the topic:** When I first had student blogs, I would post a writing prompt on the projector. However, when I had students explore real blogs, they pointed out that outside of school, bloggers write about topics they care about. So I told them to choose a topic or theme. They could create foodie blogs, sports blogs, gamer blogs, etc.
2 **Let students ask the questions:** I believe students should question answers as often as they answer questions. This is why inquiry is such a critical component of design thinking. Students need to move from awareness to curiosity in a way that will fuel their creative thinking.
3 **Let students decide the content:** I love sustained silent reading. I get it. It's old school. It won't make the list of trendy new maker space learning (where space is used to facilitate student collaboration, communication, creativity, and critical thinking). However, it works. A few years ago, I taught 8th grade self-contained. The school librarian and the upper-grade teachers had cultivated this love of silent reading. So when we went to the library, it was like going to a candy store.

4   **Let students pick the materials and resources:** In design thinking, students work through an ideation phase and then begin building a prototype. I love the idea that they guide not only the concept of what they will create, but they also figure out what materials they will use in order to build their prototype. This goes beyond physical products. In digital content, they can choose what applications they will use and what type of media they will work with. When designing an event or a service project, they can determine the venue, the materials, and the resources.

5   **Let students choose the strategies:** When I think of the most tedious things kids experience in school, there is a high likelihood that they don't get a chance to choose the strategies. Take close reading. The rigid approach says, "Use these symbols and follow this recipe." Students focus on doing things the "right way" and they fail to make sense out of the actual text.

6   **Let students choose the scaffolding:** I remember requiring students to use a set of scaffolding for the research process. A handful of students loved it because they needed it. The rest of the students viewed the scaffolding like a cage. I should have treated the scaffolding as an optional resource that they could access when they found it necessary.

7   **Let students choose the format:** When possible, allow students to choose the format for their creative work. It might be a video, a podcast, or a blog post.

8   **Let students choose the audience:** When students define the audience, they are able to clarify what they are doing and how they are going to do it. This honors student agency.

9   **Let students choose the groups:** This is the most controversial. People will often point out that in the real world, you don't always get to choose your groups. I get that. But when you work on a cool, voluntary collaboration, you often get to choose your groups. In my experience, our most functional groups were the ones where students worked with their friends. At first, they were too social. But then the challenge and the excitement of the tasks kicked in and they were able to tap into their mutual trust and go deeper in their work. While this might not be necessary for every project, it is something teachers can try out.

10   **Let students manage the projects:** This was the hardest thing for me to let go of. However, I believe that project management is a powerful, transferrable skill. Students need to learn the art of project management. Over time, I have learned to allow students to own the project management and to build their own systems to monitor their programs.

For all the talk of the "guide on the side," the truth is that guides are still guides. Even in a student-centered classroom, the teacher is still the expert. There are times when limiting choices actually increases creative thinking. Students work within the constraints to find solutions that push divergent thinking. Moreover, there are times when students don't have as much prior knowledge in an area and you, as the teacher, will expose them to new ideas, approaches, and content that they might have otherwise ignored. However, when we incorporate choice, students own the learning process. We honor their agency and empower them to become the lifelong learners we want them to be. At some point, they will leave the classroom and they won't have a guide right there by their side. They will have to take charge and make decisions about their own learning. This is why student choice is so critical.

For Hispanic/Latino students, choice is a powerful instructional tool. It is empowering and allows them flexibility in the way they use their time. Choice allows them to be self-sufficient. This is important because of the expectations often thrust upon them by their parents, their culture, and their heritage. Often, they must care for younger siblings, manage the household, and work to help support the family. Choice allows teachers to recognize and value student input. In essence, when Hispanic/Latino students' background knowledge in their interest area is recognized and allowed to develop, content standards, benchmarks, and expectations are also honored.

Recommendations

To summarize, the information presented in this chapter provides guidance on how to identify and educate gifted Hispanic/Latino students; and explains why it is important to acknowledge and promote their sense of belonging and identity. The following recommendations may assist teachers and administrators with this endeavor.

1   When teachers, administrators, and parents and families collaborate and work together to plan and evaluate programs, products, and services, student achievement is heightened. Effective meetings should be facilitated by building trust, communicating clearly, and listening carefully to others' concerns and opinions.
2   Teachers should respectfully and effectively communicate considering the background, socioeconomic status, language, culture, and priorities of the students and their families.
3   To develop a deep understanding of a gifted Hispanic/Latino student's learning needs, teachers of the gifted, and other related educators, should compile a comprehensive learner profile through the use of a variety of assessment measures and other sources (e.g., information from parents, other teachers) that are sensitive to language and culture.
4   Teachers working with gifted Hispanic/Latino students should provide scaffolded supports so students can successfully complete tasks. Teachers should also select powerful visual, verbal, and written supports; carefully calibrate them to students' performance and understanding in relation to learning tasks; use them flexibly; evaluate their effectiveness; and gradually remove them once they are no longer needed.
5   Local, state, and national leaders in the field should expand research on the importance of identifying and educating gifted Hispanic/Latino students.

Conclusion

Though progress has been made on the inclusion of Hispanic/Latino students in advanced academic programs like gifted education, the fact remains that as a group they remain under-identified and underserved. In an effort to address this problem, the National Association for Gifted Children (NAGC), in December of 2019, created a national task force to build stronger ties with the Hispanic/Latino community. This is something that has never been done before and time will tell if the task force is successful not only in creating awareness, but whether its efforts will move the needle on the numbers of Hispanic/Latino students eligible for services.

For those Hispanic/Latino students currently enrolled in gifted education programs, building a culture of achievement and sustaining programs and services are of critical importance. This importance involves a transparency of accountability rooted in the effective communication and collaboration of important stakeholder groups. Together, these groups build a "web of support" that encourages, motivates, and monitors student growth and potential. Programs for gifted Hispanic/Latino students must be strategically delivered and goal-directed. Their purpose must be clear. That is, students must feel that what they are learning is worthwhile.

To meet the needs of gifted Hispanic/Latino students, identification, assessment, and instruction cannot be one-dimensional. A variety of assessment strategies should be considered based on language proficiency patterns; a variety of instructional approaches should be used to challenge these students and to meet their instructional goals; and teachers should receive the professional development required to identify them in the first place. Creating a programmatic infrastructure that includes these practices builds a foundation which increases the possibility that the gifts, talents, and potential that gifted Hispanic/Latino students possess will be recognized, nurtured, and honored.

References

AP Chemistry Teacher (2018). Transcript of interview.

AP English teacher (2018). Transcript of interview.

Bernal, E. M. (2002). Three ways to achieve a more equitable representation of culturally diverse students in GT programs. *Roeper Review, 24*(2), 82–88.

Blad, E. (2017). Q&A: Teachers' cues shape students' sense of belonging. *Education Week*. Retrieved from: www.edweek.org/ew/articles/2017/06/21/teachers-cues-shape-students-sense-of-belonging.html

Castellano, J. A. (2018). Opening the door to hope, promise, and possibility. In J. A. Castellano (Ed.), *Educating Hispanic/Latino students: Opening the door to hope, promise, and possibility* (pp. 69–117). Learning Sciences International.

Castellano, J. A. (2020). Serving gifted, advanced, and high-ability Latino students: Programming for success. In S. J. Paik, S. M. Kula, J. J. González, & V. V. González (Eds.), *High-achieving Latino students: Successful pathways toward college and beyond* (pp. 231–246). Information Age Publishing.

Cohn, C. A. (2020). Foreword. In S. J. Paik, S. M. Kula, J. J. González, &V.V. González (Eds.), *High-achieving Latino students: Successful pathways toward college and beyond* (p. ix). Information Age Publishing.

Council for Exceptional Children. (2017). *High-leverage practices in special education*. Author.

Derman-Sparks, L., & Edwards, J. O. (2010). *Anti-bias education for young children and ourselves*. National Association for the Education of Young Children.

Dixon, L., Hassell, B., Fister-Gale, S., & Kalman, F. (2016). Talent is the world's most valuable resource: It's time for leaders to elevate its strategic importance. Talent Economy. Retrieved from: www.chieflearningofficer.com/2016/12/02/talent-valuable-resource/

Education Week Research Center. (2019). *Gifted education: Results of a national survey*. Author.

Ford, D. Y., Lawson Davis, J., Dickson, K. T., Frazier Trotman Scott, M., Grantham, T. C., Moore III, J. L., & Taradash, G. D. (2020). Evaluating gifted education programs using an equity-based and culturally responsive checklist to recruit and retain under-represented students of color. *Journal of Minority Achievement, Creativity, and Leadership, 1*(1), 119–146.

Gewertz, G. (2019). "Disadvantage" index for SAT angers counselors. *Education Week, 38*(34), 1, 21.

Lopez, M. H., Krogstad, J. M., & Passel, J. S. (2021). Who is Hispanic? Pew Research Center. Retrieved from: www.pewresearch.org/fact-tank/2021/09/23/who-is-hispanic/

National Center for Educational Statistics. (2017). *Percentage of public school students enrolled in gifted and talented programs, by sex, race/ethnicity, and state: Selected years.* Author.

Okeeheelee Middle School. (2017). Students at Okeeheelee Middle School take, pass college-level Advanced Placement test. Retrieved from: www.okeeheelee.org/students___parents/international_spanish_academy___i_s_a_

Peters, S. J., & Engerrand, K. G. (2016). Equity and excellence: Positive efforts in the identification of underrepresented students for gifted and talented services. *Gifted Child Quarterly, 60,* 159–171.

Ricciardi, C., Haag-Wolf, A., & Winsler, A. (2020). Factors associated with gifted identification for ethnically diverse children of poverty. *Gifted Child Quarterly, 64*(4), 243–258.

Rivera, M. (2018). Transcribed interview for college scholarship.

Simón, Y. (2018). *Hispanic vs. Latino vs. Latinx: A brief history of how these words originated.* Retrieved from: https://remezcla.com/features/culture/latino-vs-hispanic-vs-latinx-how-these-words-originated/

Spencer, J. (2016). Ten ways to incorporate student choice in your classroom. Retrieved from: https://medium.com/synapse/10-ways-to-incorporate-student-choice-in-your-classroom-e07baa449e55

United States Department of Education's Office for Civil Rights. (2016). Civil Rights Data Collection. 2015–16 national and state estimations. Retrieved from: https://ocrdata.ed.gov/estimations/2015-2016

United States Department of Education's Office of Planning, Evaluation, and Policy Development. (2016). *The state of racial diversity in the educator workforce.* Author. Retrieved from: www2.ed.gov/rschstat/eval/highered/racial-diversity/state-racial-diversity-workforce.pdf

VanTassel-Baska, J. (2018). Achievement unlocked: Effective curriculum interventions with low-income students. *Gifted Child Quarterly, 62*(1), 68–82.

Part IV

Reflections for Practice, Policy, and Research

Chapter 14

Shifting Paradigms for Special Populations of Gifted Learners

Kimberley L. Chandler

Introduction

The last comprehensive edited volume about special populations in gifted education was published more than ten years ago. Since that time, many paradigms have shifted in some ways relative to special populations of gifted learners: who they are, how they are identified, how they are served, and how they are viewed within an inclusive, equitable educational framework. This book provides an updated view of how we must approach the work with these historically underrepresented populations in gifted education, given the multitude of paradigm changes. Groups of students included in this book are some of the traditional ones often discussed in the extant literature: Black students, Hispanic/Latino, highly gifted, young gifted, students from low-income settings, twice-exceptional learners, and students from rural settings. As a reflection of the recognition of the needs of additional special populations, also included are chapters about gifted students from groups that are less often featured in the literature: Asian Americans, American Indian and Alaska Native Youth, military-connected students, English Language Learners, GLBT students, and children who have experienced trauma, toxic stress, and adverse childhood experiences. The call for a standing commitment to special populations in gifted education proposed in the first chapter of this book is reiterated in every chapter of this current publication through the authors' advocacy for each group and the needed services.

Examining Historically Underrepresented Populations through Two Lenses

Chapter authors examined these groups through two lenses: 1) equity; and 2) supporting the identification and education of these children. Looking through either lens, the perspectives may vary significantly from what was published a decade ago. In the case of the equity lens, in particular, there are political, social, and educational forces that have resulted in a reexamination of how we view the needs of students in American schools. During the timespan from 2020 to 2021, political, social, and educational forces created an urgency not experienced previously to make some substantive changes. The global coronavirus pandemic shed a light on disparities in access to educational resources and increased those deficits for students in certain populations, most noticeably those from low-income settings. Additionally, political and social forces brought to the forefront concerns about equity and social justice. In July of 2020, the Board of Directors of the National

DOI: 10.4324/9781003265412-20

Association for Gifted Children (NAGC) released a historic statement "denouncing systemic racism and supporting racial justice." The Board also shared an "expanded vision and plan of action to confront systemic racism and advance equity for Black students in gifted education" (NAGC, 2020, n.p.). This action represents a significant stance that the organization has taken on behalf of one historically underrepresented population. For NAGC to place equity and social justice in the forefront is important for all of the student groups discussed in this book, as it shows the importance of moving beyond rhetoric toward specific actions.

The equity lens could be considered to be the backdrop for every discussion in the book, as this must be the driving force for all decision-making; it requires a deliberate, systemic approach to make sure that every child has the opportunity to achieve success. In the case of gifted education specifically, it typically refers to the equitable representation of various student populations in programs. This book recognizes the populations that have historically often not been included in an equitable manner in gifted education programs. Additionally, it recognizes those students whose needs may not have been addressed in systematic ways to ensure their success.

The identification and education lens includes emphases on research connections, instructional connections, collaboration, social-emotional learning, and practical applications. Using this lens, like using the equity lens, represents a departure from the way in which these special populations may have been sometimes addressed previously. The instructional connections represent the current thinking about how to teach gifted students, but with an eye to the specific needs of each group; they also include information about considerations that must be made in the identification process. The collaboration component is important because of the way it nests gifted education within the context of the general education enterprise, as opposed to it existing in a separate silo not connected to the larger endeavor. The emphasis on social-emotional learning, while not new, is one that carries with it more urgency at this point in time; as American students moved from in-person learning to remote learning and/or hybrid settings during the pandemic, the need for a focus on social-emotional learning has become more obvious. The practical applications portion of each chapter provides a clear translation of the theoretical underpinnings for each group into actionable items in the school setting.

The extant research about each special population is shared briefly. In many cases, that research is, however, quite limited. This paucity of research is indicative of a need for much more work to be done in gifted education. Although the field has a rich history of research focusing on certain areas related to underserved populations, this book points to a need to recraft and expand that agenda. The shifting paradigms must be considered relative to how they affect the special populations. All of these groups of underserved students need to be studied in more depth. Equity itself must be examined to determine what the perceptions are regarding it and how it is manifested within the field as it relates to these children.

The authors of this book are issuing a clarion call to advance the education of the historically underrepresented populations in gifted education. While progress in this area has been slow to occur, the political and societal forces in the early 2020s have finally provided the much-needed impetus to implement changes. With a constant eye on equitable practices, we must improve our efforts to recognize these gifted students and meet their needs.

Reference

National Association for Gifted Children [NAGC]. (2020, July 14). Championing equity and supporting social justice for Black students in gifted education: An expanded vision for NAGC. Retrieved from: www.nagc.org/championing-equity-and-supporting-social-justice-black-students-gifted-education-expanded-vision#Plan

CPSIA information can be obtained
at www.ICGtesting.com
Printed in the USA
LVHW021611100822
725526LV00006B/391

9 781032 2082